To sand.   Or not to sand.

Any questions?

It's a question faced by boaters every year. And not just by wooden boat purists, but by fiberglass boat owners who insist on beautiful brightwork. Do you apply Epifanes Clear High Gloss Varnish and dutifully sand between coats to attain that show quality finish? Or do you use Epifanes Wood Finish Gloss so you can skip the sanding and add a few potentially glorious days to your season without sacrificing durability? Or perhaps you topcoat the Wood Finish Gloss with the Clear High Gloss Varnish for the ultimate in performance and ease. Whichever option you choose, you'll be using an Epifanes varnish packed with unmatched amounts of tung oil, alkyd resin, and UV filters to create a beautiful high gloss finish that builds up faster, lasts longer, and protects your boat better. Ask for Epifanes at your local chandlery. Or call us at 1-800-269-0961 for our free technical information package. Because no matter which Epifanes varnish you start with, the finish will always be perfect—there's no question about it.

EPIFANES (ÉPEE-FAWN-US) NORTH AMERICA, INC., 70 WATER STREET, THOMASTON, MAINE 04861
1-800-269-0961 FAX: 207-354-0387 WWW.EPIFANES.COM

SAIL TALL SHIPS!   i

✺ GREENPORT HARBOR ✺
LONG ISLAND, NEW YORK

Photo: Gil Amiaga

An authentic, working deep water port
surrounded by seaside farms & vineyards...

Tall Ships 2000® Cruise Port
Americas' Sail Host–1995 & 1998

Visit Mitchell Park & Marina.
Deep water dockage, vintage carousel, amphitheater
and boardwalk—all in the heart of the village!
Easy walk to stores, galleries, beach,
hospital & Historic District.

Special arrangements made for visiting tall ships.

Services available include hauling, shipbuilding,
welding, engine repair & hardware.

For more information contact:
Mayor David E. Kapell, Village of Greenport
236 Third Street, Greenport, New York 11944
631-477-3000 • FAX 631-477-1877
or hail the harbormaster on VHF channel 9

Concordia was the winner of the 2000 ASTA Sea
Education Program of the Year Award for Class Afloat.

The Ocean Classroom Foundation's *Harvey
Gamage*, winner of the 2000 Black Pearl Award.

Muskegon, Michigan
welcomes

Tall Ships Challenge®

August 9-13, 2001

Heritage Landing
Tall Ship Site

ASTA

American Sail Training Association

For more information on events and attractions
in Muskegon County, call **1-800-250-WAVE**

www.visitmuskegon.org
www.sailmuskegon.com

Sail Tall Ships!

**A Directory
of Sail Training
and Adventure
at Sea**

ASTA

The mission of the American Sail Training Association
is to encourage character building through sail
training, promote sail training to the North
American public, and support education under sail.

AMERICAN SAIL TRAINING ASSOCIATION
NEWPORT, RI

The mission of the American Sail Training Association is to encourage character building through sail training, promote sail training to the North American public, and support education under sail.

Published by:

American Sail Training Association (ASTA)
PO Box 1459
Newport, RI 02840 USA
Phone: (401) 846-1775; Fax: (401) 849-5400
E-mail: asta@sailtraining.org
Web site: http://tallships.sailtraining.org

Acknowledgments

Many of the photographs in this edition of *Sail Tall Ships!* were supplied by:

Thad Koza	MAX	Chuck Lauwers
Tall Ships Photography	Bywater Lodge-Pierside	Marine Photography
24 Mary St.	Lymington, Hants SO41 5SB	14A Le Corbusierln
Newport, RI 02840 USA	United Kingdom	2050 Antwerp, Belgium
Phone: (401) 846-5274	Phone: + 44 (0) 1590 672047	Phone: +44 (0) 7092 084673

We would like to thank Captain Daniel Moreland, Captain George Moffett, Captain Gregg Swanzey, Steve Christman, Bostonia, and Diane Carey for submitting material or granting permission to reprint their remarks. We would also like to thank Alex Agnew, Bart Dunbar, and Christine Highsmith for their assistance in selling advertisements, and the advertisers who made the production of this Directory possible.

Registered Trademarks

The following registered trademarks and service marks are owned
by the American Sail Training Association:

Tall Ships®
Tall Ships are Coming!®
Tall Ships 2000®
Tall Ships Challenge®

Copyright ©2001 The American Sail Training Association

Sail Tall Ships! A Directory of Sail Training and Adventure at Sea
13th edition

Compiled by Lori A. Aguiar, ASTA Program Coordinator
Edited by Lori A. Aguiar and Captain David V.V. Wood, USCG (Ret.)
Designed by Thea Drew
Consulting by Pucino Print Consultants, 631 Fletcher Road,
    North Kingston, RI 02852
Printed by Dollco Printing, Ottawa, Ontario, Canada

ISBN 0-9636483-6-5

Cover photo: *True North of Toronto*, winner of the 1998 Great Lakes Tall Ships® Race Series

TALL SHIPS CHALLENGE®
Race Series

2001 Great Lakes
2002 Pacific Coast
2003 Atlantic Coast

American Sail Training Association:
Creating Awareness of Sail Training

Tall ships prepare for last leg of Tall Ships 2000® in Halifax Harbor by John Rae

TALL SHIPS CHALLENGE®
2001 Great Lakes

Niagara by
John Rae

 Muskegon, Michigan
August 9 thru 13

Info: 800-250-WAVE
visitmuskegon@co.muskegon.mi.us
www.visitmuskegon.org or
www.sailmuskegon.com

Muskegon

Appledore IV by Stephen Kent

 Bay City, Michigan
July 26 thru 30

Info: 888-BAY-TOWN
shirley@bresanlink.net
www.tallshipcelebration.com

 Detroit, Michigan
&Windsor, Ontario
July 19 thru 22

Info: 877-DET-2001
lschmidt@detroit300.org
www.detroit300.org

Concordia by
Wojciech
Wacowski

SAIL TALL SHIPS!

Inland Seas by Chris Hamm

 Kingston, Ontario
June 28 thru July 1

Info: 613-544-2250
Toll free: 866-253-6918
kingstontallships2001@city.kingston.on.ca
www.city.kingston.on.ca

Denis Sullivan by Thad Koza

Kingston

ay City

Port Colborne

etroit/Windsor

Cleveland

Port Colborne, Ontario
July 5 thru 8

Info: 888-PORT-FUN
edo@portcolborne.com
www.portcolborne.com

Cleveland, Ohio
July 11 thru 16

Info: 216-556-0666
clevelandharborfest@imgworld.com
www.clevelandharborfest.com

*Pride of
Baltimore II*
by Veronique
LeVelley

TALL SHIPS CHALLENGE®
2002 Pacific Coast

TALL SHIPS CHALLENGE.

Victoria, BC
August 2002

Seattle, WA
August 15-19, 2002

San Francisco, CA
August 28-September 2, 2002

Los Angeles, CA
September 6-10, 2002

Lady Washington &
Hawaiian Chieftain by
Benson Lee

Pacific Swift by
Tony Anderson

San Diego, CA
September 12-16, 2002

Panoramic view of *Star of India* and The Maritime Museum of San Diego by Jim Morrison

Visit the ASTA Web site for details and updates!
www.tallships.sailtraining.org

SAIL TALL SHIPS!

Table of Contents

One of the oldest maritime traditions is the practice of decorating vessels with figureheads and other carvings. Shipcarvers were inspired by mariners' folklore, function of the vessel or political or cultural events of the day. Qualities such as swiftness, strength and courage and the belief that the carving had a mystical ability to protect the vessel and crew from the hazards of navigation might influence selection of the decoration.

Left: The figurehead of the *Christian Radich*
Below: The figurehead of the USCG Barque *Eagle*

SAIL TALL SHIPS!

Foreword

BY DAVID V.V. WOOD
CHAIRMAN, ASTA

Well, whether you celebrated the turn of the millennium on January 1, 2000 or held out with the purists for January 1, 2001, the 21st Century is here to stay and will be with us for the rest of our lives; and this year ASTA will take its biggest step ever by launching the Tall Ships Challenge® series of sail training races and port events–an annual series, rotating regularly from coast to coast in a counter-clockwise direction around the country, that will bring the message of sail training and tall ships to an ever larger–and more receptive–public.

Tall Ships 2000® has already marked the course for the future, and what an event it was! More than 10 million people visited the events of the official Tall Ships 2000® Race and Cruise-in-Company ports (three-quarters of those in Boston alone), and millions more took part in the events of OpSail 2000. If there was ever a doubt that such events would attract both ships and the public in record numbers, that doubt has surely been given the deep six (you can look that up in a nautical dictionary!).

The evidence of abiding interest in what sail training and tall ships represent is all around us–the success of the Shackleton exhibit which made its way to museums around the country last year, the rapidly expanding availability of books about polar exploration and seafaring in the 19th and early 20th centuries, the growth of the adventure travel industry–all these things and many more attest to an enduring human need to stay in touch with the reality and nobility of the perpetual struggle with the forces of nature and the indomitability of the human spirit.

Let this Directory–our largest ever–be your gangway to the adventure of a lifetime. In its pages you will find opportunities for almost any kind of seafaring experience you can imagine, and in the articles that precede the listing of ASTA's member vessels you will find abundant evidence of the variety and excitement of the sail training experience.

Welcome aboard!

Barclay Warburton III's brigantine *Black Pearl*

SAIL TALL SHIPS!

A Brief History of the American Sail Training Association

In the summer of 1972 Barclay Warburton III, of Newport, Rhode Island, his two sons, and several friends, sailed his brigantine *Black Pearl* across the Atlantic to participate in a tall ships race from Cowes on the south coast of England to Malmo in Sweden, organized by what was then known as The Sail Training Association. He was so inspired by the enthusiasm and spirit he saw in that international gathering of tall ships and young people that he set out to create a similar organization in order to bring the same kind of spirit to the United States, and through his efforts the American Sail Training Association was founded the following year. ASTA soon became the first national association to formally affiliate with what eventually became known as the International Sail Training Association–a family that has since grown to more than 16 members around the globe.

The tall ships races in which the *Black Pearl* took part had first been held in 1956, when a London solicitor, Bernard Morgan, had the idea of bringing what he imagined to be the last of the world's great square-riggers together for a race as a sort of last hurrah–a farewell salute–for the Great Age of Sail. A committee was formed, and with the support and assistance of the Portuguese Ambassador in London, a race was organized from Torbay, on England's Cornish coast, to Lisbon. Five square-rigged schoolships entered the race: Denmark's *Danmark,* Norway's *Christian Radich* and *Sorlandet*, Belgium's *Mercator*, and Portugal's first *Sagres*.

ASTA flags flying!

ASTA member vessels *Fair Jeanne* and *Liberty Clipper* in Boston during Tall Ships 2000®

The event proved to be anything but a funeral procession, however, and it has since grown into an annual series that would astonish its original organizers. Today, hundreds of tall ships from around the world come together annually for friendly competition in international and regional tall ships races organized by ISTA and national affiliates such as ASTA. These races, along with waterfront festivals in designated start and finish ports, bring together the ships and young people of most European countries, Russia and the former Soviet states, the Americas, and the Pacific Rim. The key elements uniting these events are an emphasis on youth. From the beginning, ISTA's racing rules have required that no less than half those on board participating vessels be between 15 and 25 years of age. A formula for rating participating vessels allows vessels ranging in size from the largest square-riggers down to yachts of 30 or more feet in length to compete against each other.

ASTA's efforts in its first decade were primarily focused on organizing tall ships races on the ISTA model, but from the mid-1980's to the mid-1990's (when it began intensive planning, in conjunction with ISTA, for Tall Ships 2000® it worked on a multitude of activities broadly aimed at promoting sail training and supporting education under sail in North America. Thus at the beginning of the 21st Century, the American Sail Training Association has evolved into both an organizer of tall ships races and a strong industry association for the growing numbers of vessels involved in providing opportunities for people of all ages to take part in a seagoing experience aboard a sailing vessel. With an organizational membership of over 240 vessels, ASTA serves as a forum for information exchange, professional development, and program standards. Through such initiatives as the Council of Educational Ship Owners, which worked successfully for the passage of the Sailing School Vessels Act of 1982, and the Sailing School Vessels Council, founded the following year, ASTA has continued to work with the US Coast Guard and other agencies to create and maintain a friendly regulatory climate for the development of sail training.

Safety at sea has been an enduring

emphasis, and in conjunction with the Australian bicentennial gathering of tall ships in Sydney in 1988, a group of ASTA members organized the first international discussion on safety standards, practices, and equipment for sail training programs. Since 1992, ASTA and ISTA have jointly sponsored the annual International Sail Training Safety Forum, which in 1999 drew more than 160 professional sail trainers from 16 nations. Also in the 1980s, ASTA developed the concept of the Sail Training Rally, a competition among crews both at sea and ashore, which provides trainees with an opportunity to demonstrate their seamanship skills in a friendly but competitive format. During shoreside events, the general public can observe the sort of teamwork and maritime skills that are learned on board sail training vessels at sea.

Over the years, the American Sail Training Association has undertaken many other projects to meet the needs of a rapidly growing sail training community. These include a variety of publications including this Directory, forums, an Annual Conference on Sail Training which attracts substantial international attention and participation; a Marine Insurance Program; a Billet Bank to assist vessels in finding qualified crewmembers, and vice versa; a growing program of scholarships and grants to support trainees, vessels, and professional crew; and a constantly expanding Web site. This year, building on the spectacular success of Tall Ships 2000, will see the launch of ASTA's most ambitious project to date–an annual series of tall ships races known as Tall Ships Challenge®. Starting with a series in the Great Lakes in 2001, the series will move to the Pacific Coast in 2002 and to the Atlantic Coast in 2003. It is expected to attract both significant corporate sponsorship and participation by sail training vessels and tall ships from around the world.

SEA's *Corwith Cramer* from the bow of the *Westward*

International Sail Training Association Affiliated Organizations

The following organizations have functions corresponding to those of the American Sail Training Association. Please contact them for information about sail training opportunities in their respective countries.

AUSTRALIA

Australian Sail Training Association (AUSTA)
PO Box 196
Crows Nest, NSW 2065
AUSTRALIA
Tel: +61 2 9906 1277
Fax: +61 2 9906 1030
E-mail: avboz@ozemail.com.au

BELGIUM

Sail Training Association Belgium (STAB)
Grote Singel 6
B-2900 Schoten
BELGIUM
Tel: + 32 3 6580 006

CANADA

Canadian Sail Training Association (CSTA)
Upper Canada Marine Group
29 Euclid Avenue
Toronto, Ontario M6J 2J7
CANADA
Tel: +1 416-525-6321 or 416-603-0109
Fax: +1 416-603-9270
E-mail: doug.prothero@sympatico.ca
Web site: www.uppercanadamarine.ca

DENMARK

Danish Sail Training Association (DSTA)
Attn: Mr Steen Bjerre
Soendergade 12
DK 9000 Aalborg
DENMARK
Tel: + 45 98 10 29 15
Fax: + 45 98 10 00 15
E-mail: steen-bjerre@steen-bjerre.dk

FINLAND

Sail Training Association Finland (STAF)
Risto Villikari
Hietasaarenkuja 6
FIN-00180 Helsinki
FINLAND
Tel: +358 9 685 2616
Fax:+358 9 685 2615
E-mail: purjelaivasaatio@kolumbus.fi
Web site: www.kolumbus.fi/nuorpurj/

FRANCE

Sail Training Association France (STA France)
France - Voiles - Equipages
8 rue Jean Delalande
F-35 400 Saint-Malo
FRANCE
Tel: + 33 2 99 82 35 33
Fax: + 33 2 99 82 27 47

GERMANY

Sail Training Association Germany (STAG)
Hafenhaus, Columbusbahnhof
D-27568 Bremerhaven
GERMANY
Tel: + 49 471 945 5880
Fax: + 49 471 945 8845
Web site: www.sta-g.de

INDONESIA

Sail Training Association of Indonesia (STA Ina)
APLI - Mabes TNI AI Cilangkap
Jakarta 13780
INDONESIA
Tel: +62 21 872 3162
Fax: +62 21 871 1358
E-mail: dispot@centrin_med.ld

ITALY

Sail Training Association Italia (STAI)
Yacht Club Italiano
Porticciolo Duca degli Abruzzi
I-16128 Genova
ITALY
Tel: + 39 010 254 3652
Fax: + 39 010 246 1193
Fax: + 39 010 251 6168
E-mail: staitaly@tin.it

JAPAN

Sail Training Association of Japan (STAJ)
Memorial Park Tower A
2-1-1 Minato-Mirai
Nishi-ku, Yokohama
Kanagawa 220-00 12
JAPAN
Tel: + 81 45 680 5222
Fax: + 81 45 680 5225
E-mail: LDD00622@nifty.ne.jp

THE NETHERLANDS

Sail Training Association Netherlands
  (STAN)
Postbus 55
NL-2340 AB Oegstgeest
THE NETHERLANDS
Tel and Fax: + 31 71 515 3013

NORWAY

Norwegian Sail Training Association (NSTA)
c/o Jostein Haukali
Stokkahagen 54
N-4022 Stavanger
NORWAY
Tel: +47 5156 0621
Fax: +47 5156 0621

POLAND

Sail Training Association Poland (STAP)
PO Box 113
ul.Zjednoczenia 3
PL-81-963 Gdynia
POLAND
Tel: + 48 58 20 6580
Fax: + 48 58 20 6225

PORTUGAL

Portuguese Sail Training Association
  (APORVELA)
Centro de Operacoes
Doca do Terreiro do Trigo
1100 Lisboa
PORTUGAL
Tel: +351 21 887 6854
Fax: +351 21 887 3885
E-mail: Aporvela@telepac.pt
Web site: www.Aporvela.pt

RUSSIA

Sail Training Association Russia (STAR)
Admiral Makarov State Maritime Academy
Kosaya Linia 15a, RU-199026
St. Petersburg
RUSSIA
Tel: + 7 812 217 1934
Fax: + 7 812 217 0682

SOUTH AFRICA

Sail Training Association of South Africa
  (STASA)
P O Box 479
5 Vesperdene Road
Green Point
8051 Capetown
SOUTH AFRICA
Fax: +27 21 797 3671

SWEDEN

Sail Training Association of Sweden (STAS)
Christer Samuelsson
C/O MAN B&W Diesel Sverige AB
Box 2331
403 15 Göteborg
SWEDEN
Tel: + 46 31 17 62 95
Fax: + 46 31 13 15 64

UNITED KINGDOM

Sail Training Association (STA)
2A The Hard
Portsmouth PO1 3PT
UNITED KINGDOM
Tel: + 44 23 92 832055
Fax: + 44 23 92 815769

National Representatives

National Representatives to the International Race Committee of the International Sail Training Association

Australia	Rear Admiral Rothesay Swan, AO, CBE
Belgium	Captain Roger Ghys
Canada	Captain Doug Prothero
Denmark	Captain Bo Rosbjerg
Finland	Risto Villikari
France	Philip Rousseau
Germany	Captain Manfred Hövener
Indonesia	Captain Gita Arjakusuma
Ireland	Sean Flood
Italy	Dr. Giovanni Novi
Japan	Kaoru Ogimi
Latvia	Ugis Kalmanis
The Netherlands	Commander Bernard Heppener
Norway	Gunn von Trepka
Poland	Captain Andrzej Szleminski
Portugal	Dr. Luis de Guimarães Lobato
Russia	Prof. Alexander Pimoshenko
Russia	Ivan I. Kostylev
South Africa	Patrick Fraser
Spain	Rafael Iturrioz
Sweden	Captain Ragnar Westblad
Ukraine	Captain Oleg Vandenko
United Kingdom	John Hamilton, OBE
United States	Captain David V.V. Wood, USCG (Ret.)

2001 Board of Directors

Chairman	Captain David V.V. Wood, USCG (Ret.) - Newport, RI
Vice Chairman	Mr. Thomas J. Gochberg - New York, NY
Vice Chairman	Captain Christopher Rowsom - Baltimore, MD
Secretary	Mr. Per H.M. Lofving - New York, NY
Treasurer	Mr. B. Devereux Barker III - Manchester, MA
Fund Development Committee Chair	Mr. George Lewis, Jr. - Boston, MA
Sail Training and Education Committee Chair	Nancy H. Richardson - Maplewood, NJ
Technical Committee Chair	Captain G. Anderson Chase - Castine, ME

Class of 2001

Mr. Alexander M. Agnew - Portland, ME
Captain Sean Sexton Bercaw - Woods Hole, MA
Ms. Martha Boudreau - Annapolis, MD
Ms. Alice Collier Cochran - San Rafael, CA
Captain Deborah R. Hayes - New London, CT
Ms. Alison E. Healy - Sausalito, CA
Mr. Jeffrey N. Parker - McLean, VA
Captain Nancy H. Richardson - Maplewood, NJ

Class of 2002

Captain G. Anderson Chase - Castine, ME
Mr. George Lewis, Jr. - Boston, MA
Mr. Clarke Murphy - New York, NY
Ms. Carrie O'Malley - Milwaukee, WI
Mr. Wilbert A. Pinkerton, Jr. - Newport, RI
Captain Michael J. Rauworth, Esq. - Boston, MA
Captain Walter Rybka - Erie, PA
Ms. Alix T. Thorne - Georges Mills, NH
Mr. Barclay H. Warburton IV - Newport, RI

Class of 2003

Captain Richard Bailey - Bridgeport, CT
Captain Martyn J. Clark - Victoria, BC
Chuck Fowler - Olympia, WA
Captain James Gladson - San Pedro, CA
Captain Joseph A. Maggio - Coconut Grove, FL
Captain William D. Pinkney - Mystic, CT
Captain Doug Prothero - Toronto, ONT.
Captain John C. Wigglesworth - Ipswich, MA

Commodores Council

Mr. Henry H. Anderson, Jr. - Newport, RI
Mr. Bart Dunbar - Newport, RI
Nancy H. Richardson - Maplewood, NJ
VADM Thomas R. Weschler, USN (Ret.) - Newport, RI

ASTA Staff

Mr. Peter Mello - Executive Director
Mr. Steve Baker - Race Director
Ms. Christine Highsmith - Development Coordinator
Ms. Lori Aguiar - Program Coordinator
Miss Sara Aguiar - Intern

ASTA Supporting Members

Thank you to the following ports, businesses, and individuals who have made an extra commitment to supporting ASTA:

Acheson Ventures, LLC/Robert Lafean

Alliance Marine Risk Managers, Inc./Fredric A. Silberman

Atlantic City, New Jersey and the Casino Reinvestment Development Authority/Bunny Loper

Steven Baker and family

B. Devereux Barker III

Hal Barstow

Battle of Georgian Bay/David J. Brunell

Bowen's Wharf Company/Bart Dunbar

Buffalo Place, Inc./Peggy Beardsley

Clayton Area Chamber of Commerce/Karen Goetz

Coos Bay/North Bend PCB/ Beve Saukko

Euro Products, Inc./Randers Ropeworks/Lars O. Pedersen

Fall River Area Chamber of Commerce/Donna Futoransky

Mr. and Mrs. Thomas J. Gochberg

Helena Gosling

L. K. Gosling

Greater South Haven Area Chamber of Commerce/Larry King

S. Matthews V. Hamilton, Jr.

Alison Healy

Mr. and Mrs. Frederick E. Hood, Sr.

George Lewis, Jr.

James L. Long

Peter Manigault

George L. Maxwell

Port of Oswego Authority-Oswego Harbor/Thomas H. McAuslan

Jeffrey N. Parker

Wilbert A. Pinkerton, Jr.

Piscataqua Maritime Commission/Sue Cobler

City of Port Colborne/Bill LeFeuvre

Captain Walter Rybka

Sail Baltimore/Laura McCall

Sail San Francisco/Alison Healy

H. Alexander Salm

Savannah Waterfront Association/Gordon S. Varnedoe

Societé du Vieux-Port de Montreal/Sylvain DesChamps

Mr. and Mrs. Stephen W. Spencer

David A. Steen

Tall Ships® Travel Club/ Dewey Kennell

Technology Law Offices of Virginia/James W. Hiney

Mr. and Mrs. David Evan Thomas

Alix T. Thorne

Village of Greenport/Mayor David E. Kapell

CAPT Eric J. Williams III, USCG (Ret.)

Guayas passing under
the Golden Gate Bridge

SAIL TALL SHIPS!

2000 ASTA Awards

Sail Training Program of the Year 2000
Boston University's Maritime History in the Atlantic World Course
Aboard "HMS" ROSE

Sea Education Program of the Year 2000
Class Afloat
Aboard CONCORDIA

Sail Trainer of the Year 2000
Captain George Moffett

Port City of the Year 2000
Charleston, South Carolina

Volunteer of the Year 2000
Alison Healy

Lifetime Achievement Award
Exy Johnson

Lifetime Achievement Award
Tom Weschler

Special Recognition Awards 2000
For Raising Funds and Organizing Programs Which Enabled Local Youth to Participate in One or More Legs of the Tall Ships 2000® Race Series
Tall Ships 2000® Nova Scotia
Tall Ships 2000® Bermuda

The Black Pearl Award
Awarded to the Current ASTA Member Who Places Best in an ASTA Sanctioned Shore-Side Rally Demonstrating Team Spirit, Sportsmanship and Skill.
Ocean Classroom Foundation
HARVEY GAMAGE

The Perry Bowl
Awarded to the Top Finishing Class B ASTA Member Vessel in the Summer's Tall Ships 2000® Races
PRIDE OF BALTIMORE II

Right: ASTA Chairman Captain David Wood presents Bunky Wichmann with the Port of the Year award (Charleston, South Carolina)

Left: Captain Chris Rowsom presents Captain Terry Davies with the award for Sail Training Program of the Year for Class Afloat on board the *Concordia*

Right: Mr. Don Treworgy of the Mystic Seaport Museum accepts the 2000 Sail Trainer of the Year award from Alix Thorne, on behalf of George Moffett, Captain of the *Brilliant*

Left: Nancy Richardson accepts the 2000 Lifetime Achievement award from Captain David Wood on behalf of Exy Johnson

SAIL TALL SHIPS!

"Marine insurance...not for yachtsmen, but for seamen, as they share with this and the next generation the joys of learning, on and about the traditional and historic vessels that are an inseparable part of our Nation's rich maritime heritage."

An Insurance program for member vessels of the American Sail Training Association from Alliance Marine Risk Managers, Inc.

14

Rose Island Lighthouse, Newport, RI

Tall Ships 2000®: An ASTA After-Action Report

Gone, but not forgotten . . . the Tall Ships 2000® fleet departed North American waters on 25 July, as the transatlantic race from Halifax to Amsterdam started on a near-perfect afternoon off Chebucto Head. The many tall ships events of this most superlative of tall ships summers left millions of people with bright and lasting memories, not only in North America but, indeed, in the entire North Atlantic world.

Some highlights from the final report by Paul Canter, Project Manager for Tall Ships 2000 Ltd.– the organization within ISTA which organized the overall event:

• Four-and-a-half months from the first race start at Southampton, UK in mid-April to the conclusion of Sail Amsterdam in late August
• 9,500 nautical miles sailed
• More than 70 vessels from 29 countries
• 7,000 young crewmembers from 33 countries
• An estimated 13.4 million visitors during the 7 Official Race Port events

As a full partner with ISTA for the North American component of the race, ASTA ran a race from Bermuda to Charleston in support of a first-ever tall ships event (Tall Ships® Charleston) in that lovely southern seaport, and supported numerous other events during the official Cruise-in-Company, notably Tall Ships® Delaware and Tall Ships® Newport Salute 2000. Most significantly, ASTA was responsible for organizing the Boston to Halifax Race; and of the 38 vessels that started in the Halifax-Amsterdam race, fully a third of the participants were ASTA member vessels. We are particularly proud that ASTA members took First Place in Classes A (*Kruzenshtern*), B (*Pride of Baltimore II*), and CI (*Brilliant*)-with *Brilliant* taking First Overall, and *Pride of Baltimore II* second to cross the finish line.

Tall Ships® 2000 was nearly 8 years in the planning, and was truly an enormous undertaking; but the experience gained and the lessons learned will prove invaluable as ASTA launches the Tall Ships Challenge® race series and when the next major transatlantic (or transpacific!) race takes place.

Race Results

Race 1 - Southampton to Cadiz Class Prizes

Class CIII
1st - *Peter von Danzig* - Germany

Class CII
1st - *Esprit* - Germany

Class CI
1st - *Jolie Brise* - UK

Class A
1st - *Dar Mlodziezy* - Poland

First Vessel to Cross Finish Line - *Peter von Danzig* - Germany
Overall Winner on Corrected Time - *Dar Mlodziezy* - Poland

Race 2 - Genoa to Cadiz Class Prizes

Class CIII
1st - *Hebe III* - Czech Republic

Class CII
1st - *Blitz* - Italy

Class B
1st - *Arung Samudera* - Indonesia

Class A
1st - *Kaliakra* - Bulgaria

1st ship across Finishing Line - *Blitz* - Italy
1st Overall on Corrected Time - *Blitz* - Italy

Race 3 - Cadiz to Bermuda Class Prizes

Class CIII
1st - *Hebe III* - Czech Republic

Class CII
1st - *Esprit* - Germany

Class CI
1st - *Jolie Brise* - UK

Class B
1st - *Arung Samudera* - Indonesia

Class AII
1st - *Eye of the Wind* - UK

Class A
1st - *Gorch Fock* - Germany

1st ship across Finish Line - *Peter von Danzig* - Germany
1st Overall on Corrected Time - *Jolie Brise* - UK

Race 4 - Boston to Halifax Class Prizes

Class CIII
1st - *Hebe III* - Czech Republic

Class CII
1st - *Sarie Marais of Plym* - UK

Class CI
1st - *Brilliant* - USA

Class AII
1st - *Asgard II* - Ireland

Class A
1st - *Kaiwo Maru* - Japan

1st ship across Finish Line - *Mir* - Russia
1st Overall on Corrected Time - *Kaiwo Maru* - Japan
The ASTA prize for the first North American vessel on corrected time - *Brilliant* - USA

Race 5 - Halifax to Amsterdam Class Prizes

Class CIII
1st - *NV Hamburg* - Germany

Class CII
1st - *Blitz* - Italy

Class CI
1st - *Brilliant* - USA

Class B
1st - *Pride of Baltimore II* - USA

Class AII
1st - *Eye of the Wind* - UK

Class A
1st - *Kruzenshtern* - Russia

1st ship across Finish Line - *NV Hamburg* - Germany
1st Overall on Corrected Time - *Brilliant* - USA

Tall Ships Challenge®

The Tall Ships Challenge® race series will launch ASTA and sail training in North America into the 21st Century with an exciting series of races and rallies starting in the Great Lakes in the summer of 2001, moving to the Pacific Coast in 2002, and then to the Atlantic Coast in 2003. These events will involve five to seven port cities in each region, linked by sail training races and/or cruises-in-company, over a five- to eight-week period each summer.

The aim of the Tall Ships Challenge® race series is to further ASTA's mission by creating public awareness of sail training and our member vessels throughout North America. This will help our member vessels to fill their berths and earn needed revenue; it will help ASTA to earn revenue for programs that directly support our industry, such as scholarships and grants, representing the industry on governmental advisory committees, publishing our Directory and other publications, and producing our annual Conference, Safety Forum, and Regional Meetings; it will bring tall ships from around the world to our port cities; and it will ultimately create a climate and an awareness of the benefits of sail training that will cause more vessels to be built, thereby generating more opportunities for young people of all ages to have a sail training experience.

ASTA is actively seeking title sponsors and co-sponsors for the overall series, which we have every reason to expect will repeat its cycle in the years beyond 2003. Companies interested in sponsorship, ports interested in hosting the Challenge, and sail training organizations desiring to participate in the Challenge should contact the ASTA office.

Above: Captain David V.V. Wood, USCG (Ret.), Chairman of ASTA, announces the Tall Ships Challenge® Race Series at a press conference in Boston during the spring of 2000. Right: Brig *Niagara* passing in front of the crowds during the 1998 Great Lakes Tall Ships® Race.

Following is the confirmed schedule of events for Tall Ships Challenge® 2001:

Kingston, Ontario	June 28-July 2	Port festival
Lake Ontario	July 2-5	Tall Ships Race
Port Colborne, Ontario	July 5-9	Port festival
Lake Erie	July 9-11	Tall Ships Race
Cleveland, Ohio	July 11-16	Port festival
Detroit, Michigan/ Windsor, Ontario	July 18-22	Port festival
Lake Huron	July 23-26	Tall Ships Race
Bay City, Michigan	July 26-30	Port festival
Bay City to Straits of Mackinac	July 30-August 1	Tall Ships Race
Lake Michigan	August 1-9	Cruise in Company
Muskegon, Michigan	August 9-13	Port festival

Following is the schedule of events for Tall Ships Challenge® 2002

Victoria, British Columbia	August	Port festival
Seattle, Washington	August 15-19	Port festival
Pacific Coast	August 20-28	Tall Ships Race
San Francisco, California	Aug. 28-Sept. 2	Port festival
Pacific Coast	September 2-6	Tall Ships Race
Los Angeles, California	September 6-10	Port festival
San Diego, California	September 12-16	Port festival

The Sailing Experience

On board the *Jolie Brise* off the Dutch Coast during Tall Ships 2000®.

WITH INFORMATION AND ARTICLES BY CAPTAIN DAN MORELAND OF THE *PICTON CASTLE*, CAPTAIN GEORGE MOFFETT OF *BRILLIANT*, STEVE CHRISTMAN, ERIC MCHENRY, GREGG SWANZEY AND DIANE CAREY

Remarks Given at Halifax's Celebrated Admiral's Ball on 29 April 2000

As Tall Ships 2000® gets underway, the skipper of the barque *Picton Castle* offers some reflections on the significance of the event, and on the staying power of tall ships.

BY CAPTAIN DAN MORELAND

Tonight, while we are warm, snug, well fed and under cover, a great fleet of sailing ships on the other side of this cold, dreary, storm-tossed North Atlantic is underway from England, bound for Cadiz, Spain. Vessels from 3,000-ton, four-masted barques built at the end of the Age of Sail for carrying grain around Cape Horn to 100-foot schooners, built last year to take a new generation out under sail. These vessels are at sea, taking come what may on their way to join what promises to be simply one of the greatest convoys of sailing ships the world has ever seen. Never before have there been this many sailing ships navigating the sea in such a coordinated race.

Individually and in company, the ships will participate in multi-day port festivals in Bermuda, San Juan, Miami, Norfolk, Portsmouth, Charleston, Baltimore, Wilmington, Philadelphia, New York City, Long Island, New Haven, Boston, Newport, Martha's Vineyard, Portland, Halifax, Lunenburg, Erie, Cleveland, South Haven, Wyandotte, and Chicago. Most, after leaving Boston, will cross the Gulf of Maine, sail along the southwest shore of fair Nova Scotia and into Halifax harbor. And, as in those other ports, our docks and wharves will be crowded with folks anxious to see these ships sail into one of the world's greatest natural harbors. Office buildings with sea views will

The barque *Picton Castle*

PHOTO BY DAN MORELAND

be in danger of capsizing from the unequal distribution of office workers staring out their seaward side. The grassy slopes of the Citadel Hill will be hosting many a picnic. Telephoto cameras and binoculars will be in strong evidence. All to catch a glimpse of these ships as they make entry onto Halifax's aquatic stage.

While the sight of so many ships and people may be a rare phenomenon, it is not anything new. History is replete with vignettes of people's fascination with sailing ships and those who sail them — from ancient Greek myths celebrating the return of Jason and the Argonauts to

Polynesian islanders flocking out in their canoes to visiting sailing ships hundreds of years ago. Even that great classic of the sea, *Moby Dick*, by former foc's'le hand, Herman Melville, concerning itself mostly with whalish gore and devilish pacts, describes early on the land-bound citizenry of Manhattan drawn to the fringe of their New York island to witness the shipping under sail and commune with the sea itself. This, of course, after Ishmael was done bringing up the end of funeral marches and knocking off people's hats in the dark November of his soul.

This grand tall-ship gathering — part Olympics of wind and sail, part coming-out party of fresh paint and sharp uniforms — is an event organically called into being by the combined will of people of the world as a celebration and perhaps the ultimate form of ritualistic launch of the new millennium. For years, everyone has assumed there would be a

great cavalcade of the world's windjammers at this prescribed moment. No one actually voted for it, as far as I know, but I don't think anyone voted against having a tall ship celebration either. Organizers are finding out now how hard the work is to pull these off, while the ships — without which there would be no tall ship event — have long been aware of the challenges and work they face in making this all look easy.

But it is my aim tonight to attempt to put the upcoming and much anticipated arrival and celebrations of these wonderful tall and small ships into some perspective. Said differently, to try to frame these ships and our attention and affection for them in some sort of historical, cultural and educational context.

It is clear that there is some under-the-skin, deep-in-the-marrow primal fascination not for just any old ships, but for these tall ships in particular; and, by extension, their crews and almost any-

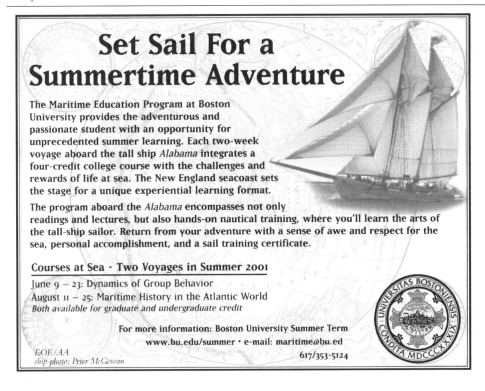

thing to do with them. History tells us that this has always been so. When we glance at old prints or paintings of sailing ships, or perhaps gaze at a fine museum vessel trussed to the pier, secured for visitors, we can be forgiven if we find ourselves thinking "how quaint, how old-fashioned, but how obsolete." Yet there was once a day when sailing ships were state-of-the-art technology for moving goods, people and ideas around most of the world—or sometimes just down the coast. That day is only now just at dusk and that day lasted for over 4000 years. Five hundred years hence, what will be said of the era of fossil fuels?

Imagine what it used to require to move 100 tons of stuff (that's about ten tractor-trailers full) the 60 miles to Halifax from that daughter of the sea, Lunenburg. One wagon, four oxen and a driver or two could move a ton about 10 to 15 miles a day. So 100 wagons, 400 oxen and a hundred or so drivers could get that 100 tons to Halifax in five or six days...if the road was good...if there was a road. But even before there was a Lunenburg/Halifax land road, a handy coasting schooner and her crew of four or five could kiss their wives goodbye, sail out of Lunenburg at dawn with a fair wind and expect to be alongside a pier ready to discharge her hold in Halifax in daylight with time enough for a pint with their friends later that evening. I think that works out to schooner technology being a thousand times more efficient than wagon technology. And that's giving the wagon a road hewn out of the forest. But the wagon technology has won this last round for the time being. Stay tuned.

The ocean is Nova Scotia's heritage. Before there was an information highway, we had an ocean highway. We still have it. Before the Internet, Nova Scotia had the schooner-net. Fast enough for me and no need for virtual reality — genuine old-fashioned reality and plenty of it. It may be a fantasy looking up at a lofty rig of a sailing ship from the wharf, but cross the rail and cast off with us and you'll find reality aplenty.

And what of the tall ship's educational role—and what is sail training? Just a little over a hundred years ago, as steam vessels eclipsed sailing vessels in how much cargo they moved about, shipping companies learned that their officers and crew brought up in sail had qualities that were good for their ships and resulted in ships that were in better repair, less in danger from the weather and, in fact, just had fewer problems. As these ships' officers and seamen went ashore, and if they weren't broken by the experience, they were inevitably in demand in any industry they pursued. It was only in the mid-1990's that the last European country repealed the law that required merchant marine officers to have time in deepwater sail. There were no ships left in which to

sail in order to fill the requirement.

Joseph Conrad's stories often place you in the company of captains of commerce and industry, former seafarers under sail all recalling their formative years. Why? What did these folks get out of that life experience that gave them the goods and what goods were these? People have been stumbling over how to express the benefits of sail training for some time. The exercise usually gets shunted off under the heading of "It builds character." That's hardly enough. We all know plenty of characters that never went to sea. But that crucible of being a working crew in a vessel of canvas, rope and wood or steel, not fighting the wind and sea but harnessing its power and riding this unnamable entity, brings out — or causes to be forged — an enviable array of characteristics.

These include teamwork and dependability. What could be more of a team than a watch on deck jibing the monster mainsail of a huge fishing schooner on the Grand Banks, swinging around to pick up a straggling dory at dusk with the fog closing in? Problem solvers: on a vessel at sea your resources are your ship, yourself and your experience. Conservationists: at sea under sail you can sail forever, cross any number of oceans without diesel fuel if you can take care of your gear. Environmentalists: seafaring under sail close to the ocean surface you will see the impact of a careless world civilization. Again, reading between the lines of *Moby Dick* you find that Melville sent out a clarion call to stop the whale-killing a hundred years before civilization took up the cause.

Sailors learn to be alert, not just on duty but all the time. A sailor's eyes, ears and nose are always working and they seem to work best when the mouth is closed. The veteran sailor is usually respectful of tradition and authority, but not blindly, and he usually holds both to a high standard. There is more along this line, but you get the idea.

Today, we have faster and more efficient ways to carry fish, pianos, bananas, rocks and rum. It is good that we have trucks, planes and trains to undertake these mundane tasks. This leaves the real unquenchable mission to sailing ships, for which no more efficient engine has yet been conceived. That, of course, is education in its many forms and that is what the tall ships of today do. To take young and not so young people to sea and along the coast, and to prepare them for the squalls and calms, doldrums and gales and even the blue sky — those puffy, white-cloud, trade-wind days of life when everything is just going right. You need a couple of cold North Atlantic gales to really appreciate the good days. Every one of these ships is an educational institution unto itself with — besides the nautical issues — all the problems of such institutions: finding funding, quali-

fied teachers, students. Even the great state vessels have to scramble for funding, qualified crew and appropriate students.

The barque *Picton Castle* is no exception. A product of Lunenburg's maritime trades, she as well has an educational mission, and it is an ambitious one. When voyaging, we are involved in four categories of education. First, there is the hands-on experience for the crew sailing a square-rigged ship around the world in the trade winds by way of the tropics. Working the ship, visiting old cultures new to us. On board, learning to steer the 300-ton barque. Rigging, sail making, spar making, boat handling and repair, chart work, piloting, celestial navigation and more are taught as a matter of course. Immersing ourselves in third world cultures is a learning experience that affects our outlook the rest of our lives. But it is hard to define. Nonetheless, learning to get along in close quarters and learning not to waste or defile are key markers along the way.

Second, we give back as we go. On this last voyage, the crew distributed donated educational materials to island schools. I was surprised to learn the demand and desire for what we could bring. We hope to fill our hold with redundant, remaindered books on our next trip. Let us know what you have and we'll be glad to take it to the South Pacific for you.

Third, we use the Internet to share our experiences with the folks back here and with classrooms around the world. Both a popular, 100-page active Web site to follow our voyage with many stories and over 2,000 photos, plus another Web site with structured classroom lesson plans to inspire school children to grasp the relevance of their basic studies. Sails, sailing and navigation are physics, math and teamwork. Buying mangoes in Zanzibar is an exercise in financial exchange, math, language and diplomacy, and young people get it when it's shown to them.

Fourth, we teach the teachers. Through our affiliate, WebED, a dot.com company dedicated to expanding professional development for the education community, we reach teachers and provide them with grist — the likes of which I just mentioned — to help them inspire young people and teach outside the lines, especially in addressing such visual teaching problems as dyslexia.

When the dust settles in Halifax — after the party is over — the wakes foaming off the bows of these brigantines, schooners, and barques will have stilled to nothing on the water's edge. Perhaps for some people. But I suggest that they will continue to pound like ocean surf in the hearts of many who let these tall "cathedrals of the seas" into their lives. These ships connect us in time to our rich past. As they sail over the horizon bound we know not where, they sail with our imaginations in tow into the unknown of the future. They do this forging forward, harnessed to the wind and sea with something much stronger than hope, yet more delicate than certainty.

As for these ships being obsolete, they will be obsolete the day the long ocean swell has been retired. They will be obsolete the hour the trade winds have been judged outdated and have been switched off. Our ships will be obsolete the minute the smoky southwester that flows along the coast of Nova Scotia, carrying the sweet salt tang of a sea breeze that clears our minds as well sails our ships, is finally worn out and retired.

Tall Ships 2000®–Ocean Racing as a Sail Training Experience

ASTA's Sail Trainer of the Year in 2000, along with members of his crew, tell the story of *Brilliant's* experience in the Tall Ships 2000 transatlantic race from Halifax to Amsterdam in which they took first place

BY CAPTAIN GEORGE MOFFETT

Within the matrix of sail training opportunities, there are numerous turns a student can take in seeking the way to the core experience. Not long ago there were only a few sail training options in the US and abroad, in contrast to the enormous expansion of programs and vessels we see today. The international growth and success of the industry, along with the anticipated continuation of this trend, demonstrates that something important has been discovered or rediscovered. With so many ships, interest has grown proportionately in organizing fleet events. Always, in devel-

The crew in Amsterdam. Back row: Dan Parke, Christine Alberi (Mate), and Frank Bohlen (Watch Leader); second row: Matt Lincoln, George Moffett (Captain), Lee Wacker (Cook & Medical Specialist), Myles Thurlow and Jon Feins; front row: Katie Olman and Chris Schmiedeskamp.

oping programs or organizing events such as the ASTA and ISTA tall ship races, the question must be asked: To what degree are we fostering the core experience? Racing, as compared to cruising-in-company or alone, shapes the experience, and some might ask if it strengthens or weakens the quality and content of what is learned at sea.

We all know that the gathering of large numbers of sailing ships in a harbor stimulates a burst of growth for the local economy. Also, with financial support to the ships for attending these events, there is benefit to the vessels as they struggle to keep their operations viable. Within this international context, youth of all ages meet and discover a larger world. These incentives are strong, so we can be sure that such events will continue. However, when sail training ships race from one spectacular harbor event to another–as was the case with Tall Ships 2000–the focus shifts to why these vessels exist and what happens at sea.

We know these ships exist to offer a worthwhile experience, but it is difficult to communicate that value to those who are not at sea experiencing the moment, or the long stretch of days into weeks. Aboard *Brilliant*, as was the case with many participating vessels, we communicated daily from the ship to shore with the global satellite system Inmarsat C. We hoped to bridge the gap between those at sea and their enthusiastic followers ashore. The ship's log was transmitted as written messages in the form of e-mails to Mystic Seaport's planetarium office; the planetarium director, Don Treworgy, then forwarded the e-mails and posted the log on our Web page. We hoped this would provide a 'real time' vicarious experience, and all reports indicate that this method of stimulating interest was very successful.

Getting close to Amsterdam! Lee Wacker (Cook & Medical Specialist) at the wheel, with Jon Feins along side, during the race from Halifax to Amsterdam.

We feel sure that the personal growth witnessed aboard *Brilliant* in the races from Boston to Halifax and Halifax to Amsterdam was similar in many ways to the development aboard other vessels in the fleet. Within the great variety of ship types, sizes, and operations, there is a common understanding. The intensity of sustained racing with unrelenting attention to sail changes, sail trim, course steered, equipment security, and many safety details results in a different experience than would be the case on a more relaxed cruise where the focus can shift away from boat performance to a broader program and course content. Our crew learned to sustain a singularly intensive focus on responding to the elements to keep the boat moving at her best speed over a wide range of wind strengths and sea states.

The following student comments, slightly edited, from *Brilliant's* e-mail log give insight into how some were finding their way to the core:

Dan Parke, 20 years old, August 3, 2000, ten days after the start of the race from Halifax, a week before crossing the finish line, following a gale: Standing on the bowsprit with surprisingly warm mid-Atlantic water up to one's waist is a strange place for an epiphany, but that was exactly my position when I realized this may be my last summer vacation. Then Myles Thurlow tugged on the jib and passed me another few feet of luff, and we got the sail changed. That was the first sail change of a series that would see us shorten all the way down to a storm trysail and forestaysail and then back to full canvas. The past few days have been a trial of stamina, concentration and teamwork. Squalls with cold rain and wind, seas slapping the hull and drenching the watch on deck; after four hours we would go below, shed our foul weather gear and find a roughly horizontal surface to collapse on. The off watches are looking forward to sleeping in a clean and ventilated cabin.

Katie Oman, 22, on reaching Amsterdam, August 23: A poster of *Brilliant* hangs over my bed. I have occasionally been known to obsessively polish household brass. I wrote my college admission essay about my first trip on *Brilliant*. A sail to Bermuda, two Opera House Cups, a summer as cook, and a transatlantic passage later, I'm still learning about the boat, the ocean, myself, and most importantly my shipmates. I have enjoyed a long, salty, and personally transforming passage.

Jon Feins, 17, Amsterdam, August 23: These past 6 weeks have enabled me to

see and experience things that few people will ever get to experience. I've learned how to tie many different knots, and I can now look in the sky at night and name many stars. Yet if you asked me what the most enjoyable part of the trip was, I'd respond by saying 'the crew'. We worked incredibly well together. If someone needed help or did not understand something, another was there to give a hand and when things needed to be done, they were done fast and well. So out of the sunsets, sunrises, stars, dolphins, whales, sea turtles, huge seas, small seas, little wind, a lot of wind, seasickness, field days, and all the onshore activities, the things that will always remain with me are my memories of this crew. I would be honored to sail with them again.

Myles Thurlow, 17, Amsterdam, Aug 23: I'll remember the days of the gale where we were wet whenever we were on deck and the struggle of trying to clean the head while we were pounding through 10' seas in 30 knots of wind. But most of all I will remember coming onto this boat with nine other people I had never met before and making it through six weeks sailing without any major incident.

We know that racing is not essential to a high quality learning experience at sea, and accept that sometimes it may stand in the way of a broader approach to program content. But there can be no doubt that living through the tempest of a seventeen day ocean race with sustained attentiveness, demanded even when least welcome, will prepare the way for the next challenge that requires similar endurance from the mind and will, indeed the heart.

Brilliant on her way to Amsterdam, Tall Ships 2000®

Millennium Voyage of the *Californian*

BY STEVE CHRISTMAN, PRESIDENT, NAUTICAL HERITAGE SOCIETY

Wednesday, October 11th 1848 - (Log of the C.W. Lawrence) - At 12 we hauled off from Easby's Ship Yard, took on board the crew and prepared the ship to be taken in tow. At 3P.M. steamer SALEM came alongside and took the vessel in tow. At 6 P.M. off the Navy Yard, cast off from the steamer and hauled into the wharf at the Navy Yard and made fast. Ends with calm and pleasant weather. Served 30 rations. W.R. Pierce 2d Lt.

One hundred and forty-eight years ago, the Revenue Cutter *C.W. Lawrence*, began an epic one-year voyage from Washington D.C. to take station in San Francisco at the height of the California Gold Rush. The *Lawrence* was the first Revenue Marine cutter to be sent to the Pacific.

Last year the *Californian*, a replica of the *Lawrence* returned to the very dock where the *Lawrence* outfitted so many years before. The purpose of the *Californian's* voyage was to participate in the ASTA and OpSail events commemorating the Millennium.

As the voyage would be a huge undertaking , the decision to send the topsail schooner *Californian* to the East Coast was one that the Nautical Heritage Society did not take lightly. But when OceanSpray committed as a sponsor for the special events, and the Coast Guard expanded the ship's authorized route, the decision was made in February of 1999 to undertake the trip.

Californian

ship and the cadets that sailed with her, so we expected the same for this "Millennium Voyage".

Twelve girls from Mercy High School in San Francisco were our cadets for the first two months.

February 22nd, 2000 - (Captain's Report SV *Californian*) - We

The voyage would cover between 15 and 16 thousand miles and six countries, and would be by far the longest ever made in the seventeen years the ship has been at sea. Nevertheless, the *Californian* had been out to Hawaii four times and to Canada and Mexico twice, and all had been great experiences for the

are heading to Santa Catalina Island tonight - we may sail all night. Seven of the twelve girls climbed aloft over the futtock shrouds and then ventured out onto the topsail yard foot ropes; we expect to cross into Mexican waters by the 27th. — Todd Burgman Captain.

Daily reports from the *Californian's* INMARSAT C provided welcome information on the ship as she worked her way toward Panama, and eventually on to the East Coast. Using satellite technology on an 1848 replica may seem anachronistic, but the peace of mind it gives those of us back at the Nautical Heritage Society is considerable, especially on the long open-water passages.

March 31, 2000 - We weighed anchor after lunch yesterday at Isla Isabela, had a swim call, and then sailed averaging 7 kts under the 4 lowers and fore top until the wind died around 1900. We then motored to the village of La Cruz de Huanacaxtle in Banderas Bay, where we anchored at 0430. We saw several sea turtles yesterday while sailing. Plan on a short day sail after lunch, then anchoring inside Pta Mita for a swim on the beach.

May 3, 2000 - At anchor Bahía Limón / Colon. Locked through Gatún at

SAIL TALL SHIPS!

2300 last night and entered Bahía Limón, at anchor in Colon now, cleared foreign. We straightened jibboom spreader that was damaged by Panama Canal operators last night and reinstalled. Setting up jibboom guys now. Will sail shortly after 1200 today for Mobile. North wind near coastal, but offshore forecast looks good so far. All's well aboard.

The passage from Acapulco through the Canal and on to Mobile, Alabama was made with crew only. Our next crew of cadets came aboard at. St. Petersburg, Florida, and various groups of cadets were aboard for most of our time on the East Coast. The parade in New York and up the Hudson was certainly a high point in a voyage filled with high points. Sailing the Atlantic coast is a far different experience than operating in the Pacific. The eastern seaboard has many more ports and anchorages to duck into, while on the West Coast safe anchorages may be hundreds of miles apart.

For the Tall Ships 2000® race to Halifax, we recruited students from California to be our cadets. Races add a real element of excitement for the cadets aboard. We also raced in New London and Baltimore. Our thanks to ASTA and all the various race organizers, win or lose: it was fun.

July 9, 2000 - New London, Today we raced with the *Pride of Baltimore II* and a group of smaller schooners. Unfortunately our start was dreadful and we never were able to recover the distance lost so the race was lost, in light winds.

September 8, 2000 - New London, Connecticut We are currently docked at Fort Trumbull. Getting off the dock this afternoon to greet the U.S.C.G. Barque *Eagle* when she returns to New London at the end of her training voyage. We will

be docking at the U.S.C.G. Academy with the *Eagle* and will be holding an open house for the Coast Guard cadets and their parents.

New London was designated as the *Californian's* honorary East Coast port due to the ship's historical ties with the Coast Guard. We very shortly found that we would be needing Coast Guard help having nothing to do with history at all.

September 22, 2000 - Atlantic City, Arrived in Atlantic City yesterday evening. Had a very lively sail down the coast, the ship reaching 10 knots at times. One of the crew had to be removed by U.S. Coast Guard 41 foot rescue boat due to a ruptured appendix, crew member arrived at the hospital and had it removed, all is well. But it was an experience we hope not to repeat any-time soon.

Our sincere thanks to our friends in the

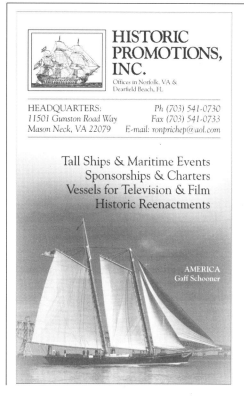

Coast Guard, those folks are great!

October 3, 2000 - Washington Navy Yard, Anchored just south of the Woodrow Wilson Bridge yesterday late afternoon to wait until the bridge could be opened to let us through. Because of the strong current and soft mud on the bottom of the river we dragged the anchor along for a little distance while making quite a bit of sternway before it decided to dig in. Transited up river this morning and passed under the South Capitol Street Bridge up to the Navy Yard. We are now at the birth place of the *C.W. Lawrence* where she was launched with all her colors flying from every elevated point of the vessel on August 20th, 1848!

We had chosen to haul out in Fairhaven Massachusetts for our annual Coast Guard inspection, but also to be inspected by the American Bureau of Shipping for the Load Line Certificate the Coast Guard is now requiring for international voyages. The *Californian* has also applied for a new dual certificate as a Sailing School Vessel to allow the ship to carry additional cadets. The folks at the Fairhaven Shipyard were very helpful and soon the ship was back visiting ports all along the Eastern seaboard.

Arriving at the Washington Navy Yard brought the saga of the *Lawrence* full circle. We held a "Welcome Home" reception with the Navy Memorial Foundation and Admiral Vern Clark, Chief of Naval Operations, was on hand to help us celebrate a bit of history.

Then, since we hadn't done well in New London, we tried again in the "Great Chesapeake Bay Schooners Race".

October 21, 2000 - Norfolk, Many of the schooners dropped out of the race due to light winds, but we continued on determined to finish before the time deadline. Fighting the light winds and tides paid off and we have finished first, winning the Chesapeake Bay Schooner's Race for class AA!!!

By November the ship was preparing to come home. No hurricanes were in the offing and we wanted to be home by New Year's Day.

November 23, 2000 - Colon, Panama, Happy Thanksgiving! We are in neither the Atlantic nor Pacific. We cleared the Gatún Locks at noon and are motoring on Lake Gatún, a fresh water lake between the oceans (fresh water showers for everyone!). We expect to arrive in Balboa by 1800. We have contacted the agent: we will pick up a mooring in Balboa. — Rinn Wright Captain.

Back in the Pacific we could reflect back on our voyage. The cadets who sailed with us had the adventure of a lifetime. The hospitality shown the crew and the ship was much appreciated. The crew enjoyed sailing and visiting with the crews of the many traditional vessels we encountered along the way. Our various sponsors were happy and, best of all, it was a safe voyage.

December 24, 2000 - At sea, Twas the night before Christmas and wherever you'd look, Not a creature was stirring, not even the cook. The deckhands were perched asleep in their racks, Dreaming of anything other than tacks. The captain was resting, as captains oft' do, The bosun was snoozing — amazing but true. The mate was looking busy writing this prose, But well looking forward to his afternoon doze. — Jesse Schaffer 1st Mate.

And one final entry:

December 30, 2000 - At anchor in San Diego Bay, in the wee hours of Saturday morning we dropped anchor in San Diego harbor. This morning we cleared

customs and are now officially home in the U.S.A. Our voyage covered 15,454 sea miles over 314 days. My leg from Virginia covered 5,000 miles, including all conditions of sailing: calms, gales and everything in between. With the help of this excellent crew and very worthy vessel it was a piece of cake. — Rinn Wright Captain.

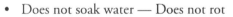

Two Weeks Before the Mast

In a new summer history course, students trade walls for trade winds.

BY ERIC MCHENRY
PHOTOGRAPHS BY VERNON DOUCETTE

Tammie Newman may be the first person in history to stand on the weather deck of an oceanbound ship and hope out loud for bad weather.

It's July 30, a Sunday, and Newman has just stepped aboard the Rose, a full-scale replica of an eighteenth-century British frigate moored for the moment in Boston's Inner Harbor. During the next two weeks, it will be her home, her school, and above all else her workplace.

"I haven't talked to anybody about the forecast yet," says Newman, a Clarion College senior and mother of four, "but I'm hoping we hit a nasty storm."

That hope is actually consistent with the aim of the course she's taking — exposure to the elements of seafaring. Designed and taught by Timothy Walker under the aegis of Metropolitan College, Maritime History in the Atlantic World is a rare opportunity, in Newman's words, "not to be a part of history, but to feel a part of it."

From Knot-Tying to Navigating

Walker began dreaming up the course five years ago, when he worked for a semester-at-sea program offered by the University of Pittsburgh. He liked the setup — 500 students aboard a modern steamship — but envisioned an even

centuries.

"Ships are the sine qua non of colonization and of empires," says Walker, a veteran MET instructor, who with his long ponytail and thick black beard could also be the world's most articulate pirate. "People tend to forget that sailing once tied everything together. Two hundred years ago, the London and Liverpool docks each employed 50,000 people. A hundred years ago, this Inner Harbor looked like a forest with all the masts."

The towering, three-masted Rose, an embarrassment to the pleasure boats in its presence, perfectly illustrates the sea's diminished importance. At 179 feet, spar to stern, and 500 tons, she is the largest active wooden sailing ship in the world. But her eighteenth-century predecessor, with exactly the same dimensions and displacement, was a sixth-rater — among the smallest of British warships.

more intensive history course "in which the students have a role in moving the vessel along, in which they really get a feel for what it was like to take a ship from port to port in a period when that was a very dodgy business."

The Rose, as one full-time deckhand puts it, "is not a passenger vessel." Students who expect the ship to take them to Nova Scotia and back are quickly reoriented: as apprentice crew members, they take it. Along with a daily sail training session in which professional crew teach everything from navigation to knot-tying, students stand watch eight hours of every twenty-four. They steer, set and strike sails, raise the 2,000-pound anchor by collectively turning the capstan, wash down the deck with saltwater, performed exhaustive boat checks, do the dishes, and clean the heads.

Into this demanding schedule Walker shoehorns his two-hour lectures on travel and trade among Europe, Africa, and South and North America from the early fifteenth through the early nineteenth

Some Negative First Impressions

Built in Hull in 1757, the early Rose menaced colonial ships in the waters off Massachusetts and Rhode Island. In 1769, several of her officers boarded the brigantine Pitt and attempted to impress four men into service. The men resisted violently, killing one of the Rose's lieutenants with a harpoon. A young John Adams won their acquittal in a special court of vice-admiralty.

Using the original drawings, a history enthusiast from Newport, Rhode Island, built the modern Rose in 1970, hoping to take part in the battle reenactments of the U.S. bicentennial. He underestimated the cost of the project, though, and the Rose remained for the most part a dockside attraction until 1985, when the nonprofit HMS Rose Foundation was formed. The new Rose, a full-time sail training vessel, differs from the old in a few small but significant ways. Walker gestures jokingly to a panel of "authentic eighteenth-century electronic controls" on the quarterdeck. Gone are all but a few of her cannons. New are a couple of diesel engines that can be engaged when the winds are against her.

"But the sails are what it's about," says Hank Moseley, the ship's rigging chief, or boatswain. With a blond goatee and a strip of T-shirt tied around his head, Moseley looks even more like a pirate than Walker, although he too is unassuming and well-spoken. "When the winds are favorable," he says, "we're much faster with sails than we are with our diesels going."

Students set and strike sails just as their Revolution-era counterparts did: climbing a rope ladder through the ship's rigging, then walking along the yard — a horizontal spar that supports the sails — on a single rope. A hundred and thirty feet separate a sailor on the highest yard from the water below, although of course that number rises and drops along with the ship. Sail trainees say it's exhilarating.

"We don't require anyone to go aloft," says Captain Richard Bailey, a Cape Cod native and dry wit who has been with the ship almost since the Rose Foundation was established. "But if we had thirty trainees and none would go aloft, it would certainly affect how much sail we could set, because the crew couldn't do it all.

"In the eighteenth century," Bailey

says, "the Rose had a crew of 160. Today, forty-nine is a full house. So we have to use our human resources very efficiently."

A Motley Crew

It's August 12, and the Rose has just returned to the Inner Harbor. Seen through the central archway of the Boston Harbor Hotel, she is a stunning anachronism. Passersby are as taken by the tall ship as they are indifferent to the streamlined yacht she has bellied up beside.

Students and crew are tanned, scruffy, and salt-encrusted. They hustle to clear the weather deck for one final knot-tying session — someone has reserved the Rose for a wedding. Bailey disappears belowdecks, emerging a few moments later in a tuxedo; he'll be performing the ceremony.

The twenty-four who signed up for Walker's course are a diverse bunch. More than a third are women. Several are high school students and one is a junior high school principal. But the experience seems to have brought out similarities rather than differences. They gab enthusiastically, not too eager to be reunited with their land legs.

"I will always understand — and never forget — the theory of mercantilism and how to tie a bowline," says Brandeis graduate student Abigail Weiner. She's picked up the sailor's inflection, stressing first syllables and softening the rest: bo´lun.

Newman got the nasty weather she'd been hoping for — a squall with plenty of pitching and rolling, "but no lashing rain or water up over the sides.

"Once you realize you actually have to be out in it, and you don't have a little picture window to look through," she admits, "it's not necessarily so cool."

She says the sheer quantity of work demanded by the ship, ironically, makes it an environment almost free of stress.

"I couldn't worry about anything that was going on at home, even though I left behind my husband and my four children. There just wasn't time," she says. "You had to catch any little bit of sleep that you could."

Aaron Berman, a College of Communication sophomore who will "definitely" be sailing again, has a different perspective.

"To me," he says, "sleep would have been a waste of time."

For Boston University Summer Term information, call 617-353-5124, or visit www.bu.edu/summerterm. To find out more about the Rose, visit www.tallshiprose.org.

Reprinted with permission from Bostonia Quarterly.

Sailing on a Mission for our Waters

BY CAPTAIN GREGG SWANZEY

We have long known that sailing ships offer powerful multi-disciplinary learning experiences to people of all ages. We have witnessed the global impact of modern civilization on water quality and the ecological health of our waterways, coastal environments and, indeed, the oceans thousands of miles from shore. Today, many ships have come to serve missions both as educators as well as flagships for protecting and restoring the health of coastal and ocean ecosystems.

In 1972 the Clean Water Act was passed. Regulatory provisions imposed progressively more stringent requirements on industries and cities in order to meet the statutory goal of zero discharge of pollutants. Other provisions authorized federal financial assistance for municipal wastewater treatment construction. Industries were to meet pollution control limits first by use of Best Practicable Technology and later by improved Best Available Technology. Cities were to achieve secondary treatment of municipal wastewater, or better if needed, to meet water quality standards.

The most recent amendments to the Clean Water Act, enacted in February 1987 as the Water Quality Act of 1987, brought to a conclusion six years of congressional efforts to extend and revise the Act, and are the most comprehensive amendments to it since 1972. They recognize that, despite much progress to date, significant water quality problems persist.

The 1987 amendments add Section 319 to the Act, under which states are required to develop and implement programs to control non-point sources of pollution, or rainfall runoff from farm and urban areas, as well as construction, forestry, and mining sites. Previously, the Act had largely focused on controlling point sources, while helping states and localities to plan for management of diverse non-point sources. Yet, as industrial and municipal sources have abated pollution, uncontrolled non-point sources have become a relatively larger portion of remaining water quality problems — perhaps contributing as much as 50% of the nation's water pollution.

Now, more than ever, on account of significant population growth along waterways and in coastal areas of the

Ships To Save The Waters, July 2000, Liberty State Park, New York.

United States, broad-based grassroots efforts are critical for the protection and restoration of water resources. Education and local planning efforts are necessary to expose and control non-point sources of pollution from sources such as septic systems, stormwater runoff, chemical use (pesticides, herbicides and fertilizers) and emissions from

Pete Seeger

marine engines such as outboards and jetskis. New approaches to planning based on 'smart growth' and 'livable communities' initiatives are helping communities as well as businesses consider sustainable approaches. Businesses are coming to realize that "anything leaving the premises as a waste stream, instead of a revenue stream, is both an environmental liability and a drain on profits." A long term effort is necessary for a lasting impact.

Another recent development centers around school reform. The Environment as an Integrating Context for learning (EIC) defines a framework for education that uses the surroundings and community as resources for learners as they construct their own learning. Assessments show that students perform better in EIC programs than traditional learning environments. What are some effects of the EIC approach?

• Students develop their capacity to examine and understand the complex inter-relationships and interactions that take place among diverse socio-cultural and natural systems.

• Students discover their own skills and appreciate those of others.

• Students learn to treat each other with more care and exhibit more self-discipline.

• Hands-on learning opportunities involving authentic problems help students understand math and physics concepts and skills more thoroughly and generate motivation and enthusiasm for the subject areas in everyday life.

• The hands-on, minds-on approach enables students of all ability levels to improve their performance and gain a better understanding and appreciation for science.

• Involvement in real-world, project-based activities helps students refine their abilities in scientific observation, data collection, analysis, and formulating conclusions.

• Engagement in learning about their community and natural surroundings builds students' interest and dedication to studying science.

• When allowed to explore the environment and related community topics,

students commonly express a growing interest in developing their language arts skills.

• When students have a chance to use math skills like measuring in a real context, they not only learn better but can apply and remember their math skills longer.

• Students learn to share ideas, discuss their reasoning, and develop new ideas that emerge from team discussions.

• Teachers and students become an enthusiastic learning-teaching team focused on the same objectives.

The effects of the EIC approach and multi-disciplinary shipboard educational experiences as we observe on the water are similar. This similarity suggests that merging compatible classroom-based and water-borne programs would reinforce each other.

There is a great example of a ship built for this new type of service in response to current needs. In 1966, a handful of river-lovers, inspired by Pete and Toshi Seeger, decided to change the course of events that was destroying the Hudson River in New York, and reclaim a natural treasure for us all. They wanted to dramatize the river's plight, recall its history, and help guide its future. They wanted to provide their fellow citizens with a first-hand look at the neglect and pollution of the river, and move them to action. So they built a sloop and named it *Clearwater*.

More than thirty years later Clearwater is still under full sail with other ships working for similar missions: to defend and restore our waters and waterways. Tens of thousands of school children are served every year in coastal and inland waterways throughout the United States. Schooner *Adventuress* sails Puget Sound (Washington), Schooners *Lady Maryland* and *Sultana* run programs in the Chesapeake, Schooner *A.J. Meerwald*, official vessel of New Jersey, plies the Delaware River, Schooners *Quinnipiack* and *SoundWaters* serve Long Island Sound (Connecticut), Schooners *Inland Seas* (Michigan) and *Denis Sullivan* (Wisconsin) sail the Great Lakes, Sloop *Providence* sails Narragansett Bay (Rhode Island) and Schooner *Ernestina*, official vessel of Massachusetts, sails the bays of the Bay State from New Bedford. *Amara Zee* sails from seaport to seaport as a stage-barge, with sail rigging becoming stage rigging and crew becoming actors alongside for shows with social and environmental messages. There are others in a growing list both in the United States and abroad.

Along with the dramatic rise in waterborne activity comes the need for exchange and sharing between organizations. In July 2000, just prior to the Parade of Sail in New York Harbor, the first annual "Ships to Save the Waters" (StStW) Conference was held thanks to the inspiration of Pete Seeger who envisioned a venue for networking water-based programs, sharing environmental educational methodologies and exposing the work of these ships to the public-at-large. Schooner *A.J. Meerwald*, Sloop *Clearwater* and Schooner *Ernestina* organized and hosted the event along with sponsorship from the Liberty State Park Development Corporation in Jersey City, New Jersey. A vision statement was developed: "The waters of the world are precious. Traditional sailing vessels are magical places where waters share their secrets and expose our vulnerability. StStW brings these special vessels together, broadcasts their message and recruits new stewards for sustainable, healthy world waters for this and future generations." The mission of the conference is to "inform and inspire the creation and sustainability of water-borne programs for protection, preservation, restoration and celebration of our waters." Madame Francine Cousteau, president of The

Cousteau Society, was the keynote speaker along with Luis Garden Acosta of El Puente Academy.

Following the successful conference held at Liberty State Park in July 2000, a second annual Ships to Save the Waters Conference will be hosted by the Schooner Ernestina Commission and regional environmental and on-the-water experiential organizations during June 1st through 3rd, 2001 at the F.A. Sowle Building in the New Bedford Whaling National Historical Park in New Bedford.

Representatives from organizations as well as interested individuals and experts in related fields will come together to form alliances and generate collaborative spirit for sharing resources and expertise. Participation is expected from tall ship organizations as well as the Riverkeepers, rowing clubs, environmental educational organizations, sailing school vessels, small boat builders, watershed alliances, etc. The conference will be open to the public-at-large.

A series of panels and workshops will be offered to focus on critical aspects of watershed and marine-based programs launched from both small boats and larger ships with special attention to the community relationships and constituency-building necessary for any initiative to grow and take hold. As a specific project, participants will use a charrette format to take a close look at the southern New England region and develop a model for using natural, cultural, and educational resources in a collaborative way to address current priorities.

This project will bring together an international community and broad expertise to bear on development of a strategy for using watersheds, coastal environments and watercraft to inspire stewardship of the fragile water ecosystems. The model will be applicable in many of the home communities of the participants and will help local and regional organizations come together in a focused way to build public awareness and stewardship in this area. Published results will serve as a template for future conferences, guide next steps within the region and as a tool for stimulating interest in the press for follow-up articles.

Please visit our webpage at http://www.ernestina.org/StStW.html for a description of the activities of last year and for registration information for this years conference June 1-3, 2001. Please consider participating even if your ship cannot attend.

A Congressional Research Service Issue Brief is made available to the public by the National Council for Science and the Environment on Water Quality: Interpreting the Clean Water Act on the Internet. Please see http://www.cnie.org/nle/h2o-15.html with more resources at http://www.cnie.org/nle for more information.

For more information about Sustainability, please see the Florida Sustainable Communities Center website at http://sustainable.state.fl.us and links through the US Department of Energy site at http://www.sustainable.doe.gov/

For more information about the Environment as an Integrating Context for Learning, please see Closing the Achievement Gap in the State Education and Environmental Roundtable website at http://www.seer.org/pages/GAP.html.

Gregg Swanzey is executive director for the Schooner Ernestina Commission and also serves as President of the Board for the Westport River Watershed Alliance, Chair of the Southeastern Environmental Education Alliance in Southeastern Massachusetts and serves on the steering committee for the Secretary's Advisory Group for Environmental Education (MA Executive Office of Environmental Affairs)

Big "A"
Little "A"

Making the Model of a Ghost Ship

BY DIANE CAREY
DECKHAND AND WATCH LEADER,
SCHOONER ALEXANDRIA

When the old schooner was lost, there had already been chit-chat about building a scale model. No one had done the most necessary task: stand on board with a well-marked measuring stick and take specific architectural photos of her, squared off and dead on. We always thought we'd have her around.

But the ship was gone, lost off Cape Hatteras in the growling December Atlantic, in 1996. Only random pictures remained—tourist shots and sentimental snaps taken by friends and crew, mostly of each other, from unhelpful angles.

Make a scale model without the ship to measure? How? The shipwright's plans we had in possession were not accurate. The shape of the bow wasn't even right. The mizzen mast was in the wrong place.

And what about the details? Who thinks to take a picture of a decklight? A tackle? An anchor? The main sheet traveler? How high was the wooden grid we stood on while piloting the ship? How far apart were the deckhouses? What was the shape of the rudder?

What was the angle of the bowsprit? The cut of her headsails? How far forward was the fo'c'sle hatch housing? Where was that little Charlie Noble we all tripped over on the mizzen topdeck?

Suddenly, we didn't remember. And our ship was gone.

A sailing ship endures many alterations in 67 years. Built in Denmark in 1929,

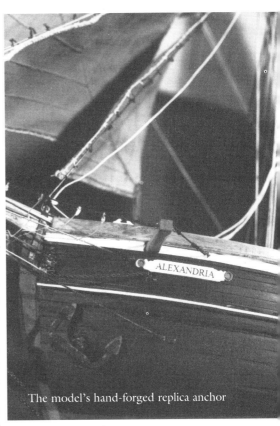

The model's hand-forged replica anchor

Alexandria was a Baltic trader, carrying cargo for a Swedish captain. Over the years she was a gaff schooner, a sloop, a topsail schooner, a Caribbean yacht, a training ship, and a movie prop. Booms and square sails came on and off as needed.

During her last four years, this pliant old vessel was second home to a family of devoted volunteers. Though she was home-berthed in Alexandria, Virginia, her crew came from Michigan, New

The schooner's hand-forged port-side anchor

York, Florida, Wisconsin, and other-wheres. She sailed Chesapeake Bay, New England, down the Carolinas to Florida and across the Gulf of Mexico to New Orleans, then sixty miles up the flooded Mississippi River. And, of course, back to the Bay. These voyages were demanding, but the ship was tough.

A favorite at many harbor festivals, the barbecue-black schooner with the red sails earned herself a reputation for surviving times both prosperous and lean. She appeared in coffee table books about tall ships and even in National Geographic. Though she now rests in the graveyard of ships, her bonding effect

upon her crew endures.

Along came the true skill and fine mind of retired engineer James Turner, a friend living near me in Michigan. An afficionado of ships, trains, and planes, Jim picked up the passion in my voice when I spoke of our schooner. A veteran model builder, he seized upon the idea of building a little *Alexandria*. He wanted photos, lots of them, squared-off shots of things nobody in his right mind would photograph.

That plan was flickering to life when the ship was sold and almost immediately sunk. There would be no pictures with nice clear markers. We couldn't even measure her spare booms and yards. She'd taken all her extra gear down with her.

Now what?

Jim gave me my orders, course and speed. I gathered every photo in my possession, then started contacting shipmates. *Alexandria's* friends from all over

began sending me whatever they had, even photos no one thought were any good. In foregrounds and backgrounds of these photos were the treasury of details no one ever records on purpose.

Further details were teased out of a video tape I made during our voyage from Miami to New Orleans. Mostly recordings of shipmates making merry and dolphins under the bow chains, the video proved a wealth of valuable shots. They include the only known clear photo of the ship's galley decklight, taken completely by accident. We thought the camera had been turned off when it swept past the decklight and captured the picture.

Jim worked miracles, like measuring the width of my hand, a five-gallon bucket, or the height of shipmates, then extrapolating the sizes and shapes of rails, lanyards, deadeyes, deckhouses, height and diameter of the masts and width of the shrouds. At one point, dissatisfied with

SAIL TALL SHIPS!

the tumblehome under the transom, he broke the model apart and completely rebuilt her stern.

The ribs, hull, and deck planking soon took shape. Every few weeks I visited Jim's spotlessly clean workshop and sifted my memory for details. How wide was this companionway? How far apart were these ratlines? Where was the samson post positioned? Was the futtock shroud angle correct? Exactly where was the kevel cleat that snapped in half on the Mississippi River and ripped out the gunwale? And port foredeck looked wrong—didn't it?

Yes, it was wrong. We scrounged for a photo of the port deck, but found none without a distorting angle. Eventually we found a photo of the main salon's interior, showing the location of the portholes. Sure enough, the starboard portholes were evenly spaced, but not on the port side. A flicker of memory pays off!

Then came the rigging—another nightmare, since the pattern of lines changed frequently and no one clearly recalled the details. Pooling of knowledge from her captain, bosuns, mates and deckhands eventually led to a viable plan, added to the blessing that *Alexandria* was a schooner—a simplicity of design that made the rigging into a logic puzzle we understood.

As with the full-sized ship, there were tedious jobs. At the age of 8, my son Gordon Brodeur was one of the ship's last crewmen. Now 13, he helped tie on nearly 200 ratlines and belay the sheets and halyards on teensy pins.

Everything works just like the real thing. Her sails swing from port to starboard tack, her lifts raise the yards, and her halyards hold the gaffs up. The little 8-spoked wheel freely turns on its ropecoiled drum. Jim Turner's sense for detail shows in the graceful flukes of a tiny hand-forged anchor, a duplicate of

Jim Turner rigging the model *Alexandria*

the *Alexandria's* vintage port side anchor.

We then discovered that the "official" sail plan didn't fit the ship. I cut new sails and dyed them to replicate *Alexandria's* weatherworn tanbark sailcloth. They were then shipped to a crewmate from *Pride of Baltimore II*, Bob Johnson of Baltimore, who expertly stitched them, added reefing points, and installed wires that would allow the sails to appear air-filled.

When the sails returned, I stitched ropework around the edges and added tiny robands to hold them to the hoops, stays, or yards, each with a micro reef knot. Soon the model began sailing across my kitchen table.

Little "A" turned out to be not so little—the model stands a mighty 2'7" tall and 3'9" long. She sits on cradles made from a block off the real thing.

Like a friendly old Clydesdale, Schooner *Alexandria* worked hard for decades, endlessly forgiving as her crew acquired sea legs, learned the ropes, and discovered how to keep her bow from swinging. Though she was a cargo vessel, she sailed with secure grace and was always true to her helm.

After 4 years of design and construction, the model of *Alexandria* was christened with a mini-bottle of champagne by Jim Turner at a boatwarming party in June of 2000. Nine people who had sailed *Alexandria* attended, some who came very far to be here, as well as many friends who knew the ship's story.

Now the Little "A" sails our memories back to life, a testimonial to the devotion of *Alexandria's* crews, captains, and one gentleman engineer who has worked on the ship—technically speaking—more than anyone else.

Ocean Classroom Foundation

Programs Under Sail Aboard the Schooners
Spirit of Massachusetts and *Harvey Gamage*

• Fully Accredited Semester at Sea for High School Students
Offered Fall, Spring and Summer Terms

• Summer Seafaring Camp Combining Sea Adventure with Maritime Studies

• Various Programs Throughout the Year Operated in Partnership
with Schools, Colleges, Research Organizations, and Museums.

Contact Information for Individuals or Institutions:

Ocean Classroom Foundation • PO Box 446 • Cornwall, NY 12518

1.800.742.SAIL   mailgamage.org   www.sailgamage.org

2000 Scholarship and Grant Recipients

During 1999, ASTA established three new scholarship and grant programs. The Henry H. Anderson, Jr. Sail Training Scholarship Fund was created to provide financial support for young people who might not otherwise be able to afford the cost of a sail training experience. Named in honor of Harry Anderson, a former Chairman of ASTA and world-renowned yachtsman, the program was launched with a highly successful fundraising event on the grounds of the International Yacht Restoration School, an ASTA member, in Newport in June, 1999. At the same time, the ASTA Sailing Vessel Assistance Grant program was announced.

The scholarships are open to youth in the 14-19 age range who wish to sail aboard an ASTA member vessel which is Coast Guard-inspected as either a Sailing School Vessel or a Small Passenger Vessel. Scholarships are awarded according to need, with priority given to students determined to reach beyond prior experience. Students must pay some part of their tuition, but the percentage is not fixed, nor is it a determining factor in the selection process. ASTA may fund up to 75% of the cost for an individual, to a maximum of $750, and up to 50% for a group, to a maximum of $1,500. Applications may be submitted at any time, but we suggest they be submitted at least four months prior to the sail training experience as applications are considered quarterly.

Recognizing that a substantial number of ASTA's Professional Members do not operate vessels required to be inspected by the Coast Guard, and that trainees on board these vessels would therefore not be eligible for scholarship awards, ASTA has also established a Sailing Vessel Assistance Grant Program. Grants of up to $1,000 may be awarded for projects that further the mission and goals of the American Sail Training Association, or are consistent with ASTA's stated mission. Applications may be submitted at any time, but we suggest they be submitted at least four months prior to need as applications are considered quarterly.

The ASTA Crew Development Grant Program supports the professional development of crewmembers who regularly serve aboard ASTA member vessels. This program, established late in 1999, supports training courses for both individuals and groups. Applications must be received by ASTA by February 15, June 15, and October 15 of each year.

Complete details and application forms for these exciting new programs are available from ASTA's Web site, or by contacting the office directly.

The Henry H. Anderson, Jr. Sail Training Scholarship Fund has been established to assist youth ages 14 - 19 in achieving a sail training experience. Scholarships will be awarded according to need, with priority given to students determined to reach beyond prior experience. Students must pay some part of their tuition, but the percentage is not fixed, nor is it a determining factor in the selection process. The Sail Training Program selected must be a current Professional Member of the American Sail Training Association and the vessel must be a US Coast Guard Inspected Sailing School or Passenger Vessel. Application deadlines: Applications may be submitted at any time. We suggest that applications be submitted at least four (4) months prior to the sail training experience.

Year 2000 Recipients - total of $7,550:

Individual

Christopher M. An - *Westward*/Sea Education Association
Andrea Bennet - *Harvey Gamage*/Ocean Classroom
Bridget C. Brett - *Westward*/Sea Education Association
Cordelia Hall-Reinhard - H. M. Bark *Endeavour*
Myles B. Matteson - *Harvey Gamage*/Ocean Classroom
Sarah Beth Maxner - *Picton Castle*/Summer Sail Training Program
Lily K. Morris - *Harvey Gamage*/Ocean Classroom
Jared K. Nunery - *Harvey Gamage*/Ocean Classroom
Sara Elizabeth Rubio - *Californian*/Mercy High School Tall Ship Semester for Girls
Myles Emery Thurlow - *Brilliant*/Transatlantic Program

Group

Mercy High School Tall Ship Semester for Girls - *Californian*
New York Restoration Project - *Cleawater*
Washington Waldorf School - *Mystic Whaler*
Wauwatosa East High School - *Denis Sullivan*/Science Under Sail

The ASTA Sailing Vessel Assistance Grant has been established to support vessels that are not necessarily operating as USCG-inspected Sailing School or Passenger Vessels. Applicant must be a Professional Member of the American Sail Training Association. Priority will be given to requests that further the mission and goals of the American Sail Training Association or are consistent with ASTA's stated mission. Application deadlines: Applications may be submitted at any time. We suggest that applications be submitted at least four (4) months prior to need.

Year 2000 Recipients - total of $7,800:

Fyrdraca - Longship Company, Ltd. - Avenue, MD
Governor Stone - Apalachicola Maritime Museum, Inc. - Apalachicola, FL
Pacific Swift - Sail and Life Training Society (S.A.L.T.S.) - Victoria, BC, Canada
Phoenix - Coastal Ecology Learning Program (CELP) - Huntington, NY
Providence - Providence Maritime Heritage Foundation - Providence, RI
Rachel B. Jackson - Downeast Sailing Adventures, LLC - Southwest Harbor, ME
SoundWaters - SoundWaters, Inc. - Stamford, CT
Sultana - Schooner Sultana Project - Chestertown, MD

The ASTA Crew Development Grant has been established to provide financial assistance to professional crewmembers of ASTA vessels in order to meet new and existing requirements for maintaining as well as advancing their USCG licenses, and to encourage the highest possible standards of safety training for individuals or groups of ASTA members. Application deadlines: Applications must be received by ASTA by February 15, June 15, and October 15 of each year.

Year 2000 Recipients - total of $4,000:

Sea Education Association, Inc. - Heavy Weather Avoidance Course presented by Maritime Institute of Technology and Graduate Studies

Tall Ship Adventures/Toronto Brigantine, Inc. - Marine Emergency Duties presented by St. Lawrence College

---

Following are some comments written by ....

"The Henry H. Anderson, Jr. Sail Training Scholarship was important to the success of this year's tall ship semester program. Thank you for sharing our vision and for helping to make this vision a reality for deserving young women." - Caitlin Schwarzman, Principal, Tall Ship Semester for Girls

"The experience aboard *Mystic Whaler* was beyond the expectations of all of the students regardless of their previous sailing experience or lack of it." - Don Bufano, Waldorf High School

"Thank you for awarding the Longship Company a grant which made it possible for us to trailer the *Fyrdraca* to Newfoundland for the Viking Sail 2000 event." - Terry L. Neill, President

"Participation in round-the-clock watch groups gave us much practical experience in all aspects of *Westward's* navigation and maintenance. Climbing aloft, sighting whales and other sea creatures, swimming in the middle of the Atlantic Ocean, being at the helm, and experiencing weather conditions of all types are adventures I will never forget." - Bridget Brett on SEA's Oceanography on the Gulf of Maine program.

"We at the Coastal Ecology Learning Program (C.E.L.P.) and the schooner *Phoenix* are most grateful for ASTA's financial assistance in helping us convert a cargo hold into usable space for our sail training cadets." - Captain Dennis F. Watson, President

"I thought the voyage would be easy. Well not only was it not easy, but it was probably the hardest thing I've ever done. I went through more emotions in one day than I think I have in my entire life, and tasks that seemed near impossible to me in the beginning of the trip became second nature by the end of the trip. Rarely do I actually notice myself changing as a person, but I noticed this time and I'm proud of myself." - sail trainee/scholarship recipient

"Thank you for the grant award to help defray the cost of replacing the masts aboard the *Governor Stone*. As our organization grows, we anticipate participating in your sail training scholarship program."-Sherrie Stokes, Director/Curator, Apalachicola Maritime Museum

"This program is incredible! I learned so much about what it takes to live on a ship, how a ship is built, line handling, knot tying, and climbing aloft." - Jon Oldt about his experience aboard *Lady Maryland* and *Sultana*

"Thank you for the association's belief in our mission. ASTA's grant award for the Schooner Sultana Project set an example for other associations to contribute to the mission of *Sultana* and the programs which will be executed aboard her." - Michael M. Thielke, Executive Director

"I'm glad I had the privilege of sailing with the crew and other cadets aboard *Lady Maryland*. I know that sometime in my future I will be sailing those open waters once again. I wish to thank ASTA for awarding me a scholarship which made this great adventure possible." - Kyle Turner

"For many of the girls this was their first sail training experience. During these five days aboard *Brilliant*, they gained self-confidence and the knowledge that some-times you need to depend on others to help achieve your goals." - Sue Wagener, Senior Girl Scout Troop 514

SOUTH STREET SEAPORT MUSEUM

Sail Training / Marine Education Opportunities

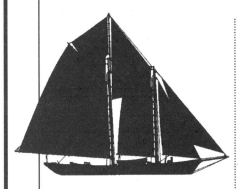

PIONEER
1885 Iron Hulled Cargo Schooner

- School Trips
- Boy Scouts / Girl Scouts
- Charters
- Volunteer Opportunities

LETTIE G. HOWARD
1893 Gloucester Fishing Schooner

- Elderhostel
- Seafaring Camp (with Harvey Gamage)
- Urban Waters
- Team Building

Recipient, ASTA's 1997 Sea Education Program Award

Come join us!
For information call (212) 748-8600
or write to us at
207 Front Street
New York, NY 10038

www.southstseaport.org

Member Vessels

The Continental
Sloop *Providence*

240 OPPORTUNITIES TO LEARN
FROM THE SEA, UNDER SAIL

777 (Triple Seven)

Association. Yacht *777*'s owner served as one of the first cadets aboard the *Black Pearl*. This excellent experience of transatlantic passage, tall ships races, and the character-building values embodied in sail training brings together the vessel and her crew to continue the tradition.

Yacht *777* was built in 1963 for the Fastnet Race of that year. Built under Lloyd's supervision and to the highest standards of UK racing rules, she has crossed the Atlantic many times, traveling the traditional cruising circuit from New England down to the lower Caribbean.

Established in 1993, Proper Yacht, Inc. follows the tradition begun by Barclay Warburton III with the formation of the American Sail Training

Flag:	USA
Rig:	Sloop
Homeport/waters:	Charleston, South Carolina: Coastal US to Caribbean
Who sails?	Individuals, students, and families of all ages.
Season:	Year-round
Cost:	$100 per person per day. $500 per person per week.
Program type:	Sail training for volunteer and paying crew and trainees. Sea education programs in marine science, maritime history, historic reenactments, and ecology in cooperation with accredited institutions and organized groups, and as informal, in-house programming.

Specifications:

Sparred length: 41' 3"	Draft: 6' 6"	Sail area: 1,400 sq. ft.
LOD: 39'	Beam: 11' 8"	Tons: 10 GRT
LOA: 41'	Freeboard: 4'	Power: diesel
LWL: 37'	Hull: wood	

Built:	1963; R J. Prior and Sons, UK
Coast Guard certification:	Sailing School Vessel (Subchapter R)
Crew:	2. Trainees: 4
Contact:	Charles Hatchell
	Proper Yacht, Inc.
	PO Box 7
	Little River, SC 29566
	Tel: 843-830-3506; Fax: 843-767-1405
	E-mail: yacht777@gte.net
	Web site: http://www.properyacht.com

Abaco was designed by John Alden in 1921 and built by W.B. Calderwood at Manchester Marine, Manchester, Massachusetts for Mr. Robert Saltonstall. She is owned and operated by Captain Peter L. Warburton, son of the late Barclay H. Warburton III, founder of ASTA.

Abaco operates half-day, day, weekend and week-long sail training, adventure cruising, chartering and team building experiences, as well as seamanship classes. Individuals, families, and groups, of all ages and types, are encouraged to plan their next voyage, vacation, adventure, outing or educational experience aboard this classic beauty!

Abaco carries up to six passengers or trainees. She operates in South Carolina, Florida, and/or the Bahamas during the winter months, and sails in Chesapeake Bay and New England waters during the summer months. When participating on the passage north or south, or for any portion of any voyage, passengers are the crew and are able to experience all aspects of ship life. Duties on board *Abaco* include steering, sail handling, cooking, watch standing, navigating, and much more. All duties are performed under the direction of *Abaco's* captain and crew. Experience is not necessary. Whether you are a novice or a seasoned sailor, you are sure to further your sailing knowledge, challenge your own abilities, develop a sense of "team," experience personal growth, and have fun!

PHOTO BY MORRIS ROSENFELD

ABACO

Flag:	USA
Rig:	Main staysail schooner
Homeport/waters:	Newport, Rhode Island: New England, Maryland, Coastal Northeast (summer), South Carolina, Florida Bahamas (winter)
Who sails?	School groups from middle school through college, individuals, families, corporate groups, charter groups
Season:	Year-round
Cost:	Call for details
Program type:	Sail training for paying trainees. Informal programming in maritime history and ecology. Passenger day sails, overnight voyages and adventure vacations.

Specifications:			
	Sparred length: 53'	Draft: 7'	Sail area: 2,000 sq. ft.
	LOD: 45' 6"	Beam: 11' 8"	Tons: 20 GRT
	LOA: 45' 6"	Rig height: 62'	Power: 85 HP diesel
	LWL: 33'	Freeboard: 5'	Hull: wood, Color: whilte

Designer:	John G. Alden
Built:	1921; W.B. Calderwood, Manchester, Massachusetts
Coast Guard certification:	Uninspected Vessel
Crew:	2. **Trainees:** 6
Contact:	Captain and Mrs. Peter L. Warburton
	East Passage Packet Co., LLC
	Fazio, 57 Palmetto Dunes
	Hilton Head Island, SC 29928
	Tel: 843-842-2432, E-mail: schoonerabaco@cs.com

Adirondack

The schooner *Adirondack* is the third of five schooners to come out of the Scarano Boat Building yard, beginning with the 59-foot schooner *Madeline* and the 61-foot *Woodwind* in 1991, and followed by the 105-foot schooner *America* in 1995 and a sister ship, *Adirondack II*, launched in August 1999. *Adirondack* combines the virtues of turn-of-the-century American schooner yachts with the latest in laminated wood technology. Offering an enviable combination of stability and speed, the *Adirondack* fulfills the builder and owner's ambition of providing a quality sail for people of all ages and experience.

Flag:	USA
Rig:	Gaff schooner
Homeport/waters:	New York, New York: New York Harbor
Who sails?	School groups from elementary school through college, individuals and families.
Program type:	Sail training with paying trainees. Passenger day sails.

Specifications:		
Sparred length: 80'	Draft: 8'	Sail area: 1,850 sq. ft.
LOD: 64' 6"	Beam: 16'	Tons: 41 GRT
LOA: 65'	Rig height: 62'	Power: twin 50 HP diesels
LWL: 58'	Freeboard: 3' 4"	Hull: wood

Built:	1996; Albany, New York, Scarano Boat
Coast Guard certification:	Passenger Vessel (Subchapter T)
Crew:	3. **Trainees/passengers:** 49
Contact:	Rick Scarano, Manager
	Sailing Excursions, Inc.
	c/o Scarano Boat, Port of Albany
	Albany, NY 12202
	Tel: 800-701-SAIL; 518-463-3401; Fax: 518-463-3403
	E-mail: mail@scaranoboat.com
	Web site: http://www.scaranoboat.com

Adirondack II

PHOTO BY BILLY BLACK

The schooner *Adirondack II* is the latest sailing vessel to be launched from the Scarano yard in Albany, New York. Launched in August of 1999, the near-sister ship of the *Adirondack* joins the fleet of schooners known for their performance-oriented design/construction combined with classic traditional aesthetics (see *Coronet*).

ADIRONDACK II

"This year's model" expands on the idea that safety, comfort, and style are paramount considerations. Passengers can experience the exhilaration of being aboard the huge new day sailer, with its wide-open cockpit that can comfortably accommodate larger groups of trainees and passengers (up to 65). While dockside, spacious cockpit doghouses double as serving space for food and beverages or classroom navigation paperwork. *Adirondack II* affirms that modern wood composite construction and 19th-century elegance blend seamlessly to the benefit of all.

Flag:	USA		
Rig:	Gaff schooner		
Homeport/waters:	Newport, Rhode Island: Narragansett Bay.		
Specifications:	Sparred length: 80'	Beam: 16'	Sail area: 1,800 sq. ft.
	LOD: 64' 6"'	Draft: 8'	Tons: 41 GRT
	LOA: 65'	Rig height: 62'	Hull: wood
	LWL: 58'	Freeboard: 3' 4"	Power: twin 50 HP diesels
Built:	1999; Albany, New York, Scarano Boat		
Coast Guard certification:	Passenger Vessel (Subchapter T)		
Crew:	3. **Trainees/passengers:** 65		
Contact:	Rick Scarano, Manager		
	Sailing Excursions, Inc.		
	c/o Scarano Boat, Port of Albany		
	Albany, NY 12202		
	Tel: 800-701-SAIL, 518-463-3401; Fax: 518-463-3403		
	E-mail: mail@scaranoboat.com		
	Web site: http://www.scaranoboat.com		

Adventure

PHOTO BY FREDERICK BODEN

ADVENTURE

The Schooner *Adventure* is one of the last of the Gloucester fishing schooners, an icon of our nation's fishing industry and Gloucester's heritage. *Adventure* was built in 1926, near the end of the commercial Age of Sail, in Essex, Massachusetts. Designed by McManus as a "knockabout", without a bowsprit for the safety of the crew, the 122' *Adventure* represents the pinnacle of schooner design, embodying grace, speed, and functionality.

Immortalized by Rudyard Kipling's novel *Captains Courageous*, Gloucester's fishing schooners, known as "Gloucestermen", were famous throughout the world. Fast and able under sail and carrying 14 dories, *Adventure* was the "highliner" of the North Atlantic fleet, earning more money than any other fishing vessel of

her era. At the time of her retirement from fishing in 1953, *Adventure* was the last American dory-fishing schooner working in the North Atlantic.

Refitted as a windjammer, *Adventure* carried passengers along the coast of Maine until 1987. Her grace, beauty, and prowess as a sailing vessel earned her the nickname "Queen of the Windjammers." In 1988, *Adventure* was given to the people of Gloucester to be preserved as Gloucester's historic tall ship. A rare survivor, *Adventure* is a unique vessel from an extraordinary era in American history. A National Historic Landmark, *Adventure* serves as a living memorial to the more than 5,000 Gloucester fishermen lost at sea, and was selected as an Official Project of "Save America's Treasures" by the National Trust for Historic Preservation.

Adventure is being restored as a 1926 Gloucester fishing schooner and will resume sailing once work is completed. The schooner will be used as a community resource for educational programming, focusing on maritime, cultural, and environmental issues, and will sail as a living symbol of Gloucester's maritime heritage. The vessel is available for dockside tours, educational programs, and maritime events.

Flag:	USA
Rig:	Gaff topsail schooner
Home port/waters:	Gloucester, Massachusetts
Program type:	Dockside interpretation. Educational programs for schools.

Specifications:			
	LOA: 122'	Draft: 13' 6"	Sail area: 6,500 sq. ft.
	LOD: 122'	Beam: 24' 6"	Tons: 130 GRT
	LWL: 109'	Rig height: 110'	Hull: wood

Designer:	Tom McManus
Built:	1926; Essex, Massachusetts, John F. James & Son Yard
Coast Guard certification:	Moored Attraction Vessel (dockside)
Contact:	Amy-Beth Healey
	Gloucester Adventure, Inc.
	PO Box 1306, Gloucester, MA 01931-1306
	Tel: 978-281-8079; Fax: 978-281-2393
	E-mail: abhealey@schooner-adventure.org
	Web site: http://www.schooner-adventure.org

SAIL TALL SHIPS!

Adventuress

In 1913 the schooner *Adventuress* sailed from Maine to the Bering Sea via the straits of Magellan and served the Bar Pilots of San Francisco Bay until 1952. Although originally commissioned to gather Arctic specimens, *Adventuress* now sails to increase awareness of the majesty and vulnerability of Puget Sound. Since 1989, Sound Experience, a nonprofit environmental education organization, has provided hands-on education aboard *Adventuress* in response to the area's urgent environmental issues. Today, *Adventuress* is a National Historic Landmark and a Puget Sound treasure—the crowning jewel of the Pacific Northwest's collection of wooden ships.

Volunteer and paid crew receive environmental and sail training. The ship's apprentice program for youth 14-18 and month-long internships for adult sailor/educators also feature extensive sail training. Sound Experience is proud to own and operate *Adventuress* and to keep her a "working" vessel—Protecting Puget Sound Through Education. The non-competitive environment fosters cooperation, teamwork, leadership, and sailing skills for Elderhostelors, Boy and Girl Scout Troops, youth groups, schools, and individuals of all ages who enjoy raising her massive sails and standing watch to hand, reef, and steer this classic tall ship. Truly a boat for the people, *Adventuress* provides empowering, life-changing experiences to more than 3,500 youth and adults each year.

Flag:	USA
Rig:	Gaff topsail schooner
Homeport/waters:	Port Townsend, Washington: Puget Sound/Salish Sea
Who sails?	School and other groups from elementary school through college, individuals and families.
Season:	March to November
Cost:	$30 per person ($20 for youth) for 3-5 hour sail, $1,260 per day for adult groups ($800 youth groups). Overnights: $2,500 per day adult groups ($1,725 youth groups). Scholarships available.
Program type:	Sail training for paying trainees. Sea education in marine science, maritime history, and ecology. Passenger day and overnight sails. Dockside interpretation during port visits.

Specifications:	Sparred length: 135'	Draft: 12'	Sail area: 5,478 sq. ft.
	LWL: 71'	Beam: 21'	Sail number: TS 15
	Rig height: 110'	Tons: 82 GRT	Power: 250 HP diesel

Designer:	B.B. Crowninshield
Built:	1913; East Boothbay, Maine, Rice Brothers
Coast Guard certification:	Passenger Vessel (Subchapter T)
Crew:	4-5, 8-10 instructors. **Trainees:** 45 day, 25 overnight. **Age:** 8-adult
Contact:	Jenell DeMatteo
	Sound Experience
	2310 Washington Street
	Port Townsend, WA 98368
	Tel: 360-379-0438; Fax: 360-379-0439
	E-mail: soundexp@olypen.com Web site: http://www.soundexp.org

A.J. Meerwald

The Delaware Bay Schooner Project operates the schooner *A.J. Meerwald*, New Jersey's official tall ship, as an experiential classroom. This authentically restored 1928 Delaware Bay oyster schooner sails from her homeport, Bivalve, New Jersey, as well as annual visits to cities and coastal towns throughout New Jersey, Pennsylvania, and Delaware (occasional special trips into the Chesapeake and the Northeast Atlantic seaboard).

Students range from fourth-graders to senior citizens; subject matter ranges from the history of Delaware Bay oystering to present water quality issues. Stewardship of the environment and preservation of our maritime heritage are the primary goals of all activities on the *A.J. Meerwald*, regardless of their target audience, length of program, and/or port of origin.

The Delaware Bay Schooner Project also conducts shore-based programs, lecture series, hosts Delaware Bay Day (the first Saturday in June), and provides leadership on watershed issues throughout the Delaware Estuary. Members and volunteers are the lifeblood of the organization and are always welcome.

Flag:	USA
Rig:	Gaff-schooner
Homeport/waters:	Bivalve, New Jersey: Delaware Bay and coastal New Jersey
Who sails?	School groups, 4th grade through college, families, scouts, teachers, businesses, associations, and anyone interested in a *Meerwald* experience.
Cost:	$25 per person per sail, $2,500 group rate per day (charter)
Program type:	Sail training for professional crew and volunteer and paying trainees. Three-hour educational sails, summer camp, family sails, teacher workshops, overnight programs, team building, and special "theme" sails (i.e. birding, oystering, etc.). Sea education in marine science, maritime history, ecology, team building, and watershed awareness in cooperation with accredited institutions and other groups, and as informal, in-house programming.

Specifications:			
	Sparred length: 115'	Draft: 6'	Sail area: 3,560 sq. ft.
	LOA: 85'	Beam: 22' 1"	Tons: 57 GRT
	LOD: 81' 7"	Rig height: 67' 8"	Power: diesel
	LWL: 78' 3"	Freeboard: 3' 6"	Hull: wood

Designer:	Charles H. Stowman and Sons, Dorchester, New Jersey
Built:	1928; Dorchester, New Jersey, Charles H. Stowman and Sons Shipyard
Coast Guard certification:	Passenger Vessel (Subchapter T)
Crew:	11, augmented by volunteers
Contact:	Meghan Wren, Executive Director
	Delaware Bay Schooner Project
	2800 High Street, Bivalve
	Port Norris, NJ 08349
	Tel: 856-785-2060; Fax: 856-785-2893
	E-mail: ajmeerwald@snip.net
	Web site: http://www.ajmeerwald.org

Alabama

The ex-pilot schooner *Alabama* is an authentic example of a typical Gloucester fishing schooner of the early 1900s. She was built for the Mobile Bar Pilot Association in Pensacola, Florida in 1926 and designed by the greatest New England designer of Gloucester schooners, Thomas F. McManus.

After a major three-year reconstruction, the summer of 1998 marked her first season sailing the waters of southern New England. She is a product of Vineyard Haven craftsmanship as the lion's share of her rebuild took place in Vineyard Haven Harbor. *Alabama* now joins *Shenandoah* in the Coastwise Packet Company fleet.

The *Alabama* runs 6-day sailing trips for kids ages 9 to 14 from late June

through late August. She also runs day sails and is available for private charter each year from June 1 through June 23 and August 25 through September.

Flag:	USA
Rig:	Gaff schooner
Homeport/waters:	Vineyard Haven, Massachusetts: Southern New England
Who sails?	School groups from elementary through college and individuals ages 25 and under.
Cost:	$700 per person per week (Sunday night through Saturday noon).
Program type:	Sail training for paying trainees.

Specifications:			
	Sparred length: 120'	Draft: 12' 6"	Sail area: 5,000 sq. ft.
	LOD: 85'	Beam: 21'	Tons: 85 GRT
	LOA: 90'	Rig height: 94'	Power: twin diesels
	LWL: 78'	Freeboard: 5'	Hull: wood

Designer:	Thomas F. McManus
Built:	1926; Pensacola, Florida, Pensacola Shipbuilding Company
Coast Guard certification:	Passenger Vessel (Subchapter T)
Crew:	6. **Trainees:** 49 (day sails), 27 (overnight)
Contact:	Captain Robert Douglas
	Coastwise Packet Company
	PO Box 429
	Vineyard Haven, MA 02568
	Tel: 508-693-1699; Fax: 508-693-1881
	Web site: http://www.coastwisepacket.com

Alaska Eagle

Winner of the 1977-78 Whitbread Round the World Race as the Dutch yacht *Flyer*, the 65-foot *Alaska Eagle* now operates as a sail training vessel for adults and college students interested in acquiring offshore passage-making skills. Since 1982, *Alaska Eagle* has made more than 22 Pacific crossings and sailed more than 200,000 miles with students aboard. Cruises and passages are generally two to three weeks in length.

Strong and fast, *Alaska Eagle* is a comfortable offshore cruiser with four private staterooms and two heads and showers. Under the guidance of two USCG-licensed skipper/instructors, *Alaska Eagle*'s nine-member crews participate in watch standing, sail handling, steering, and navigating. A professional cook handles the meals. *Alaska Eagle* is operated by the Sailing Center at Orange Coast College, a Southern California nonprofit boating education program.

Plans for 2001-2002 have *Alaska Eagle* sailing from Newport Beach to Antarctica via Hawaii, Tahiti, Pitcairn Island and Chile.

Flag:	USA		
Rig:	Sloop		
Homeport/waters:	Newport Beach, California: South Pacific, New Zealand		
Who sails?	Individual college students and adults		
Cost:	$180 per person per day		
Program type:	Sail training with paying trainees. Paying passengers on overnight passages.		
Specifications:	Sparred length: 65'	Draft: 10' 5"	Sail area: 1,500 sq. ft.
	LOD: 65'	Beam: 16' 4"	Tons: 39 GRT
	LOA: 65'	Rig height: 90'	Power: 200 HP diesel
	LWL: 50'	Freeboard: 5'	Hull: aluminum
Designer:	Sparkman & Stephens		
Built:	1977; The Netherlands, Royal Nuisman Shipyard		
Coast Guard certification:	Sailing School Vessel (Subchapter R)		
Crew:	3. Trainees: 9		
Contact:	Catherine Ellis, Adventure Sailing Coordinator		
	The School of Sailing and Seamanship		
	Orange Coast College		
	1801 West Coast Highway		
	Newport Beach, CA 92663		
	Tel: 949-645-9412; Fax: 949-645-1859		
	E-mail: sailing@occsailing.com		
	Web site: http://www.occsailing.com		

Alma

The scow schooner *Alma* was built at Hunters Point in San Francisco Bay in 1891 and is the last of approximately 400 scow schooners that carried cargo in the San Francisco Bay area at the turn of the century. She is owned and operated by the San Francisco Maritime National Historical Park and docked at Hyde Street Pier near Fisherman's Wharf. The San Francisco Maritime National Park Association supports operations of the *Alma* at the many maritime festivals and parades in the Bay area.

Alma sails from March until November and is crewed by volunteers, representing and interpreting a time when commerce moved by boat around the Bay. The *Alma* volunteer program enables trainees and apprentices to learn about traditional sailing and wooden boat maintenance. No fees are required as all crew volunteer to sail and maintain

the *Alma* and other park vessels at Hyde Street Pier.

Flag:	USA
Rig:	Schooner, two-masted
Homeport/waters:	San Francisco, California: San Francisco Bay
Who sails?	Adult education groups, individual students and adults, families.
Program type:	Sail training for crew and apprentices. Sea education based on informal, in-house programming focused on maritime history. Dockside interpretation. Affiliated groups include the National Maritime Museum Association, San Francisco National Maritime Historical Park, and National Park Service.

Specifications:	Sparred length: 88'	Draft: 3' 6"	Sail area: 2,684 sq. ft.
	LOD: 61' 4"	Beam: 23' 6"	Tons: 47 GRT
	LOA: 62'	Rig height: 76'	Power: twin diesels
	LWL: 59' 5"	Freeboard: 4'	Hull: wood

Designer:	Fred Siemers
Built:	1891; San Francisco, California, Fred Siemers
Crew:	6. **Trainees:** 28 (overnight), 40 (day). **Age:** 14+
Contact:	Captain Al Lutz
	San Francisco Maritime National Historical Park
	Building E, Fort Mason Center
	San Francisco, CA 94123
	Tel: 415-556-1659; Fax: 415-556-1624
	E-mail: al_lutz@nps.gov
	Web site: http://www.nps.gov/safr/local/alma.html

Alvei

Alvei's rig, the main topsail schooner, was the preference of privateers during the early 19th century. *Alvei* has 137 lines of running rigging to handle 16 sails, providing experience in both fore-and-aft and square-rigged sail handling.

A sailor from a hundred years ago would be at home on *Alvei*. It takes a team of people using block and tackle, to "sweat & tail" as they set and handle sails. Raising the anchor, rowing the shore boat, and laundry are all done by hand.

After an extensive 8-year refit, *Alvei*'s accommodations, deck, and rigging have been completely renewed. Underway since October 1995, *Alvei* has completed half a circumnavigation, sailing from Portugal to Australia. She now sails long trade wind passages using the old sailing ship routes.

The crew, both regular and trainees, stand watch at sea, four on and eight off; in port it's one day on and two days off. Duties include steering, lookout, sail handling, painting, tarring, sewing, cooking, and rigging. *Alvei* has a full-participation crew.

Flag:	Vanuatu
Rig:	Main Topsail Schooner
Homeport/waters:	Port Vila, Republic of Vanuatu; tropical waters worldwide
Who sails?	Adults 18 and over
Season:	Year-round
Cost:	$24 per person per day
Program type:	Sail training for volunteer and paying trainees. Sea education based on informal in-house participation. Coastal and offshore passages.

Specifications:	Sparred length: 126'	LOD: 92'	LOA: 126'
	LWL: 87'	Draft: 10'	Beam: 19'
	Rig Height: 85'3"	Freeboard: 2'6"	Sail area: 5700 sq. ft.
	Power 160 HP Diesel	Hull: steel	

Designer:	Unknown; rig, Evan Logan
Built:	1920; Montrose, Scotland
Contact:	Margy Gassel, Shore Crew
	604 Masonic Avenue
	Albany, CA 94706
	Tel: 510-526-7157
	E-mail: alvei@yahoo.com
	Web site: http://www.alvei.de

Amara Zee

The Caravan Stage Barge *Amara Zee* is the new touring vessel of the Caravan Stage Society, Inc. Built in 1997, the *Amara Zee* is based on a Thames River Sailing Barge blended with the best of contemporary marine and theater technology. With its shallow draft and lowering masts, the Stage Barge can access almost any waterfront community in North America. The spars are utilized for scenery, lights, sound equipment, and special effects. All performances are staged on deck, with the audience sitting on the shore.

The *Amara Zee* was built by the theater company with the assistance of a number of marine professional volunteers and financed by over 600 manufacturing companies with in-kind donations of equipment, materials, and services. The Caravan's original productions express contemporary concerns and issues in an engaging and compelling format that is both entertaining and inspirational.

AMARA ZEE

Flag:	Canada		
Rig:	Ketch (sailing barge)		
Homeport/waters:	East Coast of US		
Program type:	Theatrical performances.		
Specifications:	LOA: 90'	Draft: 3' 6"	Sail area: 5,100 ft.
	Rig height: 90'	Beam: 22'	Power: twin 120
	Hull: steel		HP diesels
Contact:	National Caravan Stage Company, Inc.		
	140 Seventh Avenue South		
	St. Petersburg, FL 33701		
	Tel: 917-208-6976, 727-515-8163		
	E-mail: office@caravanstage.org		
	Web site: http://www.caravanstage.org		

America

America's Cup, in honor of the original winner, and now represents the world's most coveted yachting trophy.

The schooner *America* was built in 1995 to continue the tradition of the original vessel and be a sailing ambassador for the United States. One mission for the *America* is to function as a living museum and interest the public in history and maritime traditions. This is accomplished with dockside interpretations and media coverage throughout an extensive worldwide sailing schedule. *America* sails an average of 20,000 miles a year and has visited major boat shows, classic sail regattas, Tall Ships 2000®and OpSail 2000, among other events.

In 2001, America will participate in the ASTA Tall Ships Challenge® 2001 Race Series in the Great Lakes and Sail Duluth-Superior 2001.

America is a waterline-up replica of the schooner, designed by George Steers, which successfully represented the New York Yacht Club in the 1851 challenge race with the Royal Yacht Squadron. History and racing buffs know the famous reply to Queen Victoria, when she inquired about the second-place ship, "Madam, there is no second..." The race itself was later renamed the

Flag:	USA				
Rig:	Gaff schooner				
Homeport/waters:	Key West, Florida: Worldwide.				
Program type:	America is dedicated to furthering education of the history of sail racing and yachts manship. She holds dockside interpretations at port events and offers day and overnight sails.				
Specifications:	Sparred length: 139'		Draft: 10'		Sail area: 6,400 sq. ft.
	LOA: 105'		Beam: 25'		Tons: 120 GRT
	LOD: 105'		Rig height: 108'		Power: twin diesels
	LWL: 90' 6"		Freeboard: 4'		
Designer:	George Steers, w/modifications by Scarano Boat				
Built:	1995; Scarano Boat, Port of Albany, New York				
Coast Guard certification:	Passenger Vessel (Subchapter T)				
Contact:	Ron Prichep				
	Historic Promotions, Inc.				
	11501 Gunston Road Way				
	Mason Neck, VA 22079				
	Tel: 703-541-0730; Fax: 703-541-0733				
	E-mail: ronprichep@aol.com or cawingate@aol.com				
	Web site: http://www.historicpromotions.com				

American Eagle

The 12-meter yacht *American Eagle* was launched in Stamford, Connecticut, in 1964, and won 20 out of 21 races in the June and July America's Cup defender trials. In 1968, she was bought by Ted Turner, a 31-year-old sailor from Atlanta, Georgia. During his years racing *American Eagle*, Turner became one of the finest 12-meter helmsmen in the world and was selected by the New York Yacht Club to defend and win the America's Cup with *Courageous* in 1977.

American Eagle offers a memorable experience for you and your guests. Take the wheel and sense the sheer power and exhilaration that only the big twelves provide. An experienced three-man crew will make your pleasure a priority while ensuring safety aboard. Rediscover Narragansett Bay or the historic America's Cup course on Rhode Island Sound on one of the greatest 12-meter yachts ever built. *American Eagle* is based in Newport but upon request can be available at the port of your choice from New York to Maine by the day or the week. Call or write for more information.

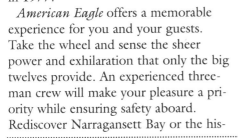

Flag:	USA
Rig:	Sloop
Homeport/waters:	Newport, Rhode Island: New England and Chesapeake Bay
Who sails?	Individual and group charters
Cost:	$1,800 group rate per day, $60 per person for evening sails
Program type:	Sail training for volunteer and paying trainees. Sea education based on informal, in-house programming. Passenger day sails.

Specifications:	Sparred length: 69'	Draft: 9'	Sail area: 1,850 sq. ft.
	LOA: 68'	Beam: 12' 8"	Tons: 28 GRT
	LOD: 68'	Rig height: 90'	Power: diesel
	LWL: 46'	Hull: wood	

Designer:	A.E. Luders
Built:	1964; Stamford, Connecticut, Luders
Coast Guard certification:	Passenger Vessel (Subchapter T)
Crew:	3. **Trainees/passengers:** 12 (day sails)
Contact:	Herb Marshall/George Hill
	America's Cup Charters
	PO Box 51
	Newport, RI 02840
	Tel: 401-849-5868; Fax: 401-849-3098
	Web site: http://www.americascupcharters.com

American Pride

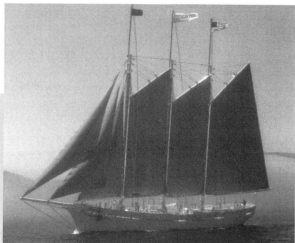

Long Beach, California.

The AHMI offers hand-on educational programs for children which stress science, marine biology, history, and sail training. Programs encourage teamwork, good communication, problem solving, and leadership. Sail training programs and private group charters are available for teens and adults, with destinations and length of voyage varying.

AHMI is actively engaged in sharing the thrill of sailing with sick or abused children, and regularly donates sails to child welfare groups and fundraising guilds. A professional crew and strong volunteer group generously gives time, talents, and resources in support of the programs.

The graceful three-masted schooner *American Pride* was built in 1941 as a two-masted "schooner-dragger." She spent over 40 years commercially fishing the Grand Banks and George's Banks. In 1986, completely restored and with a third mast added, she operated as a charter boat out of Bar Harbor, Maine. In October 1996, she was purchased by the American Heritage Marine Institute (AHMI) and sailed to her new home in

The once-successful fishing schooner now majestically sails the southern California waters, her huge red sails highly visible as she gracefully shares the adventures and romance of the tall ship with all that come aboard.

Flag:	USA
Rig:	Schooner, three-masted
Homeport/waters:	Long Beach, California: Southern California.
Who sails?	Elementary and middle school students, individuals of all ages, and families.
Season:	Year-round
Cost:	$100 per person per day, $1,800 group rate per day (charter)
Program type:	Sail training for volunteer and paying crew and trainees. Fully accredited sea education programs in marine science, maritime history, and ecology. Historic reenactments.

Specifications:			
	Sparred length: 129'	Draft: 10'	Sail area: 4,900 sq. ft.
	LOD: 101'	Beam: 22'	Tons: 203 GRT
	LOA: 105'	Rig height: 98'	Power: diesel
	LWL: 92'	Freeboard: 6'	Hull: wood

Built:	1941; Muller Boatworks, Brooklyn, New York
Coast Guard certification:	Passenger Vessel (Subchapter T)
Crew:	6 (paid and volunteer). **Trainees/passengers:** 100 (day sails), 48 (overnight)
Contact:	Helen H. Clinton, Director
	American Heritage Marine Institute
	21520 "G" Yorba Linda Blvd., # 444
	Yorba Linda, CA 92887
	Tel: 714-970-8800; Fax: 714-970-8474
	E-mail: americprd@aol.com
	Web site: http://www.americanpride.org

American Rover

The *American Rover* operates a rigorous day sailing schedule out of the Norfolk, Virginia waterfront. Cruises are generally two to three-hour sightseeing and historical tours. Special student educational field trips are also popular.

Flag:	USA
Rig:	Topsail schooner, three-masted
Homeport/waters:	Norfolk, Virginia: Chesapeake Bay and tributaries
Who sails?	Individuals, families, and student groups. Affiliated institutions include Old Dominion University.
Cost:	$12-$16 per person, two to three hours, $9-$13 per person group rate, two to three hours
Program type:	Sail training for crew and apprentices. Sea education in marine science, maritime history, and ecology in cooperation with schools and colleges. Passenger day sails. Homeport dockside interpretation.

Specifications:

Sparred length: 135'	Draft: 8' 6"	Sail area: 5,000 sq. ft.
LOA: 98'	Beam: 24'	Tons: 98 GRT
LOD: 96'	Rig height: 85'	Power: 240 HP
LWL: 80'	Freeboard: 8'	

Designer:	Merritt Walter
Built:	1986; Panama City, Florida, Kolsar & Rover Marine
Coast Guard certification:	Passenger Vessel (Subchapter T)
Crew:	4; non-crew educators: 2. **Trainees/passengers:** 49
Contact:	Captain Brook J. Smith
	Rover Marine, Inc.
	PO Box 3125
	Norfolk, VA 23514
	Tel: 757-627-7245; Fax: 757-627-6626

Amistad

Freedom Schooner *Amistad* ™ set sail in July 2000, plying the nation's waterways as an educational ambassador, teaching lessons of history, cooperation and leadership to Americans of all ages, interests, and cultural backgrounds.

Amistad ™ was launched on March 25, 2000, from Mystic Seaport Museum, the nation's leading maritime museum. The vessel will travel south along the east coast during the fall of 2001. Her homeport is Long Wharf Pier in New Haven, Connecticut.

Amistad America ®, the educational organization which owns and operates the ship, is currently raising the $10 million endowment necessary to ensure *Amistad* sails for decades. Individuals, families, and school groups learn the importance of historical identity through a variety of experiences, from onboard and dockside exhibits to half-day excursions and overnight programs. Themes for program curricula are interdisciplinary, blending communication skills, geography, math, and social studies while making history relevant and fostering cooperation among people of diverse backgrounds.

Flag:	USA
Rig:	Topsail schooner
Homeport/waters:	New Haven, Connecticut: East Coast of the United States.
Who sails?	School groups from elementary schools through college.
Program type:	Sail training for crew and apprentices and with paying trainees. Maritime history and a full range of programming are expected. Sea education in cooperation with accredited institutions and other groups. Passenger day sailing and dockside interpretation during home and port visits.

Specifications:	Sparred length: 129'	Draft: 10' 2"	Sail area: 5,000 sq. ft.
	LOA: 85'	Beam: 22' 4"	Power: twin diesels
	LOD: 81'	Rig height: 90'	Hull: wood
	LWL: 79'		

Designer:	Tri-Coastal Marine
Built:	1998-2000, Mystic Seaport, Mystic, Connecticut
Coast Guard certifications:	Sailing School Vessel (Subchapter R), Passenger Vessel (Subchapter T)
Crew:	8, combination paid and volunteer. **Trainees/passengers:** 49
Contact:	Christopher Cloud, Executive Director
	Amistad America, Inc. c/o Mystic Seaport
	PO Box 6000
	Mystic, CT 06355
	Tel: 860-536-6003; Fax: 860-536-4861
	E-mail: ccloud@mysticseaport.org
	Web site: http://www.amistadamerica.org

SAIL TALL SHIPS!

Aphrodite

Named for the Greek goddess of the sea, Aphrodite, this trim 100' brig arose from the "sea-foam" dreams of her captain, Aent Kingma. Scion of a family of cargo and charter canal boat captains, Captain Kingma designed this unique 16-passenger vessel when the opportune time presented itself in 1995.

Crewed by Captain Kingma, a cook, first mate, and one or two of his own children, the *Aphrodite* is a popular addition to the tall ship fleet of northern Europe. Offering deluxe, informal cruises along the coasts of the North and Baltic seas, and also visiting the English and French coasts, the *Aphrodite* has participated in the major maritime festivals at Douarnenez, France; Rostock, Germany; Ebsjerg, Denmark; and of course, Amsterdam, The Netherlands.

With eight double cabins, the brig affords opportunities for "adventure sailing" in an intimate and collegial setting. Each cabin is equipped with bathroom facilities and showers. Guests on board can help with the sail lines or retire to cozy nooks on deck or below with a

favorite book. Cruises are generally 5 to 7 days in duration, but often seem far too short for a true appreciation of this neat, comfortable sailing brig.

Flag:	The Netherlands
Rig:	Brig
Homeport/waters:	Stavoren, The Netherlands: European coastal waters.
Who sails?	Individuals of all ages, families, corporate groups.
Season:	March to November
Cost:	$200 per person per day, $2500 group rate (or charter) per day.
Program type:	Sail training and sea education for individuals, groups, families, and companies as informal programming. Sail training for adults as paying trainees. Passenger day sails and overnight passages.

Specifications:

Sparred length: 100'	Draft: 6' 4"	Sail area: 4,162 sq. ft.
LOD: 77'	Beam: 21' 3"	Tons: 94 GRT
LOA: 81'	Rig height: 74'	Power: Iveco 360 HP
LWL: 70'	Freeboard: 7'	Hull: steel
Hull color: white	Spar: steel/wood	

Designer:	J. M. de Vries/M. Bekebrede/A. Kingma
Built:	1994; Lemmer, The Netherlands
Certification:	Passenger vessel, Holland and Dutch shipping inspection.
Crew:	3-6. **Trainees/passengers:** 50 (day sails), 16 (overnight)
Contact:	Captain Aent Kingma, Owner
	Koeweg 3
	NL-8715 JW Stavoren, The Netherlands
	Tel: +31-514-68-1989; Fax: +31-514-68-1302
	E-mail: aentkingma@tref.nl
	Web site: http://www.maritime.org.nz/aphrodite

Appledore II

McIntosh circumnavigated the world on her maiden voyage, an adventure documented in Herbert Smith's *Dreams of Natural Places and Sailing Three Oceans*. *Appledore II* makes day sails from her homeport of Camden, Maine from late June until mid-October. During the winter months, she undertakes snorkel trips on North America's only living coral reef, as well as sunset cruises from Key West, Florida. She carries up to 49 passengers on day sails and can accommodate up to 26 overnight.

The crew of the *Appledore II* is committed to sail training, and they are trained in sailing, celestial navigation, and marlinespike seamanship through operation of the vessel on day sails as well as two 2,000-mile offshore voyages yearly. Interested persons are encouraged to contact us for possible payroll or volunteer positions. We have opportunities for not only crew, but business positions on an entry level.

The *Appledore II* is a traditional gaff-rigged schooner designed for ocean sailing. Launched in 1978 at the Gamage Ship Yard in South Bristol, Maine, Bud

Flag:	USA
Rig:	Gaff topsail schooner.
Homeport/waters:	Camden, Maine: Maine to the Florida Keys
Season:	June to October (Maine); December to May (Florida)
Cost:	$20 per person per trip
Who sails?	School groups from elementary school through college, individuals and families.
Program type:	Sail training for crew and apprentices. Sea education based on informal, in-house programming. Passenger day sails. Dockside interpretation.

Specifications:		
Sparred length: 86'	Draft: 10' 6"	Sail area: 2,815 sq. ft.
LOA: 82'	Beam: 18' 9"	Tons: 63 GRT
LOD: 65'	Rig height: 75'	Power: 210 HP diesel
LWL: 53'	Freeboard: 8'	Hull: wood

Designer:	Bud McIntosh
Built:	1978; Gamage Shipyard, South Bristol, Maine, Herb Smith
Coast Guard certification:	Passenger Vessel (Subchapter T)
Crew:	7. **Trainees/passengers:** 49 (day), 26 (overnight)
Contact:	John P. McKean, President
	Schooner Exploration Associates, Ltd.
	"0" Lily Pond Drive
	Camden, ME 04843
	Tel: 207-236-8353, 800-233-PIER (summer)
	PO Box 4114, Key West, FL 33041-4114; Tel: 305-296-9992 (winter)

Appledore IV

The schooner *Appledore IV* is owned and operated by BaySail, a private, non-profit organization. Tall ship adventures aboard the *Appledore IV* help to support BaySail's mission: "To foster environmental stewardship of the Saginaw Bay watershed and the Great Lakes ecosystem and to provide personal development opportunities for learners of all ages through shipboard and land based educational experiences."

BaySail's environmental education program begins and ends in the classroom with materials designed to prepare students for their sailing experience and reinforce the lessons learned while on board the *Appledore IV*. During the three-and-a-half-hour excursion, trained volunteer teachers lead small groups of students through activities including collecting and analyzing water, sediment, and plankton samples. Land use, maritime history, navigation, and weather observation are also discussed.

BaySail is developing a sail training program, which is envisioned to be an intensive training experience on board the *Appledore IV*. It will be designed to teach at-risk youth about the importance of self-reliance, teamwork and respect for authority in an environment few have ever experienced. Communication skills and self-esteem will be enhanced as trainees work independently and as a team on every aspect of *Appledore IV*'s operations.

Appledore IV is available for private charter to companies, organizations, and other groups of up to 48 people and for public sails on weekends from May through September.

Flag:	USA
Rig:	Topsail schooner
Homeport/waters:	Bay City, Michigan: Saginaw Bay and Lake Huron
Who sails?	Elementary students through adults.
Season:	April to October
Cost:	$25 per person per day (3 hour sail)
	$1000 group rate (or charter) per day (3 hour cruise)
Program type:	Marine science and ecology education in cooperation with accredited institutions. Sail training for volunteer and paying trainees .Affiliated with K-12 public schools, Saginaw Valley State University, Boys & Girls Clubs of Michigan.

Specifications:

Sparred length: 85'	Draft: 8' 6"	Sail area: 3,500 sq. ft.
LOD: 65'	Beam: 18' 5"	Tons: 70 GRT
LOA: 65'	Rig height: 76'	Power: 135 HP diesel
LWL: 53'	Freeboard: 6'	Hull: steel

Designer:	Bud McIntosh
Built:	1989; Palm Coast, Florida, Treworgy Yachts
Coast Guard certification:	Passenger Vessel (Subchapter T)
Crew:	4. **Trainees/passengers:** 48 (day sails)
Contact:	Shirley Roberts, President, BaySail
	901 Saginaw Street, Bay City, MI 48708
	Tel: 517-893-1222; Fax: 517-893-7016
	E-mail: Shirley@bresnanlink.net, Web site: http://www.tourbaycitymi.org

Arethusa

Arethusa is a 72-foot ketch owned and operated by the Shaftesbury Homes & Arethusa charity, which runs homes for disadvantaged young people and orphans, mainly in southeast London. Her predecessor was a four-masted barque (*Peking*) which was a training ship moored on the Medway River providing training for up to 200 boys destined for careers in the British Royal Navy and the British Merchant Fleet. In 1974 *Peking* was towed to the South Street Seaport Museum in New York (where she is still moored), but it was decided to continue the fine sailing record of the Shaftesbury Homes Society with the construction of a new boat.

Arethusa's normal program is to run weekly cruises for groups of up to 12 young people ages (13-25), either from the Shaftesbury Homes or from similar underprivileged groups. She is home-ported at Upnor near Chatham/Rochester on the River Medway, but she cruises extensively in European waters and every second year deploys to the Canary Islands for the winter months. She is ever-present in the Cutty Sark Tall Ship Races each year. *Arethusa* visited the US in 1987, and returned last year to New York and Boston as a participant in Tall Ships 2000®. Several young people from the US participated in different legs of the race and the organization is keen to take more as participants in the European tall ship races in 2001.

Flag:	UK
Rig:	Bermuda-rigged ketch
Homeport/waters:	Upnor, near Rochester, Kent, England, UK: Europe, Baltic Sea, Biscay Bay, Canary Islands (biennially)
Who sails?	Students and individuals over 13. Affiliated with many UK school groups.
Program type:	Sail training for volunteer and paying crew and trainees. Dockside interpretation while in homeport.

Specifications:			
	Sparred length: 72'	Draft: 8'	Sail area: 1,856 sq. ft.
	LOD: 72'	Beam: 17' 4"	Tons: 43 GRT
	LOA: 72'	Rig height: 86'	Power: 130 HP diesel
	LWL: 58'	Freeboard: 4'	Hull: wood

Designer:	David Cannell
Built:	1982; Fox's, Ipswich, Suffolk, England
Certification:	SCV2 (Small Commercial Vessel), issued by YBDSA (Yacht Brokers Design and Surveyors Association)
Crew:	5. Trainees: 12
Contact:	Nicko Franks, Ketch Manager
	Shaftesbury Homes and Arethusa
	Lower Upnor Rochester
	Kent ME2 4XB, United Kingdom
	Tel: 44-1634-711566; Fax: 44-1634-295905
	E-mail: angela.arethusa@bigwig.net

Aries

Aries was built in 1962 to the highest possible standards by C.A. Crosby Co. in Osterville, Massachusetts. Materials include mahogany carvel planking from Honduras on Connecticut white oak frames with Sitka spruce masts and spars. Virtually everything else on board is teak, from the hand-carved ram figurehead tucked beneath the bowsprit to the raised eagle on the transom. Solid and comfortable with a large cockpit and berths for four, the classic cabin is a testimony to the fine yacht-builder's art. In addition to the schooner's four working sails, she hoists a flying jib, two jib-cut topsails and a powerful fisherman. With dead-eyes and ratlines on both masts, fifty belaying pins on board, and a dozen gun ports (alas, no cannon), the *Aries* has the look and feel of a two-hundred year old privateer. Having seen only light day sailing duty in her early years, the *Aries* languished in a shed for more

than fifteen years before being discovered by her present owner, re-powered, and put back to sea. In addition to private excursions up and down the New England coast, the *Aries* is available for charter out of Plymouth and Duxbury harbors in Massachusetts, and is used for traditional sail training at the Duxbury Bay Maritime School.

Flag:	USA
Rig:	Schooner
Homeport/waters:	Duxbury, Massachusetts: New England
Who sails?	Groups and individuals of all ages.
Program type:	Sail training and sea education in cooperation with the Duxbury Bay Maritime School and other organized groups. Private charters. Dockside interpretation during port visits.

Specifications:			
	Sparred length: 45'	Draft: 4' 5"	Sail area: 900 sq. ft.
	LOD: 36'	Beam: 12'	Tons: 10 GRT
	LOA: 37'	Rig height: 45'	Power: 51 HP diesel
	LWL: 30'	Freeboard: 2'6"	Hull: wood
	Hull color: black w/white stripe	Spar material: wood	

Designer:	W. D. Knott, Barnstable, Massachusetts
Built:	1962; Osterville, Massachusetts, C. A. Crosby Co.
Crew:	3. **Trainees/passengers:** 6
Contact:	Andrew Olendzki, Owner
	C. Barnes Davis, Charter Captain
	152 James Street
	PO Box 192
	Barre, MA 01005
	Snug Harbor Station, Duxbury, MA 02331
	Tel: 978-355-2985 or 781-789-SAIL

Aurora

PHOTO BY ONNE VAN DER WAL

AURORA

Aurora, formerly known as the *Francis Todd*, is a two-masted schooner built in 1947 by Newbert & Wallace of Thomaston, Maine, for work in the fishing industry. *Aurora* retired from fishery work in 1991. The vessel has been rebuilt to offer ample seating, a spacious deck plan, and amenability to catering arrangements. *Aurora* is the perfect venue for entertaining and special occasions. The vessel is inspected and certified by the US Coast Guard as a Passenger Vessel. She is stable, seaworthy, and professionally maintained for comfort and safety. *Aurora* is based in Newport, Rhode Island and sails Narragansett Bay.

Flag:	USA
Rig:	Gaff topsail schooner
Homeport/waters:	Newport, Rhode Island: Narragansett Bay
Who sails?	School groups from elementary school through college, as well as individuals and families.
Program type:	Passenger day sails and informal sail training.

Specifications:			
Sparred length: 101'	Draft: 8'	Sail area: 2,800 sq. ft.
LOD: 80'	Beam: 17'6"	Tons: 53 GRT
Rig height: 82'	Hull: wood	Hull color: black/green w/gold stripe

Designer:	Newbert & Wallace
Built:	1947; Newbert & Wallace, Thomaston, Maine
Crew:	3. **Trainees/passengers:** 80
Contact:	IDC Charters, Inc.
	Goat Island Marina
	Newport, RI 02840
	Tel: 401-849-6999
	Web Site: http://www.newportexperience.com

SAIL TALL SHIPS!

Avon Spirit

Avon Spirit was named to celebrate the intrepid spirit of those New England Planters (1760) who settled the lands along the Avon River and who built, sailed, and managed 650 large ships during the "Golden Age of Sail." She was constructed in the Avon Spirit Shipyard, Avondale/Newport Landing, Nova Scotia, by the same shipwrights of Snyder's Shipyard Limited, who gave *Bluenose II* new life in 1991 and by local skilled craftsmen of Hants County, Nova Scotia. The sails are by Michele Stevens Sail Loft, 2nd Peninsula. *Avon Spirit* is a 55-foot version of the "F.G.B.", the last cargo schooner built in Nova Scotia, and in 1929, the last vessel registered on the Windsor Registry of Shipping. The traditional 64 shares are registered to Avon Spirit, Inc., which was founded to help preserve the skills of the wooden shipwright in Nova Scotia.

She has been traditionally built with sawn oak frames, oak keel, stem, sternpost, and deadwood, and planked with oak and Eastern White Pine. The masts are Black Spruce. Her draft and traditional rig make her an ideal vessel for sailing the waters of beautiful Mahone Bay. *Avon Spirit* operates from the Mahone Bay Town Wharf (home of the Mahone Bay Wooden Boat Festival), conducting daily cruises or private charters.

Flag:	Canada
Rig:	Square topsail schooner
Homeport/waters:	Lunenburg, Nova Scotia, Canada: Mahone Bay, Nova Scotia, Canada
Program type:	Sail training program being developed for volunteer and paying trainees.

Specifications:			
	Sparred length: 70' 6"	Draft: 5' 6"	Sail area: 1,216 sq. ft.
	LOD: 53'	Beam: 16' 6"	Tons: 16.3 GRT
	LOA: 55'	Rig height: 50'	Power: 300 HP diesel
	LWL: 44'	Freeboard: 2' 6"	Hull: wood

Built:	1998; Snyder's Shipyard, Ltd.
Certification:	Canadian Coast Guard certified passenger vessel
Crew:	4
Contact:	Hugh MacNeil, VADM (Ret.)
	Avon Spirit Shipyard, Ltd.
	15 Belmont Road, RR # 2
	Newport, Nova Scotia B0N 2A0, Canada
	Tel/Fax: 902-757-1718
	E-mail: arhs@glinx.com
	Web site: http://www.glinx.com/users/arhs

Bagheera

Built in 1924 for Newport, Rhode Island millionaire Marion Eppley, *Bagheera* represents a time when unlimited wealth and classical tastes combined to produce some of the finest vessels in the history of yachting and yacht racing. For many years, *Bagheera* was the boat to beat in campaigns from the Great Lakes to the Bahamas, and as far as Morocco and the Mediterranean. She twice won the prestigious Chicago-Mackinac Race, and was used for the training of naval cadets during the Second World War. After the war *Bagheera* cruised extensively all over the world, eventually making her way to the West Coast.

Throughout the 1980's, *Bagheera* was a familiar sight along the San Diego waterfront, sailing for hire, and competing in many classic yacht races.

Now, after an extensive six-month restoration, *Bagheera* is in San Francisco Bay, certified by the US Coast Guard, and operated by an experienced, well trained crew. She can comfortably carry 30 passengers for day sails.

Flexible programs and schedules are available for group charters.

Bagheera sails primarily from Richmond, in the East Bay.

Flag:	USA
Rig:	Staysail schooner
Homeport/waters:	San Francisco, California: San Francisco Bay, California
Who sails?	School groups from elementary school through college, individuals and families.
Program type:	Sail training for volunteer and paying trainees. Sea education based on informal, in-house programming. Passenger day sails.

Specifications:		
Sparred length: 72'	Draft: 7' 6"	Tons: 21 GRT
LOD: 54'	Beam: 14' 6"	Power: 72 HP diesel
LOA: 55' 6"	Rig height: 65'	Hull: wood
LWL: 44'	Freeboard: 4'	

Designer:	John G. Alden
Built:	1924; East Boothbay, Maine, Rice Brothers
Coast Guard certification:	Passenger Vessel (Subchapter T)
Crew:	2. Trainees/passengers: 25-30
Contact:	Captain Jonathan Friedberg and Becky Waegell
	Bagheera Charters, LLC
	7700 Fagle's Nest Road
	Sacramento, CA 95830
	Tel: 916-683-4915, 1-87-SCHOONER (toll-free)
	E-mail: bagheera@theship.com
	Web site: http://www.bagheera.theship.com

Balclutha

In 1886, Charles Connell & Company built a three-masted, riveted steel ship "to the highest class in Lloyd's registry" near Glasgow, Scotland. Her owner, Robert McMillan, named that 256-foot vessel *Balclutha*—the Gaelic name for Dumbarton, Scotland.

As a deepwaterman, *Balclutha* and a 26-man crew rounded Cape Horn with grain for Great Britain, and later ran Pacific Coast lumber to Australia. Each year as a salmon packet, the vessel carried hundreds of men (with boats and supplies) to the salmon-fishing grounds of Alaska. *Balclutha* even had a brief Hollywood career. The vessel was rescued from decay by the San Francisco Bay Area community in 1954, and has been restored as a memorial to the men and times of the grand days of sail.

Today, *Balclutha* (now designated a National Historic Landmark) is open to the public daily as part of the San Francisco Maritime National Historical Park. Park Service rangers conduct regular tours and present a variety of history programs aboard, and the vessel hosts special events such as the Park's annual Sea Music Concert Series, and maritime-related theater productions.

PHOTO BY STEVE DANFORD

BALCLUTHA

Flag:	USA		
Rig:	Full-rigged ship		
Homeport/waters:	San Francisco, California		
Program type:	Dockside sea education in maritime history.		
Specifications:	Sparred length: 301'	Draft: 22' 7"	Tons: 1,689 GRT
	LOD: 256' 6"	Beam: 38' 6"	Hull: steel
	Rig height: 145'		
Designer:	Charles Connell		
Built:	1886; Scotland, Charles Connell		
Contact:	William G. Thomas, Superintendent		
	San Francisco Maritime National Historical Park		
	Building E, Fort Mason Center		
	San Francisco, CA 94123		
	Tel: 415-556-1659; Fax: 415-556-1624		
	Web site: http://www.nps.gov/safr		

Bat'kivshchyna

The *Bat'kivshchyna* is a converted steel-hull Russian fishing supply boat which has been reinforced with ferro-cement. The design and conversion was accomplished by Dmytro Biryukovich, a civil engineer in Kyiv, Ukraine and an expert in ferro-cement applications.

Captain Biryukovich intends to circumnavigate the world promoting tourism and foreign business investments in his beloved Ukraine. During the Tall Ships Challenge® in the summer of 2001, the *Bat'kivshchyna* will partner with the Children of Chernobyl Relief Fund in raising funds for, and awareness of, the medical and health needs of Ukrainian children affected by the radioactive fallout caused by the Chernobyl nuclear power plant explosion in 1986. (This power plant was permanently closed on 15 December 2000.)

The *Bat'kivshchyna* has become an icon for a free Ukraine, which will be celebrating its 10th year of independence in 2001.

Flag:	Ukraine
Rig:	Gaff rigged schooner
Homeport/waters:	Kyiv, Ukraine: Dnipro River, Black Sea (summer)
Season:	April through October
Who sails?	Trainees of all ages.
Program type:	Sail training for volunteer and paying trainees. Sea education as informal in-house programming. Dockside interpretation at every opportunity.
Cost:	$100 per person per day, $1500 (day sails) group rate per day (20 max.)
Specifications:	Sparred length: 97' Draft: 10' LOD: 80'
	LOA: 87' LWL: 68' Beam: 17'
	Tons: 80 GRT Rig height: 68' Freeboard: 3'6"
	Hull: steel reinforced with ferrous cement
	Power: 150 HP diesel Hull color: black
Designer:	Dmytro Biryukovich
Built:	1991; Kyiv, Ukraine, Dmytro Biryukovich
Crew:	3. **Trainees:** 20 (day sails), 10 (over night)
Contact:	Fleet Teachout, Liaison
	S/V Bat'kivshchyna
	PO Box 684
	Great Mills, MD 20634
	Tel: 301-994-2593
	E-mail: fleet@batkivshchyna.org
	Web site: http://www.batkivshchyna.org

HMS Bee

The *HMS Bee* is a replica of a Royal Navy transport schooner which operated on the Upper Great Lakes in the years immediately following the War of 1812. Commissioned by the Province of Ontario, the vessel was constructed in 1984 by provincial staff and volunteers on the naval site where the original schooner sailed.

Although incorporating modern technology, *HMS Bee* is a faithful reproduction of an early 19th century naval vessel. Her exterior and interior reflect the realities of a sailor's life of that time. The schooner *Bee* proudly sails from the Discovery Harbour Provincial Historic Site in Penetanguishene, Ontario, under an "Honorary Warrant" of the Royal Navy.

The volunteers and staff of the Marine Heritage Association operate the vessel on beautiful Georgian Bay, June through September. Families and individuals are invited to sail 3-hour cruises departing weekday evenings and weekend afternoons. The program emphasizes living history and hands-on sail training for sailors of all ages. Our rig is in the 19th century tradition, as is the dress and manor of the crew. During your visit to Ontario, join the officers and crew in the naval fashion of 1812. Step back in time and run away to sea on Georgian Bay!

Flag:	Canada
Rig:	Gaff schooner
Homeport/waters:	Penetanguishene, Ontario, Canada: Georgian Bay and upper Great Lakes
Who sails?	Individuals and groups
Season:	June to September
Cost:	$29 (3-hour sail). Expeditions and attractions by arrangement.
Program type:	Living history and seamanship. Sail training for paying trainees. Dockside interpretation during port visits.

Specifications:	Sparred length: 78'	Draft: 5' 6"	Sail area: 1,672 sq. ft.
	LOA: 48' 6"	Beam: 14' 6"	Tons: 25 GRT
	LWL: 42'	Hull: GRP and wood	Power: 90 HP diesel

Certification:	Operates under the Canadian Sail Training Association guidelines
Designer:	Steve Killing
Built:	1985; Penetanguishene, Ontario, Canada, Charlie Allen
Crew:	5 officers and leading hands. **Trainees:** 14
Contact:	The Marine Heritage Association
	PO Box 353
	Midland, Ontario L4R 4L1 Canada
	Tel: 705-549-5575/800-MHA-5577; Fax: 705-549-5576
	E-mail: marineheritage@on.aibn.com
	Web Site: http://www.discoveryharbour.on.ca

Bill of Rights

The Los Angeles Maritime Institute is the educational affiliate of the Los Angeles Maritime Museum. Through the Topsail Youth Program, the Institute provides character-building sail training adventures for youth. The schooners *Swift of Ipswich* and *Bill of Rights* are learning environments that nurture the development of knowledge, skills, and attitudes that are necessary for the education of today's youth, but difficult to teach in a traditional classroom.

The schooners sail with crews of mariner-educators who encourage the growth of awareness, understanding, communication, and teamwork, along with maturing of the traits of persistence, patience, endurance, courage, and caution.

Topsail can be adjusted to fit the age, interests, and abilities of any participants. Single-day events are for exploration, fun, and an introduction to the sea and sailing. Multi-day programs typically provide a life-changing experience for participants.

The Los Angeles Maritime Museum and all of its affiliates take pleasure in offering hospitality, on an as-available basis, to visiting tall ships and other "educationally significant" vessels.

Flag:	USA
Rig:	Gaff-rigged topsail schooner, two-masted
Homeport/waters:	Los Angeles, California: coastal California and offshore islands.
Who sails?	Referred youth-at-risk and groups catering to students and adults.
Season:	Year-round
Program type:	Educational

Specifications:	Sparred length: 136'	Draft: 10'	Sail area: 6,300 sq. ft.
	LOD: 94'	Beam: 23'	Tons: 95 GRT
	LOA: 129'	Rig height: 100'	Power: 210 HP diesel
	LWL: 85'	Freeboard: 5' 8"	Hull: wood

Designer:	McCurdy, Rhodes & Bates
Built:	1971; South Bristol, Maine, Harvey F. Gamage
Coast Guard certification:	Passenger Vessel (Subchapter T)
Crew:	5 (day); 8 (overnight); 5 instructors. **Trainees:** 52 (day sails); 39 (overnight)
Contact:	Captain Jim Gladson
	Los Angeles Maritime Institute
	Berth 84, Foot of Sixth Street
	San Pedro, CA 90731
	Tel: 310-833-6055; Fax: 310-548-2055

Black Jack

PHOTO BY CLIFF PATTERSON

Rebuilt in 1952 from the hull of a 1904 tugboat by the late Captain Thomas G. Fuller, *Black Jack* is an 87-foot brigantine. Carrying 3,000 sq. ft. of sail, the ship is now used as a centerpiece for a sail training program operated on Canada's historic Ottawa River. Up to 30 youth, aged 12 to 16, participate in 12-day sail training programs which depart from Canada's capital city for the river and voyage to an 18-acre wilderness island camp. At the island, trainees live aboard traditional logging barges from where they set out to explore the river. In addition to sailing aboard *Black Jack*, trainees also sail 27-foot traditional Navy Whalers and share a variety of other camp activities.

Thomas Fuller was one of Canada's most decorated war heroes, earning the name "Pirate of the Adriatic" and holding the distinction of the longest time served in offensive war action. His wartime experience taught him the value of instilling confidence and resourceful-

ness in our youth through adventure at sea. Captain Fuller founded the nonprofit Bytown Brigantine in 1983 to provide these opportunities to young people.

BLACK JACK

Flag:	Canada
Rig:	Brigantine
Homeport/waters:	Ottawa, Ontario, Canada: Ottawa River.
Who sails?	Middle school, high school, and college students as well as individuals of student age.
Cost:	$60 per person per day
Program type:	Sail training for paying trainees. Overnight voyages.
Season:	April to October

Specifications:			
	Sparred length: 90'	Draft: 6'	Sail area: 3,000 sq. ft.
	LOD: 68'	Beam: 15'	Tons: 42.25 GRT
	LOA: 87'	Rig height: 80'	Power: 235 HP diesel
	LWL: 57'	Freeboard: 3'	Hull: steel

Built:	1904; Scotland
Crew:	6
Contact:	Simon A.F. Fuller, President
	Bytown Brigantine, Inc.
	2700 Queensview Dr.
	Ottawa, Ontario K2B 8H6, Canada
	Tel: 613-596-6258; Fax: 613-596-5947
	E-mail: tallshipinfo@tallshipsadventure.org
	Web site: http://tallshipsadventure.org

Black Pearl

Built in 1938 by Lincoln Vaughan for his own use, *Black Pearl* was purchased by Barclay H. Warburton III in 1958. Long a believer in the sea as a teacher, Warburton selected the rig as a good one for sail training. In 1972

Warburton sailed the *Black Pearl* to England to participate in that summer's European tall ships race, becoming the first American to do so. On his return to Newport, Warburton founded the American Sail Training Association.

Black Pearl is currently owned and operated by the Aquaculture Foundation, a nonprofit trust formed to promote quality education in marine studies. Her programs take her throughout Long Island Sound, as well as into the North Atlantic, Gulf of Mexico, and Caribbean. At present, the Foundation is engaged in a capital campaign to raise $1.25 million for *Black Pearl*'s complete renovation.

Flag:	USA
Rig:	Brigantine
Homeport/waters:	Bridgeport, Connecticut: Atlantic Ocean and Caribbean Sea
Who sails?	School and other groups and individuals aged 16 to 65. Affiliated groups include University of Bridgeport, Housatonic Community College, and seven Connecticut school districts.
Season:	May to October
Program type:	Sail training for crew and paying trainees. Sea education in marine science, maritime history, and ecology in cooperation with accredited schools and colleges. Passenger day sails and overnight voyages.

Specifications:	Sparred length: 79'	Draft: 9'	Sail area: 2,000 sq. ft.
	LOD: 52'	Beam: 14'	Tons: 28 GRT
	LWL: 43'	Rig height: 63'	Sail number: TS US-33
	Freeboard: 6'	Power: diesel	

Designer:	Edson Schock
Built:	1938; Wickford, Rhode Island, C. Lincoln Vaughan
Crew:	3-4 (day), 4-8 (overnight). **Trainees:** 6
Contact:	Edwin T. Merritt, Executive Director
	The Aquaculture Foundation
	525 Antelope Trail
	Shelton, CT 06484
	Tel: 203-372-4406; Fax: 203-372-4407
	E-mail: tmerritt@pcnet.com
	Web site: http://www.tallshipblackpearl.org

Bluenose II

The original *Bluenose*, launched on March 26, 1921, was a typical Nova Scotian Grand Banks fishing schooner. Built at Lunenburg both for fishing and for the International Fishermen's Trophy series of races between Canada and the US, *Bluenose* was undefeated under her legendary Master, Captain Angus J. Walters of Lunenburg. Her likeness became a national emblem and it is depicted on stamps and the ten-cent coin of Canada. Launched on July 24, 1963, *Bluenose II* was built from the same plans at the same yard and by some of the same men. The only difference lies in the accommodations for the co-ed crew of 18 and the modern navigation and communication instruments. She serves as a goodwill ambassador for the Province of Nova Scotia, participating in tall ship events throughout the Western Hemisphere.

Bluenose II's 12 deckhands receive instructions from the officers in all manners of seamanship. Today she sails in the best *Bluenose* tradition, and all officers and deckhands are encouraged to enhance their skills and certifications.

Flag:	Canada
Rig:	Gaff topsail schooner
Homeport/waters:	Lunenburg, Nova Scotia, Canada: East Coast of Canada and the US.
Who sails?	Individuals and groups. Affiliated institutions include the Fisheries Museum of the Atlantic, Lunenburg; the Maritime Museum of the Atlantic, Halifax; Nova Scotia Nautical Institute, Port Hawkesbury; and the Canadian Navy, Halifax.
Season:	April to November
Cost:	Adults, $20, children under 12, $10 (per two-hour sail).
Program type:	Sail training for crew. Passenger day sails. Dockside interpretation.

Specifications:	Sparred length: 161'	Draft: 16'	Sail area: 11,139 sq. ft.
	LOD: 143'	Beam: 27'	Tons: 285 GRT
	LWL: 112'	Rig height: 132'	Power: twin 250
	Hull: wood		HP diesels

Designer:	William J. Roué, Halifax, Nova Scotia, Canada
Built:	1963; Lunenburg, Nova Scotia, Canada, Smith & Rhuland Shipyards
Certification:	Canadian Coast Guard certified
Crew:	18
Contact:	Senator Wilfred P. Moore, Chairman
	Bluenose II Preservation Trust
	PO Box 1963
	Lunenburg, Nova Scotia B0J 2C0, Canada
	Tel: 902-634-1963; Fax: 902-634-1995
	E-mail: ship@bluenose2.ns.ca
	Web site: http://www.bluenose2.ns.ca

BLUENOSE II

Bonnie Lynn

Bonnie Lynn is one of the most unique of the Maine Windjammer fleet. She is a modified version of designer Merrit Walter's *Trade Rover*, the hull being built by Treworgy Yachts and then the interior and rigging completed in Maine. Being a serious offshore cruising vessel, she is built to very high standards. The steel hull is 57' on deck, with an overall length of 72'. She was completed in July of 1998 and has been actively chartering since then.

Bonnie Lynn charters from the Virgin Islands through the Grenadines in the winters, and returns to her homeport of Islesoboro, Maine in the summers, where she charters from New England to Nova Scotia. She is Coast Guard certified for 38 passengers for day sail and 10 for ocean. Extraordinary means have been taken to make this a most comfortable and seaworthy vessel. Although she has a very traditional look, passengers rest in the serenity and luxury of modern day technology and amenities. Her charters range from day sails and term charters to offshore cruising. Future plans include a circumnavigation with guests.

Flag:	US
Rig:	Schooner
Homeport/waters:	Islesboro, Maine: New England (summer), Caribbean (winter).
Who sails?	Families and groups.
Program type:	Sail training for volunteer crew and for volunteer and paying trainees. Dockside interpretation during port visits.

Specifications:			
	Sparred length: 72'	Draft: 7'	Sail area: 2,500 sq. ft.
	LOD: 57'	Beam: 15'3"	Tons: 32 GRT
	LWL: 49'	LOA: 57'	Rig height: 63'
	Power: diesel 220 HP	Hull: steel	Hull color: black

Designer:	Merrit Walter
Built:	1997;: Palm Coast, Florida, Islesboro, Maine; Treworgy
Certification:	Passenger Vessel (Subchapter T)
Crew:	3
Contact:	Captains Bonnie and Earl MacKenzie
	PO Box 41
	Islesboro, ME 04848
	Tel: 401-862 1115 (summer)
	E-mail: mack@midcoast.com
	Web site: http://www.bonnielynn.com

Bounty

Built for the 1962 movie "Mutiny on the *Bounty*" by MGM Studios, the *Bounty* was later purchased by Turner Broadcasting System in 1986 and once again put to sea. Donated to the Tall Ship Bounty Foundation in 1993, the *Bounty* was successfully operated as a sail training vessel for many years under the auspices of the nonprofit educational organization. Due to the her commitment to sail training and preserving the art of square-rigged sailing, the US Navy selected the *Bounty* to help prepare the officers and crew to sail the USS CONSTITUTION for the first time in more than 100 years!

Recently acquired by the Long Island-based HMS Bounty Organization, LLC, the *Bounty's* new owner will continue the tradition of teaching 18th century seamanship skills through sail training voyages that will be open to the public. The organization will operate teen sailing and personal development programs throughout the year, and the ship will also be available for port festival appearances, corporate entertaining, film

appearances and private charter.

The Organization plans to restore the *Bounty* to her former "movie star" glory while providing safe accommodations and passage for future trainees. Due to the tremendous task of restoring and reviving this famous tall ship, the owners are seeking donations, volunteers and sponsors. After extensive restoration, the group plans to sail in the northeast in the summer months and Florida and the Caribbean in the winter months.

BOUNTY

Flag:	USA
Rig:	Full-rigged ship, three-masted
Homeport/waters:	Long Island, NY and the waters to northeast US (summer); Florida and Caribbean (winter)
Who sails?	Students, individuals, and groups of all ages
Season:	Year-round
Program type:	Sail training for paying trainees. Sea education in marine science, maritime history, and ecology in cooperation with organized groups and as informal, in-house programming. Passenger overnight passages. Dockside interpretation during port visits.

Specifications:			
	Sparred length: 169'	Draft: 13'	Sail area: 10,000 sq. ft.
	LOD: 120'	Beam: 30'	Tons: 412 GRT
	LOA: 130'	Rig height: 115'	Power: twin 200 HP diesels
	Hull: wood		

Designer:	The British Admiralty
Built:	1960; Lunenburg, Nova Scotia, Smith & Rhuland
Coast Guard certification:	Uninspected Vessel
Crew:	18. **Trainees/passengers:** 12
Contact:	Robert E. Hansen, President or
	Margaret Ramsey, Director of Seaside Operations
	HMS Bounty Organization, LLC
	PO Box 141
	Oakdale, NY 11769
	Tel: 8631-588-7900 or 66-HMSBounty (866-467-2686) Fax: 631-471-4609
	E-mail: mailbox@tallshipbounty.org
	Web site: http://www.tallshipbounty.org

Bowdoin

The schooner *Bowdoin* is the flagship of Maine Maritime Academy's sail training fleet, and the official sailing vessel of the state of Maine. Built in 1921 specifi- cally for cruising in Arctic waters, she is one of the strongest wooden vessels ever constructed. Between 1921 and 1954 she made 26 voyages to the far north under the command of her first master, explorer Donald B. MacMillan.

Today, with the characteristic ice barrel on her foremast, *Bowdoin* serves the students of the Maine Maritime Academy and the educational community of New England with a broad range of programs in seamanship, ocean studies, and curriculum development. Offerings begin at the high school level, and range from cruises on Penobscot Bay to extended passages to Greenland and Labrador. These semi-annual cruises represent a unique opportunity in the world of sail training.

Flag:	USA
Rig:	Schooner
Homeport/waters:	Castine, Maine: Gulf of Maine, Canadian Maritimes
Who sails?	School groups from high school through college as well as individuals of all ages. Affiliated institutions include the Maine Maritime Academy.
Season:	May to October
Cost:	$1,500 group rate per day (charter)
Program type:	Sail training for professional crew and paying trainees. Fully accredited sea education in marine science, maritime history, and ecology as well as informal, in-house programming. Passenger overnight passages. Limited dockside interpretation during port visits.

Specifications:	Sparred length: 100'	Draft: 10'	Sail area: 2,900 sq. ft.
	LOD: 83'	Beam: 20'	Tons: 66 GRT
	LOA: 88'	Rig height: 70'	Power: 190 HP diesel
	LWL: 72'	Freeboard: 4'	Hull: wood

Designer:	William Hand
Built:	1921; East Boothbay, Maine, Hodgdon Brothers Shipyard
Coast Guard certification:	Sailing School Vessel (Subchapter R), Passenger Vessel (Subchapter T)
Crew:	6. **Trainees:** 40 (day), 11 (overnight)
Contact:	Virginia Comiciotto, Continuing Education Coordinator Maine Maritime Academy Castine, ME 04420 Tel: 207-326-2211; Fax: 207-326-2218 E-mail: vcomo@mma.edu Web site: http://www.mainemaritime.edu

Brandaris

Brandaris, the 63-foot Dutch-design sailing vessel was launched in 1938 as the private yacht of William De Vries Lentsch, Jr., shipyard owner and famous Dutch designer. After a colorful escape from German occupation in WW II, *Brandaris* participated in the evacuation of Dunkirk. Now berthed in Wickford, RI, she is available for public excursions, sailing charters, and special occasion functions from weddings to funerals.

Brandaris also offers a Classroom Afloat program featuring educational field trips and curriculum based experiential learning programs. Many of these programs have received sponsorship from corporate and grant-based underwriters at no charge to schools.

Flag:	USA
Rig:	Cutter/Sloop
Homeport/waters:	Wickford, Rhode Island: Narragansett Bay, Rhode Island
Who sails?	School groups from elementary school through college, individuals, families, charter groups.
Season:	Year-round
Program type:	Sail training for volunteer and paying trainees. Sea education in marine science, maritime history and ecology in cooperation with organized groups. Passenger day sails and overnight voyages, dockside interpretation during port visits.

Specifications:			
	Sparred length: 63'	Draft: 2'6"	Sail area: 1,317 sq. ft.
	LOD: 55'	Beam: 18'	Tons: 60 GRT
	LOA: 58'	Rig height: 59'	Power: 135 HP Ford
	LWL: 53'	Freeboard: 4'6"	Hull: riveted iron
	Spar: spruce	Hull color: white	

Designer:	William De Vries Lentsch, Jr.
Built:	1938; Amsterdam Shipyard, Amsterdam, The Netherlands
Coast Guard certification:	Passenger vessel (Subchapter T), Inland, Near Coastal
Crew:	2. **Trainees:** 32 (day sails)
Contact:	Captain Douglas Somers, Owner
	Brandaris Sailing Charters/Friends of Brandaris
	7 Main Street
	Wickford, RI 02852
	Tel: 401-294-1481; Fax: 401-294-1938

Brilliant

Winner of the Tall Ships 2000® transatlantic race from Halifax to Amsterdam and captained by ASTA's 2000 "Sail Trainer of the Year," George Moffett, *Brilliant* is the traveling ambassador of Mystic Seaport, our nation's leading maritime museum. In service for more than 45 years – the oldest sail-education program in the nation – *Brilliant* has introduced more than 8,000 people to the lessons a sailing ship naturally teaches. Board this classic schooner and become the crew; steer, handle sails, cook and clean as you learn the venerable maritime tradition of "for the good of the ship." *Brilliant* has two other ASTA awards to her credit: "First in Class" in the 2000 Boston to Halifax race and "Sail Training Vessel of the Year" in 1996. She also won the 1997 Nantucket Lighthouse Opera Cup.

Her 2001 sailing schedule includes: Mystic to Mystic, July 1-6 and August 26-31 (ages 15-16), Mystic to Marblehead, July 8-13 (ages 15-16), Marblehead to Rockland, July 22-27 (ages 17-19), Rockland to Halifax and Halifax to Rockland (ages 17-19), Marblehead to Mystic, August 12-22 (ages 17-19), and Mystic to Mystic, September 7-10, September 14-17, September 28-October 1, and October 5-8 (adult, 20+).

Flag:	USA
Rig:	Gaff schooner, two-masted
Homeport/waters:	Mystic, Connecticut: New England, Nova Scotia, Chesapeake Bay.
Who sails?	Transatlantic and Europe 2000, ages 18-25. Participants must be physically fit, agile, and competent swimmers. Affiliated institution is Mystic Seaport.
Season:	May to October.
Cost:	$1,400 and up for *Brilliant* 2000 trips. Financial assistance is available.
Program type:	Sail training with paying trainees. Sea education in cooperation with organized groups such as Scouts, based on informal, in-house programming.

Specifications:			
	Sparred length: 74'	Draft: 9'	Tons: 30 GRT
	LOD: 61' 6"	Beam: 14' 8'	Power: 97 HP diesel
	LOA: 61' 6"	Rig height: 81'	Hull: wood
	LWL: 49'		

Designer:	Sparkman & Stephens
Built:	1932; City Island, New York, Henry B. Nevins
Coast Guard certification:	Sailing School Vessel (Subchapter R), Passenger Vessel (Subchapter T)
Crew:	3 (day), 4 (overnight). **Trainees:** 9-10 (day); 6 (overnight)
Contact:	Brilliant Program, Museum Education Department
	Mystic Seaport
	PO Box 6000
	Mystic, CT 06355-0990
	Tel: 860-572-5323; Fax: 860-572-5395
	Web site: http://www.mysticseaport.org/brilliant

Californian

Owned and operated by the nonprofit Nautical Heritage Society, the *Californian* is a recreation of the 1849 Campbell-class Revenue Marine Cutter *C.W. Lawrence*. *Californian*'s sail training programs immerse trainees in a unique and valuable education in which they experience the forces of nature and develop skills that relate directly to life ashore. Self-reliance, teamwork, American history, coastal ecology, and sailing are the cornerstones of the *Californian* programs. The Sea Chest Program provides curriculum materials for classroom use, ship tours, and day sails for elementary school students. High school students can receive academic credit for time spent aboard, and college level programs are also available.

The ship has been designated as the official tall ship ambassador for the state of California. In addition to its coastal sail training programs, the *Californian* has sailed to Hawaii and Canada, and to Mexico to offer humanitarian aid after Mexico's 1986 earthquake.

Flag:	USA
Rig:	Square topsail schooner, two-masted
Homeport/waters:	Long Beach, California: coastal California and Pacific Ocean
Who sails?	School groups and individuals.
Season:	Year-round
Cost:	$150 per person per day
Program type:	Sail training for professional crew, and volunteer, and paying trainees. Sea education includes marine science, maritime history, and ecology in cooperation with other groups, and informal, in-house programming.

Specifications:	Sparred length: 145'	Draft: 9' 5"	Sail area: 7,000 sq. ft.
	LOD: 93' 5"	Beam: 24' 6"	Tons: 130 GRT
	LWL: 84'	Freeboard: 6'	Power: 100 HP diesel
	Rig height: 101'	Hull: wood	

Designer:	Melbourne Smith
Built:	1984; San Diego, California, Nautical Heritage Society
Coast Guard certification:	Passenger Vessel (Subchapter T), Sailing School Vessel (Subchapter R)
Crew:	8. **Trainees:** 45 (day sails), 16 (overnight)
Contact:	Steve Christman, President
	Nautical Heritage Society
	1064 Calle Negocio, Unit B
	San Clemente, CA 92673
	Tel: 949-369-6773; Fax: 949-369-6892
	E-mail: nhs@californian.org
	Web site: http://www.californian.org

Camelot

The sailing vessel *Camelot* was built in 1961 by American Marine. She was an inspiration and collaboration of two designers: Angelman and Davies. They named the design Mayflower, *Camelot* is hull # 7. She is professionally maintained and operated by a licensed Coast Guard Captain with more than 20 years experience. *Camelot* is an uninspected vessel that is very well maintained.

Camelot has been used in a variety of programs and activities, from leisure sunset cruises to sail training programs, and to just share the joy of living under sail. The main focus of *Camelot* is in sail training and team building for corporate and government executives. She is perfect for small groups of six or less.

Flag:	USA
Rig:	Gaff-ketch
Homeport/waters:	Hilton Head, South Carolina: East Coast US, Gulf of Mexico, Caribbean.
Who sails?	High school and college groups, individuals, groups, and families.
Season:	Year-round
Cost:	$400 per person per day, $1,200 group rate per day (charter), $2,000 per person per week (minimum of two people)
Program type:	Sail training for paying trainees. Sea education in cooperation with organized groups and as informal, in-house programming. Corporate team building.

Specifications:			
	Sparred length: 54'	Draft: 7'	Sail area: 978 sq. ft.
	LOD: 40'	Beam: 13' 6"	Tons: 22 GRT
	LOA: 54'	Rig height: 53' 6"	Power: diesel
	LWL: 36' 6"	Freeboard: 3'	Hull: Burmese teak

Designer:	Angleman & Davies
Built:	1961; Hong Kong, American Marine
Coast Guard certification:	Uninspected Vessel
Crew:	2. **Trainees/passengers**: 6 (day), 2 (overnight)
Contact:	Captain Armour Rice
	Camelot Excursions
	13862 Lazy Lane
	Fort Myers, FL 33905
	Tel: 941-694-0576
	E-mail: ssavalon@aol.com
	Web site: http://www.mgtaylor.com/camelot

Cape Rose

Cape Rose, the ex-*Danielle Louise*, was restored to her original launch name in the spring of 2001. She sailed the entire eastern seaboard in the year 2000, from historic Key West to the scenic ports of Downeast Maine, participating in maritime festivals and nautical events along the way. She is seaworthy, comfortable, and a good boat on all points of sail.

Hull construction is of multi-chine steel with the topside radiused in sections, giving the appearance of a round bilge boat when on the water. Below the waterline, she was given a modern underbody, for good performance and maneuverability. The combination of traditional gaff rig, her modern underbody; and her spacious deck area give her performance, helm response and comfort, which surprises most who sail on her.

This rugged schooner is a perfect platform for sail training programs. Wellness and personal growth are the focus of professionally-facilitated workshops. The training fosters team-building, cooperation, self-sufficiency, and leadership. Awareness and appreciation for the shipboard and marine environments are emphasized. Programs are customized to meet the specific needs of the participants.

CAPE ROSE

Flag:	USA
Homeport/waters:	Wickford, Rhode Island; Narragansett Bay/North Atlantic (summer), Florida coast/Caribbean (winter)
Who sails:	Individuals and groups of all ages
Program type:	Sail training for volunteer and paying trainees. Sea education in marine science, maritime history, and ecology as informal in-house programming, and in cooperation with accredited institutions and other organized groups. Dockside interpretation while in port.
Season:	Year-round

Specifications:

Sparred length: 72'	LOD: 50'	LWL: 39'6"
LOA: 52'	Draft: 6'6"	Beam: 16'
Tons: 32 GRT	Rig height: 56'	Sail area: 1,284 sq. ft.
Freeboard: 4'	Power: 212 HP diesel	Hull: steel
Hull color: teal green	Spar material: steel	

Designer:	Dudley Dix
Built:	1987; South Africa, Brian Alcock
Crew:	3. **Trainees/passengers:** 6
Contact:	Diane Luchild, CEO
	Sail into Wellness
	PO Box 865
	North Kingston, RI 02852
	Tel: 401-419-6155; Fax: 401-295-9628
	E-mail: dluchild@ids.net
	Web site: http://www.sailintowellness.com

C.A. Thayer

Once, hundreds of sailing schooners carried lumber to San Francisco from Washington, Oregon, and the California Redwood Coast. Built in 1895, *C.A. Thayer* was part of that mighty Pacific Coast fleet. *C.A. Thayer* usually sailed from the E.K. wood mill in Grays Harbor, Washington, to San Francisco, but she also carried lumber as far south as Mexico, and even ventured offshore to Hawaii and Fiji. Later, the vessel supplied the Alaskan salt-salmon canneries, anchoring out during the summer, then returning in September with the season's catch packed in her hold. From 1925-1950, *C.A. Thayer* carried men north to the Bering Sea cod-fishing grounds. In fact, *C.A. Thayer*'s last voyage in that trade marked the end of commercial sail on the West Coast. Purchased by the State of California in 1957, and transferred to the National Park Service in 1977, this National Historic Landmark is a rare survivor from the days when strong canvas sails billowed over tall deckloads of freshly-milled fir and redwood.

Today, the vessel hosts a slate of unique school education programs presented by the San Francisco Maritime National Park Association, and is open to the public as part of the San Francisco Maritime National Historical Park.

Flag:	USA
Rig:	Schooner, three-masted
Homeport/waters:	San Francisco, California
Program type:	Dockside sea education programs in maritime history.

Specifications:	Sparred length: 219'	Draft: 11' 3"	Tons: 453 GRT
	LOD: 156'	Beam: 36'	Hull: wood
	Rig height: 105'		

Designer:	Hans Bendixsen
Built:	1895; Fairhaven, California, Hans Bendixsen
Contact:	William G. Thomas, Superintendent
	San Francisco Maritime National Historical Park
	Building E, Fort Mason Center
	San Francisco, CA 94123
	Tel: 415-556-1659; Fax: 415-556-1624
	Web site: http://www.nps.gov/safr

Challenge

Challenge is a 96-foot three-masted schooner. Her hull was built on the lines of the famous schooners that once dominated the Great Lakes. She operates a very unique day sail training program in conjunction with The Pier – Toronto's Waterfront Museum. The cooperative program enables teachers to bring the life of a 19th-century sailor to their students. The *Challenge* voyage is also an opportunity for children to learn about other sail training programs. In 1998 over 6,000 schoolchildren from Canada and the US took part in *Challenge*'s day sail training program.

Flag:	Canada
Rig:	Staysail schooner, three-masted
Homeport/waters:	Toronto, Ontario, Canada: Lake Ontario
Who sails?	Individuals and groups of all ages. Challenge operates a day sail training program in conjunction with The Pier – Toronto's Waterfront Museum.
Season:	April to October.
Program type:	Day sail training program. Vessel also conducts corporate charter and public day sails.

Specifications:

Sparred length: 96'	Draft: 8'	Sail area: 3,500 sq. ft.
LOD: 86'	Beam: 16' 6"	Tons: 76 GRT
Rig height: 96'	Hull: steel	Power: Volvo 160
Freeboard: 5'		

Designer:	Bob Johnston
Built:	1984; Port Stanley, Ontario, Kanter Yachts
Certification:	Transport Canada Certified Passenger Vessel
Crew:	6 professional paid crew. **Trainees:** 70 (day sails)
Contact:	Roger Nugent, President
	Great Lakes Schooner Company
	249 Queen's Quay West, Suite 111
	Toronto, Ontario M5J 2N5, Canada
	Tel: 416-260-6355; Fax: 416-260-6377
	E-mail: roger@greatlakesschooner.com
	Web site: http://www.greatlakesschooner.com

Clearwater

The *Clearwater* is the only full-sized replica of the 18th and 19th-century merchant vessels known as Hudson River sloops. Since 1969, *Clearwater* has served both as a platform for hands-on environmental education and as a symbol for grassroots action. The sloop is owned and operated by Hudson River Sloop Clearwater, Inc., a non-profit membership organization dedicated to defending and restoring the Hudson River and related waterways.

The sloop sails seven days a week, carrying as many as 50 passengers for three to five-hour education programs. Adults and children take part in a wide range of activities involving water life, water chemistry, sail raising, steering, piloting, and more. A US Coast Guard-licensed captain is in charge, and an education specialist directs the program. The permanent crew are complemented by apprentices aged 16 and older, an education assistant, and volunteers. During a month on board, apprentices are given in-depth training in many aspects of sailing and maintaining a wooden ship and in the education program.

Flag:	USA
Rig:	Gaff topsail sloop
Homeport/waters:	Poughkeepsie, NY: Hudson River, New York Harbor and Long Island Sound
Who sails?	Individuals, families, and groups.
Season:	April 15 to November 15 (daily education program); winter maintenance program.
Cost:	$6-$30 per person per day, $40 per week for crew/trainee bunk, $850-$2500 group rate. Membership is $30 per year for individuals, $10 for low-income.
Program type:	Sail training for crew and apprentices. Sea education in marine science, maritime history, and ecology. Passenger day sails. Dockside interpretation during port visits. Clientele includes school groups from elementary school through college and individuals of all ages.

Specifications:			
	Sparred length: 106'	Draft: 6' 6"	Sail area: 4,350 sq. ft.
	LOD: 76' 6"	Beam: 24'	Tons: 69 GRT
	LOA: 76' 6"	Rig height: 108'	Power: 190 HP diesel
	LWL: 67'	Hull: wood	

Designer:	Cy Hamlin
Built:	1969; South Bristol, Maine, Harvey Gamage Shipyard
Coast Guard certification:	Passenger Vessel (Subchapter T)
Crew:	6 (4-month), 3 (1-month), 6 (1-week). **Trainees:** 50 (day sails)
Contact:	Captain, Hudson River Sloop Clearwater, Inc.
	112 Little Market Street
	Poughkeepsie, NY 12601
	Tel: 845-454-7673; Fax: 845-454-7953
	E-mail: captain@mail.clearwater.org
	Web site: http://www.clearwater.org

Clipper City

Clipper City is a replica of a Great Lakes lumber schooner of the same name, which sailed from 1854 until 1892. The plans for the *Clipper City* of 1985 were obtained from the Smithsonian Institution and adapted for modern use. *Clipper City* sails Baltimore's Inner Harbor and the waters of the Chesapeake Bay from April through October each year. providing two and three-hour public excursions for tourists in the Baltimore area and private charters for corporate groups and families. She sails up to 21 times each week and has carried over 30,000 passengers in a single season. *Clipper City* is also available for winter charter.

Flag:	USA			
Rig:	Gaff topsail schooner			
Homeport/waters:	Baltimore, Maryland: Chesapeake Bay (summer), Caribbean Sea (winter)			
Who sails?	Individuals and groups			
Season:	Year-round			
Specifications:	LOD: 120'	Draft: 14'	Sail area: 10,200 sq. ft.	
	LOA: 158'	Beam: 27' 6"	Tons: 210 GRT	
	Hull: steel	Rig height: 135'	Power: CAT 3208 SS	
Built:	1985; Jacksonville, Florida			
Contact:	William L. Blocher, General Manager			
	Clipper City, Inc.			
	5022 Campbell Blvd., Suite F			
	Baltimore, MD 21236			
	Tel: 410-931-6777; Fax: 410-931-6705			
	E-mail: info@sailingship.com			
	Web site: http://www.sailingship.com			

Columbia

The beautiful Sparkman and Stephens-designed *Columbia* was the first 12-meter to defend the America's Cup. Skippered by legendary sailor and auto racing champion Briggs Cunningham, she was a refinement of the successful 1939 *Vim*. Close competition in the defender's trials of 1958 prepared her for an easy win over British challenger *Spectre*. Now, after many years in Europe, where she received a well-appointed interior and teak decks, *Columbia* has joined the America's Cup Charters 12-meter fleet in Newport, Rhode Island. She is perfect for leisure sails, racing, and team building from any port between Maine and the Chesapeake. Sail aboard a winner—no sailing experience necessary!

Flag:	USA
Rig:	Sloop
Homeport/waters:	Newport, Rhode Island: New England and Chesapeake Bay
Who sails?	Individuals of all ages.
Cost:	$1,800 group rate per day, $60 per person evening sail
Program type:	Sail training for volunteer or paying trainees. Sea education based on informal, in-house programming. Passenger day sails.

Specifications:			
	LOD: 67'	Draft: 9'	Sail area: 1,800 sq. ft.
	LOA: 67'	Beam: 11' 6"	Tons: 28 GRT
	LWL: 46'	Rig height: 92'	Power: diesel
	Hull: wood		

Designer:	Sparkman and Stephens
Built:	1958; City Island, New York, Nevens
Coast Guard certification:	Passenger Vessel (Subchapter T)
Crew:	3. **Trainees/passengers:** 14
Contact:	George Hill/Herb Marshall
	America's Cup Charters
	PO Box 51
	Newport, RI 02840
	Tel: 401-849-5868; Fax: 401-849-3098
	Web site: http://www.americascupcharters.com

Concordia

Over 700 international students have joined Class Afloat and sailed the world for an entire academic year. Applications from 11th and 12th-grade coeds are encouraged, and applicants who are seeking a unique and challenging "year out" program are also accepted. Crewmembers are selected on the basis of strong academic profiles, demonstrated strength of character and social suitability, health and fitness, and on their degree of commitment and dedication.

Class Afloat is a nonprofit educational program affiliated with high schools across the United States and Canada. Its mission is to broaden students' understanding of international issues while preparing them for responsible global citizenship in the 21st century.

The concept of "taking the classroom to the world" is intended to encourage self-sufficiency, cooperation, and a clear awareness of other cultures. Each semester, 48 qualifying students work as crew and study aboard the *Concordia*, a modern tall ship.

A fully-certified faculty instructs stu-

dents in a full curriculum including social studies and global issues, anthropology, marine biology, and physical education. Optional, non-credit enrichment courses are also offered in seamanship, celestial navigation, and the history and traditions of the sea.

CONCORDIA

Flag:	Bahamas
Rig:	Barquentine, three-masted
Homeport/waters:	Nassau, Bahamas: worldwide, unrestricted
Who sails?	11th and 12th-grade high school and college students. Affiliated institutions include West Island College (high school), College Marie-Victorian, Hingham High School, I.S.A.M, and A.I.E.S.
Season:	Academic year. Summer programs offered for students and adults
Cost:	$15,200 per student per semester, $25,800 per student per year.
Program type:	Full-curriculum academics and marine biology for high school students.

Specifications:

Sparred length: 188'	Draft: 13' 6"	Sail area: 10,000 sq. ft.
LOA: 154'	Beam: 31'	Tons: 495 GRT
LOD: 152' 6"	Rig height: 115'	Power: 570 HP diesel
Freeboard: 8'	Hull: steel	

Certification:	Lloyds 100A1 and LMC
Built:	1992; Poland
Crew:	8, 8 instructors. **Trainees:** 48. **Age:** 16-19, coed
Contact:	Sherri Holcman, Executive Director Class Afloat 851 Tecumseh, Dollard des Ormeaux Montreal, Quebec H9B 2L2, Canada Tel: 514-683-9052; Fax: 514-683-1702 E-mail: discovery@classafloat.com Web site: http://www.classafloat.com

USS Constellation

The *USS Constellation*, the last all-sail warship built by the US Navy, was launched in 1854 at the Gosport Naval Shipyard in Portsmouth, Virginia. *Constellation* served the country for over ninety years in both military and non-military roles. Before the Civil War, she was flagship of an international squadron charged with the mission of intercepting vessels engaged in the illegal slave trade along the coast of West Africa. While on patrol in these waters, *Constellation* captured three vessels and set free over seven hundred men, women, and children, landing them safely back in Africa. During the Civil War, *Constellation* saw duty in the Mediterranean Sea protecting American interests there, and as part of the Gulf Coast Blockading Squadron.

During her later years the *Constellation* sailed as a training or "practice" ship for the US Naval Academy and then as a stationary training ship at the Naval War College in Newport, Rhode Island. She was last under sail in 1896. Her final role as a commissioned vessel came during World War II when *Constellation* served as Flagship of the Atlantic Fleet.

In 1955, *Constellation* was brought to Baltimore to be preserved as a national shrine. The ship recently has undergone a $9 million reconstruction that has restored the ship to her original 1854 configuration. The ship made her triumphant return to Baltimore's Inner Harbor on July 2, 1999 and she is now open for public tours, offering a wide array of living history and education programs under the management of the Living Classrooms Foundation.

Flag:	USA
Rig:	Full-rigged ship
Homeport/waters:	Baltimore, Maryland
Program type:	Dockside interpretation and educational programming.

Specifications:			
	Sparred length: 282'	Draft: 21'	Sail area: 20,000 sq. ft.
	LOD: 176'	Beam: 42'	Hull: wood
	LOA: 200'	Rig height: 165'	Freeboard: 16'
	LWL: 179'		

Designer:	John Lenthall
Built:	1854; Portsmouth, Virginia, US Navy
Contact:	Christy Schmitt, Visitor Services Coordinator
	The Constellation Foundation
	Pier 1, 301 East Pratt Street
	Baltimore, MD 21202
	Tel: 410-539-1797; Fax: 410-539-6238
	E-mail: E-mail: rowsom@constellation.org
	Web site: http://www.constellation.org

USS *Constitution*

"Old Ironsides" is the oldest commissioned warship afloat in the world. One of six ships ordered by President George Washington to protect America's growing maritime interests in the 1790s, *Constitution* earned widespread renown for her ability to punish French privateers in the Caribbean and thwart Barbary pirates of the Mediterranean. The ship's greatest glory came during the War of 1812 when she defeated four British frigates. During her first engagement, against *HMS Guerriére* in 1812, seamen nicknamed her "Old Ironsides" when they saw British cannonballs glance off her 21-inch-thick oak hull.

In the 1830s, the ship was slated to be broken up, but a public outcry sparked by the publication of a poem by Oliver Wendell Holmes saved her. Over the following century, the ship undertook many military assignments and served as a barracks and as a training ship. She was restored in 1927, and after a coast-to-coast tour, *Constitution* was moored in the Charlestown Navy Yard in 1934 where she is now open year-round for free public tours. She again underwent an extensive restoration from 1992-96, and on July 21, 1997, launching a year-long celebration of her bicentennial, *Constitution* sailed under her own power for the first time in 116 years. As flagship of the Sail Boston celebration, she led the Tall Ships 2000® fleet into Boston Harbor during the Grand Parade of Sail on July 11, 2000.

USS CONSTITUTION

Flag:	USA		
Rig:	Full-rigged ship		
Homeport/waters:	Charlestown, Massachusetts: Boston Harbor		
Program type:	US naval history		
Specifications:	Sparred length: 306'	Draft: 22'	Sail area: 42,710 sq. ft.
	LOD (gun deck): 174' 10"	Beam: 43' 6"	
	Tons: 2,200 GRT	LOA: 204'	Rig height: 189' 2"
	Hull: wood	LWL: 175'	Freeboard: 15'
Built:	1797; Boston, Massachusetts, US Navy, Edmond Hartt Shipyard		
Certification:	Commissioned US Navy ship		
Crew:	48		
Contact:	Commander William F. Foster, Jr., USN, Commanding Officer		
	USS Constitution, Charlestown Navy Yard		
	Charlestown, MA 02129-1797		
	Tel: 617-242-5670; Fax: 617-242-2308		
	Web site: http://www.ussconstitution.navy.mil		

Coronet

In 1995 *Coronet* was acquired by the International Yacht Restoration School (IYRS) in Newport, RI. Founded in 1993, IYRS teaches the skills, history and related sciences needed to restore classic yachts. Over the next several years, IYRS will carry out a comprehensive and well-documented restoration to return *Coronet* to her late 19th century condition. She will have no engines, electricity or modern equipment. When completed, she will sail as the school's flagship and a living museum of yachting history.

Coronet is America's most historic yacht, and the last remaining grand yacht from the gilded age. Built in 1885, she has voyaged far and wide during her career, twice circumnavigating the globe. She won the 1887 transatlantic race against the schooner *Dauntless*. She also transported a scientific expedition to Japan in 1896 to view a total eclipse of the sun.

Coronet is open to visitors dockside at IYRS from May to October each year. The public will also be able to view the ship once restoration begins. For history, photographs, documentation drawings, updates on the restoration project and information about IYRS's programs, visit www.iyrs.org.

Flag:	USA
Rig:	Gaff topsail schooner
Homeport/waters:	Newport, Rhode Island
Season:	May to October
Program type:	Walk-on visitation and dockside interpretation for individuals and groups of all ages.

Specifications:	Sparred length: 190'	Draft: 12'	Sail area: 8,300 sq. ft.
	LOD: 133'	LOA: 133'	LWL: 125'
	Beam: 27'	Tons: 174 GRT	Freeboard: 6'
	Hull: wood	Hull color: white	

Designer:	Smith & Terry, Christopher Crosby, William Townsend
Built:	1885; Brooklyn, New York, C & R Poillon
Contact:	John Summers, Curator/Editor
	International Yacht Restoration School
	449 Thames Street
	Newport, RI 02840
	Tel: 401-848-5777; Fax: 401-842-0669
	E-mail: info@iyrs.org
	Web site: http://www.iyrs.org

Corsair

Corsair is a sailing whaleboat, an open boat designed to be launched from a larger ship while at sea. She was built at Puget Sound Naval Shipyard in 1939 for use in the Navy's fleet sailing program. As the US prepared for war, the Navy stripped its ships and our whaleboats were sent ashore. The sailing program was never reinstated, and surplus Navy whaleboats found their way to Sea Scout units around the country, offering thousands of youth the opportunity to learn sailing, seamanship, and teamwork on the water. Of those boats, only a handful remain.

The Sea Scout Ship *Corsair* has been serving the youth of the Bay Area for over 60 years, offering programs that teach sailing, seamanship, and leadership to young men aged 14-21. Her sister ship, *Viking*, offers similar programs for young women. The two ships sponsor many joint activities. In addition to the annual two-week summer cruise in the Sacramento Delta, the Bay Area Sea Scouts organize day sails, races, weekend outings, dances, and regattas. New members are always welcome, both young and adult.

Flag:	USA
Rig:	Ketch
Homeport/waters:	San Francisco, California: San Francisco Bay and tributaries
Who sails?	High school students and individuals. Affiliated institutions include Sea Scouting, Boy Scouts of America, San Francisco Bay Area Council.
Program type:	Sail training for male trainees, aged 14-21. Sea education in marine science and maritime history in cooperation with other groups.

Specifications:		
Sparred length: 30'	Draft: 4' 6"	Sail area: 600 sq. ft.
LOD: 30'	Beam: 8'	Freeboard: 2'
LOA: 30'	Rig height: 35'	Hull: wood
LWL: 28'		

Designer:	US Navy
Built:	1939; US Navy, Puget Sound Naval Shipyard
Crew:	Up to 18
Contact:	Nick Tarlson, Skipper
	Sea Scout Ship Viking
	220 Sansome Street, Ste. 900
	San Francisco, CA 94104
	Tel: 415-956-5700; Fax: 415-982-2528
	E-mail: seascouts@dictyon.com
	Web site: http://www.tbw.net/~chriss/scouts/

CORSAIR

Corwith Cramer

Sailing School Vessels. The Sea Education Association (SEA), working through ASTA, was instrumental in helping the Coast Guard shape these regulations. The *Cramer* was built in Bilbao, Spain, and it took the largest floating crane in northern Spain to launch her. She is a safe, stable vessel and an excellent platform for SEA's educational and oceanographic research missions. The *Corwith Cramer* is owned and operated by the SEA, Woods Hole, Massachusetts. See also *Westward*.

The *Corwith Cramer* was the first ship built to the USCG's regulations for

Flag:	USA
Rig:	Brigantine
Homeport/waters:	Woods Hole, Massachusetts: worldwide
Who sails?	Educators and students who are admitted by competitive selection. Over 150 colleges and universities award credit for SEA programs.
Season:	Year-round
Program types:	Marine and maritime studies including oceanography, nautical science, history, literature, and contemporary maritime affairs. SEA programs include SEA Semester (college level, 12 weeks long, 17 credits), SEA Summer Session (college level, 8 weeks long, 12-credits), and SEA Seminars for high school students and K-12 teachers. All programs include a seagoing component on board the Sailing School Vessels *Westward* and/or *Corwith Cramer*.

Specifications:			
	LOA: 134'	Draft: 13'	Sail area: 7,380 sq. ft.
	LWL: 87' 6"	Beam: 26'	Power: 500 HP diesel
	Hull: steel	Tons: 158 GRT	

Designer:	Woodin & Marean
Built:	1987; Bilbao, Spain, ASTACE
Coast Guard certification:	Sailing School Vessel (Subchapter R)
Crew:	6 professional mariners and 4 scientists. **Trainees:** Up to 25 in all programs
Contact:	Sea Education Association, Inc.
	PO Box 6
	Woods Hole, MA 02543
	Tel: 508-540-3954, 800-552-3633; Fax: 508-457-4673
	E-mail: admission@sea.edu
	Web site: http://www.sea.edu

Cutty Sark sails the waters of the State of Washington from historic Captain Whidbey Inn on the shores of Penn Cove, Whidbey Island. *Cutty Sark* operates as a commercial charter sailing ship, as well as offering volunteer educational opportunities for local school districts and scout groups. Charterers are encouraged, although not required, to lend a hand at running the ship as she slips past the sylvan shores of the San Juan Islands. School groups, however, stand watches, navigate the ship, and sing sea chanteys as they raise the sails, while learning the history, ecology, and lore of these enchanting islands. A ship provides an excellent platform for learning by experience: communication skills are honed and teamwork is established as the rule rather than the exception. The interdependence of shipboard life renders a microcosm of the world which gives the student sailors transferable skills.

Programs can be designed for groups of any type, from gourmet country inn cruises, small business retreats, overnight excursions for middle school, high school, and college students, to day sails for elementary school students.

CUTTY SARK

Flag:	USA
Rig:	Gaff ketch
Homeport/waters:	Coupeville, Washington: Whidbey Island and San Juan Islands, Washington
Who sails?	School groups from elementary school through college. Individuals and families of all ages. Affiliated groups include the Coupeville, South Whidbey, and Sedro Wooley School Districts, and Troop 58 BSA.
Cost:	$350 group rate per day, $250 per day for schools.
Program type:	Sail training for volunteer or paying trainees. Sea education in marine science, maritime history, ecology, and other subjects in cooperation with other groups and as informal, in-house programming.

Specifications:			
	Sparred length: 52'	Draft: 6' 6"	Sail area: 1,100 sq. ft.
	LOD: 40'	Beam: 13' 6"	Tons: 19 GRT
	LOA: 40'	Rig height: 55'	Hull: teak
	LWL: 33' 4"	Freeboard: 3' 6"	

Designer:	Hugh Angleman/Charlie Davies
Built:	1957; Hong Kong, American Marine
Contact:	Captain John Colby Stone
	Æolian Ventures, Ltd., SV *Cutty Sark*
	2072 West Captain Whidbey Inn Road
	Coupeville, WA 98239
	Tel: 800-366-4097, 360-678-4097; Fax: 360-678-4110
	E-mail: Captjohn@whidbey.net
	Web site: http://www.captainwhidbey.com/cutty.htm

Dariabar

Dariabar, launched in 1992, is a custom-built sailing research vessel. Her lines are those of a John Alden schooner and her design incorporates both traditional and modern aspects. She is built from steel with watertight subdivisions and a double bottom. She has a generous lab and workspace amidships with lifting gear above deck. *Dariabar* is presently involved in bioacoustic research and marine mammal observation. She is associated with Pelagikos, a California-based marine research organization. Pelagikos, in conjunction with Mendocino College, conducts courses in marine mammal ecology and behavior aboard *Dariabar*. These classes offer students the opportunity to engage in active research while learning about sailing and life at sea. Pelagikos also employs *Dariabar* as a platform for research conducted by other college and scientific organizations.

Flag:	USA
Rig:	Schooner
Homeport/waters:	Sausalito, California: California and northeast Pacific
Who sails?	College students and adults involved in ocean research
Program type:	Sea education, marine science, ecology, and bioacoustic research in cooperation with accredited institutions.

Specifications:			
	LOA: 84'	Draft: 10'	Sail area: 3,000 sq. ft.
	LOD: 84'	Beam: 18'	Tons: 84 GRT
	LWL: 64'	Rig height: 90'	Power: diesel
	Freeboard: 6'	Hull: steel	

Designer:	John Alden
Built:	Oakland, California, E.A. Silva
Coast Guard certification:	Ocean Research Vessel (Subchapter U)
Crew:	4 (educators). **Trainees:** 30 (day); 10 (overnight)
Contact:	Dr. Urmas Kaldveer, Executive Director
	Pelagikos
	3020 Bridgeway # 155
	Sausalito, CA 94966
	Tel: 707-462-5671; Fax: 707-468-3120
	E-mail: silva@well.com

Denis Sullivan

Construction of the newest member of the tall ship fleet, the Wisconsin Lake Schooner Education Association's schooner *Denis Sullivan*, was completed in the fall of 2000.

From June to October, she will operate as a floating, traveling classroom and as a goodwill ambassador for the State of Wisconsin from her homeport of Milwaukee on Lake Michigan. She winters in Florida and the Bahamas.

The Association exists to offer hands-on learning for people of all ages and backgrounds, inspire interest in marine science and maritime heritage, increase appreciation, understanding, and protection of our freshwater resources, and provide opportunities to develop self-knowledge, teamwork and leadership. Diverse dockside and onboard educational programs are offered for learners of all ages, from "Fish Tales" for preschoolers to four-hour on board Lakewatch Expeditions for 5th through 12th graders, to the adventure-based,

intensive "Florida Science Under Sail" program for high school students, to the "Small Boat Building" program for adults and Field Learning opportunities for educators.

The *Denis Sullivan* is also available for three-hour day sails from her homeport, adult and youth overnight discovery expeditions, charters and dockside receptions, and exciting learning adventure cruises in the Bahamas and Florida.

Flag:	USA
Rig:	Schooner, three-masted
Homeport/waters:	Milwaukee, Wisconsin: Great Lakes, Bahamas, Florida
Who sails?	Schools and other groups from elementary school through college, individuals, families and other interested adult groups.
Cost:	Varies
Program type:	Sail training for crew, volunteers, and paying trainees. Learning expeditions under sail in marine science, maritime studies, and ecology in cooperation with accredited schools, colleges and other organized groups. Science Under Sail (high school level, 2 weeks long). Summer Schooner School, professional development for educators, and special "themed" sails. Passenger day-sails and dockside interpretation.

Specifications:	Sparred Length: 133'	Draft: 8'9"	Sail area: 5,000 sq. ft.
	LOD: 93'	Beam: 23'6"	Tons: 100 GRT
	LOA: 99'	Hull: wood	Power: twin diesels
	LWL: 88'4"		

Designer:	Timothy Graul
Built:	2000; Milwaukee, Wisconsin, Rob Stevens
Coast Guard certification:	Sailing School Vessel (Subchapter R), Passenger Vessel (Subchapter T)
Contact:	Therese Hamilton
	Wisconsin Lake Schooner Education Association
	500 North Harbor Drive
	Milwaukee, WI 53202
	Tel: 414-276-7700; Fax: 414-276-8838; Schooner Hotline: 414-276-2001
	E-mail: info@lakeschooner.org
	Web site: http://www.lakeschooner.org

Dewa Ruci

in the Indonesian Navy. *Dewa Ruci* was built in 1952 by H.C. Stulchen and Son, Hamburg, Germany. After being launched in 1953, she was sailed to Indonesia by the Indonesian Navy. Since then the ship has served the Indonesian Navy as a sail training vessel and a successful ambassador of goodwill for the people of Indonesia. *Dewa Ruci*'s name comes from a Hindu epic play: Dewa Ruci is the name of a character representing the God of truth and courage.

Dewa Ruci, the beautiful barquentine flying the red and white (the colors of Indonesia's flag), is the largest tall ship

Flag:	Indonesia
Rig:	Barquentine
Homeport/waters:	Surabaya, Indonesia: Indonesian waters, Indian Ocean, Pacific Ocean
Who sails?	Cadets of the Indonesian Naval Academy
Season:	Year-round
Program type:	Sail training and sea education for Indonesian Naval cadets.

Specifications:	Sparred length: 191'	Draft: 13'	Sail area: 11,738 sq. ft.
	LOD: 163' 1"	Beam: 31'	Tons: 847 GRT
	LOA: 165'	Rig height: 119' 7"	Power: 986 HP diesel
	LWL: 138' 4"	Freeboard: 15' 1"	Hull: steel

Built:	1952; Hamburg, Germany, H.C. Stulchen & Sohn
Certification:	Indonesian Sailing School Vessel
Crew:	70. **Trainees:** 80
Contact:	(1) Commanding Officer, *Dewa Ruci*
	KRI Dewa Ruci – Sabatan – Armartim – Ujung,
	Surabaya 60155, Indonesia
	Tel: 62-31-3294000; Fax: 62-31-3294171
	(2) Indonesian Naval Attaché, Defense Attaché Office
	2020 Massachusetts Avenue NW
	Washington, DC 20036

SAIL TALL SHIPS!

Distant Star

The *Distant Star* will conduct a mixture of sail training programs, including middle school and junior high school programs, as well as offering adventure vacation opportunities. Programs will focus on team building while teaching traditional seamanship and the sailor's arts in the unique setting of a traditional, square-rigged vessel. In port and underway, the ship will simulate the atmosphere of the early American Navy, depicting the life aboard ships of that era and passing on sea-going military tradition and heritage within a fun and challenging historical framework.

Designed and built by James D. Rosborough in his Nova Scotia yard, *Distant Star* (formerly the *Meghan D*) was launched in 1978. She completed minor repairs in Port Townsend, Washington, and during the summer of 1999, she voyaged to her new homeport of San Diego. Her first operations will be in the spring of 2001.

The Foundation is seeking U. S. Coast Guard certification as a sailing school vessel. As such, all who sail aboard her will be involved in sailing her. If you've ever dreamed of sailing aboard a traditional square-rigger, this is your chance!

DISTANT STAR

Flag	USA
Rig:	Brigantine
Homeport/waters:	San Diego, California: Eastern Pacific off Southern California
Season:	Year-round
Who sails?	School groups from elementary through high school and individuals of all ages.
Program type:	Sail training for paying trainees. Team building within a framework of maritime history, sea education, and naval science programs. Education programs featuring traditional seamanship and tailored multi-disciplinary subjects as requested.

Specifications:		
Sparred length: 56'	LOA: 46'	LOD: 45'
LWL: 36'6"	Draft: 7'	Beam: 14'
Rig height: 55'	Sail area: 1,490 sq. ft.	Tons: 27 GRT
Power: diesel 84 HP	Hull: wood	Hull color: white

Designer:	James D. Rosborough
Built:	1978; Parrsboro, Nova Scotia; James D. Rosborough
Coast Guard certification:	Sailing School Vessel (Subchapter R) pending.
Crew:	2-4. Trainees: 6-10 (day sails), 4 (overnight)
Contact:	Tom Wing, Executive Director
	Continental Navy Foundation
	11054 Melton Court
	San Diego, CA 92131
	Tel/Fax: 858-271-4883
	E-mail: tmwing@sprintmail.com
	Web site: http://home.sprintmail.com/~tmwing/

Dorothea

For generations, Nova Scotians have traveled the coast in small boats, learning wisdom and courage from the sea. The Nova Scotia Sea School takes young people to sea in small boats today for fun and personal challenge. The Sea School teaches traditional seamanship and navigation, and gives teenagers the chance to discover the Nova Scotia coast, and to discover themselves.

Young people 14-18 years old, male and female, from all over North America and Europe sail on voyages ranging from five days to three weeks, living in an open boat powered by sails and oars. They explore the coast, live with the elements, visit the islands, and learn to take command of the boat, and of their lives. As one student said, "I don't always understand things at home—out here they make sense."

Professional enrichment programs for experiential educators, sail trainers and outdoor leaders are also offered as well as programs exploring how to work with youth and the sea (or any demanding environment) in the most powerful way possible.

Flag:	Canada
Rig:	Ketch
Homeport/waters:	Halifax, Nova Scotia, Canada: coastal Nova Scotia
Who sails?	Individuals and groups associated with accredited schools and colleges as well as summer camps and other youth organization participation.
Cost:	$95 per person per day
Program type:	Sail training with paying trainees. Sea education programs in marine science, maritime history, and ecology, and informal, in-house programming.

Specifications:	LOD: 28' 6"	Draft: 5'	Hull: wood
	LOA: 28' 6"	Beam: 7'	Tons: 4 GRT

Designer:	E.Y.E. Marine
Built:	1995; Halifax, Nova Scotia, Canada
Crew:	2. Trainees: 10
Contact:	Crane W. Stookey, Program Director
	The Nova Scotia Sea School
	PO Box 546, Central C.R.O.
	Halifax, Nova Scotia B3J 2S4 Canada
	Tel: 902-423-7284; Fax: 902-423-7241
	E-mail: nsseaschool@attglobal.net
	Web site: http://www.seaschool.org

Dream Catcher

Dream Catcher is a 72-foot steel schooner built by Treworgy Yachts in Palm Coast, Florida in 1996. Designed by marine architects Woodin and Marean, from Maine, her conception, design factors and interior design came from Captain John Duke. John grew up on the waters of Biscayne Bay in Miami, Florida, has been USCG licensed since 1979, and has been sailing the waters of the lower Florida Keys, South Florida and the Bahamas for 30 years. During this time he has worked with scientific research groups, youth groups, and environmental groups, and has introduced hundreds of marine enthusiasts to the many wonders of the sea.

The *Dream Catcher* provides sailing adventures designed to be informative for both environmental professionals and individuals interested in marine habitat. Ideal for large families and groups (scouts, clubs, students) interested in participating in and learning all aspects of sailing and navigation, *Dream Catcher* is looking for groups that want to be a part of the adventure!

Flag:	USA		
Rig:	Schooner		
Homeport/waters:	Oceanside Marina, Key West, Florida: Florida Keys		
Who sails?	Students, individuals, families and groups of all ages.		
Program type:	Sail training for volunteer crew and trainees. Sea education in cooperation with accredited institutions and other organized groups.		
Cost:	$75 per person per (8 hr) day, $850 group rate (charter) per day		
Specifications:	Sparred length: 74'	Draft: 5'	Sail area: 1,700 sq. ft.
	LOD: 65'	Beam: 20'	Tons: 49 GRT
	LOA: 69'	Rig height: 73'	Power: 130 John Deere
	LWL: 62'	Freeboard: 5'	Hull: steel
	Hull color: turquoise	Spar material: aluminum	
Designer:	Woodin and Marean		
Built:	1996; Hammocks, Florida, Treworgy Yachts		
Cost Guard certification:	Passenger Vessel (Subchapter T)		
Crew:	**Trainees/passengers:** 49 (day sails), 19 (overnight)		
Contact:	Captain John Duke		
	Coastal Sailing Adventures, Inc.		
	28555 Jolly Roger Drive		
	Little Torch Key, FL 33042		
	Tel: 305-295-8844		
	E-mail: saildreamcatcher@mindspring.com		
	Web site: http://www.keywest.com/dreamcatcher/		

Eagle, USCG

navigation, engineering, and other skills they are taught at the Coast Guard Academy. As underclassmen, they fill positions normally taken by the enlisted crew of a ship, including watches. They handle the more than 20,000 square feet of sail and more than 20 miles of rigging. Over 200 lines must be coordinated during a major ship maneuver, and the cadets must learn the name and function of each. As upperclassmen, they perform officer-level functions. For many, their tour of duty aboard *Eagle* is their first experience of life at sea; but it is here that they learn to serve as the leaders they will one day become in the Coast Guard.

One of five sister ships built for sail training in Germany in the 1930s, *Eagle* was included in reparations paid to the United States following World War II and the Coast Guard took her over as a training ship. Aboard the *Eagle*, cadets have a chance to put into practice the

Flag:	USA
Rig:	Barque, three-masted
Homeport/waters:	New London, Connecticut: Atlantic Ocean, Caribbean, and Pacific Ocean
Who sails?	US Coast Guard Academy Cadets, US Coast Guard Officer Candidates, and other Coast Guard personnel.
Season:	Year-round
Cost:	Included in school tuition
Program type:	Seamanship

Specifications:		
Sparred length: 295'	Draft: 17'	Sail area: 22,245 sq. ft. (23 sails)
LOA: 266' 8"	Beam: 40'	Tons: 2,186 GRT
LWL: 231'	Rig height: 147' 4"	Power: 1,000 HP diesel
Hull: steel		

Built:	1936; Hamburg, Germany, Blohm & Voss
Contact:	Commanding Officer
	USCGC EAGLE (WIX-327)
	45 Mohegan Avenue
	New London, CT 06320
	Tel: 860-444-8595; Fax: 860-444-8445
	E-mail: Kboda@cgceagle.uscg.mil
	Web site: http://www.cga.edu/eagle

Earl of Pembroke

The second-largest vessel of the Square Sail fleet was originally named *Orion* and built in Pukavik, Sweden, in 1945 as one of the last three-masted sailing schooners. She traded timber in the Baltic and British East Coast until being laid up in Thisted, Denmark in 1974. Square Sail purchased her in 1979 and she underwent a complete restoration, which commenced in 1985. In 1994 she was commissioned as the three-masted wooden barque that she is today.

All of Square Sail's ships are fully commissioned and work throughout the year. When not filming, they have a regular sailing program, giving people the chance to experience traditional square-rig sailing first-hand. These voyages typically run between four and seven days, and occasionally longer. They are either based from Square Sail's homeport of Charlestown, Cornwall, UK, or they work around the annual schedule offering voyages between the various ports.

Square Sail runs an annual course from February to October where trainees are given the opportunity to learn the skills associated with sailing these ships, and in addition to maintenance and shore-based instruction, they form part of the regular crew throughout the season.

Flag:	UK
Rig:	Barque, three-masted, single topsail
Homeport/waters:	Charlestown Harbour, St. Austell, Cornwall, UK: UK and Europe
Who sails?	Individuals of all ages and families. Affiliated institutions include Falmouth Marine School and Cornwall College.
Cost:	$200 per person per day, $8,000 group rate per day (charter)
Program type:	Sail training for professional crew, volunteer and paying trainees. Sea education in maritime history in cooperation with accredited institutions and as informal, in-house programming. Worldwide film work and corporate charters.

Specifications:	Sparred length: 145'	Draft:10' 6"	Sail area: 9,500 sq. ft.
	LOD: 115'	Beam: 24'	Tons: 174 GRT
	LOA: 145'	Rig height: 93'	Power: 300 HP diesel
	LWL: 108'	Freeboard: 7'	Hull: oak on oak

Built:	1948, Pukavik, Sweden, Albert Svenson
Certification:	MCA Oceans (UK)
Crew:	15. **Trainees/passengers:** 50 (day sails), 12 (overnight)
Contact:	Chris Wilson, Marketing Manager, Square Sail
	Charlestown Harbour
	St. Austell, Cornwall PL25 3NJ, United Kingdom
	Tel: 44-1726-67526; Fax: 44-1726-61839
	E-mail: info@square-sail.com
	Web site: http://www.square-sail.com

Eastwind

Schooner *Eastwind*, built in Albion, Maine, is the sixth schooner built by Herb and Doris Smith. The other five were all named *Appledore*, two of which the Smiths sailed around the world. *Eastwind* is built of native white oak and planked with Port Orford cedar. She is fastened with copper rivets and bronze screws. In November of 1999, the Smiths left with *Eastwind* for South America. They have since returned to Boothbay Harbor, Maine, where they take passengers during the summer months.

Flag:	USA
Rig:	Topsail schooner
Homeport/waters:	Boothbay Harbor, Maine: Boothbay Harbor (summer), southern waters (winter)
Who sails?	Individuals of all ages
Cost:	$22 per person per two-hour sail
Program type:	Sail training for paying passengers. Dockside interpretation while in homeport.

Specifications:			
	Sparred length: 64'	Draft: 7'	Sail area: 1,600 sq. ft.
	LOD: 56'	Beam: 14'	Tons: 31 GRT
	LOA: 56'	Rig height: 75'	Hull: wood
	LWL: 47'	Freeboard: 4'	
	Hull color: white	Spar Material: wood	

Designer:	McIntosh
Built:	1999; Albion, Maine, Herb Smith
Coast Guard certification:	Passenger Vessel (Subchapter T)
Crew:	1 **Trainees/passengers:** 28 (day sails)
Contact:	Captain Herb Smith
	Eastwind Cruises
	20 Commercial St.
	Boothbay Harbor, ME 04538
	Tel: 207-633-6598
	Web site: http://www.fishermanswharfinn.com

Ebb Tide

Ebb Tide is a delightful topsail schooner, built by Peter Legnos of Legnos Boatbuilding in Groton, Connecticut. Forty feet overall, *Ebb Tide* is one of the smallest and one of the few trailerable square-riggers, and also one of the few fiberglass boats to carry square sails. Small but quick, and undefeated in her division at the marvelous Gloucester schooner races, *Ebb Tide* carries a complement of three ten-gauge and one four-gauge cannons.

Ebb Tide participates in classic and antique vessel events in the Boston area, as well as reenactment events such as the birthday of the United States Navy in Beverly, Massachusetts and the birthday of the United States Coast Guard in Newburyport, Massachusetts. *Ebb Tide* is privately owned and does not offer a formal sail training program, but is always eager for crew for reenactments or classic sailboat events.

Flag:	USA
Rig:	Topsail schooner
Homeport/waters:	Gloucester, Masschusetts: Gloucester and North Shore waters
Who sails?	Fund development personnel from area nonprofit institutions, Salem Maritime National Historic Site, Forbes Museum, and trainees involved in military reenactments and classic sailing events.
Season:	April to November
Program type:	Sail training for crew and apprentices. Sea education in maritime history in the form of military reenactments and gunnery practices. Dockside interpretation.

Specifications:			
	Sparred length: 40'	Draft: 4' 6"	Tons: 4.5 GRT
	LOA: 40'	Beam: 10' 3"	Power: 6 HP diesel
	LOD: 30'	Freeboard: 2'	Hull: fiberglass

Built:	1975; Groton, Connecticut, Legnos Boatbuilding
Crew:	2. **Trainees:** 4 (day), 4 (overnight).
Contact:	Captain Keating Willcox
	Longmeadow Way – Box 403
	Hamilton, MA 01936-0403
	Tel/Fax: 978-468-3869
	E-mail: kwillcox@shore.net
	Web site: http://www.shore.net/~kwillcox/spirit.html

Elissa

In 1975, a rusted iron hulk lay in the waters of Piraeus, Greece. Nearly 100 years earlier, she had sailed the world's oceans as a proud square-rigged sailing ship. Cut down, leaking, and decrepit, she waited a cable's length from the scrap yard.

Today, *Elissa* remains one of the hallmarks of maritime preservation. Lovingly restored and maintained, she sails again, continuing a far longer life than most ships are ever granted. She tests her readiness annually in a series of sea trials amid the oilrigs and shrimpers off Galveston Island. Working under professional officers, her volunteer crew completes an extensive dockside training program. As funds allow, she makes longer voyages, such as her journey to New York to participate in Operation Sail 1986/Salute to Liberty.

Flag:	USA
Rig:	Barque, three-masted
Homeport/waters:	Galveston, Texas: coastal waters near Galveston
Who sails?	School groups from middle school through college and individuals of all ages.
Season:	April to November
Cost:	Volunteers and guests only
Program type:	Sail training for crew and apprentices. Sea education in maritime history based on informal, in-house training. Dockside interpretation.

Specifications:			
	Sparred length: 205'	Draft: 10'	Sail area: 12,000 sq. ft.
	LOA: 155'	Beam: 28'	Tons: 411 GRT
	LOD: 150'	Rig height: 110'	Power: 450 HP diesel
	Freeboard: 10'	Hull: iron	

Built:	1877; Aberdeen, Scotland, Alexander Hall and Sons Yard
Coast Guard certification:	Cargo and Miscellaneous Goods (Subchapter I)
Crew:	40. **Trainees:** 85 (day)
Contact:	Kurt Voss, Director
	Texas Seaport Museum/Galveston Historical Foundation
	Pier 21, No. 8
	Galveston, TX 77550
	Tel: 409-763-1877; Fax: 409-763-3037
	E-mail: elissa@galvestonhistory.org
	Web site: http://www.tsm-elissa.org

Elizabeth II

Built with private funds to commemorate the English colonization of America's 400th anniversary, *Elizabeth II* is named for a vessel that sailed from Plymouth, England, on the second of the three Roanoke voyages sponsored by Sir Walter Raleigh between 1584 and 1587. She probably carried marines, colonists, and supplies to establish a military garrison to support England's claim to the New World.

Elizabeth II's sail training program teaches volunteer crew about America's 16th-century maritime heritage. In addition to classroom instruction and dockside training, crew members participate in the care and maintenance of wooden vessels. The 24-foot ship's boat, *Silver Chalice*, is used for underway training and travels with *Elizabeth II* when she sails. Voyages are scheduled during the spring and fall seasons. Sponsorship for the volunteer crew program is provided by the nonprofit Friends of Elizabeth II, Inc.

ELIZABETH II

Flag:	USA
Rig:	Barque, three-masted (lateen mizzen)
Homeport/waters:	Manteo, North Carolina: inland sounds of North Carolina
Who sails?	Volunteer crew
Season:	Spring and fall
Cost:	$8 for adults, $5 students (dockside visits), free for children under 6 accompanied by an adult
Program type:	Sail training for volunteer crew and apprentices. Dockside interpretation.

Specifications:					
	Sparred length: 78'		Draft: 8'		Sail area: 1,920 sq. ft.
	LOA: 68' 6"		Beam: 16' 6"		Tons: 97 GRT
	LOD: 55'		Rig height: 65'		Hull: wood
	LWL: 59'				

Designer:	W.A. Baker and Stanley Potter
Built:	1983; Manteo, North Carolina, O. Lie-Nielsen, Creef-Davis Shipyard
Age:	16+
Contact:	Captain Horace Whitfield
	Roanoke Island Festival Park
	One Festival Park
	Manteo, NC 27954
	Tel: 252-475-1500; Fax: 252-475-1507
	Web site: http://www.schoonerman.com/e12.htm

Empire Sandy

As Canada's largest sailing ship, the *Empire Sandy* cruises Toronto Harbor and the Great Lakes in summer and Nassau, Bahamas in winter. The *Empire Sandy* is certified by Transport Canada and the Bahamian government to carry up to 275 passengers, and offers sailing cruises and dockside receptions to the public, corporations, and charitable organizations. In Canada, the *Empire Sandy* is a popular attraction at numerous waterfront festivals and events. During her passages between Canada and the Bahamas, the *Empire Sandy* offers a unique sail training program where up to 30 participants learn basic seamanship, sailing, navigation, and pilotage from her professional crew. The *Empire Sandy* makes weekly port visits along the eastern seaboard during her passages north and south and is an ideal venue for hosting dockside promotional events, charity fundraisers, and arts and entertainment events. While in the Bahamas, she sails from Nassau on three and four-hour ocean day sails and dinner charters, pleasing tourists and private groups alike.

Flag:	Canada
Rig:	Schooner
Homeport/waters:	Toronto, Ontario, Canada: Toronto (summer), Nassau, Bahamas (winter)
Who sails?	Students, individuals, and families of all ages.
Season:	Year-round
Cost:	$650 per person per week
Program type:	Sail training for paying trainees. Sea education in cooperation with organized groups and as informal, in-house programming. Passenger day sails. Dockside interpretation during port visits.

Specifications:			
	Sparred length: 200'	Draft: 13'	Sail area: 10,000 sq. ft.
	LOD: 145'	Beam: 30'	Tons: 338 GRT
	LWL: 137'	Rig height: 116'	Power: 400 HP diesel
	Hull: steel		

Built:	1943; Willington Quay-on-Tyne, UK
Certification:	Canadian Coast Guard certified passenger vessel, Bahamas "Class A" certificate (passenger vessels)
Crew:	25. **Trainees/passengers:** 60 (day sails), 30 (overnight)
Contact:	Sharon Rogers, Sail Training Coordinator
	Nautical Adventures
	1 Yonge Street, Suite 104
	Toronto, Ontario M5E 1E5, Canada
	Tel: 416-364-3244; Fax: 416-364-6869
	E-mail: nautical@yesic.com
	Web site: http://www.valuenetwork.com/nautical

Endeavour

Endeavour is an exact museum standard replica of the ship Captain James Cook used on the first of his three famous voyages. On that voyage, from 1768 to 1771, Cook solved the geography of the Pacific, defeated scurvy, was the first to accurately calculate his longitude at sea, and successfully charted the islands of New Zealand and the east coast of Australia.

Built in Fremantle, Western Australia, from Australian hardwoods and American Douglas Fir, the ship is the result of over five years of painstaking research coordinated by the National Maritime Museum, Greenwich, UK. The original ship was very accurately recorded in the 18th century and hence the replica is virtually a reincarnation of that ship, not a 20th-century designer or historian's view of what she may have been like. The only concessions to the 20th century are modern heads and showers, and electric galley and mess, locker, machinery, and freezer spaces. All of these are housed in what was the capacious hold on the original ship. The crew live, sleep, and work the ship exactly as they did in the 18th century.

ENDEAVOUR

Flag:	Australia
Rig:	Full-rigged ship
Homeport/waters:	Sydney, Australia: international
Who sails?	Adults of all ages
Program type:	Sail training for volunteer crew and trainees. Sea education in maritime history based on informal, in-house programming. Passenger day sails.
Cost:	Varies, average $100 per person per day

Specifications:			
	Sparred length: 145' 6"	Draft: 12' 6"	Sail area: 15,800 sq. ft.
	LOD: 105'	Beam: 29' 2'	Tons: 397 GRT
	LOA: 109' 3"	Rig height: 121' 4"	Power: diesel
	LWL: 101' 5"	Freeboard: 13' 6"	Hull: wood

Designer:	David White/Bill Leonard
Built:	1993; Fremantle, Western Australia, HM Bark Endeavour Foundation
Certification:	USL 2A Ocean
Crew:	16. **Trainees/passengers:** 70 (day sails), 40 (overnight)
Contact:	Dominic Hannelly, Sydney Manager
	HM Bark Endeavour Foundation
	Australian National Maritime Museum
	PO Box 4537, Sydney, NSW, 2001, Australia
	Tel: 61-2-9298 3872; Fax: 61-2-9298 3849
	E mail: crewman@attglobal.net
	Web site: http://www.barkendeavour.com.au

Ernestina

On February 5, 1894, a single line in a corner of the *Gloucester Daily Times* recorded an addition to the Massachusetts fishing fleet: "The new schooner for J.F. Wonson and Co. has been named *Effie M. Morrissey.*" This marked the birth of a schooner that would become famous as a Grand Banks fisher, an arctic expeditionary vessel under the command of Captain Robert Abrams Bartlett, and as a World War II survey vessel under Commander Alexander Forbes. After a fire in 1946, the *Morrissey* was raised and renamed *Ernestina* to serve in the transatlantic Cape Verdean packet trade. In 1982 she was gifted by the Republic of Cape Verde to the people of the United States as a symbol of the close ties between lands.

The essence of *Ernestina*'s educational mission today extends from the vessel's phenomenal track through history. Aboard *Ernestina*, learners of all ages use the ship as a platform to study the marine environment and human impacts during structured underway and dockside programs. They gain confidence and self-esteem by learning how to orient themselves in the natural world while solving real-world problems.

Additionally, a membership program presents special sailing opportunities including both day sails as well as multiple day sails.

Flag:	USA
Rig:	Gaff topsail schooner, two-masted
Homeport/waters:	New Bedford, Massachusetts: East Coast US, Canada (summer); Caribbean and West Africa (winter)
Who sails?	School groups from elementary through college, and individuals of all ages.
Season:	Year-round
Cost:	$125 per person per day, $2,700 group rate or charter per day/$1,600 half-day
Program type:	Sail training for volunteer or paying trainees. Sea education in marine science, maritime history, and ecology in cooperation with accredited schools and colleges, Scouts, and other groups. Passengers carried on day and overnight sails. Dockside interpretation.

Specifications:		
Sparred length: 156'	Draft: 13'	Sail area: 8,323 sq. ft.
LOD: 106'	Beam: 24' 5"	Tons: 98 GRT
LWL: 94'	Rig height: 115'	Power: 259 HP diesel
LOA: 112'	Hull: wood	

Designer:	George M. McClain
Built:	1894; Essex, Massachusetts, Tarr and James Shipyard
Coast Guard certification:	Sailing School Vessel (Subchapter R), Passenger Vessel (Subchapter T)
Crew:	11. **Trainees/passengers:** 80 (day), 24 (overnight)
Contact:	Gregg Swanzey, Executive Director
	Schooner Ernestina Commission
	PO Box 2010
	New Bedford, MA 02741-2010
	Tel: 508-992-4900; Fax: 508-984-7719
	E-mail: swanzey@ ma.ultranet.com
	Web site: http://www.ernestina.org

Esprit

Esprit was launched in 1995. Honored in 1997 for her work promoting international understanding with mixed 50:50 German/host country crews, she is the only German sail training vessel to win the Cutty Sark Trophy. Since then *Esprit* has sailed as a sail training vessel between England, Portugal, the Lofoten Islands in northern Norway, and Russia, taking part in all European Cutty Sark Tall Ships Races. In 2000 she took part in the Tall Ships 2000 Race Around the Atlantic, winning honors in class Southampton/ Cadiz, and Cadiz/ Bermuda, with mixed German/American/Bermudan/ Norwegian/Australian crew, several on scholarships from HANSA and ISTA. Esprit returns to Gulf of Maine in 2003. *Esprit's* 2001 program: Cutty Sark Tall Ship Races: Antwerp, Belgium; Alesund, Bergen, and Oslo Norway; Esbjerg and Copenhagen Denmark; Gdansk, Poland; Kiel Race Week.

Esprit is a "cold-molded" wooden boat. Built for safe sailing with good handling qualities and high speed potential, she is easily sailed by novice crews, with her modern rig: gaff fore, Bermuda main.

Living on board is comfortable in a bright modern atmosphere - from the galley, mess, and state-of-the-art navigation area there is a panoramic view of the sea. Trainee berths are in three four-berth cabins, each with its private head. *Esprit's* owner, BBV seeks to teach teamwork and traditional and contemporary boat-building skills, to develop self confidence through experiential education, and to further international understanding through exchanges of young participants.

BBV's 95' sailing ship *Franzius*, new in 2000, is available on the Weser, Elbe and Baltic for 32 in school groups, incentive and corporate trainings as well as individuals.

ESPRIT

Flag:	Germany
Rig:	Schooner, two-masted
Homeport/waters:	Bremen-Vegesack: North Sea, Baltic, and Atlantic
Who sails?	Youth trainees, individuals, and groups.
Cost:	$70 for youth trainees, $110 for trainees over 26 per day
Program type:	Sail training for students, apprentices, and adults as paying trainees.

Specifications:	LOA: 64' 9"	Draft: 9' 9"	Sail area: 1,800 sq. ft.
	Beam: 16' 6"	Hull: wood	Power: 212 HP diesel

Designer:	Volker T. Behr, N.A.
Built:	1995; Bremen, Germany, Bremer Bootsbau Vegesack
Certification:	Constructed to specifications of German Lloyd
Crew:	4. **Trainees:** 4 (day sails), 12 (overnight)
Contact:	**North Americans:** HANSA Foundation
	PO Box 69, North Reading, MA 01864
	Tel: 781-944 0304; Fax: 781-944 2469
	E-mail: ESPRIT@sailtraining.com
	Web site: http://www.sailtraining.com
	Others: BBV Sailing
	Teerhof 46
	D-28199 Bremen, Germany
	Tel: 49-421-50-50-37; Fax: 49-421-59-14-00
	E-mail: info@bbv-sailing.de
	Web site: http://www.bbv-sailing.de

Europa

The barque *Europa* was built for the city of Hamburg in 1911 at the Stulcken Shipyard. Between 1987 and 1994, she was rebuilt into a fine square-rigger by Harry Smit.

The ship represents the end of the famous clipper era and is one of the few ships in the world that carries a full set of studding sails. Below decks you will find a classic romantic interior with lounge, bar, and saloon. All cabins have their own shower and toilet, and modern necessities for safety and comfort are hidden by the historic appearance.

For part of the year, *Europa* is the official sail training vessel of the Enkhuizen Nautical College, which educates officers and masters for commercial oceangoing sailing vessels.

In 2000 she sailed the entire Tall Ships 2000® race, finishing third in her class at her homeport of Amsterdam. From Amsterdam, *Europa* sailed for the southern summer in Antarctica. After four expeditions to the Antarctic peninsula the barque will return to Europe to participate in the Cutty Sark Tall Ships race from Antwerp to Esbjerg in Denmark via Alesund and Bergen in Norway. *Europa* will return to the USA in October 2001 as a participant in the Sea Trek Project. In the autumn of 2001 *Europa* will undertake sail training voyages along the East Coast of the USA and Canada heading South in November to Bermuda and the Caribbean for her winter program.

Flag:	The Netherlands
Rig:	Barque, three-masted
Homeport/waters:	Amsterdam, The Netherlands: world wide
Who sails?	Youth trainees, individuals, families, and groups of all ages.
Cost:	$110 - $175 per person per day (overnight). Special rates for youth trainees.
Program type:	Sail training for paying trainees. Fully accredited sea education in maritime history. Special expeditions. Dockside interpretation during port visits.

Specifications:			
	Sparred length: 185'	Draft: 12'	Sail area: 11,000 sq. ft.
	LOD: 143'	Beam: 24'	Tons: 303 GRT
	LOA: 150'	Rig height: 109'	Hull: steel
	LWL: 132'	Freeboard: 4'	

Built:	1911; Hamburg, Germany, Stülcken
Certification:	Bureau Veritas Worldwide
Crew:	12. **Trainees:** 100 (day sails), 50 (overnight)
Contact:	Smit Tall Ship b.v.
	Oostelijke Handelskade 1
	NL-1019 BL Amsterdam, The Netherlands
	Tel: +31-20-4197668; Fax: +31-20-4196134
	E-mail: info@barkeuropa.com
	Web site: http://www.barkeuropa.com

Evangelyn

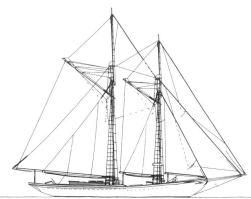

The schooner *Evangelyn* and her sister ship *Narragansett* are an adaptation of the style of fast fishing schooner once common along the New England coast prior to the World War II. Designed for the Newport Schooner Project, these schooners will be used for sail training, maritime related courses, and private charters on the waters surrounding Narragansett Bay.

The students of the Aquidneck Island School of Boatbuilding, Newport, RI will conduct construction of these schooners, over the next two years beginning mid-2001.

Students enrolled in this full time course will be involved in the design, displacement, and stability calculations, lofting, construction, commissioning, and certification of these schooners. Once in operation, there will be six paid sail training berths available.

Flag:	USA
Rig:	Schooner
Homeport/waters:	Newport, Rhode Island: Narragansett Bay and vicinity
Who sails?	Individuals and groups of all ages.
Program type:	Sail training for volunteer crew/trainees in cooperation with accredited institutions and other organized groups.

Specifications:		
Sparred length: 86'	Draft: 9'	LOD: 57'6"
Beam: 15'4"	Tons: 40 GRT	LOA: 62'10"
Rig height: 65'	LWL: 46'10"	Hull: wood
Power: 100HP CAT		

Designer:	Jeff Szala
Built:	Fall 2000; Newport, Rhode Island, Aquidneck Island School of Boatbuilding
Coast Guard certification:	Passenger Vessel (Subchapter T) approved
Crew:	5. Trainees/passengers: 45 (day sails), 4 (overnight)
Contact:	Jeff Szala, Project Manager
	Newport Schooner Project
	c/o The Aquidneck Island School of Boatbuilding
	PO Box 913
	Newport, RI 02840
	Tel: 401-849-5034
	E-mail: Jeff@aisbinc.org
	Web site: http://www.aisbinc.org

Exy Johnson

(Work in Progress)

The Los Angeles Maritime Institute is constructing two 90-foot brigantines. The vessels will be named *Irving Johnson* and *Exy Johnson* in honor of the Johnsons and their life-long commitments to character-building sail training. The voyages of Irving (1905-1991) and Electa (b. 1909) Johnson aboard *Yankee* are well known by nearly everyone familiar with the sea.

When asked, "How does your wife feel about all this voyaging?" Captain Irving Johnson's reply was, "It was her idea!"

As his extraordinary wife-mate, Exy distinguished herself as a full partner on their three *Yankees*. Her skills and talents complimented and completed the excellence of their joint endeavors. Exy is a multi-lingual, cultural ambassador extraordinaire, whether exploring remote islands of the vast Pacific, leading her pre-teen granddaughter out on the bowsprit of SEA's *Corwith Cramer*, or going aloft, at 85, when she sailed on the *Swift of Ipswich*.

Construction is taking place at the Los Angeles Maritime Museum in John Gibson Park, San Pedro. The brigantine design, based on one developed in the 1930's, has been adapted by W.I.B. Crealock to meet US Coast Guard and LAMI program requirements.

The shipyard is visitor-friendly, set up as a living history exhibit of the museum. Construction is carried out by professional, paid shipwrights, working with trained volunteers. Funding for this project will come from private donations, corporate sponsorships, and foundation grants.

Flag:	USA
Rig:	Brigantine
Homeport/waters:	Los Angeles, California: Southern California and offshore islands
Who sails?	Referred youth-at-risk and groups catering to students and adults
Season:	Year-round
Cost:	Based on ability to pay
Program type:	Educational sailing adventures for youth and adult groups.

Specifications:			
	Sparred length: 110' 8"	Draft: 11'	Sail area: 4,540 sq. ft.
	LOA: 90'	Beam: 21' 9"	Tons: 99 GRT
	LWL: 72' 6"	Rig height: 87' 8"	Power: diesel

Coast Guard certification:	Sailing School Vessel (Subchapter R), Passenger Vessel (Subchapter T)
Contact:	Captain Jim Gladson, President
	Los Angeles Maritime Institute
	Berth 84, Foot of Sixth Street
	San Pedro, CA 90731
	Tel: 310-833-6055; Fax: 310-548-2055

Eyrie

The ketch *Eyrie* was built in Marblehead, MA and launched in 1967 as a private yacht. She is strip-planked fir over oak frames coated with fiberglass mat.

Eyrie has been owned and operated by Captains Stuart and Stella Korpela since 1974, and provides a hands-on learning platform for abused and disadvantaged children connected with the Children's Embassy of Fort Lauderdale, Florida.

Flag:	USA
Rig:	Ketch
Homeport/waters:	Dinner Key, Miami, Florida: Florida (summer), Bahamas (winter)
Who sails?	Individuals and groups of all ages.
Program type:	Sail training for volunteer crew/trainees in cooperation with other organized groups.

Specifications:			
	Sparred length: 57'	Draft: 6'	Beam: 13"
	LOD: 45'	LWL: 36'	Freeboard: 5'
	Hull: wood	Power: 85 HP diesel	

Designer:	Coluin
Built:	1968; Marblehead, Massachusetts, Bromfield
Coast Guard certification:	Uninspected Vessel
Crew:	2. **Trainees/passengers:** 6 (day sails)
Contact:	Stuart Korpela
	Atlantis Marine
	PO Box 1655, 3400 Pan Am Drive
	Miami, Fl 33133
	Tel: 305-854-6198; Fax: 305-854-0832
	E-mail: vesselassistsl@aol.com

EYRIE

Fair Jeanne

Built in 1982, *Fair Jeanne* is a 110-foot brigantine originally built by the late Captain Thomas G. Fuller as a private yacht. Carrying 4,000 square feet of sail, the ship is now in service as a sail training vessel carrying up to 30 youths aged 14 to 24. Programs are also available for adults and seniors. During the summer months, the ship operates in the Great Lakes, St. Lawrence Seaway, and the East Coast. During 2000, *Fair Jeanne* participated in a range of activities, including the Boston to Halifax Race Leg of Tall Ships 2000.®

The program reflects Captain Fuller's belief in using sail training as a means of building confidence and resourcefulness in our youth. He was one of Canada's most decorated war heroes, earning the name "Pirate of the Adriatic" and holding the distinction of the longest time served in offensive war action. His wartime experience taught him the value of instilling confidence and resourcefulness in our youth through adventure at sea. Captain Fuller founded the nonprofit Bytown Brigantine, Inc. in 1983 to provide these opportunities to young people.

Flag:	Canada
Rig:	Brigantine
Homeport/waters:	Ottawa, Ontario, Canada: Great Lakes, Maritime Provinces (summer), Caribbean (winter)
Who sails?	Students between 14 and 24.
Program type:	Sail training for paying trainees. Sea education in maritime history in cooperation with organized groups and as informal, in-house programming. Dockside interpretation during port visits.

Specifications:			
	Sparred length: 110'	Draft: 6'	Sail area: 4,000 sq. ft.
	Rig height: 80'	Beam: 24' 6"	Tons: 135 GRT
	Freeboard: 8'	Hull: steel & fiberglass	Power: 235 HP

Designer:	T.G. Fuller
Built:	1982; Ottawa, Ontario, Canada, T.G. Fuller
Crew:	6. **Trainees/passengers:** 50 (day sails), 21 (overnight)
Contact:	Simon A.F. Fuller, President
	Bytown Brigantine, Inc.
	2700 Queensview Dr.
	Ottawa, Ontario K2B 8H6, Canada
	Tel: 613-596-6258; Fax: 613-596-5947
	E-mail: tallshipinfo@tallshipsadventure.org
	Web site: http://tallshipsadventure.org

Fantasy

Originally named *Isla De Ibiza*, the *Fantasy* has had a colorful history. Planned in 1870, the *Fantasy* was not built until 1913. During that time, trees were planted and grown specifically for this ship, bent and bound during growth and earmarked for various parts of the vessel. In 1998, *Isla De Ibiza* became *Fantasy*, and a new era in her history began. Today's ship is an elegant mixture of old-world shipbuilding techniques and modern amenities.

Flag:	USA				
Rig:	Topsail schooner, two-masted				
Homeport/waters:	Castries, St. Lucia: Caribbean				
Who sails?	High school and college students, and individuals.				
Program type:	Sail training for paying trainees. Sea education in marine science, maritime history, and culture and language studies in cooperation with accredited institution and as part of informal, in-house programming.				
Cost:	$3,000 per person per month				
Specifications:	Sparred length: 120'		Draft: 8' 10"		Sail area: 4,000 sq. ft.
	LOD: 90'		Beam: 19'		Tons: 150 GRT
	LOA: 96'		Rig height: 75'		Power: Caterpillar 342
	LWL: 90'		Freeboard: 3'		Hull: wood
Built:	1912; Spain, Palma Sues Shipyard				
Contact:	Tom Gibbs				
	Experiential Learning				
	210 Dixon Street				
	Henderson, KY 42420				
	Tel: 502-827-8291; Fax: 502-827-8006				
	E-mail: tgibbs@cooltides.com				
	Web site: http://cooltides.com				

Fiddler

The 65' sloop, *America II*, was the
third boat built for the New York Yacht
Club's 1987 Americas Cup Challenge.
She was featured in the movie "WIND".
Acquired by Alfred B. Van Liew in the
fall of 1993, she was re-named *Fiddler*.

Flag:	USA
Rig:	Sloop
Homeport/waters:	Newport, Rhode Island: Southern New England
Who sails?	Individuals of all ages.
Program type:	Sail training for volunteer crew/trainees from local colleges and universities. Training for Corinthian Racing and events in cooperation with the Newport Museum of Yachting's Courageous Program.

Specifications:	Sparred length: 65'	Draft: 9'	Beam: 12'
	LOA: 65'	LOD: 65'	LWL: 50'
	Rig height: 90'	Tons: 28 GRT	Freeboard: 4'
	Power: Volvo 100 HP		

Designer:	S & S
Built:	1986; Newport, Rhode Island, Williams & Manchester
Crew:	15. **Trainees/passengers:** 4
Contact:	Alfred B. Van Liew, Owner
	306 Indian Avenue
	Middletown, RI 02842
	Tel: 401-272-2510 ext. 106; Fax: 401-272-6590
	E-mail: avanliew@vanliewtrust.com

Formidable

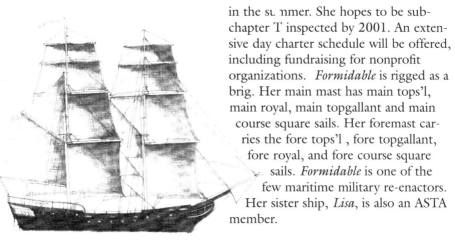

in the summer. She hopes to be sub-chapter T inspected by 2001. An extensive day charter schedule will be offered, including fundraising for nonprofit organizations. *Formidable* is rigged as a brig. Her main mast has main tops'l, main royal, main topgallant and main course square sails. Her foremast carries the fore tops'l , fore topgallant, fore royal, and fore course square sails. *Formidable* is one of the few maritime military re-enactors. Her sister ship, *Lisa*, is also an ASTA member.

Formidable has an active re-enactment schedule in the St. Petersburg, Florida area in the winter, and the Boston area

Flag:	USA		
Rig:	Brig		
Homeport/waters:	Gloucester, Massachusetts		
Specifications:	Sparred length: 72'	Draft: 6'	Sail area: 3,000 sq. ft.
	LOA: 55'	Beam: 18'	Rig height: 55'
	LWL: 49'		
Contact:	Captain Keating Willcox		
	Longmeadow Way - Box 403		
	Hamilton, MA 01936-0403		
	Tel: 866-921-9674; Fax: 978-468-1954		
	E-mail: kwillcox@shore.net		
	Web site: http://www.tallshipformidable.com		

Friendship

Friendship, a full size replica of a Salem East Indiaman built for the National Park Service and berthed at Salem Maritime National Historic Site in Salem, Massachusetts, was launched in August 1998. Although she represents a specific vessel built in Salem in 1797, she is typical of a class of commercial carriers commonly employed in both the East India and transatlantic trades during the early years of the new American republic.

Friendship's historic predecessor is credited with 15 voyages to the Far East, South America, the Mediterranean, and northern Europe. She had the misfortune of being taken as a prize of war by the Royal Navy on a return voyage from Archangel, Russia, in 1812. Sold by the British government in 1813, her ultimate fate remains a mystery. Today's *Friendship* is built from wood laminates and solid timbers and was designed to meet all requirements as a passenger carrying and sail training vessel while exhibiting the look and function of an historic vessel.

Currently under construction, *Friendship* is expected to be accessible to the public by mid-2001. The National Park Service and the "Friends of Friendship" are developing interpretive and sailing programs jointly. Ongoing outfitting and rigging activities may be viewed from adjacent wharves at Salem Maritime National Historic Site.

Flag:	USA
Rig:	Full-rigged ship
Homeport/waters:	Salem, Massachusetts
Program type:	Informal sea education in maritime history as an historic site exhibit. Dockside interpretation.

Specifications:			
	Sparred length: 171'	Draft: 11' 3"	Sail area: 9,409 sq. ft.
	LOD: 104'	Beam: 30'	Tons: 99 GRT
	LOA: 116'	Rig height: 112'	Power: twin 300 HP diesels
	LWL: 99'	Freeboard: 10'	Hull: wood

Designer:	Bay Marine, Inc., Barrington, Rhode Island
Built:	1998; Port of Albany, New York, Scarano Boatbuilding, Inc.: 1999; Dion Yacht Yard, Salem, Massachusetts
Contact:	Colleen Bruce, Project Manager Salem Maritime National Historic Site, 174 Derby Street Salem, MA 01970 Tel: 978-740-1694; Fax: 978-740-1685 E-mail: colleen_Bruce@nps.gov

Fritha

In 1999, Phillip Fuller purchased *Fritha* in Auckland, New Zealand, then sailed her to Bermuda, where she met up with the Tall Ships 2000® fleet arriving from Europe. The voyage took *Fritha* and her crew to Fiji, Hawaii, San Diego, Mexico, Costa Rica, the Panama Canal, Fort Lauderdale, and Bermuda. From Bermuda, *Fritha* raced to Charleston, South Carolina as part of ASTA's Bermuda to Charleston Race. She then cruised in company up the eastern seaboard to Boston, Massachusetts, where she participated in Sail Boston 2000®. *Fritha* then raced to Halifax, Nova Scotia as a part of the Tall Ships 2000® fleet. She completed the voyage with her arrival in Mackeral Cove, Maine, only a few nautical miles from her place of origin, the drawing board of her designer, Murray Peterson.

FRITHA

Flag:	USA		
Rig:	Hermaphrodite brigantine		
Homeport/waters:	Harpswell, Maine: Maine (summer)		
Who sails?	High school and college students, and individuals under 25.		
Program type:	Sail training for volunteer and paying trainees. Informal sea education in marine science and maritime history.		
Specifications:	Sparred length: 74'	Draft: 6' 10"	Tons: 39 GRT
	LOD: 57'	Beam: 15'	Hull: wood
	Rig height: 51'	Freeboard: 5'	Power: GM 4-71
	LWL: 46'		
Designer:	Murray Peterson		
Built:	1983-1984; Auckland, New Zealand, McMullen & Wing		
Coast Guard certification:	Sailing School Vessel (Subchapter R)		
Crew:	2. Trainees: 6		
Contact:	Philip Fuller, Owner		
	SeaMe.Sail		
	304 Chestnut Street		
	North Andover, MA 01845		
	Tel: 207-363-0048		
	E-mail: fritha@mediaone.net		

Fyrdraca

Fyrdraca is a copy of a small 10th-century Viking warship found near Ralswiek on the German Island of Rügen in the Baltic Sea. The Longship Company seeks to rediscover the lost art of Viking sailing and navigation. To that end, *Fyrdraca* sails twice a month from March through November with a volunteer crew.

Fyrdraca also appears at waterfront and cultural festivals near the Potomac River and Chesapeake Bay and also participates in living history demonstrations in concert with the Markland Medieval Mercenary Militia's Viking reenactment camps. Voyage and demonstration schedules are published on the Longship Company's Web site.

Fyrdraca and her consort *Gyrfalcon* are both owned and operated by The Longship Company, Ltd., a member-supported nonprofit educational organization.

Flag:	USA
Rig:	Viking longship
Homeport/waters:	Oakley, Maryland: Potomac River and Chesapeake Bay
Who sails?	School groups from elementary school through college as well as individuals of all ages.
Season:	March to November
Program type:	Sail training for volunteer crew and apprentices. Sea education in maritime history based on informal, in-house programming. Non-paying passengers for day sails. Dockside interpretation during port visits.

Specifications:			
	Sparred length: 34'	Draft: 2'	Sail area: 240 sq. ft.
	LOA: 32'	Beam: 9' 2"	Tons: 3 GRT
	LWL: 29'	Rig height: 25'	Hull: wood
	Freeboard: 2' 6"		

Designer:	Traditional Norse design
Built:	1979; Keyport, New Jersey, Hans Pederson & Sons
Coast Guard certification:	Uninspected Vessel
Crew:	18 (day sails), 10 (overnight). **Trainees:** 4-12
Contact:	Bruce E. Blackistone, Registered Agent
	Longship Company, Ltd.
	21924 Oakley Road
	Avenue, MD 20609
	Tel: 301-390-4089
	E-mail: longshipco@hotmail.com
	Web site: http://www.wam.umd.edu/~eowyn/longship

Gallant

Pete Cullers' schooner *Gallant* was designed and built for Richard Tilghman in 1966, who cruised her on the East Coast until 1983, at which time she was donated to the Chesapeake Bay Maritime Museum. In 1986 the present owners, Tuck and Anne Elfman, purchased her from the Museum and put her back into service sailing the Chesapeake Bay and coastal waters, participating in the Great Chesapeake Bay Schooner Races in 1994 and 1997, the 1986 salute to the Statue of Liberty, and OpSail 2000 in New York Harbor. *Gallant* is based on a Chesapeake Bay pilot schooner with quite a bit of coaster influence. Her designer described her as being a "main topmast flying jib-boomer."

Gallant is of unusually rugged build by today's standards, using very traditional construction features such as standing rigging of iron cable, tarred, parceled and served, maintained with pine tar, and fastened to lignum vitae deadeyes. She has plenty of deck area to enjoy a stable sail. *Gallant* is privately owned and maintained, offering guests day trips on the lower Hudson and East River, teaching the workings of the schooner rig, safety, and traditional maintenance, among other subjects. Based at Liberty Landing Marina across from lower Manhattan, *Gallant* carries a 10-gauge cannon for saluting notable vessels.

GALLANT

Flag:	USA		
Rig:	Main topsail schooner, two-masted		
Homeport/waters:	Jersey City, New Jersey; Hudson River, East River and East Coast		
Who sails?	Individuals of all ages and families		
Program type:	Sail training for volunteer crew or trainees. Informal, in-house programming in vessel maintenance. Dockside interpretation while in homeport.		
Specifications:	Sparred length: 62'	Draft: 6' 6"	Sail area: 1,450 sq. ft.
	LOD: 40' 6"	Beam: 12' 6"	Tons: 20 GRT
	LOA: 43' 8"	Rig height: 62'	Power: 68 HP diesel
	LWL: 35'	Freeboard: 2'	Hull: wood
Designer:	Pete Culler		
Built:	1966; South Dartmouth, Massachusetts, Concordia – Waldo Howland		
Coast Guard certification:	Uninspected Vessel		
Crew:	1. **Trainees/passengers:** 6		
Contact:	A. Tuck Elfman, Owner		
	51 Elfman Drive		
	Doylestown, PA 18901		
	Tel: 215-348-2731: Fax: 215-348-4178		

Gazela Philadelphia

Philadelphia, the Commonwealth of Pennsylvania, and the Ports of Philadelphia and Camden, New Jersey. A new initiative is the maritime education of Philadelphia's disadvantaged youth. *Gazela* and her volunteer crew have also taken part in the filming of *Interview with the Vampire*, the documentary *The Irish in America*, and *The Widow of St. Pierre*.

The century-old *Gazela Philadelphia* was built as a Grand Banks fishing vessel. She is one of many Portuguese ships that fished for cod there for hundreds of years. Now owned and operated by the Philadelphia Ship Preservation Guild, a nonprofit organization, the *Gazela* sails as a goodwill ambassador for the City of

Gazela is maintained and sailed by a very active and knowledgeable volunteer group participating in maintenance and sail training activities throughout the year. After 25 hours of work on the vessel, a volunteer is eligible for a crew position on the next available voyage.

Flag:	USA
Rig:	Barquetine, three-masted
Homeport/waters:	Philadelphia, Pennsylvania: Delaware River and Atlantic Coast
Who sails?	Volunteers who support the maintenance of the ship. Dockside visitors include school groups from elementary school through college, as well as individuals and families.
Program type:	Sail training for crew and apprentices. Sea education based on informal, in-house programming. Dockside interpretation during outport visits.

Specifications:			
	Sparred length: 178'	Draft: 17'	Sail area: 8,910 sq. ft.
	LOD: 140'	Beam: 27' 9"	Tons: 299 GRT
	LOA: 150'	Rig height: 100'	Power: diesel
	LWL: 133'	Hull: wood	

Built:	1883; Cacilhas, Portugal
Coast Guard certification:	Attraction Vessel and Uninspected Vessel
Crew:	35 (volunteer)
Contact:	Karen H. Love, Executive Vice President
	Philadelphia Ship Preservation Guild
	Pier 36 South, 801 S. Columbus Blvd., 2nd floor
	Philadelphia, PA 19147-4306
	Tel: 215-218-0110; Fax: 215-463-1875
	E-mail: gazela@usa.net
	Web site: http://www.gazela.org

Geronimo

Geronimo makes three six-to-eight week trips during the school year, carrying students from St. George's School. Marine biology and English are taught on board, and the students continue their other courses by correspondence with the faculty at St. George's. Students receive full academic credit for their time on board. These cruises usually include operations along the eastern seaboard and in the waters of the Bahamas and northern Caribbean.

Geronimo's marine biology research has always included tagging sharks and collecting biological samples for the Apex Predator Investigation of the National Marine Fisheries Service. *Geronimo* also tags sea turtles in cooperation with the Center for Sea Turtle Research of the University of Florida. Their recent work has included the use of satellite transmitters on loggerhead turtles in Bahamian waters.

In the summer, *Geronimo* makes two three-week cruises, usually to the waters south of New England, to Bermuda, or to the Bahamas. Each summer cruise includes a series of lectures on marine biology and fisheries management as well as sail training, snorkeling, and the collecting of data on turtles and/or sharks.

GERONIMO

Flag:	USA
Rig:	Sloop
Homeport/waters:	Newport, Rhode Island: North Atlantic and Caribbean
Who sails?	Enrolled students at St. George's School.
Season:	Year-round
Cost:	Regular school tuition (winter); inquire for summer 2001 cruise
Program type:	Full curriculum academics, marine biology, and environmental studies for high school students.

Specifications:	Sparred length: 69' 8"	Draft: 6' 8" 13' 5",	Sail area: 2,091 sq. ft.
	LOD: 68'	Beam: 18' 7"	Tons: 53 GRT
	LOA: 69' 8"	Rig height: 85' 6"	Power: diesel
	LWL: 53' 11"	Freeboard: 5'	Hull: fiberglass

Designer:	Ted Hood Design Group
Built:	1998; Portsmouth, Rhode Island, New England Boatworks
Coast Guard certification:	Sailing School Vessel (Subchapter R)
Crew:	2. Trainees: 8
Contact:	Captain Stephen Connett
	St. George's School
	372 Purgatory Road, PO Box 1910
	Newport, RI 02840
	Tel: 401-847-7565; Fax: 401-842-6696
	Web site: http://www.stgeorges.edu

Gleam

The eleventh 12-meter vessel built for the United States, *Gleam* is beautifully restored and has her original pre-World War II interior. She has been painstakingly maintained by the same owner for 25 years. Together with her near sister ship *Northern Light, Gleam* offers a unique team-building program called "Your Own America's Cup Regatta." Each boat accommodates 13 guests plus three crewmembers. No previous sailing experience is necessary to participate. Group and corporate outings are available in Newport, Rhode Island, and other New England ports.

GLEAM

Flag:	USA
Rig:	Sloop
Homeport/waters:	Newport, Rhode Island: Narragansett Bay
Who sails?	Corporations who charter the vessel for team building and client entertaining.
Program type:	Sail training with paying trainees. Passenger day sails.

Specifications:			
	Sparred length: 67' 11"	Draft: 9'	Sail area: 1,900 sq. ft.
	LOD: 67' 11"	Beam: 12'	Tons: 30 GRT
	LOA: 67' 11"	Rig height: 90'	Power: diesel
	LWL: 46' 11"	Freeboard: 3'	Hull: wood

Designer:	Clinton Crane and Olin Stephens
Built:	1937; City Island, New York, Henry Nevins
Coast Guard certification:	Passenger Vessel (Subchapter T)
Crew:	3. **Trainees:** 14
Contact:	Elizabeth Tiedemann, Director of Sales and Marketing

Seascope Systems, Inc.
103 Ruggles Ave.
Newport, RI 02840
Tel: 401-847-5007; Fax: 401-849-6140
E-mail: aboard@earthlink.net
Web site: http://www.seascopenewport.com

Glenn L. Swetman

The *Glenn L. Swetman* is the first of two replica Biloxi oyster schooners built by the Biloxi Schooner Project under the auspices of the Maritime and Seafood Industry Museum. She is available for charter trips in the Mississippi Sound and to the barrier islands, Cat Island, Horn Island, and Ship Island. Walk-up day sailing trips are made when she is not under charter. Groups can learn about the maritime and seafood heritage of the Gulf Coast and about the vessels that began Biloxi's seafood industry. The *Glenn L. Swetman* is an integral part of the museum's Sea and Sail Summer Camp, and sailing classes are also offered through local colleges. *Glenn L. Swetman* also accommodates weddings, parties, and Elderhostel and school groups.

Money for construction and equipping the *Glenn L. Swetman* and her sister ship, *Mike Sekul*, has come from donations by interested individuals, businesses, civic groups, and a variety of museum-sponsored fundraising events.

Flag:	USA
Rig:	Gaff topsail schooner, two-masted
Homeport/waters:	Biloxi, Mississippi: northern Gulf of Mexico
Who sails?	Individuals and groups of all ages. Affiliated institutions include William Carey College, Mississippi State University, J.L. Scott Marine Education Center, and Seashore Methodist Assembly.
Season:	Year-round
Cost:	$15 per adult or $10 per child (2-1/2 hours), $750 per day group rate, $500 for half-day
Program type:	Sail training for volunteer and paying trainees. Sea education in maritime history, marine science, and ecology for college students and adults in cooperation with accredited institutions, organized groups, and as informal, in-house programming. Children's summer camp and private charters.

Specifications:	Sparred length: 76'	Draft: 4' 10"	Sail area: 2,400 sq. ft.
	LOD: 50'	Beam: 17'	Tons: 21 GRT
	LOA: 65'	Freeboard: 4' 6"	Power: 4-71 Detroit diesel
	LWL: 47'	Hull: Juniper	

Designer:	William Holland
Built:	1989; Biloxi, Mississippi, William T. Holland
Coast Guard certification:	Passenger Vessel (Subchapter T)
Crew:	3. **Trainees:** 49 (day sails)
Contact:	Robin Krohn, Executive Director
	Maritime and Seafood Industry Museum of Biloxi
	PO Box 1907
	Biloxi, MS 39533
	Tel: 228-435-6320; Fax: 228-435-6309
	E-mail: schooner@maritimemuseum.org
	Web site: http://www.maritimemuseum.org

Gloria

PHOTO BY THAD KOZA

Built in Bilbao, Spain, and purchased in 1966 by the Colombian Navy, the three-masted barque *Gloria* is used today as a school ship for the Colombian Navy. She has proudly served for 33 years training more than 700 officers and 4,500 enlisted men and women.

Gloria carries a complement of 150 men and women, ranging from enlisted to midshipmen and officers. The cruise is aimed at training officers, in their third year at the Naval Academy, to implement their academic knowledge in the areas of navigation, seamanship, leadership, and teambuilding. *Gloria* is a proud goodwill ambassador of the Colombian Navy.

Flag:	Colombia
Rig:	Barque
Homeport/waters:	Cartegena, Colombia
Who sails?	Colombian Naval Academy cadets and officers of the Colombian Navy.
Season:	Year-round
Program type:	Sail training for Colombian Naval Academy cadets.

Specifications:

Sparred length: 249' 4"	Draft: 14' 9"	Sail area: 15,075 sq. ft.
LOD: 189'	Beam: 34' 9"	Tons: 934 GRT
LOA: 212'	Rig height: 126' 4"	Power: twin 256 KV
LWL: 184'	Freeboard: 21' 7"	Hull: steel

Designer:	Sener
Built:	1968; Bilbao, Spain, Celaga S. A. Shipyards
Certification:	Colombian Naval vessel
Crew:	160
Contact:	Naval Attaché, Colombia
	2118 Leroy Place NW
	Washington, DC 20008
	Tel: 202-387-8338; Fax: 202-232-8643
	E-mail: arcgloria@yahoo.com

SAIL TALL SHIPS!

Governor Stone

The *Governor Stone* was built for Charles Greiner in Pascagoula, Mississippi, in 1877 as a cargo freighter and named for John Marshall Stone, the first elected Governor of Mississippi after the Civil War. This gaff-rigged, shallow draft schooner represents a class of sailing vessels unique to the Gulf Coast and is the oldest vessel of the American south afloat. Possibly the last of her type, the *Governor Stone* has seen service from an oyster buy-boat to yacht club committee boat to pleasure craft. The vessel has been declared a National Historic Landmark by the National Park Service.

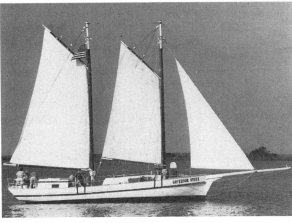

Governor Stone sails year-round. Sailing times vary. Reservations are suggested and can be obtained by calling the Apalachicola Maritime Museum.

Flag:	USA
Rig:	Gaff schooner, two-masted
Homeport/waters:	Apalachicola, Florida: Gulf of Mexico, upper coast
Who sails?	School groups from elementary school through college as well as individuals and families. Affiliated institutions include Gulf Coast Community College, Panama City, Florida.
Season:	Year-round
Cost:	$20 per person per day; $900 group rate; $450 half day. Overnight trips by special arrangements.
Program type:	Sea education in marine science, maritime history, and ecology based on informal, in-house programming, with special attention given to at-risk students. Passenger day sails and overnight passages. Dockside interpretation.

Specifications:			
	Sparred length: 68'	Draft: 2' 6"	Sail area: 1,400 sq. ft.
	LOD: 42'	Beam: 13' 6"	Tons: 12 GRT
	LOA: 44'	Rig height: 52'	Power: 80 HP diesel
	LWL: 38'	Freeboard: 5'	Hull: wood

Built:	1877; Pascagoula, Mississippi
Coast Guard certification:	Passenger Vessel (Subchapter T)
Crew:	3, 1 instructor. **Trainees:** 6
Contact:	Joe Terrell, Assistant Administrator Apalachicola Maritime Museum, Inc. 268 Water Street, PO Box 625 Apalachicola, FL 32329-0625 Tel: 850-653-8700

Grand Nellie

Designers Parker Marean III and Russel Woodin of Boothbay, Maine balanced traditional Maine schooner lines with modern technology for comfort, safety and performance in creating the classic schooner *Grand Nellie*. Top quality materials and equipment were chosen throughout the building process to meet the highest standards of compliance with US Coast Guard Oceans and SOLAS International regulations for passenger vessels.

Owner operated *Grand Nellie* provides tall ship sailing experience for beginner to advanced sailors of all ages and abilities. Participation in all aspects of vessel operation is encouraged to allow passengers and trainees to gain experience and increase their abilities while on board. Offshore and multiple day voyages provide participants the opportunity to be an integral part of sail handling, navigation and watchkeeping.

On deck, *Grand Nellie* is free of clutter, providing plenty of room to move about or just lounge in the sun or the shaded cockpit. Below deck, the open interior is beautifully appointed with cherry and maple custom woodwork.

Grand Nellie winters in the Caribbean, based out of St. Thomas, USVI, and during the summer months, she joins various festivals and races, such as OpSail 2000, Tall Ships 2000®, Tall Ships Challenge® Great Lakes 2001 and the Great Chesapeake Bay Schooner Race.

Flag:	USA
Rig:	Topsail schooner
Homeport/waters:	St. Thomas, USVI
Season:	Year-round
Who sails?	Families and individuals of all ages.
Program type:	Sail training for paying trainees. Sea education in cooperation with accredited institutions and other organized groups. Dockside interpretation. Participation in festivals and special events.

Specifications:			
	Sparred length: 75'	Draft: 8'	Beam: 16'
	LOA: 60'	LOD: 57'	LWL: 49'
	Rig height: 75'	Freeboard: 5'	Sail area: 3,000 sq. ft.
	Hull: steel	Power: 140 HP Yanmar	Tons: 42 GRT
	Hull color: white	Spar material: aluminum	

Designer:	Parker Marean III and Russel Woodin
Built:	1998; Merritt, North Carolina, Custom Steel Boats
Coast Guard certification:	Passenger Vessel (Subchapter T)
Crew:	3. **Trainees/passengers:** 49 (day sails), 6 (overnight)
Contact:	Jeff and Ellen Troeltzsch
	Schooner Grand Nellie
	525 Lake Avenue South
	Suite 405
	Duluth, MN 55802
	Tel: 340-513-4643; Fax: 218-723-1918
	E-mail: ellen@grandnellie.com
	Web site: http://www.grandnellie.com

Guayas

Guayas was built in the Celaya Shipyard in Bilbao, Spain, with construction beginning in 1974. She is named after the Chief of Huancavilcas, a native culture in the Ecuadorian coastal region. The general arrangement was the same as *Gloria* of Colombia. *Simon Bolivar* of Venezuela and *Cuahtemoc* of Mexico were also built using the same design. *Guayas* was commissioned on July 23, 1977, and since that date has proudly served for more than 20 years training more than 500 officers and 3,000 enlisted men.

Guayas has participated in many tall ship events over the years. This representation has led her to be referred to as Ecuador's Afloat Embassy. The ship carries a complement of 16 officers, 43 midshipmen, and 94 enlisted men, including the ship's band. During a cruise, considered one semester at the Ecuadorian Naval Academy, midshipmen apply—in a very challenging environment—theoretical principles of navigation, seamanship, and other subjects learned in the classroom.

GUAYAS

Flag:	Ecuador
Rig:	Barque
Homeport/waters:	Guayaquil, Ecuador: cruises to various destinations worldwide
Who sails?	Ecuadorian Naval Academy cadets.
Season:	Year-round
Program type:	Sail training for Ecuadorian Naval Academy cadets.

Specifications:	Sparred length: 257' 1"	Draft: 15' 4"	Sail area: 15,784 sq. ft.
	LOD: 218'	Beam: 34' 9"	
	LOA: 221'	Power: diesel	
	LWL: 184'	Hull: steel	

Designer:	Celaya
Built:	1976; Celaya Shiupyard, Bilbao, Spain
Certification:	Ecuadorian Naval Vessel
Crew:	76
Contact:	Naval Attaché, Ecuador and Captain, "Buque Escuela Guayas"
	2535 15th St. NW
	Washington, DC 20009
	Tel: 202-265-7674; Fax: 202-667-3482
	E-mail: Aembassyec@aol.com

Gyrfalcon

Gyrfalcon is a copy of the faering buried with the Gokstad ship in Norway in the 9th century. She was built by the boat building program at the Hampton Mariner's Museum (now the North Carolina Maritime Museum) in Beaufort, North Carolina under the direction of Geoffrey Scofield.

Gyrfalcon is often seen at cultural, water, community, and boat festivals, historic reenactment events, and school demonstrations. She also participates in living history demonstrations in concert with the Markland Medieval Mercenary Militia's Viking reenactment camps, where the public enjoys the spectacle of crews dressed in historic costume and armor, offering historic interpretation.

As an enticement to school children and adults to discover more about the Viking Age, *Gyrfalcon* spends off-season time on display at area libraries and schools. *Gyrfalcon* and her consort, *Fyrdraca*, are both owned and operated by The Longship Company, Ltd., a member-supported nonprofit educational organization.

Flag:	USA
Rig:	Viking faering boat
Homeport/waters:	Avenue, Maryland: East Coast and Chesapeake Bay
Season:	March to November
Who sails?	School groups from elementary school through college as well as individuals of all ages.
Season:	March to November
Program type:	Sail training for crew and apprentices. Sea education in maritime history as well as informal, in-house programming. Dockside interpretation at outport visits.

Specifications:	Sparred length: 21'	Draft: 1'	Sail area: 80 sq. ft.
	LOA: 21'	Beam: 5'	Tons: 200 lbs.
	Freeboard: 1'	Rig height: 10'	Hull: wood

Built:	1981; Hampton Mariner's Museum (now the North Carolina Maritime Museum), Beaufort, North Carolina
Coast Guard certification:	Uninspected Vessel
Crew:	4. Trainees: 1-3
Contact:	Bruce E. Blackistone, Registered Agent
	Longship Company, Ltd.
	21924 Oakley Road
	Avenue, MD 20609
	Tel: 301-390-4089
	E-mail: longshipco@hotmail.com
	Web site: http://www.wam.umd.edu/~eowyn/longship

GYRFALCON

Half Moon (Halve Maen)

The replica ship *Half Moon (Halve Maen)* was launched on June 20, 1989, to draw attention to the exploration and colonization of the Mid-Atlantic States. The 1609 voyage of the original *Halve Maen,* under the command of Henry Hudson, led to the first European settlements by the Dutch in what are now the States of New York, New Jersey, Connecticut, Delaware, and Pennsylvania. In 1614, the Dutch named the area "Nieu Nederlandt."

Since her launch, the replica *Half Moon* has visited over 40 ports along the eastern seaboard and the Great Lakes. She has been boarded by over 100,000 visitors and participated in port festivals and a yearly New Netherland Festival. The *Half Moon* is featured in the 1994 Walt Disney movie, *Squanto: An Indian Warrior's Tale.*

The ship's design is based on original Dutch East India Company documents, including the resolution of 1608 ordering the original ship's construction and *Juet's Journal.* Hudson sailed the *Halve Maen* up the Hudson River as far as present-day Albany in 1609.

The *Half Moon*'s program offers the public both an active sail training program and instruction on the history of New Netherland. Thus, the crew is trained in both historical presentation and ship handling.

HALF MOON (HALVE MAEN)

Flag:	USA
Rig:	Full-rigged ship
Homeport/waters:	Croton-on-Hudson, New York: East Coast and Great Lakes
Who sails?	School groups from elementary school through high school, individuals and adults.
Program type:	Sail training and maritime history based on informal programs. Dockside interpretation.

Specifications:			
	Sparred length: 95'	Draft: 8' 5"	Sail area: 2,757 sq. ft.
	LOD: 64' 3"	Beam: 17' 6"	Tons: 112 GRT
	LOA: 65'	Rig height: 78'	Power: diesel
	LWL: 84'	Freeboard: 10' 5"	Hull: wood

Designer:	Nicholas S. Benton
Built:	1989; Albany, New York, New Netherland Museum
Coast Guard certification:	Attraction Vessel
Crew:	7-12 (day sails), 8-15 (overnight)
Contact:	Dr. Andrew Hendricks, Chairman
	New Netherland Museum and Half Moon Visitor Center
	PO Box 10609
	Albany, NY 12201-5609
	Tel: 518-443-1609
	Web site: http://www.newnetherland.org

Harvey Gamage

The schooner *Harvey Gamage* is owned by the Ocean Classroom Foundation (formerly the Schooner Harvey Gamage Foundation). She sails on sea education programs ranging from four month semesters-at-sea to weeklong programs with schools and youth groups. All programs use the power of the sea and the challenge of traditional seafaring as the basis for the academic curriculum taught on board.

Ocean Classroom, a fully accredited high school semester-at-sea, is a true voyage of discovery for qualified sophomores, juniors, and seniors. Young people come from all over the US to join this outstanding learning adventure. The voyage covers more than 4,000 nautical miles, connecting South American shores to the Canadian Maritimes. Students live and work as sailors while they study maritime history, maritime literature, marine science, applied mathematics, and navigation. Ocean Classroom is offered fall, spring, and summer terms.

Some other programs include SEAmester (a complete semester-at-sea for college credit), Marine Awareness Research Expeditions (also for college credit), and Summer Seafaring Camp (for teens age 13-17).

The Ocean Classroom Foundation also owns and operates the schooner *Spirit of Massachusetts.*

Flag:	USA
Rig:	Gaff topsail schooner, two-masted
Homeport/waters:	Islesboro, Maine: Eastern US and Canada (summer), Caribbean and South America (winter)
Who sails?	School groups from middle school through college. Affiliated institutions include Proctor Academy, Long Island University, Franklin Pierce College, and other schools.
Season:	Year-round
Cost:	Varies with program
Program type:	Sail training with paying trainees/students. Fully accredited sea education in marine science, maritime history, maritime literature, marine applied mathematics and navigation.

Specifications:			
	Sparred length: 131'	Draft: 9' 7"	Sail area: 4,200 sq ft.
	LOD: 90'	Beam: 23' 7"	Tons: 94 GRT
	LOA: 95'	Rig height: 91'	Power: 220 HP diesel
	LWL: 85'	Hull: wood	

Designer:	McCurdy & Rhodes
Built:	1973; South Bristol, Maine, Harvey Gamage Shipyard
Coast Guard certification:	Sailing School Vessel (Subchapter R), Passenger Vessel (Subchapter T)
Crew:	7-10, including instructors. **Students:** 27 (overnight)
Contact:	Bert Rogers, Director
	Ocean Classroom Foundation, Inc.
	PO Box 446
	Cornwall, NY 12518
	Tel: 800-724-7245 or 845-615-1412; Fax: 845-615-1414
	E-mail: mail@sailgamage.org
	Web site: http://www.sailgamage.org

Hawaiian Chieftain

PHOTO BY BENSON LEE

The *Hawaiian Chieftain* is a 103-foot square topsail ketch. A replica of an 18th century European trading vessel, she was built in Hawaii in 1988. She is a contemporary interpretation of a traditional design and is an excellent classroom for the teaching of traditional sailing skills. The hands-on history program "Voyages of ReDiscovery" teaches 4th and 5th grade students about the exploration of the West Coast during the 1790's. A summertime, weeklong day camp, "Buccaneers & Explorers Camp" is offered for youth from 9 – 12 years.

Debuting in the summer of 2001 is our expeditionary longboat program. The boats, two 25-foot Pinky schooners and a 23-foot Royal Navy launch, will be sailed by 7th to 9th grade students on the Sacramento/San Joaquin River Deltas. The program will focus on empowering the students through experience, education and exploration.

For the past five winters, *Hawaiian Chieftain* has toured Californian ports in company with the *Lady Washington*, providing the "Voyages of ReDiscovery" sailing and dockside educational programs. *Hawaiian Chieftain* coordinates with many organizations to develop self-esteem building programs for youth in a challenging environment. She also offers sail training and team building for adults, private charters, natural history cruises and Naval Battle Reenactments with visiting vessels.

HAWAIIAN CHIEFTAIN

Flag:	USA
Rig:	Square topsail ketch
Homeport/waters:	Sausalito, California: San Francisco Bay (summer), southern California coast (winter)
Who sails?	Elementary and middle school groups, individuals and families.
Season:	Year-round
Cost:	$35 to $100 per person per day, $1,050-$2,400 group rate per day
Program type:	Sail training for volunteer or paying trainees. Sea education in maritime history in cooperation with accredited schools and colleges. Passenger day sails. Dockside interpretation during port visits.

Specifications:

Sparred length: 103'	Draft: 6'	Sail area: 4,200 sq. ft.
LOD: 65'	Beam: 22'	Tons: 64 GRT
Rig height: 75'	Freeboard: 3'	Power: twin diesels
LWL: 62'	Hull: steel	

Designer:	Raymond R. Richards
Built:	1988; Lahaina, Maui, Hawaii, Lahaina Welding Co.
Coast Guard certification:	Passenger Vessel (Subchapter T)
Crew:	8. **Trainees:** 47
Contact:	Captain Ian McIntyre
	Hawaiian Chieftain Inc.
	Suite #266, 3020 Bridgeway
	Sausalito, CA 94965
	Tel: 415-331-3214; Fax: 415-331-9415
	E-mail: tallship@hawaiianchieftain.com
	Web site: http://www.hawaiianchieftain.com

Heritage

The beautiful varnished-hulled *Heritage* was built in 1970, the last year of the wooden twelve-meters. Designed, built, and sailed by Charlie Morgan, her tank tests showed her to be a technological breakthrough. However, by the end of the summer's racing, the redesigned *Intrepid* won the right to defend the Cup.

Heritage avenged her earlier defeat to *Intrepid* when they met on the Great Lakes in the 1980s. There she dominated the Great Lakes racing circuit, scoring multiple wins in the Chicago to Mackinac, Port Huron to Mackinac, Trans-Superior, and Queen's Cup races. In 1988 she sailed from the Lakes to California and in 1991 returned to New England. She is now part of the America's Cup Charters twelve-meter fleet in Newport, Rhode Island. *Heritage* is available for charter in New England and New York and is a perfect platform for family outings and corporate entertaining or team building.

Flag:	USA
Rig:	Sloop
Homeport/waters:	Newport, Rhode Island: New England and Chesapeake Bay
Who sails?	Individuals of all ages.
Cost:	$1,800 group rate per day, $60 per person evening sail
Program type:	Sail training for volunteer or paying trainees. Sea education based on informal, in-house programming. Passenger day sails.

Specifications:			
LOD: 65'	Draft: 10'	Sail area: 1,700 sq. ft.
LOA: 65'	Beam: 12'	Power: diesel
LWL: 46'	Rig height: 90'	Hull: wood

Designer:	Charles Morgan
Built:	1970; Clearwater, Florida, Morgan Custom Yachts
Coast Guard certification:	Passenger Vessel (Subchapter T)
Crew:	3. Trainees: 14
Contact:	George Hill/Herb Marshall
	America's Cup Charters
	PO Box 51
	Newport, RI 02840
	Tel: 401-849-5868; Fax: 401-849-3098
	Web site: http://www.americascupcharters.com

Heritage of Miami II

The *Heritage of Miami II* is an 83-foot square topsail schooner that is modern in materials and construction but traditional in style. Built specifically for crossing wide expanses of open water, she has a wide, spacious deck that provides ample room for working the sails, lounging in the sun, and sleeping in the evening. Her shoal draft makes even small islands accessible while her long bowsprit, topmasts, and yards allow extra sails for speed between them.

Heritage of Miami II's travels take her to Garden Key and the famous Fort Jefferson in the Dry Tortugas, the coral reefs of the Florida Keys, and Key West. Sea Explorer cruises last for six days and five nights. Her professional captain and crew help the Explorers experience the life of the sea: setting and furling sails, manning the helm, and even catching, cleaning, and cooking fish. The program offers a unique opportunity to explore a part of the Florida Keys while enjoying a hands-on sailing experience.

Flag:	USA
Rig:	Square topsail schooner, two-masted
Homeport/waters:	Miami, Florida: Biscayne Bay, Florida Keys, Gulf of Mexico
Who sails?	School groups from elementary school through college as well as individuals. Affiliated institutions include Dade County Schools, Broward County Schools, area private schools, and the Boy Scouts of America.
Season:	Year-round
Cost:	$75 per person per day; $1,000 group rate per day
Program type:	Sail training for crew, apprentices, and paying trainees. Sea education in maritime history and ecology in cooperation with accredited schools and colleges and other organized groups. Passenger day sails and overnight passages. Dockside interpretation.

Specifications:	Sparred length: 85'	Draft: 6'	Sail area: 2,200 sq. ft.
	LOD: 65'	Beam: 17' 9"	Tons: 47 GRT
	LOA: 68'	Rig height: 64'	Power: 140 HP diesel
	LWL: 62'	Freeboard: 8'	Hull: steel

Designer:	Merritt Walters
Built:	1988; Norfolk, Virginia, Howdy Bailey
Coast Guard certification:	Passenger Vessel (Subchapter T)
Contact:	Captain Joseph A. Maggio The Schooner Heritage of Miami, Inc. 3145 Virginia St. Coconut Grove, FL 33133 Tel: 305-442-9697; Fax: 305-442-0119 E-mail: heritage2@mindspring.com Web site: http://www.heritageschooner.com

Hewitt R. Jackson

On May 12, 1792 Captain Robert Gray sailed his ship, *Columbia Rediviva*, over the bar of the "Great River of the West" and named it Columbia's River in honor of his ship. Robert Gray never would have entered that river had it not been for the information he received from the first American vessel to enter the river, *Columbia*'s longboat.

Unnamed and unheralded, ship's boats were the workhorses of the 16th to 19th century. Powered by either oars or sails, these versatile seaworthy craft carried all manner of cargo from ship to shore and back again.

Grays Harbor Historical Seaport Authority built two 18th-century ship's longboat reproductions in 1993. The design for the Seaport longboats was painstakingly researched by noted maritime historian and artist Hewitt R. Jackson, who worked closely with naval architect Stuart Hoagland and Seaport Director Les Bolton to ensure both historical accuracy and the meeting of specific program needs.

Powered by ten oars or up to a three-masted dipping lugsail rig, these versatile vessels are ideal for exploring the protected inland waterways of Washington. Programs are customized to the needs and interests of specific groups. Half-day, full-day, and weeklong programs are available to organized groups as well as to individuals.

Flag:	USA
Rig:	Dipping lug
Homeport/waters:	Aberdeen, Washington: Western Washington, Grays Harbor, Washington
Who sails?	School groups from middle school through college, individuals under 25.
Program type:	Sail training for volunteer and paying trainees. Sea education in marine science, maritime history, ecology, and team building in cooperation with accredited institutions and as part of informal, in-house programming. Passenger day sails, dockside interpretation.
Cost:	$95 per person per day, $600 group rate per day. Residential programs, $55 per person per day (five-day minimum).

Specifications:				
	Sparred length: 36'	Draft: 20"		Sail area: 310 sq. ft.
	LOD: 25'	Beam: 7'		Tons: 3,800 lbs. (dsp)
	LOA: 26'	Rig height: 16'		Hull: wood
	LWL: 26'	Freeboard: 20"		

Designer:	Stuart Hoagsland/Hewitt Jackson
Built:	1993; Aberdeen, Washington, Grays Harbor Historical Seaport Authority
Coast Guard certification:	Sailing School Vessel (Subchapter R)
Crew:	2. Trainees: 8-13
Contact:	Les Bolton, Executive Director
	Grays Harbor Historical Seaport
	PO Box 2019
	Aberdeen, WA 98520
	Tel: 800-200-LADY (5239); Fax: 360-533-9384
	E-mail: ghhsa@techline.com
	Web site: http://www.histseaport.org

Hibiscus

Polynesian multi-hull ships were among the earliest long distance travelers. A catamaran experience is unique and one of the longest-standing ways to sail the seas. The catamaran is stable and provides a more comfortable platform to learn sail handling skills. Captain Larry and First Mate Nikki White share their experiences-traveling the Southeast Pacific, the US Pacific Coast and the Caribbean including extensive knowledge of the Bahamas. Each summer is spent training the Boy Scouts of America in their High Seas Adventure in the Abacos.

Flag:	USA
Rig:	Sloop
Homeport/waters:	Miami, Florida: Bahamas and Caribbean cruising areas.
Season:	Year-round
Who sails?	Families and individuals of all ages. Affiliated groups include the Boy Scouts of America.
Program type:	Sail training for paying trainees. Bareboat certification, corporate team building & charters. Day sailing for groups, overnight 3 queen berths and room for 6 on deck under the stars.
Cost:	$80-$150 per person per day. Group rates available.

Specifications:		
LOA: 39'	Draft: 3'8"	Sail area: 1,180 sq. ft.
LWL: 36'	Beam: 21'	Rig height: 59"
Power: 54 HP diesel	Freeboard: 6'	Hull: fiberglass

Designer:	Phillip Jeantot
Built:	1990
Coast Guard certification:	Uninspected Vessel
Contact:	Larry K. White, Captain
	8305 SW 39th Street
	Miami, FL 33155
	Tel: 305-793-4487; Fax: 242-367-2033
	E-mail: whibiscus@oii.net

Highlander Sea

programs have been created to provide marine career awareness training for high school and college students.

The crew consists of six professionals, accompanied by 9-12 deck cadets. Some cadets have already been trained at various nautical institutions, others are looking to gain some sea experience before committing to gaining the education required to start a career in this industry. The goal of this program is to seek out and prepare cadets who are suitable for work offshore. Serving as a cadet on the *Highlander Sea* acts as an extended interview for the Human Resources Department and allows them to evaluate his or her seafaring skills and adaptability to the offshore. It also allows cadets who have already begun their training to earn valuable sea time, thus helping them to progress with their career.

Highlander Sea was welcomed to the Secunda fleet in 1998. Along with being an ambassador for Secunda Marine Services, Ltd., she is used primarily as a sail training vessel. Various

Flag:	Canada
Rig:	Grand Banks topsail schooner
Homeport/waters:	Halifax, Nova Scotia, Canada: Eastern Seaboard including Atlantic Provinces (summer), Caribbean (winter)
Who sails?	High school and college students, individuals of all ages, and marine institute students.
Season:	Year-round
Program type:	Sail training for volunteer trainees. Informal, in-house sea education. Dockside interpretation during port visits and in homeport.

Specifications:			
	Sparred length: 154'	Draft: 14'	Sail area: 10,000 sq. ft.
	LOD: 124'	Beam: 25' 8"	Tons: 140 GRT
	LOA: 126'	Rig height: 109'	Power: twin 380 HP
	LWL: 116'	Hull: wood	
	Power: twin 400 HP	Hull color: black	Spar material: douglas fir

Designer:	Sterling Burgess
Built:	1924; Essex, Massachusetts, F.W. James & Son
Certification:	Canadian Coast Guard certified
Crew:	6. **Trainees:** 12-14
Contact:	Sean Leet, Marketing
	Secunda Marine Services, Ltd.
	1 Canal Street
	Dartmouth, Nova Scotia B2Y 2W1 Canada
	Tel: 902-465-3400; Fax: 902-463-7678
	E-mail: stevew@secunda.com
	Web site: http://www.secunda.com

Hindu

Hindu was designed by William Hand, Jr. and built as a private yacht in 1925 in East Boothbay, Maine, by the Hodgdon Brothers. She is a 79-foot wooden vessel designed as a half-scale model of a 19th-century Grand Banks fishing schooner. In her long career she has been a private yacht, a cargo ship transporting spice from India, and as a US Navy U-boat tracker in World War II on the Eastern Seaboard. *Hindu* has also participated in many blue water races, including two of the Newport-Bermuda classics.

Hindu is Coast Guard inspected for coastwise navigation, carrying 49 passengers overnight. She is privately owned and available for charter. In the past, *Hindu* has called on such ports as Bermuda; Port Antonio, Jamaica; Grand Cayman; Havana, Cuba; Porta Plata, Dominican Republic; and Key West, Florida. *Hindu* has been conducting

two-hour day sails out of Provincetown, Massachusetts for over fifty years.

Flag:	USA
Rig:	Gaff schooner
Homeport/waters:	Provincetown, Massachusetts: Provincetown, Massachusetts (summer), Caribbean (winter)
Who sails?	Elementary and middle school students, and individuals of all ages.
Season:	Year-round
Cost:	$60 per person per day, $1,500 group rate per day
Program type:	Sail training for paying trainees. Sea education as informal, in-house programming.

Specifications:			
	Sparred length: 73'	Draft: 9'	Sail area: 2,500 sq. ft.
	LOD: 61' 3"	Beam: 15'	Tons: 29 GRT
	LOA: 64'	Rig height: 60'	Power: 90 HP diesel
	LWL: 47'	Freeboard: 4'	Hull: wood

Designer:	William Hand, Jr.
Built:	1925; Boothbay Harbor, Maine, Hodgdon Brothers
Coast Guard certification:	Passenger Vessel (Subchapter T)
Crew:	3. **Trainees/passengers:** 49 (day sails), 6 (overnight)
Contact:	John Bennett, President
	Hindu of Provincetown, Inc.,
	333R Commercial Street
	Provincetown, MA 02657
	Tel: 508-487-3000
	E-mail: jbennett1@capecod.net
	Web site: http://www.schoonerhindu.com

Hjørdis

The schooner *Hjørdis* was acquired for the Freshwater Studies at North House Folk School in 1997. This gaff-rigged vessel serves as an educational platform for youth, college groups, and the general public. With the *Hjørdis*, North House seeks to apply its unique and skills-based philosophy to a program based in the physical, biological, cultural, and historical elements of Lake Superior. Coursework on the *Hjørdis* focuses on nautical science, maritime history, limnology, environmental stud-

ies, and personal growth. North House Folk School's Freshwater Studies offers two-hour, half-day, and multi-day programs from Grand Marais Harbor to the near coastal waters and as far as Grand Portage National Monument and Isle Royal National Park. Each sail is limited to six trainees, with two crewmembers affording each personal attention and experiences.

Special programs include The Craft of Sail, The Great Lakes Schooner Trade, Navigation and Weather Studies, and two teacher programs; Experiential Lake Studies for Teachers, and Ten-Day Experiential Lake Studies for Teachers and Wilderness Education Experience. Fall Color Tours give participants the opportunity to experience the spectacular nature of the North Shore of Lake Superior as it changes from the green of summer to the reds, oranges, and yellows of autumn from offshore.

Flag:	USA
Rig:	Gaff schooner, two-masted
Homeport/waters:	Grand Marais, Minnesota
Who sails?	Students of all ages, individuals, and groups.
Program type:	Sail training for paying trainees. Sea education in nautical science and maritime history.

Specifications:	Sparred length: 50'	Draft: 3' 10'	Sail area: 1,100 sq. ft.
	LOD: 42' 2"	Beam: 11' 4"	
	LOA: 42' 2"	Rig height: 42'	Power: 36 HP diesel
	LWL: 33'	Hull: steel	

Designer:	Thomas Colvin
Built:	1978; Mt. Clement, Michigan, Kenneth R. Woodward
Coast Guard certification:	Uninspected Vessel
Contact:	Captain Matthew Brown or Peter Barsness, Curriculum Director
	North House Folk School/Freshwater Studies
	PO Box 759
	Grand Marais, MN 55612
	Tel: 218-387-9762 (office), 218-370-0675 (vessel); Fax: 218-387-9760
	E-mail: info@northhouse.org
	Web site: http://www.northhouse.org

H. M. Krentz

One of the last skipjacks to be built, and still commercially dredging oysters during the winter months (November – March), the *H. M. Krentz* offers day sails on the Chesapeake's Eastern Shore waters near St. Michaels, Maryland from April through October.

Get the feel of a true working vessel and learn about the history of the working fleet of sailing vessels on the Chesapeake Bay. Experience dragging for oysters, and then explore the ecology and economic development of the Chesapeake region through discussing the past and present status of this once abundant natural resource.

What we can learn about ourselves and about our surrounding world through sailing is what makes the present the greatest age of sail. By working with the technologies and traditions of the past, perhaps we can have a better vision for the future. Since 1972, Captain Ed Farley has been a commercial oysterman

and has worked to preserve several of the working skipjacks; since 1985, he has been sharing his life experience with school children, business leaders, politicians and family groups.

Flag:	USA
Rig:	Skipjack/sloop
Homeport/waters:	Potomac River, Maryland; Chesapeake Bay
Season:	Mid-April to late October
Who sails?	School groups from elementary through college as well as families and individuals of all ages.
Program type:	Sail training for professional and volunteer crew/trainees. Sea education in marine science, maritime history and ecology as informal in-house programming. Dockside interpretation while in port.
Cost:	$30 per person per 2-hour day sail ($15 children under 12)
	$400 per school group (3-hour day sail), Group rate: $25 per person per 2-hr day sail (12 person minimum)

Specifications:			
	Sparred length: 70'	Draft: 4'8"	Sail area: 1,850 sq. ft.
	LOD: 48'	Beam: 16'	Tons: 8 GRT
	LOA: 54'	Rig height: 65'	Hull: wood
	LWL: 45'	Hull color: white	Spar material: wood
	Power: 150 HP diesel; yawl boat		

Designer:	Krentz/Skipjack
Built:	1955; Harryhogan, Virginia, Herman M. Krentz
Coast Guard certification:	Passenger Vessel (Subchapter T)
Crew:	1 Passengers/trainees: 32 (day sails)
Contact:	Captain Ed Farley
	Chesapeake Skipjack Sailing Tours, LLC
	PO Box 582
	St. Michaels, MD 21663
	Tel: 410-745-6080
	E-mail: hmkrentz@bluecrab.org
	Web site: http://www.oystercatcher.com

Howard Blackburn

Howard Blackburn is a fine example of a classic John G. Alden design. Built in 1951 in Cristobal, Panama, her hull design and construction are reminiscent of the fishing vessels that sailed from New England in the 1900s. She is a very able and seaworthy vessel. Originally built as a private yacht, *Howard Blackburn* also spent some time in the charter trade, sailing in waters from South America to New England. She also did some campaigns for the Greenpeace organization.

In 1995 Mark Roesner and Terry Westhead took ownership and brought her to the Chesapeake Bay area. Mark and Terry both have years of experience sailing and teaching aboard sail training vessels. *Howard Blackburn* can take up to six trainees on day and overnight trips. During the summer camp program, youths between the ages of 13-18 come aboard to learn all aspects of seamanship, marine science, and ecology of the Chesapeake Bay. The vessel is also available for individual, family, and group charters.

Flag:	USA
Rig:	Ketch
Homeport/waters:	Baltimore, Maryland: Chesapeake Bay, New England
Who sails?	Students from elementary school through college, individuals, and families.
Cost:	$100 per person per day
Program type:	Sail training for volunteer and paying trainees. Informal, in-house sea education in marine science and ecology.

Specifications:	Sparred length: 58'	Draft: 6' 6"	Sail area: 1,100 sq. ft.
	LOD: 45'	Beam: 14'	Tons: 22'
	LOA: 58'	Rig height: 57'	Power: 80 HP diesel
	LWL: 36' 6"	Freeboard: 4'	Hull: wood

Designer:	John G. Alden
Built:	1951; Cristobal, Panama Canal Zone
Crew:	1. **Trainees:** 6
Contact:	Captain Mark Roesner, Owner
	925 Bowleys Quarters Road
	Baltimore, MD 21220
	Tel/Fax: 410-335-7357
	E-mail: 4roesner@msn.com
	Web site: http://www.maritime_charters.com

Hurricane (#1-22)

Hurricane Island Outward Bound® School

For 35 years The Hurricane Island Outward Bound School's sailing expeditions aboard unique 30-foot ketch-rigged pulling boats modeled after traditional whaling vessels have challenged both novice and seasoned sailors. Students experience open-ocean adventure and island living sailing the coast of Maine, one of the world's greatest cruising grounds. Nearly 3,000 islands and 3,500 miles of shoreline make this one of the last intact coastal wildernesses in America. As trainees navigate rugged shores they rotate responsibilities, learning sail handling, navigation, and boat handling.

Founded in 1964, the Hurricane Island Outward Bound School is the largest Outward Bound School in the United States. From its headquarters in Rockland, Maine, the school operates in 14 locations stretching from Maine through Maryland and Philadelphia, all the way to the Florida Keys. The school is a nonprofit educational organization

whose mission is to conduct safe, adventure-based courses structured to encourage growth and discovery, and to inspire confidence, self-reliance, concern for others, and care for the environment.

By combining the school's mission with Outward Bound's motto, "To serve, to strive, and not to yield," the school hopes to better society by providing people with positive experiences that can change their outlook, their attitudes, and their lives.

HURRICANE ISLAND OUTWARD BOUND® SCHOOL

Flag:	USA
Rig:	Ketch-rigged pulling boat
Waters:	Maine Coast, Chesapeake Bay, and Florida Keys.
Who sails?	Students and individuals (age 14+, coed), corporations, educational, and civic organizations.
Program type:	Sail training and seamanship taught to impel students into confidence-building, life-enhancing experiences.

Specifications:	LOA: 30'	Draft: 18"	Sail area: 366 sq. ft.
	LWL: 28'	Beam: 8'	Freeboard: 2'
	Rig height: 20'	Hull: wood	

Designer:	Cyrus Hamlin, Kennebunk, Maine
Built:	1965-1988; Maine Coast and Maryland
Crew:	2. **Trainees:** up to 13
Contact:	Admissions/Hurricane Island Outward Bound School
	75 Mechanic Street
	Rockland, ME 04841
	Tel: 800-341-1744; Fax: 207-594-8202
	E-mail: admissions@hurricaneisland.org
	Web site: http://www.hurricaneisland.org

Idea Due

Launched in 1986, *Idea Due* is a custom-built schooner able to accommodate 12 passengers for overnight voyages and 25 for day sails. The design guarantees a high level of safety and comfort. *Idea Due* is operated by a specialized company as a school and charter vessel in the Mediterranean Sea. She participated in the 1992 Columbus Regatta and other international events. Fully certified by R.I.Na. (Registro Italiano Navale), *Idea Due* has been mentioned in the official publication for the celebration of "A Hundred Years of Lega Navale Italiana".

Flag:	Italy
Rig:	Schooner
Homeport/waters:	Otrano, Italy: Mediterranean Sea
Who sails?	High school and college students, individuals of all ages, and families.
Cost:	$1,000 - $1,500 group rate per day
Program type:	Sail training for volunteer crew and trainees. Sea education in marine science and ecology in cooperation with accredited institutions. Dockside interpretation while in homeport.

Specifications:			
	Sparred length: 78'	Draft: 10'	Sail area: 4,130 sq. ft.
	LOD: 73'	Beam: 15'	Tons: 49 GRT
	LOA: 75'	Rig height: 85'	Power: twin 145 HP
	LWL: 63'	Freeboard: 6'	Hull: steel

Designer:	Stefano Rossi
Built:	1986; Fano (Pesaro), Italy, Bugari
Certification:	R.I.Na. (Registro Italiano Navale)
Crew:	4. **Trainees/passengers:** 12
Contact:	Captain Pantaleo Coluccia
	Otranto Navigazione s.a.s.,
	Via G. Galilei, n. 2
	Casamassella, Lecce 73020, Italy
	Tel/Fax: 39-337-701451

Imagine...!

The 76-foot schooner *Imagine...!* was built and put into service in 1997 to provide high quality leadership and team performance training programs to corporate executives and managers. Using two to five-day cruises, clients are challenged with a variety of "dock to destination" exercises, where their success is contingent upon operating individually as effective leaders and collectively as an efficient team. Ultimately the participants are expected to master the skills necessary to safely operate the vessel from point to point, using one another as resources. Facilitated debriefing sessions by professional corporate trainers transfer the experience from the "boat to the boardroom."

Imagine...! also operates educational sails for school groups, adjudicated youth, special need students, and other young people. These programs provide a wide spectrum of learning experiences, ranging from pure science-based curriculum to a full-fledged sail training offering. Cruises range from several hours to several days in duration.

Imagine...! operates primarily in the Baltimore/Annapolis, Maryland area, but throughout a March-November season travels as far north as Philadelphia, Pennsylvania and as far south as Norfolk, Virginia.

Flag:	USA
Rig:	Gaff schooner
Homeport/waters:	Annapolis, Maryland: Chesapeake Bay, eastern US
Who sails?	School groups, individuals, and corporate groups.
Program type:	Sail training for paying trainees. Corporate team building.

Specifications:	LOD: 65'	Draft: 7' 9"	Sail area: 1,900 sq. ft.
	LOA: 76'	Beam: 16'	Power: twin 50 HP diesels
	LWL: 55'	Hull: cedar	

Built:	1997; Port of Albany, New York, Scarano Boat Building
Coast Guard certification:	Passenger Vessel (Subchapter T)
Contact:	Captain Michael Bagley
	Imagine Yacht, LLC
	PO Box 1469
	Annapolis, MD 21404
	Tel: 410-626-0900 or 888-252-6639
	E-mail: Captimagin@aol.com
	Web site: http://www.schoonerimagine.com

Inland Seas

hulled with detailing similar to traditional tall ships. The vessel is equipped with scientific gear for studying the Great Lakes ecosystem. ISEA's popular Schoolship Program, which began in 1989, offers half-day Great Lakes educational opportunities for students aboard *Inland Seas* and chartered schooners *Westwind* and *Manitou*. A variety of summer shipboard programs are offered for students and adults aboard *Inland Seas*, all of which foster an appreciation for and a commitment to the natural and cultural heritage of the Great Lakes.

The Inland Seas Education Association's schooner *Inland Seas* was launched in 1994 to be a hands-on laboratory for students to learn about the Great Lakes. The schooner is steel

Flag:	USA
Rig:	Gaff schooner, two-masted
Homeport/waters:	Suttons Bay, Michigan: Grand Traverse Bay, Lake Michigan
Who sails?	School groups and individuals of all ages.
Season:	May through early October.
Program type:	Sail training for volunteer and paying trainees. Sea education in marine science, maritime history, and ecology for students from elementary school through college, adults, and at-risk-youth. Dockside interpretation during port visits.

Specifications:

Sparred length: 77'	Draft: 7'	Sail area: 1,800 sq. ft.
LOD: 61' 6"	Beam: 17'	Tons: 41 GRT
LWL: 53'	Rig height: 66'	Power: 130 HP
Freeboard: 4'	Hull: steel	

Designer:	Charles W. Wittholz, Woodin & Marean
Built:	1994; Palm Coast, Florida, Treworgy Yachts
Coast Guard certification:	Passenger Vessel (Subchapter T)
Crew:	5. **Trainees:** 30 (day sails), 11 (overnight), 5 (volunteer instruction)
Contact:	Thomas M. Kelly, Executive Director
	Inland Seas Education Association
	PO Box 218
	Suttons Bay, MI 49682
	Tel: 231-271-3077; Fax: 231-271-3088
	E-mail: isea@traverse.com
	Web site: http://www.schoolship.org

Internet Explorer

(Work in Progress)

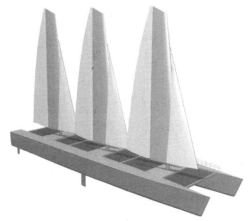

The aircraft industry makes giant wings of over 2,600 square feet that must be retired after 18,000 flights. These used 747 wings will become the wing-masts of the 270-foot aluminum catamaran, *Internet Explorer*. Using industrial crane bearings to support and rotate the wings, a highly engineered and reliable mechanism will be built. A vessel of this size and the weight will make a very impressive package indeed—the naval architects have indicated that the vessel is capable of reaching speeds of 40 knots in 20 knots of wind.

A ferry boat with these hulls could carry more than 150 cars and 800 passengers at 50 knots, so how fast is this wing ship capable of going, and perhaps more importantly, what is she capable of being? This question is why Aeronautics joined ASTA. These hulls are capable of so much more than speed records—they can be classrooms and research labs. Aeronautics plans to use *Internet Explorer* as a sail training vessel, carrying 150 trainees and 50 faculty. The vessel will be 270 feet long, 74 feet wide, and have as much as 19,980 square feet of deck space.

Flag:	USA
Rig:	Schooner, three-masted
Waters:	Worldwide
Who sails?	College students and other groups.
Program type:	Sail training for paying trainees. Sea education in marine science and ecology. Passenger sails overnight. Dockside interpretation during port visits.
Specifications:	Sparred length: 270' Draft: 3' (hull), 18' (centerboard)
	Sail area: 15,000 sq. ft. (upwind), 48,000 sq. ft. (downwind)
	LOD: 270' Beam: 72'
	LOA: 270' Rig height: 136'
	LWL: 244' Freeboard: 21' Hull: aluminum
Designer:	Aeronautics, LLC
Crew:	10. **Trainees:** 150
Contact:	Brad Cavanagh, Project Manager
	Aeronautics
	195 West Long Pond Rd.
	Plymouth, MA 02360
	Tel/Fax: 508-224-9416
	E-mail: b.s.c@worldnet.att.net

Intrepid

The incomparable two-time America's Cup winner *Intrepid* is close to the hearts of all sailors. Designed by Sparkman and Stephens and built by Minneford's in City Island, New York in 1967, *Intrepid* represents a tremendous breakthrough in twelve-meter design. She was the first twelve to separate the rudder from the keel, include a "bustle" or "kicker" and use a trim tab. *Intrepid*'s underbody type, with relatively minor refinements, was used on every subsequent Cup boat until *Australia II*'s winged keel of 1983.

After 32 years of hard sailing she has been rebuilt to "as new" condition. America's Cup Charters' George Hill and Herb Marshal worked with Sparkman and Stephens, Brewer's Cove Haven Marina, and master shipwright Louis Sauzedde to restore this landmark yacht. *Intrepid* proudly joins the twelve-meter fleet at America's Cup Charters, offering leisure sails, racing, and corporate team building charters from any port between Maine and the Chesapeake.

Flag:	USA
Rig:	Sloop
Homeport/waters:	Newport, Rhode Island: New England and Chesapeake Bay
Who sails?	Individuals of all ages
Cost:	$1,800 group rate per day, $60 per person for evening sails.
Program type:	Sail training for volunteer or paying trainees. Sea education based on informal, in-house programming. Passenger day sails.

Specifications:	Sparred length: 69'	Draft: 9'	Sail area: 1,850 sq. ft.
	LOD: 65'	Beam: 12'	Tons: 28 GRT
	LOA: 65'	Rig height: 90'	Power: diesel
	LWL: 46'	Hull: wood	

Designer:	Sparkman and Stephens
Built:	1967; City Island, New York, Minneford
Coast Guard certification:	Passenger Vessel (Subchapter T)
Crew:	3. **Trainees/passengers:** 12
Contact:	George Hill/Herb Marshall America's Cup Charters, PO Box 51 Newport, RI 02840 Tel: 401-849-5868; Fax: 401-849-3098 Web site: http://www.americascupcharters.com

Irving Johnson
(Work in Progress)

The Los Angeles Maritime Institute is building two 90-foot brigantines to be named *Irving Johnson* and *Exy Johnson* in honor of the Johnsons and their life-long commitments to character-building sail training.

Irving McClure Johnson began training for a sailor's life as a teenager. In 1929 he sailed around Cape Horn on the four-masted barque *Peking*, a voyage he documented in a film entitled "Around Cape Horn."

Captain Johnson met Electa on his next voyage aboard the *Wander Bird*. The Johnsons sailed around the world seven times in two different *Yankees* and cruised European and African waters in their third *Yankee*, a ketch, sharing their skill and knowledge of the sea with a hand-picked crew generally composed of four young women, 16 young men, a doctor, a cook, and a mate.

Construction is taking place at the

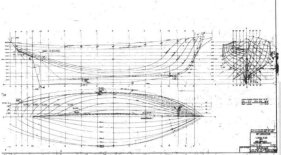

Los Angeles Maritime Museum in John Gibson Park, San Pedro. The brigantine design, based on one developed in the 1930's, has been adapted by W.I.B. Crealock to meet US Coast Guard and LAMI program requirements.

The shipyard is visitor friendly, set up as a living history exhibit of the museum. Construction is carried out by professional, paid shipwrights, working with trained volunteers. Funding for this project will come from private donations, corporate sponsorships, and foundation grants.

IRVING JOHNSON

Flag:	USA		
Rig:	Brigantine		
Homeport/waters:	Los Angeles, California: Southern California and offshore islands		
Who sails?	Referred youth-at-risk and groups catering to students and adults.		
Season:	Year-round		
Cost:	Based on ability to pay		
Program type:	Educational sailing adventures for youth and adult groups.		
Specifications:	Sparred length: 110' 8"	Draft: 11'	Sail area: 4,540 sq. ft.
	LOA: 90'	Beam: 21' 9"	Tons: 99 GRT
	LWL: 72' 6"	Rig height: 87' 8"	Power: diesel
Coast Guard certification:	Sailing School Vessel (Subchapter R), Passenger Vessel (Subchapter T)		
Contact:	Captain Jim Gladson, President		
	Los Angeles Maritime Institute		
	Berth 84, Foot of Sixth Street		
	San Pedro, CA 90731		
	Tel: 310-833-6055; Fax: 310-548-2055		

Isaac H. Evans

The schooner *Isaac H. Evans*, designated a National Historic Landmark, was built in 1886, in the era when oystering was the biggest fishing industry in the country. She spent many years on the Delaware Bay, fishing and freighting. In 1973, she was completely rebuilt to suit her for her new trade of carrying passengers on 3, 4, and 6-day cruises in mid-coast Maine.

Her captain and crew (first mate, cook, and deck hand) provide hands-on training to eager passengers from late May through early October. She has a shallow draft for ghosting alongside Maine's granite islands. There is no engine on board, although a yawl boat is carried for windless days. The minimum age for passengers is six, and youngsters are encouraged to get involved in all aspects of running the vessel.

From the deck hand working toward a captain's license, to armchair sailors on vacation, to wide-eyed youth experiencing a turn at the helm, the *Isaac H. Evans* continues to provide historic maritime experiences.

Flag:	USA
Rig:	Gaff topsail schooner, two-masted
Homeport/waters:	Rockland, Maine: Penobscot Bay and surrounding area.
Season:	May to October
Who sails?	Families and individuals ages 6 and older.
Program type:	Sail training for paying trainees.
Cost:	$125 per person per day, $390-$780 (3, 4, and six day trips)

Specifications:			
	Sparred length: 99'	LOD: 65'	LOA: 65'
	LWL: 52'	Draft: 6'	Beam: 20'
	Tons: 53 GRT	Rig height: 82'	Sail area: 2,600 sq. ft.
	Hull: wood	Hull color: white	Spar material: wood
	Freeboard: 4'		

Builder:	1886; Mauricetown, New Jersey, George Vannaman
Coast Guard certification:	Passenger Vessel (Subchapter T)
Crew:	4. **Trainees/passengers:** 46 (day sails), 26 (overnight)
Contact:	Brenda Grace Walker, Captain/Owner
	PO Box 791
	Rockland, ME 04841
	Tel: 207-594-7956
	E-mail: evans@midcoast.com
	Web site: http://www.midcoast.com/evans

Isabelle

Isabelle is a classic yacht built and designed in 1924 by the renowned William Fife. Her construction is teak over sawn-oak frames. *Isabelle* is a beautiful reminder of the glamour and romance of the "Golden Age" of yachting.

Isabelle has recently been sold to Fife Holdings LLC and her name has been changed back to her original Adventuress. She is currently undergoing a complete refit and plans are to have her ready and available for charter in New England this summer.

Flag:	USA		
Rig:	Ketch		
Specifications:	Sparred length: 83'	Draft: 10' 5"	Sail area: 3,000 sq. ft.
	LOD: 83'	Beam: 18'	Tons: 96 GRT
	LOA: 83'	Rig height: 105'	Hull: wood
	LWL: 65'	Freeboard: 4'	
Designer:	William Fife & Sons		
Built:	1924; Scotland, William Fife		
Coast Guard certification:	Passenger Vessel (Subchapter T)		
Contact:	James Lynch, President		
	Fife Holdings LLC		
	23 West Shore Drive		
	Old Saybrook, CT 06475		
	Tel: 917-991-2386		

Jeanie Johnston

Over the past 3 years, a full size replica of the famous Irish immigrant ship, *Jeanie Johnston* (1847-58), has been under construction at Blennerville, Tralee, County Kerry, Ireland.

The timber hulled *Jeanie Johnston* is due for completion early in 2001. Following sea-trials, she will set sail in the spring of 2001 on an historic North American voyage, visiting several ports in the United States and Canada. At each port the ship will be open to the public and the 'tween deck will recreate life on board an Irish immigrant ship of the 19th century. Under sail, the vessel will offer opportunities to individuals and groups for sail training on both the transatlantic crossings and the inter-city legs of the voyage.

The original *Jeanie Johnston* was built in Quebec. On over 16 transatlantic voyages she carried thousands of Irish immigrants to America and Canada. Unlike the infamous "Coffin-Ships" of the time, the *Jeanie Johnston* never lost a passenger or crewmember to disease or to the sea.

Young people from Ireland North and South have worked side-by-side with skilled shipwrights to build the *Jeanie Johnston*. A further 70 young trainees will help sail the ship throughout her North American voyage.

Flag:	Ireland
Rig:	Barque
Program type:	Sail training for volunteer and paying crew/trainees. Dockside interpretation during port visits.

Specifications:			
	Sparred length: 148'	LOD: 123'	LOA: 123'
	Rig height: 94'	Beam: 26'3"	Draft: 14'
	Sail area: 6,490 sq. ft.	Tons: 450 GRT	Freeboard: 6'
	Hull: wood	Spar material: wood	Hull color: black
	Power: 2/280 HP	Sail number: 18	

Designer:	Fred Walker
Built:	2000; Blennerville Shipyard, Tralee, County Kerry, Ireland, Jeanie Johnston Co.
Certification:	Department of Ireland Marine Sail Training Vessel
Crew:	11. Trainees: 29
Contact:	Ann Martin, Marketing Executive
	The Jeanie Johnston Project
	Blennerville Shipyard
	Blennerville, Tralee, County Kerry, Ireland
	Tel: +353-66-7129999; Fax: +353-66-7181888
	Web site: http://www.jeaniejohnston.com

John E. Pfriem

The *John E. Pfriem* is a classic Chesapeake Bay bugeye ketch design built in Gloucester, Massachusetts in 1964. She operates as a marine environmental education vessel sailing the waters of Long Island Sound from April through November.

Flag:	USA
Rig:	Chesapeake Bay bugeye ketch
Homeport/waters:	Bridgeport, Connecticut: Long Island Sound
Who sails?	Affiliated institutions include the University of Bridgeport, Housatonic Community College, and seven Connecticut school districts.
Season:	April to November
Program type:	Sail training for crew and apprentices. Sea education in marine science and ecology in cooperation with accredited institutions. Dockside interpretation.

Specifications:

Sparred length: 65'	Draft: 3'	Sail area: 1,200 sq. ft.
LOA: 55'	Beam: 14' 6"	Tons: 14 GRT
LWL: 47'	Rig height: 49'	Hull: wood
Freeboard: 2' 6"		

Designer:	Russell Grinnell
Built:	1964; Gloucester, Massachusetts, Russell Grinnell
Coast Guard certification:	Research Vessel (Subchapter U)
Crew:	2-3. **Trainees:** 22
Contact:	Edwin T. Merritt, Executive Director
	The Aquaculture Foundation
	525 Antelope Trail
	Shelton, CT 06484
	Tel: 203-372-4406; Fax: 203-372-4407
	E-mail: tmerritt@pcnet.com
	Web site: http://www.tallshipblackpearl.org

Jolie Brise

1930. In 1932 she rescued thirty crew from the American yacht *Adriana*, which had caught fire during the Bermuda Race, earning her the Blue Water Medal. *Jolie Brise* was also the last vessel to carry the Royal Mail under sail.

Jolie Brise sails with up to ten trainees, aged 13 and up, throughout northern Europe, with a different program each summer. In the year 2000 she came to Bermuda, Boston and Halifax as part of Tall Ships 2000®, then sailed back across the Atlantic to Amsterdam. Traditionally rigged, sailing her is very much a hands-on experience, requiring everyone to be involved. The atmosphere is very friendly, informal, and relaxed.

Dauntsey's School Sailing Club was established in the mid-1970s by the boys and girls at Dauntsey's School. The Sailing Club operates *Jolie Brise*, a 1913 Le Havre Pilot Cutter in conjunction with the Exeter Maritime Museum. *Jolie Brise* became famous in 1925 when she won the first ever Fastnet Race. She again won the Fastnet Race in 1929 and

Flag:	UK
Rig:	Cutter
Homeport/waters:	Southampton, England: Northern Hemisphere, British South Coast
Who sails?	School groups from high school through college, as well as individuals of all ages.
Program type:	Sail training for volunteer and paying trainees. Dockside interpretation during port visits.

Specifications:	Sparred length: 76'	Draft: 11'	Sail area: 3,750 sq. ft.
	LOD: 56'	Beam: 15'	Tons: 44 GRT
	LOA: 60'	Rig height: 77'	Power: 60 HP
	LWL: 50'	Freeboard: 4'	Hull: oak

Designer:	Paumelle
Built:	1913; LeHavre, France, Paumelle
Certification:	British MCA Cat. '0' - Sail Training
Crew:	3. **Trainees:** 15 (day sails), 10 (overnight)
Contact:	Captain T.R. Marris, Head of Sailing
	Dauntsey's School Sailing Club
	West Lavington, Near Devizes
	Wiltshire, SN10 4HE, United Kingdom
	Tel: 44-1380-818-216; Fax: 44-1380-818-216
	E-mail: marrist@dauntsey's.wilts.sch.uk

Joseph Conrad

For over 50 years young people have come to Mystic Seaport, our nation's leading maritime museum, to learn to sail and live on board the tall ship *Joseph Conrad*. Each morning, campers tackle the wind and current of the Mystic River and then set off for an active afternoon investigating the Museum's unique exhibitions. After a late-day sailing session, some "R and R" and dinner, campers spend their evenings with new friends, stargazing in a planetarium, climbing the rigging of the *Conrad* or enjoying a lively sea music sing-a-long.

The *Joseph Conrad* program is open to individual boys and girls and organized groups ages 10 through 15. Groups must have one adult leader per 10 participants. No prior experience is required for beginner sessions, only a desire to participate and learn. Intermediate sessions are for those who have attended a previous beginner session or have had sailing experience. All must hold current Red Cross swimmers certification or its equivalent.

PHOTO BY RUSSELL A. FOWLER

JOSEPH CONRAD

Flag:	USA
Rig:	Ship, three-masted
Homeport:	Mystic, Connecticut
Who sails?	Individuals and organized groups ages 10 through 15.
Season:	June through August
Cost:	$525 per person per six-day program
Program type:	Sail training. Dockside visitation for school groups and individuals.
Specifications:	Sparred length: 118' 6" Draft: 12' Tons: 213 GRT
	LOA: 100' 8" Beam: 25' 3" Hull: iron
	Rig height: 98' 6"
Designer:	Burmeister and Wain
Built:	1882; Copenhagen, Denmark, Burmeister & Wain
Trainees:	32-50
Contact:	Museum Education Department
	Mystic Seaport
	PO Box 6000
	Mystic, CT 06355-0990
	Tel: 860-572-0711; Fax: 860 572-5395
	Web site: http://www.mysticseaport.org/sailing

Ka'iulani

and lots of varnish and polished bronze in her cabins and state-rooms. Originally launched in 1984 as a private family yacht, she has sailed over 60,000 ocean miles under the command of her original captain.

In conjunction with the non-profit Coloma Outdoor Discovery School, *Ka'iulani* offers sail training programs for grades 4 through 12. These half-day programs may combine a visit to the neighboring Bay Model, operated by the Army Corps of Engineers, or a visit to the nearby Marine Mammal Center.

Ka'iulani is a modern luxury replica of an 1850s Pacific Coast gaff topsail schooner. Designed for long distance, deep ocean cruising and to sail around Cape Horn in the greatest safety and comfort, she was deliberately overbuilt to the highest possible standards. *Ka'iulani* features a mahogany hull, traditional teak decks, rig, and hardware,

Ka'iulani is also available for a wide variety of corporate and private adventures and celebrations, and ticketed Sunday morning cruises. Weddings are performed on board by the captain. Catering and beverage packages are also available.

Flag:	USA
Rig:	Gaff topsail schooner
Homeport/waters:	Sausalito, California: San Francisco Bay
Who sails?	School groups from middle school through high school. Affiliated with the Coloma Outdoor Discovery School.
Cost:	$45 per person for three-hour sail; $425 group rate per hour
Program type:	Sail training for paying trainees. Sea education as informal, in-house programming. Passenger day sails.

Specifications:			
	Sparred length: 86'	Draft: 7' 6"	Sail area: 1,436 sq. ft.
	LOD: 65'	Beam: 18'	Tons: 63 GRT
	LOA: 67'	Rig height: 75'	Power: GM 671 diesel
	LWL: 53'	Freeboard: 4'	Hull: mahogany

Designer:	W.I.B. Crealock
Built:	1984; San Diego, California, Coast
Coast Guard certification:	Passenger Vessel (Subchapter T)
Crew:	4. **Trainees:** 49 (day sails)
Contact:	Captain Robert Michaan, President
	Discovery Yacht Charters
	PO Box 1145
	Sausalito, CA 94966
	Tel: 415-331-1333; Fax: 415-331-6190
	E-mail: sail@sfyacht.com
	Web site: http://www.sfyacht.com

Kajama

Kajama is a 165' three-masted schooner built in Rendsburg, Germany in 1930. She was launched as *Wilfrid* and sailed under Captain Wilhelm Wilckens of Hamburg until 1960. The ship traded in general cargo throughout Europe and Scandinavia. In 1960 she was sold to Danish flag.

Her second owners, the Asmussens of Egernsund, Denmark renamed the vessel *Kajama* after members of the family. The Asmussens' ownership saw the ship's gradual transition to a motor vessel. In 1996 Captain Asmussen suffered a cardiac arrest while running down the Swedish coast, near Malmo. He was alone on watch and the vessel went ashore. The Asmussen family elected to leave the business and the ship was in and out of trade for the next two years. In November of 1998 she made her

last cargo voyage with a load of grain within Denmark. In January of 1999 she was purchased by Great Lakes Schooner Company and delivered to Toronto. After an intensive ten-and-a-half month refit, the ship was re-launched as a near-perfect image of her original form. Sailing from her berth at Harbourfront she makes educational trips for students, day sails for the general public, and corporate charters.

Flag:	Canada
Rig:	Gaff rig schooner, three-masted
Homeport/waters:	Toronto, Ontario, Canada: Lake Ontario
Who sails?	Individuals and groups of all ages. Kajama operates a day sail training program in conjunction with The Pier - Toronto's Waterfront Museum.
Season:	April to October
Program type:	Day sail training program, passenger voyages, corporate, charter, maritime events.

Specifications:			
	Sparred length: 165'	Draft: 9'	Sail area: 7000 sq. ft.
	LOD: 142'	Beam: 24'	Tons: 263 GRT
	Rig height: 100'	Hull: steel	Power: 400 HP
	Freeboard: 7'		

Designer:	Nobiskrug
Built:	1930; Rendsburg, Germany, Nobiskrug Shipyard
Certification:	Transport Canada Certified Passenger Vessel
Crew:	8. **Trainees/passengers:** 225 (day sails)
Contact:	Roger Nugent, President
	Great Lakes Schooner Company
	249 Queen's Quay West, Suite 111
	Toronto, Ontario M5J 2N5, Canada
	Tel: 416-260-6355; Fax: 416-260-6377
	E-mail: roger@greatlakesschooner.com
	Web site: http://www.greatlakesschooner.com

Kalaha

1975. Her cruising area is the Bahamas in the summer with the Sea Base program (Boy Scouts). Trainees learn sail handling, how to use ground tackle, prepare meals, and basic coastal navigation. *Kalaha* also travels to the Tortugas, Key West, and the Florida Keys. She day sails on the Gulf of Mexico and Pine Island Sound, and is available for charter for special events and overnight trips.

Designed by W.I.B. Crealock to be a world cruiser, the ketch *Kalaha* was built by the Westsail Corporation in

Flag:	USA
Rig:	Ketch
Homeport/waters:	Bokeelia, Florida: Bahamas (summer), Caribbean (winter)
Who sails?	Individuals and families of all ages. Affiliated groups include the Boy Scouts of America.
Season:	Year-round
Cost:	$80 per person per day, $480 group rate (charter)
Program type:	Sail training for paying trainees. Sea education in cooperation with Boy Scouts of America.

Specifications:			
	Sparred length: 47'	Draft: 6'	Sail area: 990 sq. ft.
	LOD: 42' 11"	Beam: 13'	Tons: 13 GRT
	LOA: 47'	Rig height: 56'	Power: 85 HP diesel
	LWL: 33' 4"	Freeboard: 6'	Hull: fiberglass

Designer:	W.I.B. Crealock
Built:	1975; California, Westsail
Coast Guard certification:	Uninspected Vessel
Crew:	1
Contact:	Captain Bill Misenheimer
	Pine Island Yacht Service
	11943 Oakland Dr.
	Bokeelia, FL 33922
	Tel/Fax: 941-283-7129

Kalmar Nyckel

The *Kalmar Nyckel* is a recreation of the first colonial Swedish settlement ship to arrive in America at what is now Wilmington, Delaware. Launched in the fall of 1997, commissioned in May 1998, and USCG-certified in June 2000, this ornately carved 17th century Dutch built pinnace sails seasonally, carrying out her mission of goodwill.

With the support of a colonial shipyard, Colonial History-Living TodayTM, *Kalmar Nyckel* transforms Delaware's history into hands-on educational opportunities for school children through adults. She provides economic development opportunities, tourism & convention development, corporate charters, public sails and statewide marketing initiatives on a national scale, fulfilling her role as Delaware's official tall ship ambassador. *Kalmar Nyckel* is quickly becoming a "film star", having participated in several films and documentaries.

The *Kalmar Nyckel* is manned by a professional captain, mates, engineer and volunteer crew. The vessel sails the Northern and Mid-Atlantic regions. She

is available for charter to school groups, corporations, and private parties both underway and dockside. Kalmar Nyckel FoundationTM is planning a trip to Europe in the near future to recreate her historical voyages and re-connect with her European heritage.

Flag:	USA
Rig:	Full-rigged ship
Homeport/waters:	Wilmington, Delaware: Mid-Atlantic
Who sails?	School groups from elementary through college, as well as individuals and families. Affiliated institutions include the Challenge Program.
Cost:	$40 per person per day sail, $7000 group rate per day
Program type:	Sail training for volunteer or paying trainees. Dockside interpretation during port visits.

Specifications:			
	Sparred length: 139'	Draft: 12' 2"	Sail area: 7,600 sq. ft.
	LOD: 93'	Beam: 24' 11"	Tons: 160 GRT
	LOA: 97' 4"	Rig height: 65'	Power: diesel
	LWL: 89' 2"	Freeboard: 8'	Hull: wood
	Rig height: 105'	Hull color: natural/colonial blue	
	Spar material: wood		

Designer:	Tom Gillmer
Built:	1997; Wilmington, Delaware, Allen C. Rawl
Coast Guard certification:	Passenger Vessel (Subchapter T)
Crew:	8. **Trainees/passengers:** 49 (day sails), 31 (overnight)
Contact:	Captain Robert C. Glover III, Executive Director
	Kalmar Nyckel Foundation™
	1124 East Seventh Street
	Wilmington, DE 19801
	Tel: 302-429-7447; Fax: 302-429-0350
	E-mail: execdir@kalnyc.org Web-site: http://www.kalnyc.org

Kaskelot

The flagship of the Square Sail fleet, *Kaskelot* is a three-masted barque and one of the largest remaining wooden ships in commission. Built by J. Ring Andersen in 1948 for the Royal

Greenland Trading Company, *Kaskelot* supplied the remote East Greenland coastal settlements. In the late 1960s *Kaskelot* then worked as a fisheries support vessel in The Faroes. Square Sail purchased her in 1981 and totally redesigned and re-rigged her to replicate the *Terra Nova*, returning to East Greenland to make a film about Captain Scott's ill-fated expedition to the South Pole.

All of Square Sail's ships are fully commissioned and work throughout the year. When not filming, they have a regular sailing program, giving people the chance to experience traditional square-rig sailing first-hand. These voyages typically run between four and seven days, and occasionally longer. They are either based from Square Sail's homeport of Charlestown, Cornwall, UK, or they work around the annual schedule offering voyages between the various ports.

Square Sail runs an annual course from February to October where trainees are given the opportunity to learn the skills associated with sailing these ships, and in addition to maintenance and shore-based instruction, they form part of the regular crew throughout the season.

Flag:	UK
Rig:	Barque, three-masted
Homeport/waters:	Charlestown, Cornwall, UK: UK and Europe
Who sails?	Individuals of all ages and families. Affiliated institutions include Falmouth Marine School and Cornwall College.
Cost:	$180 per person per day, $8,000 per day group rate (corporate charter)
Program type:	Sail training for professional crew and volunteer and paying trainees. Sea education in maritime history in cooperation with accredited institutions and as informal, in-house programming. Worldwide film work and corporate charters.

Specifications:			
Sparred length: 153'	Draft: 12'	Sail area: 9,500 sq. ft.
LOD: 120'	Beam: 28'	Tons: 226 GRT
LOA: 124'	Rig height: 105'	Power: 375 HP diesel
LWL: 115'	Freeboard: 9'	Hull: oak on oak

Built:	1948; Denmark, J. Ring Anderson
Certification:	Bureau Veritas and MCA Class VI certificate (UK)
Crew:	14. **Trainees/passengers:** 50 (day sails), 12 (overnight)
Contact:	Chris Wilson, Marketing Manager, Square Sail, Charlestown Harbour, St. Austell, Cornwall PL25 3NJ, United Kingdom Tel: 44-1720-67526; Fax: 44-1726-61839, E-mail: info@square-sail.com Web site: http://www.square-sail.com

Kathryn B.

A brand-new classic, the *Kathryn B.* is a rugged, ocean-going, steel-hulled 105-foot, three-masted, gaff-rigged topsail schooner. Her huge sails propel her with grace and swiftness, and when the winds refuse to cooperate, her powerful engine carries her comfortably to her next port.

Most cabins have queen-size berths, writing desks, and their own private heads with hot shower.

Relax on a tufted-velvet settee with a good book or take tea on the afterdeck and dine on delicious dishes carefully prepared using the best local seafoods and other fresh ingredients. Accommodations are available for ten passengers in queen cabins, all with hot and cold running water. Skylights and dorades in every cabin offer plenty of light and air. Launched in 1995, the *Kathryn B.* meets or exceeds all U.S. Coast Guard safety requirements. She is operated by a fully qualified, licensed professional captain and crew. The *Kathryn B.* is also available for charter for weddings, reunions, corporate retreats, and other memorable times.

Flag:	USA
Rig:	Gaff schooner, three-masted
Homeport/waters:	Hope, Maine: Maine (summer), St. Vincent and Virgin Islands (winter)
Who sails?	Adult individuals and groups.
Season:	Year-round
Cost:	$3,600 group rate (charter)
Program type:	Sail training for professional crew. Sea education as informal, in-house programming.

Specifications:			
	Sparred length: 105'	Draft: 8'	Sail area: 3,000 sq. ft.
	LOD: 80'	Beam: 20'	Tons: 80 GRT
	LOA: 105'	Rig height: 64'	Power: 135 HP diesel
	LWL: 65'	Freeboard: 8'	Hull: steel

Designer:	Tom Colvin
Built:	1995; Palm Coast, Florida, Treworgy Yachts
Coast Guard certification:	Passenger Vessel (Subchapter T)
Crew:	4. Trainees/passengers: 60
Contact:	Kathryn Baxter, Owner, Schooner Kathryn B.
	391 Hatchet Mountain Road
	Hope, ME 04847
	Tel/Fax: 207-763-4255
	E-mail: kathrynb@midcoast.com
	Web site: http://www.kathrynb.com

Kathryn M. Lee

The last working fishing schooner under sail in the Chesapeake Bay oyster dredging fleet, the *Kathryn M. Lee* is listed on the National Register of Historic Places. Pulled off a mud bank where she had been left to perish, this schooner was rescued by Captain Jim McGlincy a decade ago and, after much rebuilding and re-rigging, brought back to life. Originally built in 1923 in Dorchester, New Jersey for dredging on the Delaware Bay, the *Kathryn M. Lee* is back once more working under sail.

Recently purchased by Captain Ed Farley and Captain Steve Pagels, the schooner continues to oyster on the Bay during dredge season (starting November 1). After additional rebuilding during the winter of 2000-2001, the *Kathryn M. Lee* will operate educational, marine ecology, and sail training programs on the Chesapeake Bay during the months (spring, summer and mid-fall) that she is not oystering. Sailing under her impressive traditional schooner rig and an occasional assist from her motor yawl boat in calms, the schooner *Kathryn M. Lee* maintains a working heritage from the last century that is truly unique.

Flag:	USA		
Rig:	Schooner		
Homeport/waters:	St. Michaels, Maryland: Chesapeake Bay		
Season:	Year-round		
Who sails?	Individuals and groups of all ages.		
Program type:	Sail training for volunteer crew/trainees.		
Specifications:	Sparred length: 85'	LOA: 62'	Rig height: 60'
	Draft: 6'	Beam: 20'	Sail area: 2,000 sq. ft.
	Hull: wood	Hull color: white	Spar material: wood
	Tons:	37 GRT	Power: Yawl boat
Built:	1923; Dorchester, New Jersey, Harry Stowman & Sons		
Coast Guard **certification:**	Passenger Vessel (Subchapter T)		
Crew:	3. **Trainees:** 49 (day sails)		
Contact:	Captain Steve Pagels		
	Downeast Windjammer Cruises		
	PO Box 28		
	Cherryfield, ME 04622		
	Tel: 207-546-2972 (winter); 207-288-4585 (summer); Fax: 207-546-2023		
	Email: decruise@midmaine.com		
	Website: http://downeastwindjammer.com		

Keewatin

Keewatin is a sea-kindly, comfortable vessel with all of the classic features typical of 19th and 20th century schooners with the addition of modern conveniences. She is a great platform for educating young people in sail and line handling, knot work, helmsmanship, piloting and more. The activities aboard and the teamwork necessary to sail her promote not only strong physiques but also sterling character traits.

Her location in Abaco allows for controlled cruising in semi-protected waters abounding with marine mammals, fish, turtles, shellfish and bird life. Clean dry air and open horizons offer opportunities for astronomy. Uninhabited cays allow a first hand introduction to unique Bahamian flora. Abaco is home to settlements established in Loyalist times that present a very real insight into the historical narrative of that age.

A *"Keewatin"* has been in the Turner family since 1968. An identical schooner, built in Newfoundland, served until 1989, when she was sailed to Alabama where her hardware and rig were removed to outfit a new hull utiliz-

KEEWATIN

ing modern materials and building techniques in conjunction with traditional design. Her captain and crew delight in their opportunities to instruct and assist new sailing enthusiasts and to share the wonder of the Bahamas' unique marine environment.

Flag:	USA
Rig:	Gaff schooner
Homeport/waters:	Marsh Harbor, Abaco, Bahamas
Who sails?	Individuals, families, charter groups.
Season:	Year-round
Program type:	Sail training for volunteer and paying trainees. Sea education in marine science, maritime history and ecology in cooperation with accredited institutions and other organized groups. Passenger day sails, overnight voyages, dockside interpretation.

Specifications:			
	Sparred length: 72'	Draft: 6'	Sail area: 1,650 sq. ft.
	LOA: 56'	Beam: 16'	Tons: 60 GRT
	LWL: 48'	Rig height: 67'	Power: GM 125
	Freeboard: 6'6"	Hull: wood	Spar: spruce
	Hull color: white		

Designer:	John Alden
Built:	1992; Coden, Alabama, Zirlott
Certification:	Bahamian License
Crew:	3. Trainees: 16, Passengers: 8
Contact:	Captain Ron Turner
	Box SS 5219
	Nassau, Bahamas
	Tel: 242-477-0292
	E-mail: keewatin@oii.net
	Web site: http://www.bahamasVG.com/keewatin.html

Kruzenshtern

Kruzenshtern was built as *Padua* in 1927 in Bremerhaven, Germany. The sister ship to *Peking*, she is the last of the "Flying P" liners still under sail. These vessels were engaged in the grain trade from Australia to Europe. In 1933 *Kruzenshtern* sailed from her homeport of Hamburg to Port Lincoln in Australia in only 67 days. At the end of World War II she was handed to the USSR and converted into a sail training ship.

Since 1990, up to 40 trainees of all ages have been welcomed on board to sail along with the Russian students of the Baltic Academy in Kalingrad, Russia, learning the ropes, manning the helm, or climbing the rigging to set more than 30,000 square feet of sail. No previous experience is necessary.

Kruzenshtern is supported by Tall Ship Friends, a nonprofit organization in Hamburg, Germany. The goals of Tall Ship Friends are to promote sail training on square-riggers, to contribute to the further existence of these beautiful ships, and to provide an unforgettable experience for the participants. Members of Tall Ship Friends receive the quarterly *Tall Ships News* (English/German) and a personal sailing log.

Flag:	Russia
Rig:	Barque, four-masted
Homeport/waters:	Kalingrad, Russia: Western European waters (summer), Southern European waters (winter)
Who sails?	Individuals and groups of all ages.
Cost:	$50-$100 per person per day. Group charters by appointment
Program type:	Sail training for paying trainees. Fully accredited sea education in traditional seamanship.

Specifications:			
	Sparred length: 376'	Draft: 19	Sail area: 36,380 sq. ft.
	LOA: 346'	Beam: 46'	Power: twin 600 HP
	LOD: 329'	Rig height: 176'	Hull: steel
	LWL: 311' 6"	Freeboard: 27' 9"	

Built:	1927; Bremerhaven, Germany, J.C. Tecklenborg
Certification:	Special Purpose (School Vessel), Russia
Crew:	45-70. **Trainees:** 250 (day sails), 60 (overnight)
Contact:	Wulf Marquard, Managing Director
	Tall Ship Friends Germany
	Schweriner Str. 17
	Hamburg, D22143, Germany
	Tel: 49-40-675 635 97; Fax: 49-40-675 635 99
	E-mail: tallship1@aol.com
	Web site: http://www.tallship-friends.de

Lady Maryland

Lady Maryland is an authentic pungy schooner, an elegant boat designed to haul cargo, fish, dredge for oysters, and carry luxury items quickly from port to port on Chesapeake Bay and along the Atlantic Coast. Instead of carrying watermelons and oysters, her mission today is to provide students with the opportunity to experience sailing a historic vessel while studying history, sailing, seamanship, marine science, and ecology on her traditional waters from Maryland to Maine.

The Living Classrooms Foundation has developed a flexible educational program that can fit the needs of a variety of school and community groups. More than 50,000 students participate in LCF programs each year. The *Lady Maryland* operates educational day experiences for 32 trainees and extended live-aboard sail training and marine science programs for up to 14 people.

LADY MARYLAND

Flag:	USA
Rig:	Pungy schooner (gaff rigged), two-masted
Homeport/waters:	Baltimore, Maryland: Chesapeake and Delaware Bays, East Coast between Maryland and Maine
Who sails?	Student and other organized groups, individuals, and families.
Season:	March through November
Cost:	Rates vary depending on program, please call
Program type:	Sail training with paying trainees. Sea education in marine science, maritime history, and ecology for school groups from elementary school through colleges as well as adults.

Specifications:	Sparred length: 104'	Draft: 7'	Sail area: 2,994 sq. ft.
	LOD: 72'	Beam: 22'	Tons: 60 GRT
	LWL: 64' 3"	Rig height: 85'	Power: twin 80 HP diesels
	Freeboard: 3'		

Designer:	Thomas Gilmer
Built:	1986; Baltimore, Maryland, G. Peter Boudreau
Coast Guard certification:	Passenger Vessel (Subchapter T)
Crew:	6 (day sails), 8 (overnight). **Trainees:** 32 (day sails), 12-14 (overnight)
Contact:	Steve Bountress
	Living Classrooms Foundation
	802 South Caroline Street,
	Baltimore, MD 21231-3311
	Tel: 410-685-0295; Fax: 410-752-8433
	Web site: http://www.livingclassrooms.org

Lady Washington

Built at Grays Harbor Historical Seaport in Aberdeen, Washington and launched in 1989 as a Washington State Centennial project, the reproduction *Lady Washington* sails the waters of Washington State and the West Coast of North America as the tall ship ambassador for the state of Washington. With a busy year-round sailing schedule, *Lady Washington* regularly tours the West Coast, providing shipboard education programs for schools in 89 port communities in Washington, Oregon, California, British Columbia, and Alaska. More than 15,000 school children visit *Lady Washington* each year to learn about the rich and colorful maritime heritage of our nation.

As a privateer during the American Revolution, the original *Lady Washington* fought to help the colonies gain their independence from England. In 1788 she became the first American vessel to visit the West Coast of North America, opening trade between the colonies and the native peoples of the Northwest Coast. As the first American vessel to visit Honolulu, Hong Kong, and Japan, she played a key role in developing American involvement in Asian Pacific trade.

Crew are both paid professionals and volunteer trainees. The Historical Seaport regularly partners with a number of entities to provide unique shipboard education opportunities for trainees with independent learning contracts.

Flag:	USA
Rig:	Brig
Homeport/waters:	Aberdeen, Washington: Grays Harbor, Washington, West Coast of North America
Who sails?	School groups from elementary school through college, individuals and families.
Season:	March to January
Cost:	$35 per person for a three-hour sail, $105 per person per day, $3,500 for a full-day charter.
Program type:	Sail training for crew, apprentices, and paying trainees. Sea education in maritime history in cooperation with accredited institutions, based on informal, in-house programming. Passenger day sails overnight passages and family camps. Dockside interpretation.

Specifications:

Sparred length: 112'	Draft: 11'	Sail area: 4,400 sq. ft.
LOD: 66' 9"	Beam: 24'	Tons: 99 GRT
LOA: 87'	Rig height: 89'	Power: diesel
LWL: 58'	Freeboard: 6'	Hull: wood

Designer:	Ray Wallace
Built:	1989; Aberdeen, Washington, Grays Harbor Historical Seaport Authority
Coast Guard certification:	Passenger Vessel (Subchapter T)
Crew:	12. **Trainees:** 48 (day sails), 8 (overnight)
Contact:	Grace Hagen, Operations Director
	Grays Harbor Historical Seaport
	PO Box 2019, Aberdeen, WA 98520
	Tel: 800-200-LADY (5239); Fax: 360-533-9384
	E-mail: ghhsa@techline.com, Web site: http://www.ladywashington.org

Larinda

Designed and built as a modified replica of a 1767 Boston schooner, *Larinda* is a unique sailing vessel with modern safety features yet she retains traditional wood appointments and museum quality. Much of her construction is done with recycled 100-year-old hard pine. A restored seven-ton 1928 Wolverine 100 HP diesel provides auxiliary power. 300-pound bronze cannons add period excitement.

Featured in publications worldwide, *Larinda* has also starred in several documentaries shown on national and local television. Awards have been won at boat shows including the 1997 Wooden Boat Show and the 1998, 1999, and 2000 Antique and Classic Boat Show. Private charters are welcomed and *Larinda* is available for special events. Seaport festivals and other maritime gatherings have enjoyed her unique presence.

Flag:	USA
Rig:	Schooner
Homeport/waters:	Cape Cod, Massachusetts: Canada to the Caribbean
Who sails?	School groups from elementary through college and individuals of all ages
Cost:	Varies with program
Program type:	Sail training for volunteer and paying trainees. Sea education in marine science, maritime history, and ecology in cooperation with organized groups and as informal, in-house programming.

Specifications:			
	Sparred length: 86'	Draft: 8'	Sail area: 2,900 sq. ft.
	LOD: 56'	Beam: 16' 6"	Tons: 46 GRT
	LOA: 64'	Rig height: 62'	Power: 100 HP diesel
	LWL: 52'	Freeboard: 5'	Hull: wood and ferrocement

Designer:	Hallowell/Mahan
Built:	1996; Marstons Mills, Massachusetts, Wolverine Motor Works and Shipyard, LLC
Coast Guard certification:	Attraction Vessel
Crew:	6-8
Contact:	Captain Lawrence Mahan, President
	Schooner Larinda – Wolverine Motor Works and Shipyard LLC
	163 Walnut Street
	Marstons Mills, MA 02648
	Tel/Fax: 508-428-8728
	E-mail: tslarinda@capecod.net
	Web site: http://www.larinda.com

Lark

Forbes family and was kept in Hadley Harbor at Naushon Island in Vineyard Sound.

Over the years, *Lark* fell into disrepair. She was purchased in 1971 by Captain Eric Little of Woods Hole, Massachusetts, who painstakingly restored her over the next 10 years to her original splendor.

Since then, *Lark* has sailed the East Coast from Marblehead to Miami, competing in classic yacht regattas and antique boat shows. Distinguished by her tanbark sails and gaff rig, *Lark* has been a successful racer and elegant cruising boat for more than 60 years, and is available for day and weekend charter.

Lark is a gaff-rigged cutter built in 1932 by F.D. Lawley for John Alden. She was designed as a day sailer for the

Flag:	USA
Rig:	Cutter
Homeport/waters:	Woods Hole, Massachusetts: Marblehead, Massachusetts to New York City
Who sails?	Individuals and adults.
Program type:	Sail training for volunteer trainees. Sea education as informal, in-house programming. Passenger day sails.

Specifications:			
	Sparred length: 52'	Draft: 5' 5"	Sail area: 1,200 sq. ft.
	LOD: 44' 10"	Beam: 10' 9"	Tons: 18 GRT
	LOA: 52'	Rig height: 55'	Power: 44 HP diesel
	LWL: 30'	Freeboard: 4'	Hull: mahogany over oak

Designer:	John Alden
Built:	1932; Quincy, Massachusetts, F. D. Lawley
Crew:	5
Contact:	Captain Eric Little
	2 Huettner Road
	Woods Hole, MA 02543-1506
	Tel: 508-540-7987, 508-548-9207; Fax: 508-540-5710
	E-mail: caplittle@aol.com

Lettie G. Howard

The *Lettie G. Howard* is a Fredonia model fishing schooner, a type of vessel once widely used along the Atlantic seaboard from Maine to Texas. She was built in 1893 at Essex, Massachusetts, where the majority of the schooners for the fishing fleets of Gloucester, Boston, and New York were produced. She operated out of Gloucester for her first eight years. The fishing would have been done with hand lines set either from the vessel's deck or from small boats called dories. The *Howard* was similar to the schooners that carried their Long Island and New Jersey catches to New York City's Fulton Fish Market.

In 1901 the *Howard* was purchased by Pensacola, Florida owners for use off Mexico's Yucatan Peninsula. Completely rebuilt in 1923, she was fitted with her first auxiliary engine a year later. She remained in the Gulf of Mexico until

1968, when she was sold to the South Street Seaport Museum.

The *Lettie G. Howard* was designated a National Historic Landmark in 1988. Between 1991 and 1993 the museum completely restored her to her original 1893 appearance, while outfitting her to accommodate trainees on educational cruises.

Flag:	USA
Rig:	Gaff topsail schooner, two-masted
Homeport/waters:	New York City: Northeast United States
Who sails?	School groups, Elderhostel, individual adults, and families.
Program type:	Sail training for volunteer and paying trainees. Sea education in marine science, maritime history, and ecology in cooperation with accredited institutions and other groups.
Specifications:	Sparred length: 129' Draft: 11' Sail area: 5,017 sq. ft. LOD: 83' Beam: 21' Tons: 52 GRT LWL: 71' Rig height: 91' Power: twin 85 HP diesels Hull: wood
Built:	1893; Essex, Massachusetts, A.D. Story (restored at South Street Seaport Museum in 1993).
Coast Guard certification:	Sailing School Vessel (Subchapter R)
Crew:	7. **Trainees:** 14 (overnight)
Contact:	Captain Stefan Edick, Marine Education South Street Seaport Museum 207 Front Street, New York, NY 10038 Tel: 212-748-8596; Fax: 212-748-8610 Web site: http://www.southstseaport.org

Libertad

knowledge and cultural background of her midshipmen while integrating them to life at sea and instructing them on the fundamentals of the art of sailing. *Libertad* also serves as a floating ambassador representing the Argentine Republic, establishing professional and friendly ties with navies around the world while preparing her cadets academically, physically and spiritually.

In 1966 *Libertad* established the world record for speed crossing the North Atlantic sailing from Cape Race (Canada) to Dursey Island (Ireland) in six days and 21 hours. This record is officially recognized by the International Sail Training Association (ISTA), and *Libertad* flies a pennant commemorating this achievement.

Her figurehead was made by a Spanish sculptor and depicts Liberty, for which the ship is named. *Libertad* has sailed the seven seas and participates in regattas and port visits around the world, most recently winning ISTA's Boston Teapot Trophy (an award she's garnered seven times) as part of her voyage during Tall Ships 2000®.

The frigate A.R.A. *Libertad* was built in 1963 as a training ship for the Argentine Navy. As a training ship, her mission is to enhance the maritime

Flag:	Argentina		
Rig:	Full-rigged ship		
Homeport/waters:	Buenos Aires, Argentina: world-wide		
Who sails?	Argentinian Naval cadets		
Specifications:	LOA: 356'	Beam: 45' 3"	Draft: 21' 9"
	Sail area: 28,546 sq. ft.	Power: 2/1,200 HP diesel	
	Hull: steel		
Built:	1956:		
Contact:	Fragata A.R.A. LIBERTAD	Fragata A.R.A. LIBERTAD	
	Estado Mayor General de la Armada	Apostadero Naval Buenos Aries	
	Comodor Py 2055	Avenida Antartida Argentina No. 401	
	1104 Buenos Aries, Argentina	1104 Buenos Aires, Argentina	
	E-mail: libertad@interar.com.ar		
	Web site: http://www.fragatalibertad.ar		
	http://www.ara.mil.ar		

Liberty is modeled on early 1800s coastal schooners used by New England fisherman and as cargo vessels along the East Coast to the Florida Keys. She is based in Key West, where she offers three two-hour sails each day. *Liberty* is kept "shipshape and Bristol fashion" and is available for charter day and evening for every occasion.

PHOTO BY ALAN MALTZ

LIBERTY

Flag:	USA
Rig:	Gaff topsail schooner
Homeport/waters:	Boston, Massachusetts (summer), Key West, Florida (winter): East Coast US
Who sails?	School groups from elementary through high school, individuals and families.
Cost:	$25-$35 per person per two-hour harbor cruise, $175 per person per day, $3,600 group charter rate per day.
Program type:	Passenger day sails and overnight passages. Corporate and private charters.

Specifications:			
	Sparred length: 80'	Draft: 7'	Sail area: 1,744 sq. ft.
	LOD: 61'	Beam: 17'	Tons: 50 GRT
	LOA: 64'	Rig height: 65'	Power: diesel
	LWL: 53'	Freeboard: 5'	Hull: steel

Designer:	Charles Wittholz
Built:	1993; Palm Coast, Florida, Treworgy Yachts
Coast Guard certification:	Passenger Vessel (Subchapter T).
Crew:	3 (day sails), 4 (overnight). **Trainees:** 49 (day sails), 8 (overnight)
Contact:	Gregory E. Muzzy, President
	The Liberty Fleet of Tall Ships
	Hilton Resort & Marina
	Key West, FL 33040
	Tel: 305-295-0095; Fax: 305-292-6411
	Web site: http://www.libertyfleet.com

rty Clipper

The Schooner ★ ★ ★

famous for their fast passages around Cape Horn on their way to California and other Pacific ports. The *Liberty Clipper* joined the *Liberty* in Boston in the summer of 1996. She is available for charter, with up to 110 passengers, in Boston Harbor and Key West, for day and evening cruises. Her spacious decks and on-board hospitality create an ambiance under sail that will meet the expectation of the most discriminating clients. Guests are invited to join in hoisting the sails, steering the boat, and otherwise joining in the fun. During the winter, *Liberty Clipper* joins *Liberty* in Key West, offering day sails, dinner sails, and charters. Traveling to Key West in October, *Liberty Clipper* offers four one way trips along the East Coast and two one week trips in the spring as she returns to Boston.

The *Liberty Clipper* is a replica of the mid-19th century Baltimore Clippers

Flag:	USA
Rig:	Gaff topsail schooner
Homeport/waters:	Boston, MA (summer), Key West, FL (winter); East Coast US
Who sails?	School groups from elementary through high school, individuals, and families.
Cost:	$175 per person per day; $8,000 group charter rate per day.
Program type:	Passenger day sails and overnight passages. Corporate and private charters.

Specifications:	Sparred length: 125'	Draft: 8' (min.), 13' (max.)	Sail area: 4,300 sq. ft.
	LOD: 86'	Beam: 25'	Tons: 99 GRT
	LWL: 76'	Rig height: 78'	Power: diesel
	Freeboard: 5'	Hull: steel	

Designer:	Charles Wittholz
Built:	1983; Warren, Rhode Island, Blount Marine Corporation
Coast Guard certification:	Passenger Vessel (Subchapter T)
Crew:	5 (day sails), 10 (overnight). **Trainees/passengers:** 115 (day sails), 24 (overnight)
Contact:	Gregory E. Muzzy, President
	The Liberty Fleet of Tall Ships
	67 Long Wharf
	Boston, MA 02210
	Tel: 617-742-0333; Fax: 617-742-1322
	Web site: http://www.libertyfleet.com

Lisa

The brig *Lisa* offers teenagers the opportunity to sail before the mast in a new brig. Students can spend an academic year learning geography, history, and math by direct experience, all while experiencing the disciplines of life at sea and the thrill of manning a traditional vessel.

Flag:	USA
Rig:	Brig
Homeport/waters:	Wilmington, Delaware: worldwide
Season:	Year-round
Program type:	Full academic curriculum and special education programs for high school students and youth-at-risk.

Specifications:			
	Sparred length: 72'	Draft: 6' 3"	Sail area: 3,000 sq. ft.
	LOA: 55'	Beam: 18'	Tons: 40 GRT
	LWL: 45'	Rig height: 55'	Hull: steel
	Freeboard: 5'		

Coast Guard certification:	Uninspected Vessel
Crew:	4. Trainees: 6
Contact:	Mrs. Leibolt
	P.O. Box 161510
	Altamont Springs, FL 32716
	Tel: 407-884-8333

Little Jennie

One of the oldest surviving examples of a Chesapeake Bay Bugeye, the *Little Jennie* was built in 1884 and is listed on the National Register of Historic Places. Originally built for oystering and freighting, the *Little Jennie* now carries passengers on educational trips designed to highlight our maritime history and the ecology of coastal waters.

Undergoing extensive restoration over the winter of 2000-2001, the *Little Jennie* will again be showing her distinctive profile on the waters between Maine and the Chesapeake Bay. Her trips will offer both day sails and occasional overnight cruises where her crew can gain an appreciation for traditional watercraft and coastal estuaries.

Flag:	USA
Rig:	Bugeye ketch
Homeport/waters:	Cherryfield, Maine: Bar Harbor, Maine (summer), Chesapeake Bay (winter).
Program type:	Sail training for volunteer or paying trainees. Dockside interpretation during port visits

Specifications:

Sparred length: 86'	Draft: 4'6"	Sail area: 1,600 sq. ft.
LOA: 62'	LOD: 62'	LWL: 57'
Beam: 17'	Tons: 22 GRT	Rig height: 60'
Hull: wood	Hull color: white	Power: 100 HP diesel

Designer:	J.T. Marsh
Built:	1884; Solomons, Maryland, J.T. Marsh
Coast Guard certification:	Passenger Vessel (Subchapter T)
Crew:	2. Trainees/passengers: 32 (day sails), 6 (overnight)
Contact:	Captain Steven F. Pagels, Owner
	Downeast Windjammer Cruises
	PO Box 28
	Cherryfield, ME 04622
	Tel: 207-546-2927; Fax: 207-546-2023
	E-mail: decruise@midmaine.com
	Web site: http://downeastwindjammer.com

Lord Nelson

The 180-foot, three-masted barque *Lord Nelson* was built in 1986 for the Jubilee Sailing Trust to encourage integration between able-bodied and physically disabled people by offering them the opportunity to experience the excitement of tall ship sailing together.

Voyages last from 4 to 11 days, departing from a wide variety of ports and sailing in the English Channel and the North and Irish Seas. A winter season of voyages based in the Canary Islands is also available.

Above deck the ship's equipment enables physically disabled crew to work alongside their able-bodied crewmates. Features include power steering, wide decks to accommodate wheelchairs, a speaking compass, powered lifts between decks, and Braille marking. Below are specially designed wheelchair-accessible cabins, showers, and heads.

Voyages are open to anyone between 16 to 70+ with or without sailing experience. 20 people with physical disabilities, including eight wheelchair users, serve alongside an equal number of able-bodied people. There is a permanent crew of 10, including a medically trained person and a cook.

Flag:	UK
Rig:	Barque, three-masted
Homeport/waters:	Southampton, United Kingdom: United Kingdom (summer), Canary Islands (winter)
Who sails?	Physically disabled and able-bodied people, aged 16 to 70+.
Cost:	Ranges from $65 to $133 per person per day, plus insurance
Program type:	Sail training for paying trainees. Integration of physically disabled and able-bodied people through the medium of tall ship sailing.

Specifications:			
	Sparred length: 180'	Draft: 13' 6"	Sail area: 11,030 sq. ft.
	LOD: 133'	Beam: 29' 6"	Tons: 368 GRT
	LOA: 140' 5"	Rig height: 108'	Power: twin 260 hp
	LWL: 121' 5"	Freeboard: 6' 8"	Hull: steel

Designer:	Colin Mudie
Built:	1986; Wivenhoe, UK, James W. Cook & Co., Ltd.
Certification:	Lloyds 100A1
Crew:	10. **Trainees:** 40
Contact:	Mrs. Lindsey Neve
	Jubilee Sailing Trust
	Jubilee Yard, Hazel Road, Woolston
	Southampton, Hampshire SO19 7GB, United Kingdom
	Tel: 44-23-8044-9108; Fax: 44-23-8044-9145
	E-mail: jst@jst.org.uk
	Web site: http://www.jst.org.uk

Lycia

Lycia is a splendid custom-built wooden cutter launched in 1996. The yacht has been built over a period of four years using epoxy resins to give extreme solidity to her 19-meter mahogany hull. Her slender and graceful lines, light displacement, and large and powerful rig make for outstanding sailing abilities. This yacht is equipped with two separate cockpits, large galley and modern amenities such as warm water, showers and privacy.

Lycia carries a professional crew of two, captain and mate, handling all aspects of navigation and charter activity. The yacht can accommodate up to ten guests, who are welcome to join in steering the boat or just relaxing on her spacious deck. Her schedule brings her to navigate in diverse destinations ranging from the Caribbean area to the Mediterranean basin, offering a wealth of opportunity to explore and meeting the expectations of even the most discriminating charter clients. Her programs include sail training trips for expert trainees involving long-distance voyages and ocean passages, educational sailing, and recreational cruises including delightful charters open to anyone regardless of sailing experience. Children are most welcome aboard.

Flag:	Italy
Rig:	Cutter
Homeport/waters:	Monfalcone, Italy: Northeast America, Bermuda, Azores, Mediterranean.
Who sails?	Individuals of all ages, families, groups.
Cost:	$150 per person per day, $1000 group rate per day
Season:	Year round
Program type:	Sail training for volunteer and paying trainees based on informal, in-house programming.

Specifications:			
	Sparred length: 65'	Draft: 10'	LOD: 60'
	Beam: 15'	LWL: 58'	Tons: 24 GRT
	Rig height: 80'	Power: 95HP diesel	Freeboard: 4'6"
	Hull: wood	Hull color: white	Spar material: aluminum

Designer:	Giulio Raines
Built:	1996; Italy, Cantiere Bellini
Certification:	R.I.M.A.
Crew:	3. **Trainees/passengers:** 10
Contact:	Antonio Penati, Captain
	ARCA sas
	P2A San Tomaso 17
	Verona, VR 37129 Italy
	Tel: +39 045 8012631; Fax: +39 045 593881
	E-mail: lycia@micanet.it
	Web site: http://www.yachtlycia.com

Lynx

The square topsail schooner *Lynx* has been designed and built to interpret the general configuration and operation of a man-of-war vessel from the War of 1812. Designed by noted marine architect and historian Melbourne Smith and built by Rockport Marine for the American Clipper Schooner Foundation, *Lynx* represents a medium-sized privateer or "letter of marque" Baltimore Clipper Schooner.

LYNX

The original *Lynx* was built at Fells Point, Maryland in 1812. She was captured by the British in the Rappahannock River in 1813 and served as a Royal Navy vessel until 1820. Based at Halifax, she operated along the coast of Nova Scotia under the name *Mosquidobit*. *Lynx* will be fitted with period guns and stands of small arms and will fly historic pennants from the 1812 period. To complement the historical character of the vessel, members of the crew will wear period uniforms and operate the ship in keeping with the traditions of the early 19th century.

Lynx will operate as a sail training and adventure vessel, preserving seafaring traditions and serving as a classroom for the study of historical, environmental, and ecological issues. In addition, she will undertake "cruises of opportunity" providing youth and adult participants challenges leading to personal growth and awareness through the historical experience of life at sea aboard a traditional 1812 privateer.

Flag:	USA
Rig:	Square topsail schooner
Who Sails?	School groups from elementary school through college, individuals, families
Season:	Year-round
Program type:	Sail training for volunteer and paying trainees. Sea education in maritime history in cooperation with accredited institutions and other organized groups. Passenger day sails and overnight voyages, dockside interpretation.

Specifications:			
	Sparred length: 122'	Draft: 8'6"	Sail area: 4,669 sq. ft.
	LOD: 76'	Beam: 23'	Tons: 98.6 GRT
	LOA: 80'	Rig height: 94'	Power: CAT 290 HP
	LWL: 72'	Freeboard: 4'	Hull: wood
	Spar: Wood	Hull color: Black	

Designer:	Melbourne Smith
Built:	2001; Rockport, Maine, Rockport Marine
Coast Guard certification:	Passenger Vessel (Subchapter T), Near Coastal, Ocean
Crew:	3. **Trainees:** 40 (day sails), 10 (overnight)
Contact:	Woodson K. Woods, Director of Operations
	American Clipper Schooner Foundation
	509 29th Street
	Newport Beach, CA 92663
	Tel: 949-723-7814; Fax: 949-723-7815
	E-mail: whiskeykng@aol.com
	Web site: http://www.privateerlynx.org

Mabel Stevens

The ketch *Mabel Stevens* offers charter services in the Washington, DC, and Chesapeake Bay areas. Sail training cruises, group and individual charters, and other tailored sailing and maritime education programs are offered by Captain Chalker aboard the *Mabel Stevens*.

Built by Captain Dick Hartge of Galesville, Maryland, the *Mabel Stevens* holds a special place in the Washington metropolitan area. During the 1980s, the *Mabel Stevens* officially represented the District of Columbia at the tall ships events in Boston (350th anniversary) and New York (Statue of Liberty centennial), and in 1992 in New York at the Christopher Columbus Quincentennial Celebrations. She is the District of Columbia's goodwill ambassador vessel at major historic events. The *Mabel Stevens* competes in ASTA rallies and has in the past raced with the best of the Class C tall ships. In 1986, she led the fleet of sail training vessels engaged in friendly competition en route to New York's Statue of Liberty festivities and participated in Philadelphia and Tall Ships® Newport '92.

Flag:	USA
Rig:	Ketch
Homeport/waters:	Cobb Island, Maryland: Lower Potomac River, Chesapeake Bay.
Who sails?	Individuals and groups
Season:	April to October
Cost:	$70 per person per day; inquire for group rates
Program type:	Maritime history and environmental studies.

Specifications:			
	Sparred length: 47' 6"	Draft: 4' 6"	Sail area: 1,200 sq. ft.
	LOA: 35'	Beam: 11' 6"	Sail number: TS-US 159
	LWL: 31' 9"	Rig height: 45'	Tons: 17 GRT
	Freeboard: 3'	Hull: wood	Power: 52 HP diesel

Built:	1935; Galesville, Maryland, Ernest H. Hartge
Coast Guard certification:	Uninspected Vessel
Crew:	1. Trainees: 4
Contact:	Captain Ned Chalker
	Ketch Mabel Stevens
	119 Fifth St. NE
	Washington, DC 20002
	Tel: 202-543-0110, 301-259-4458; Fax: 202-554-3949
	E-mail: Nchalker@aol.com

Madeline

The *Madeline* is a reconstruction of a mid-19th-century schooner, typical of the trading schooners that once sailed the upper Great Lakes. The original *Madeline* was once the first Euro-American school in the Grand Traverse region and for a short time served as a lightship in the Straits of Mackinac.

The modern *Madeline*, launched in 1990, was built over period of five years by volunteers of the Maritime Heritage Alliance (MHA), using traditional methods and materials. From her homeport, Traverse City, Michigan, she has sailed with her volunteer crew on all five Great Lakes, visiting over 60 ports with dockside tours and historical interpretation. *Madeline* is the State of Michigan's official tall ship and is designated as the City of Traverse City's goodwill ambassador.

Madeline's dockside programs bring visitors on board to learn about schooners and Great Lakes history first-hand. Crewmembers, trained as historical interpreters, share their knowledge of history, marlinespike skills, and wooden boat building. School programs with special

hand-on activities are also available.

The Maritime Heritage Alliance, a nonprofit organization, fosters the study and practice of upper Great Lakes's maritime history. MHA programs, focusing on building and operating indigenous crafts, include crew training, traditional boat carpentry, and other wooden boat maintenance skills.

Flag:	USA
Rig:	Gaff topsail schooner, two-masted
Homeport/waters:	Traverse City, Michigan: upper Great Lakes
Who sails?	Trained crewmembers of the Maritime Heritage Alliance. *Madeline* is associated with the Association for Great Lakes history.
Program type:	Adult sail training and maritime history.

Specifications:			
	Sparred length: 92'	Draft: 7' 7"	Sail area: 2,270 sq. ft.
	LOA: 55' 6"	Beam: 16' 2"	Tons: 42 GRT
	LWL: 52'	Rig height: 65'	Freeboard: 2' 2"

Designer:	Robert Core
Built:	1990; Traverse City, Michigan, Maritime Heritage Alliance
Coast Guard certification:	Uninspected Vessel
Crew:	9
Contact:	Laura Quakenbush, Madeline Coordinator
	Maritime Heritage Alliance
	322 Sixth
	Traverse City, MI 49684
	Tel: 231-946-2647; Fax: 231-946-6750
	E-mail: mha.tc@juno.com
	Web site: http://www.traverse.com/maritime/

Maine

Maine's design and construction was conceived by Lance Lee at the Maine Maritime Museum. Master builders Dave Foster, Will Ansel, and Phil Shelton guided her construction by Museum apprentices between keel laying in 1981 and launching in 1986. She evolved as a project employing many skilled and experienced maritime historians, boat designers, and builders. Her lines were taken by Jim Stevens of Goudy & Stevens from a half-model dating from 1832 in East Boothbay, Maine. Marine draftsman Sam Manning drew the plans. The deck layout and rig are based on Howard Chapelle's research, with input from, among others, Maynard Bray and naval architect Jay Paris. A fast and able sailor, *Maine* serves the Museum as a floating exhibition, a sail training vessel, and a roving ambassador. *Maine* travels along the Maine coast in the summer from Portland to Penobscot Bay.

Flag:	USA
Rig:	Pinky schooner, two-masted (gaff-rigged)
Homeport/waters:	Bath, Maine: coastal Maine and southern New England.
Program type:	Sea education in maritime history.

Specifications:			
	Sparred length: 56'	Draft: 8'	Tons: 14 GRT
	LOD: 40'	Beam: 12'	Power: diesel
	LOA: 43'	Freeboard: 2' 6"	Hull: wood

Built:	1985; Bath, Maine, Maine Maritime Museum
Coast Guard certification:	Uninspected Vessel
Contact:	Tom Wilcox/Will West
	Maine Maritime Museum
	243 Washington Street
	Bath, ME 04530
	Tel: 207-443-1316; Fax: 207-443-1665

Malabar

The 105-foot topsail schooner *Malabar* is now once again based on the East Coast in the historic village of Greenport. After major restoration work in 2000, the *Malabar* is now offering a variety of educational and sail training cruises, and we can customize a charter to suit a group's individual needs. We have been told by a number of guests that the *Malabar* is ideally suited for these programs, not only because of her salty rig and appearance, but also because of her spacious interior with its large and well laid out great cabin and galley aft.

Flag:	USA				
Rig:	Gaff topsail schooner, two-masted				
Homeport/waters:	Cherryfield, Maine: Greenport, Long Island, New York				
Who sails?	Individuals and groups.				
Program type:	Sail training for crew and apprentices. Passenger day sails and overnight passages.				
Specifications:	Sparred length: 105'	Draft: 8' 6"	Sail area: 3,000 sq. ft.
	LOD: 65'	Beam: 21'	Tons: 73 GRT
	LWL: 60'	Rig height: 75'	Power: 136 HP diesel
	Freeboard: 6'	Hull: ferro/steel	
	Hull color: green	Spar material: wood	
Designer:	M.D. Lee				
Built:	1975; Bath, Maine, Long Beach Shipyard				
Coast Guard certification:	Passenger Vessel (Subchapter T)				
Crew:	3. **Trainees/passengers:** 49 (day sails), 21 (overnight)				
Contact:	Captain Steve F. Pagels, Owner				
	Downeast Windjammer Cruises				
	PO Box 28				
	Cherryfield, ME 04622				
	Tel: 207-546-2927 (winter), 631-477-3698 (summer); Fax: 207-546-2023				
	E-mail: decruise@midmaine.com				
	Web site: http://www.downeastwindjammer.com				

Mallory Todd

Named for Captain Mallory Todd, who served as master on American vessels during the Revolutionary War, the *Mallory Todd* is a modern 65-foot schooner built in the classic style with fireplaces and exceptionally fine woodwork. Designed for long distance voyages, she has sailed the West Coast from Mexico to Alaska for 18 years. When at homeport in Seattle, she relieves the tedium of long term cancer treatment with recreational outings for hospital patients and their caregivers under the auspices of the nonprofit Sailing Heritage Society.

Sail training trips to the San Juan Islands, Canada, and Alaska via the Inside Passage are blessed with the full bounty of nature. Humpback whales, Orcas, sea lions, dolphins, and sea otters cavort while bears forage ashore, eagles soar the winds, and fjord hillsides entice the naturalist with breathtaking wildflowers. These trips are open to anyone between 18 and 80 with or without sailing experience. Together, part time volunteers, trainees, and professionals get the job done. Hands on tending the sails, steering, scrubbing, navigating, fishing, or clamming, each contributes where a need fits their abilities.

Schooner *Mallory Todd* also offers corporate and private charters that provide a unique and delightful venue for business or recreational activities—be it exclusive executive meeting or picnic outing.

Flag:	USA
Rig:	Staysail schooner
Homeport/waters:	Seattle, Washington: Pacific Northwest, Canada, and Alaska
Who sails?	All ages for volunteers, paying trainees, and apprentices.
Cost:	Based on ability to pay
Program type:	Sail training for crew volunteers, trainees, and apprentices. Sea education based on programmed and day to day events. Passenger day sails for corporate team building or recreational events.

Specifications:	Sparred length: 65'	Draft: 5' (min.), 8' (max.)	Sail area: 1,545 sq. ft.
	LOD: 65'	Beam: 16'	Tons: 38 GRT
	LOA: 60'	Rig Height: 65'	Power: diesel
	LWL: 50'	Freeboard: 5'	Hull: composite

Designer:	Perry & Todd
Built:	1981; Seattle, Washington
Coast Guard certification:	Passenger Vessel (Subchapter T).
Crew:	2. **Trainees:** 6 (overnight), 25 (day sails)
Contact:	Captain George Todd
	Sailing Heritage Society
	10042 NE 13th Street
	Bellevue, WA 98004
	Tel: 425-451-8160; Fax: 425-451-8119
	E-mail: mallorytodd@email.msn.com
	Web site: http://www.sailseattle.com

Manitou

Owned and operated by Traverse Tall Ship Company, the schooner *Manitou* is one of the largest sailing vessels on the Great Lakes. She can accommodate 24 overnight guests and 56 passengers for day excursions. *Manitou* is fully certified by the US Coast Guard and offers 3, 4, and 5-day windjammer cruises to the islands, bays, and coastal villages of Lakes Michigan and Huron.

In conjunction with Inland Seas Education Association, *Manitou* offers the Schoolship Program, which provides an environmental, historical, and sail training education for students during the spring. Three day family packages are also available on two separate cruises during the regular season. Primarily offered as adult vacation, the windjammer season runs from June through October 1.

MANITOU

Flag:	USA		
Rig:	Gaff topsail schooner, two-masted		
Homeport/waters:	Northport, Michigan: Great Lakes		
Who sails?	Science and marine biology student groups from elementary school through junior high. Individual, family, and corporate groups for multi-day windjammer cruises.		
Season:	May to October		
Program type:	Sail training for crew. Sea education in marine science, maritime history and ecology. Corporate team-building workshops. Individual and group windjammer cruises.		
Specifications:	Sparred length: 114'	Draft: 7' (min.), 11' (max.)	Sail area: 3,000 sq. ft.
	LOD: 77'	Beam: 21'	Tons: 82 GRT
	LWL: 65'	Rig height: 80'	Power: 150 HP diesel
	Freeboard: 6'	Hull: steel	Rig height: 75' 6"
	Hull color: white	Spar material: wood	
Designer:	Woodin & Marean.		
Built:	1982; Portsmouth, New Hampshire, Roger Gagnon Steel Ship Company		
Coast Guard certification:	Passenger Vessel (Subchapter T)		
Crew:	5. **Trainees/passengers:** 56 (day sails), 24 (overnight)		
Contact:	Captain David P. McGinnis, President		
	Traverse Tall Ship Co.		
	13390 S.W. Bay Shore Drive		
	Traverse City, MI 49684		
	Tel: 231-941-2000; Fax: 231-941-0520		
	E-mail: tallship@traverse.com		
	Web site: http://www.traverse.com/tallship/		

Margaret Todd

Launched new in 1998, the 4-masted schooner *Margaret Todd* is the first 4-master to be based and operate in New England in over half a century. With her distinctive tanbark sails, this 151-foot schooner is becoming a legend on the Maine coast. Based in Bar Harbor, adjacent to Acadia National Park, the *Margaret Todd* can accommodate groups of up to 150 on day sails, educational, and sail training cruises.

Captain Pagels built the *Margaret Todd* (named after his grandmother) to replace his 3-masted schooner *Natalie Todd*, which he ran for ten years. The *Margaret Todd* routinely sails by some of the most spectacular scenery on the Maine coast. With her tandem centerboards and shallow draft this schooner also has a good turn of speed and offers her crew, trainees, and guests a unique and memorable experience under traditional sail.

Flag: USA
Rig: Schooner, four-masted
Homeport/waters: Cherryfield, Maine: Bar Harbor, Maine.
Program type: Sail training for paid or volunteer crew or trainees. Passenger day sails. Dockside interpretation during port visits.
Specifications:

Sparred length: 151'	Draft: 5' 9"		Sail area: 4,800 sq. ft.
LOD: 121'	Beam: 23'		Tons: 99 GRT
LOA: 121'	Hull: steel		Power: diesel
Power: 400 HP diesel	Hull color: white		Spar material: steel/wood

Designer: Woodin and Marean
Built: 1998; St. Augustine, Florida, Schreiber Boats
Coast Guard
  certification: Passenger Vessel (Subchapter T)
Crew: 8. **Trainees/passengers:** 150
Contact: Captain Steve F. Pagels, Owner
Downeast Windjammer Cruises
PO Box 28
Cherryfield, ME 04622
Tel: 207-546-2927; Fax: 207-546-2023
E-mail: decruise@midmaine.com
Web site: http://www.downeastwindjammer.com

Mary Day

Built in 1962 by Harvey Gamage, *Mary Day* combines the best aspects of the New England centerboard coaster with modern design thinking. *Mary Day* operates out of Camden, Maine, in the windjammer trade from late May to early October. She carries 30 passengers on weeklong vacation cruises in mid-coast Maine. *Mary Day* is a pure sailing vessel. She has no engine and depends on a small yawl boat when winds fail. She has a large and powerful rig and exhibits outstanding sailing abilities.

Mary Day carries a professional crew of six, including captain, mate, cook, two deckhands, and one galley hand. The galley and one deck position are considered entry-level positions, and a great many sailing professionals have started out or gained valuable experience on board the schooner *Mary Day*.

MARY DAY

Flag:	USA
Rig:	Gaff topsail schooner, two-masted
Homeport/waters:	Camden, Maine: Mid-Coast and Downeast Maine
Who sails?	Individuals and families.
Season:	May to October
Cost:	$129 per person per day
Program type:	Sail training for crew and apprentices. Passenger overnight passages. Dockside interpretation in homeport.

Specifications:			
	Sparred length: 125'	Draft: 7' 6"	Sail area: 5,000 sq. ft.
	LOD: 90'	Beam: 22'	Tons: 86 GRT
	LOA: 92'	Rig height: 102'	Hull: wood
	LWL: 81'	Freeboard: 5'	

Designer:	H. Hawkins
Built:	1962; South Bristol, Maine, Harvey Gamage
Coast Guard certification:	Passenger Vessel (Subchapter T)
Crew:	7. **Trainees:** 49 (day sails), 29 (overnight)
Contact:	Captains Barry King and Jen Martin
	Penobscot Windjammer Company
	PO Box 798
	Camden, ME 04843
	Tel: 800-992-2218
	E-mail: captains@schoonermaryday.com
	Web site: http://www.schoonermaryday.com

Mike Sekul

The *Mike Sekul* is one of the two Biloxi oyster schooner replicas built as part of the Biloxi Schooner Project under the auspices of the Maritime and Seafood Industry Museum. She was launched in April of 1994 as part of the effort to preserve the maritime and seafood industry of the Mississippi Gulf Coast. Money for construction and fitting out of the *Mike Sekul* and her sister ship, *Glenn L. Swetman*, has come from donations and fundraising events.

The *Mike Sekul* is available for charter for two-and-a-half hours, half-day, and full-day trips in the Mississippi Sound and to the barrier islands, Cat Island, Horn Island, and Ship Island. Walkup day sailing trips are made when she is not under charter. Groups of up to 45 passengers learn about the maritime and seafood heritage of the Gulf Coast and about the vessels working in Biloxi's seafood industry.

Sailing classes are offered through local colleges and the museum's Sea and Sail Adventure summer camp. Wedding parties, Elderhostel, and school groups are also accommodated.

Flag:	USA
Rig:	Gaff topsail schooner, two-masted
Homeport/waters:	Biloxi, Mississippi: coastwise Gulf of Mexico
Who sails?	Elementary students through college age, adults, and families. Affiliated institutions include William Carey College, Seashore Methodist Assembly, J.L. Scott Marine Education Center, and Mississippi State University
Season:	Year-round
Cost:	$15 per adult or $10 per child (2 hour sail). Group rate (up to 45 people) $500 for half-day, $750 per day.
Program type:	Sail training for paying and volunteer trainees. Sea education in marine science, maritime history, and ecology in cooperation with accredited institutions and organized groups and as informal, in-house programming.

Specifications:	Sparred length: 78'		Draft: 5' 10"		Sail area: 2,499 sq. ft.
	LOD: 50'		Beam: 17'		Tons: 24 GRT
	LOA: 78'		Hull: wood		Power: 4-71 Detroit diesel
	LWL: 43'				

Designer:	Neil Covacevich
Built:	1993; Biloxi, Mississippi, Neil Covacevich
Coast Guard certification:	Passenger Vessel (Subchapter T)
Crew:	3. **Trainees:** 45 (day). **Age:** 15+
Contact:	Robin Krohn, Executive Director Maritime and Seafood Industry Museum of Biloxi PO Box 1907 Biloxi, MS 39533 Tel: 228-435-6320; Fax: 228-435-6309 E-mail: schooner@maritimemuseum.org Web site: http://www.maritimemuseum.org

Minnie V.

The skipjack *Minnie V.*, built in Wenona, Maryland, was used to dredge oysters on the Chesapeake Bay for many years. The vessel was rebuilt by the City of Baltimore in 1981 and is now owned and operated by the Living Classrooms Foundation. The Foundation uses the vessel for educational programs and as a tourist attraction offering interpretive tours of the historic port of Baltimore. While on board the *Minnie V.*, students learn about the oyster trade, its importance to the economy of Maryland, and the hard life of a waterman as they relive history by raising the sails on one of the Chesapeake's few remaining skipjacks.

MINNIE V.

Flag:	USA
Rig:	Sloop
Homeport/waters:	Baltimore, Maryland: Baltimore Harbor
Who sails?	School groups from middle school through college as well as individuals and families.
Season:	April through October
Cost:	Rates vary depending on program. Please call for more information.
Program type:	Sea education in marine science, maritime history, and ecology in cooperation with accredited schools, colleges, and other organized groups. Passenger day sails. Dockside interpretation.

Specifications:					
	Sparred length: 69'		Draft: 3'		Sail area: 1,450 sq. ft.
	LOD: 45' 3"		Beam: 15' 7"		Tons: 10 GRT
	Rig height: 58'		Freeboard: 2'		Hull: wood

Built:	1906; Wenona, Maryland, Vetra
Coast Guard certification:	Passenger Vessel (Subchapter T)
Crew:	2. **Trainees:** 24
Contact:	Steve Bountress
	Living Classrooms Foundation
	802 South Caroline Street
	Baltimore, MD 21231-3311
	Tel: 410-685-0295; Fax: 410-752-8433
	Web site: http://www.livingclassrooms.org/facilities/minniev.html

Mir

MIR

1997, and 1998 under the command of Captain Victor Antonov. *Mir* was launched in 1989 at the Lenin shipyard in Gdansk, Poland, the builders of five more of the M 108 type ships: *Dar Mlodziezy, Pallada, Khersones, Druzhba,* and *Nadezhda.*

Mir is the school ship of the Makaroz Maritime Academy in St. Petersburg, Russia, training future navigators and engineers for the Russian merchant fleet. Since 1990 up to 60 trainees of all ages are welcomed on board to sail along with the Russian students, learning the ropes, manning the helm, or climbing the rigging to set the sails. No previous experience is necessary.

Mir is supported by Tall Ship Friends, a nonprofit organization in Hamburg, Germany. The goals of Tall Ship Friends are to promote sail training on square-riggers, to contribute to the further existence of these beautiful ships, and to provide an unforgettable experience for the participants. Members of Tall Ship Friends receive the quarterly *Tall Ships News* (English/German) and a personal sailing log.

Mir is regarded by many as the fastest Class A sail training ship in the world. She was the overall winner of the 1992 Columbus Race and the winner of the Cutty Sark Tall Ship Races in 1996,

Flag:	Russia
Rig:	Full-rigged ship
Homeport/waters:	St. Petersburg, Russia: west and southwest European waters
Who sails?	Students and individuals of all ages. Affiliated with Tall ShipFriends clubs in France, UK, Switzerland, Austria, Ireland, and Italy.
Cost:	$50-$100 per person per day
Program type:	Sail training for paying trainees. Fully accredited sea education in traditional seamanship. Dockside interpretation during port visits.

Specifications:			
	Sparred length: 345' 9"	Draft: 18'	Sail area: 29,997 sq. ft.
	LOA: 328'	Beam: 44' 9"	Tons: 2,856 GRT
	LOD: 300' 9"	Rig height: 149'	Power: twin 570 HP diesels
	LWL: 254'	Freeboard: 34' 6"	Hull: steel

Designer:	Z. Choren
Built:	1987; Gdansk, Poland, Stocznia Gdanska
Certification:	Russian registered Sailing School Vessel
Crew:	45-70. **Trainees/passengers**: up to 250 (day sails), 60 (overnight)
Contact:	Wulf Marquard, Managing Director, Tall Ship Friends Germany
	Schweriner Str. 17
	Hamburg, D22 143, Germany
	Tel: 49-40-675 635 97; Fax: 49-40-675 635 99
	E-mail: tallship1@aol.com
	Web site: http://tallship-friends.de

Miss Mavis

Make your own itinerary or follow one of ours. We make your dream vacation come true! Sail, snorkel, and dive while you explore the islands of the Florida Keys, the Abacos, the Dry Tortugas, and beyond. Let us help design a trip for you.

Flag:	USA
Rig:	Ketch
Homeport/waters:	Fort Lauderdale, Florida: Abaco, Bahamas (summer); Florida Keys (winter)
Who sails?	Families and adults of all ages.
Program type:	Sail training for paying trainees. Sea education in marine science and ecology as informal in-house programming.
Season:	May through August

Specifications:

Sparred length: 42'	Draft: 4'2"	Sail area: 880 sq. ft.
LOD: 40'	LOA: 41'3"	LWL: 34'
Beam: 13'10"	Rig height: 63'	Freeboard: 5'
Power: diesel	Hull: fiberglass	Hull color: white
Sail number: 3	Spar material: aluminum	

Designer:	Charles Morgan
Built:	1981; Florida, Morgan Co.
Crew:	1 **Passengers/trainees:** 6
Contact:	Captain Barry Stanley, Owner
	7464 Charleston Run Cove
	Memphis, TN 38125
	Tel: 901-757-7895; Fax: 901-757-1278
	E-mail: capbarry@mindsouth.rr.com

Misty Isles

The *Misty Isles*, a 1915 gaff rigged ketch, has relocated to the Chesapeake Bay, and will soon operate out of Hampton Roads. But she is at a channel crossing (crossroads to landlubbers) as she prepares for the 2001-2002 season. The owners will be starting a family, with a new sailor arriving in August 2001, and are undecided which channel to take; raise a farmer and sell the boat, or raise a sailor and keep charting courses on the seas.

On one course *Misty Isles* will be available (for lease or sale) to some person or program that would like to supplement their fleet with a real classic. But the active sailing course we still must chart, or be caught by a lack of planning too near the rocks and docks. A mission trip to Haiti in the winter/spring of 2002 is in the planning, followed by a summer itinerary taking *Misty Isles* from Key West to New England.

Misty Isles' motto remains "Serving Fishers of Men", as services are offered primarily to Christian churches, youth groups, missionary organizations and Sea Scouts. The preparation and serving of food underway is part of the teamwork building, as well as sail handling, navigation, anchor setting and hauling, and standing watch.

The lower Chesapeake Bay will see the start of her sailing season in May 2001, and she is seeking crew and skippers to train for her 2002 Haiti mission trip. The goal will be to deliver volunteers and logistical support to Partners In Development, of Ipswich, MA and their Habitat-like home building program in Cite Soleil, Port Au Prince. The return trip from Haiti will give additional skippers and crew experience while exploring the Florida Keys, and then navigating the Gulf Stream back to New England. The return to New England waters will bring another outreach to the Lewis Middle School in Roxbury, MA. Subsequent projects include the same Christian youth and missionary services, and an early start on the *Misty Isles* full restoration project.

Flag:	USA
Rig:	Gaff ketch
Homeport/waters:	Hampton, Virginia/Ring's Island, Salisbury, Massachusetts: East Coast and Carribean.
Who sails?	Sea Scouts, affiliated church groups
Season:	Year-round
Program type:	Sail training for crew and apprentices.

Specifications:			
	Sparred length: 60'	Draft: 9'	Sail area: 1,500 sq. ft.
	LOD: 49'	Beam: 12'	Tons: 30 GRT
	LOA: 50'	Rig height: 60'	Power: 80 HP diesel
	LWL: 44'	Hull: wood	

Built:	1915
Crew:	3 (day sails), 6 (overnight). **Trainees:** 20 (day sails), 12 (overnight)
Contact:	Ray and Wendy Pike, Owners
	133 N. First Street
	Ring's Island, Hampton, VA 23664
	or 2 Second Street, Salisbury, MA 01952
	Tel: 757-850-0890 or 978-465-7953

Mystic Whaler

Built in 1967 and rebuilt in 1994, the *Mystic Whaler* carries passengers and trainees on a variety of cruises, ranging from one day to one week. In April and May, the schooner will be on the Hudson River, conducting environmental education programs in conjunction with the *Clearwater*. Sailing from Mystic, Connecticut, in the summer months, the *Mystic Whaler* will visit New York and Boston on one-week cruises with trainees, then finish the season with Elderhostel programs in September and October. Some of the two of three-day cruises during the season focus on specific topics, such as lighthouses, sea music, art, and photography. Lobster cruises are popular during the summer. Two-week apprenticeship programs run throughout the season.

Flag:	USA
Rig:	Gaff-rigged schooner
Homeport/waters:	Mystic, Connecticut: southeast New England
Who sails?	School groups from elementary school through college, as well as individuals and families.
Program type:	Sail training for crew and apprentices. Sea education in maritime history and ecology based on informal programming with organized groups such as Scouts. Passenger day sails and overnight passages.

Specifications:	Sparred length: 110'	Draft: 7' 6" (min.), 13' (max.)	Sail area: 3,000 sq. ft.
	LOD: 83'	Beam: 25'	Tons: 97 GRT
	LOA: 83'	Rig height: 90'	Power: 6-71 diesel, 175 HP
	LWL: 78'	Freeboard: 7'	Hull: steel

Designer:	"Chub" Crockett
Built:	1967; Tarpon Springs, Florida, George Sutton
Coast Guard certification:	Passenger Vessel (Subchapter T)
Crew:	5. **Trainees:** 65 (day), 36 (overnight)
Contact:	Captain John Eginton
	Mystic Whaler Cruises, Inc.
	PO Box 189
	Mystic, CT 06355-0189
	Tel: 860-536-4218; Fax: 860-536-4219
	E-mail: mysticwhaler@bigplanet.com
	Web site: http://www.mysticwhaler.com

Nefertiti

PHOTO BY LAURA SAWALL

Anderson Syndicate at the Graves yard in Marblehead, Massachusetts for the 1962 America's Cup. She was designed and skippered by Ted Hood, who ousted both *Easterner* and *Columbia* before being eliminated by Bus Mosbacher's *Weatherly* in the defender's finals.

Following her Cup challenge, *Nefertiti* was converted for cruising and traversed the globe. She crossed the Atlantic to the Mediterranean and chartered out of Greece for several years. By 1983 she was back in Newport as a spectator of the last America's Cup series held in Newport. *Nefertiti* then traveled down to the West Indies, to Fremantle, Australia in 1987, and crossed the Indian Ocean to South Africa where she remained until September 1997. She has been restored to racing trim by America's Cup Charters.

The 1962 12-meter class sloop *Nefertiti* has returned to Newport, Rhode Island. Brought back by America's Cup Charters' George Hill and Herb Marshall, owners of the America's Cup defender *Weatherly* and Ted Turner's former *American Eagle*, *Nefertiti* is part of their charter fleet of former cup contenders.

Nefertiti was built for the Ross

Flag:	USA
Rig:	Sloop
Homeport/waters:	Newport, Rhode Island: New England and Chesapeake Bay
Who sails?	Individuals of all ages.
Cost:	$1,800 group rate per day, $60 per person for evening sails
Program type:	Sail training for volunteer and paying trainees. Sea education based on informal, in-house programming. Passenger day sails.

Specifications:			
	Sparred length: 69'	Draft: 9'	Sail area: 1,850 sq. ft.
	LOD: 67'	Beam: 13' 6"	Tons: 28 GRT
	LOA: 67'	Rig height: 90'	Power: diesel
	LWL: 46'	Freeboard: 4'	Hull: wood

Designer:	Ted Hood
Built:	1962; Marblehead, Massachusetts, Graves
Coast Guard certification:	Passenger Vessel (Subchapter T)
Crew:	3. **Trainees/passengers:** 14
Contact:	George Hill/Herb Marshall, America's Cup Charters
	PO Box 51
	Newport, RI 02840
	Tel: 401-849-5868; Fax: 401-849-3098
	Web site: http://www.americascupcharters.com

NEFERTITI

Nehemiah

Crosscurrent Voyages is a sail training program operated onboard the Class C tall ship *Nehemiah*. Emulating the training style used on such vessels as the USCG Barque *Eagle*, the program attempts to awaken and cultivate leadership skills by challenging students to learn various disciplines and to manage different types of information and technical matters. Traditional knowledge and skills are used to integrate educational disciplines such as math, reasoning, English, and history. The object is to utilize the pace and style of administering a large sailing vessel as a tool for equipping trainees to develop personal styles for dealing with the sea of information, knowledge, and options which saturate their daily lives. The program rounds out the training by enhancing personal character development in the areas of family and community values.

The primary target age is 12 through 18. The training personnel often come from the USCG and professional maritime fields. The sailing vessel *Nehemiah* has circumnavigated the globe a number of times under previous ownership, thus adding a context to the learning.

NEHEMIAH

Flag:	USA
Rig:	Ketch
Homeport/waters:	Richmond, California: San Francisco Bay and Pacific Coast
Who sails?	Groups from elementary school through college, youth organizations, individuals, and families. Court referrals are also accepted. Emphasis is on at-risk youth.
Program type:	Sail training emphasizing character and community building. Sea education in marine science, maritime history, and ecology. Passenger day sails and overnight passages.

Specifications:			
	Sparred length: 57'	Draft: 6' 5"	Tons: 23 GRT
	LOD: 46' 8"	Beam: 14' 3"	Power: Perkins 4-236
	LOA: 50'	Rig height: 58'	Hull: wood
	LWL: 39'	Freeboard: 5'	

Designer:	William Garden (modified)
Built:	1971; Santa Barbara, California, Joseph Meyr
Coast Guard certification:	Passenger Vessel (Subchapter T)
Crew:	2. **Trainees:** 25 (day sails), 12 (overnight)
Contact:	Captain Rod Phillips
	Crosscurrent Voyages
	92 Seabreeze Drive
	Richmond, CA 94804-7410
	Tel/Fax: 510-234-5054
	E-mail: captain@sailingacross.com
	Web site: http://www.sailingacross.com

Niagara

The US Brig *Niagara* was built in 1988 as a reconstruction of the warship aboard which Oliver Hazard Perry won the Battle of Lake Erie in 1813 during the War of 1812. Her mission is to interpret War of 1812 history, promote the Commonwealth of Pennsylvania and the Erie Region, and preserve the skills of square-rig seafaring.

The present *Niagara* has auxiliary power and modern navigation equipment, but lacks modern amenities such as warm water, showers and privacy. She is sailed by a crew of 18-20 professionals supplemented by 20 volunteers willing to live under Spartan conditions such as hammock berthing and living out of a duffel bag. Volunteers do not need to have experience, but a minimum sign-on of three weeks is required.

Niagara is inspected as an Attraction Vessel in port, and sails as an Uninspected Vessel. During "home summers" (odd numbered years) there are typically two day sails per week from early May to late September/early October, with a short voyage of three to four weeks sometime in the season. In the even years, the ship is away from seven to eighteen weeks on voyages to ports in the Great Lakes, US East Coast, and Canadian Maritimes. A typical schedule is public visitation in port for three days and four-day passage between ports. When not on extended voyages, she makes her home at the Erie Maritime Museum in Erie, Pennsylvania.

Flag:	USA
Rig:	Brig
Homeport/waters:	Erie, Pennsylvania: Coastwise and Great Lakes
Who sails?	School groups from middle school through college, as well as individuals and families.
Program type:	Sail training for crew and apprentices. Sea education based on informal, in-house programming. Dockside interpretation.

Specifications:	Sparred length: 198'	Draft: 11'	Sail area: 12,600 sq. ft.
	LOD: 116'	Beam: 32' 6"	Tons: 162 GRT
	LOA: 123'	Rig height: 121'	Power: twin 180 HP diesels
	LWL: 110'	Hull: wood	

Designer:	Melbourne Smith
Built:	1988; Erie, Pennsylvania
Coast Guard certification:	Uninspected Vessel and Attraction Vessel
Crew:	40
Contact:	Captain Walter P. Rybka
	Pennsylvania Historical and Museum Commission
	150 East Front Street, Suite 100
	Erie, PA 16507
	Tel: 814-452-2744; Fax: 814-455-6760
	E-mail: sail@brigniagara.org
	Web site: http://www.brigniagara.org

Nighthawk

Built in 1980 as a replica of a 19th-century coastal schooner, *Nighthawk* sails the waters of the Chesapeake Bay and its tributaries from April 1 through November 1 each season. She voyaged to Caribbean, Mexico, and South America prior to arriving in Baltimore in 1986.

Nighthawk operates as a private charter vessel as well as offering basic sail training to local school and scout groups. Docked in the historic Fells Point section of Baltimore's Inner Harbor, the *Nighthawk* and her captain and crew provide an ideal opportunity for character and team building through hands-on exploration.

Nighthawk is also available for wide variety of corporate and private charters and celebrations, as well as public excursions. "Murder Mystery" and other theme cruises are featured. Weddings are performed aboard by the captain and catering is available.

Flag:	USA
Rig:	Schooner
Homeport/waters:	Baltimore, Maryland: Chesapeake Bay
Who sails?	Students from middle school through college. Affiliated institutions include Girl Scouts and church and youth organizations.
Season:	April through November
Program type:	Sail training for paying trainees based on informal, in-house programming.

Specifications:			
	Sparred length: 82'	Draft: 5'	Sail area: 2,000 sq. ft.
	LOD: 65'	Beam:20'	Tons: 45 GRT
	LWL: 60'	Rig height: 55'	Power: twin diesels
	Freeboard: 6'	Hull: steel	

Designer:	Haglund
Built:	1980; Florida, Haglund Schooner Company
Coast Guard certification:	Passenger Vessel (Subchapter T)
Crew:	4. **Trainees/passengers:** 49 (day sails), 6 (overnight)
Contact:	Captain Martin D. Weiss, President
	Schooner Nighthawk Cruises, Inc.
	1715 Thames St., Box 38153
	Baltimore, MD 21231
	Tel: 410-276-7447; Fax: 410-327-7245
	E-mail: schoonernighthawk@erols.com
	Web site: http://www.a1nighthawkcruises.com

Niña (Santa Clara)

Jonathon Nance, a noted British designer and archaeologist, finished the vessel and designed the sailplan and rig.

She was built in Valenca, Bahia, Brazil, using only traditional tools and techniques of the 15th century. Her mission today is to educate the public on the "space shuttle" of the 15th century, and over one million students and teachers have visited the *Nina* since her completion in 1992. Starting in 2001, the *Nina* will be in Grand Cayman Island taking passengers on day sails from December through May. She is available for films, documentaries, and charters.

The *Nina* is a historically accurate replica of a 15th century caravel. John Sarsfield, the leading authority on caravels, was designer and builder until his death halfway through the project.

Flag:	USA
Rig:	15th century caravel redonda
Homeport/waters:	Wilmington, Delaware: Great Lakes/Midwestern rivers (summer), Cayman Islands (winter)
Who sails?	School groups from elementary through college. Families and adults of all ages.
Program type:	Sail training for professional and volunteer crew and trainees. Sea education in maritime history as informal in-house programming. Dockside interpretation while in port.

Specifications:

Sparred length: 92'	Draft: 7'	Sail area: 1,919 sq. ft.
LOD: 65'	Beam: 18'	Tons: 37 GRT
LOA: 68'	Rig height: 54'	Power: 128 HP diesel
LWL: 58'	Freeboard: 5'	Hull: wood
Hull color: brown/black	Spar material: wood	

Designer:	John Sarsfield/Jonathon Nance
Built:	1988-1991; Valenca, Brazil, John Sarsfield/Jonathon Nance/Ralph Eric Nicholson
Coast Guard certification:	Attraction Vessel
Crew:	6. **Trainees/Passengers:** 45-50 (day sails)
Contact:	Morgan P. Sanger, Captain/Director
	Columbus Foundation
	Box 5179
	St. Thomas, VI 00803
	Tel: 284-495-4618; Fax: 284-495-4616
	E-mail: columfnd@surfbvi.com
	Web site: http://www.thenina.com

Norfolk Rebel

Captain Lane Briggs' "tugantine" is a favorite flagship for sail-assisted working vessels and is credited with a 1984 "circumnavigation of Virginia." The *Norfolk Rebel* is a familiar site to all involved in sail training and tall ships events up and down the Chesapeake. In 2000 she participated in Tall Ships 2000®, traveling as far as Halifax, Nova Scotia from her homeport of Norfolk, Virginia.

Flag:	USA
Rig:	Gaff schooner, 2-masted
Homeport/waters:	Norfolk, Virginia; East Coast from Canada to the Gulf of Mexico
Season:	Year round
Who sails?	Individuals of all ages
Program type:	Sail training for crew and apprentices. Sea education in local maritime history and ecology based on informal, in-house programming. Dockside interpretation.

Specifications:	Sparred length: 59'	LOA: 51'	LOD: 51'
	LWL: 48'	Draft: 6'6"	Beam: 15'3"
	Rig height: 50'	Freeboard: 4'6"	Sail area: 1,700 sq. ft.
	Tons: 38 GRT	Power: diesel	Hull: steel

Designer:	Merritt N. Walter
Built:	1980; Howdy Bailey, Norfolk, Virginia
Crew:	3 (day), 6 (overnight) Trainees: 3
Contact:	Captain Lane Briggs, Owner/Master
	Rebel Marine Service, Inc.
	1553 Bayville Street
	Norfolk, VA 23503
	Tel: 804-588-6022; Fax: 804-588-7102

Norseman

The Leif Ericson Viking Ship, Inc. and the *Norseman* celebrated the millennium anniversary of the first European to set foot on the North American continent when in the late summer of 2000, the *Norseman*, in the company of approximately 16 other Viking ship Replicas from the US and Europe, sailed from the only known site of Viking habitation, L'anse aux Meadows, Newfoundland and down the East Coast of Canada and the US, stopping at selected cities as part of "Viking Sail 2000."

Built in 1992, *Norseman* offers people a glimpse of Viking culture and reminds everyone of the first discovery of North America by Europeans; Leif Ericson and his fellow Vikings, who sailed from Greenland in about the year 1000 to explore new lands to the west.

Crewmembers appear in full Viking costume, share their interests in Viking culture and their Scandinavian heritage, and practice their sailing and rowing skills. *Norseman* has appeared in sailing events on the East Coast of the US and in Sweden. In 1995 she appeared in productions shown on the History Channel and A & E cable channels. The 1999 season was spent in preparation for the voyage from Newfoundland, developing a training manual from crewmembers, and training on board the ship.

Flag:	USA
Rig:	Viking longship (single square sail)
Homeport/waters:	Wilmington, Delaware: Chesapeake Bay, Delaware River, Jersey Shore, New York Bay, Hudson River, and Long Island Sound
Who sails?	Students and individuals of all ages.
Program type:	Sail training for volunteer crew and apprentices. Sea education in maritime history relevant to Viking period. Dockside interpretation during port visits.

Specifications:

Sparred length: 42'	Draft: 3'	Sail area: 297 sq. ft.
LOD: 32'	Beam: 9'	Tons: 2 GRT
LOA: 40'	Rig height: 30'	Power: 25 HP outboard
LWL: 30'	Freeboard: 3'	Hull: fiberglass

Designer:	Applecraft, Inc.
Built:	1992; Isle of Man, UK, Applecraft, Inc.
Crew:	7-12. **Trainees:** 7-12
Contact:	Dennis Johnson, President
	Leif Ericson Viking Ship, Inc.
	4919 Township Line Road #303
	Drexel, PA 19026
	Tel: 215-242-3063; Fax: 215-242-3119
	E-mail: viking@libertynet.org
	Web site: http://www.libertynet.org~viking

Northern Light

Northern Light, a 12-meter sloop, was built in 1938 as a gift to young Lee Loomis from his father. She was later owned by the Greek shipping tycoon Steven Niarchos, during her involvement in the America's Cup under the name of *Nereus*.

A long-time racing rival of *Gleam*, the beautiful *Northern Light* sank at the dock in Lake Michigan after her Cup service. She was bought and raised by Bob Tiedemann 15 years ago, after which she underwent extensive renovation before returning to Newport. Together, *Gleam* and *Northern Light* offer a unique team building program called "Your Own America's Cup Regatta", created over 12 years ago. Each boat accommodates thirteen guests plus three crewmembers. No previous sailing experience is necessary to participate. Group and corporate outings are available in Newport, Rhode Island and other New England ports.

Flag:	USA
Rig:	Sloop (12-meter)
Homeport/waters:	Newport, Rhode Island: Narragansett Bay
Who sails?	Corporations who charter the vessels for team building and client entertaining.
Program type:	Sail training with paying trainees. Passenger day sails.

Specifications:	Sparred length: 70'	Draft: 9'	Sail area: 1,900 sq. ft.
	LOD: 70'	Beam: 12'	Tons: 30 GRT
	LOA: 70'	Rig height: 90'	Power: diesel
	LWL: 45' 6"	Freeboard: 3'	Hull: wood

Designer:	Clinton Crane and Olin Stephens
Built:	1938; City Island, New York, Henry Nevins
Coast Guard certification:	Passenger Vessel (Subchapter T)
Crew:	3. **Trainees:** 14
Contact:	Elizabeth Tiedemann, Director of Sales & Marketing
	Seascope Systems, Inc.,
	103 Ruggles Avenue
	Newport, RI 02840
	Tel: 401-847-5007; Fax: 401-849-6140
	E-mail: aboard@earthlink.net
	Web site: http://www.seascopenewport.com

Ocean Classroom Foundation Schooner Project (Work in Progress)

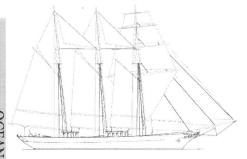

The Ocean Classroom Foundation (formerly the Schooner Harvey Gamage Foundation) is working to build a new steel ship, to meet the growing demand for the Ocean Classroom program. TriCoastal Marine is designing the vessel (as yet unnamed), to be a superb platform for teaching as well as an excellent sailer for major voyages. The new ship's detail design is nearing completion, bids are being reviewed from building yards, and fund raising continues. Keel laying and launch dates to be announced.

Ocean Classroom is a fully accredited semester-at-sea for high school students. Young people come from all parts of the country to join this award-winning program, and gain an unparalleled learning and growth experience. The new ship, conceived specifically to fulfill the mission of Ocean Classroom, will allow us to include more worthy students, to teach them better, and to increase the amount of financial aid we can award each semester.

As a non-profit organization, we gratefully accept contributions of equipment, materials, or funds for this project or the Scholarship Endowment. Ocean Classroom also owns and operates the *Harvey Gamage* and the *Spirit of Massachusetts*. For more information about Ocean Classroom and its programs, or to make a contribution, please contact our office.

Flag:	USA
Rig:	Square topsail schooner, three masted
Homeport/waters:	Islesboro, Maine: Eastern US and Canada (summer), Caribbean and South America (winter)
Who sails?	School groups from middle school through college. Affiliated institutions include Proctor Academy, Long Island University, Franklin Pierce College, and other schools.
Season:	Year-round
Cost:	Varies with term
Program type:	Sail training with paying trainees/students. Fully accredited sea education in marine science, maritime history, maritime literature, marine applied mathematics and navigation.

Specifications:			
	Sparred length: 158'	Draft: 12' 6"	Sail area: 8,000 sq. ft.
	LOD: 112' 6"	Beam: 27'	Tons: 99 GRT
	LOA: 124'	Rig height: 108'	Power: 500 HP diesel
	LWL: 100'	Hull: steel	

Designer:	TriCoastal Marine
Coast Guard certification:	(planned) Sailing School Vessel (Subchapter R), Passenger Vessel (Subchapter T)
Crew:	10-15, including instructors. **Trainees:** 30 (overnight)
Contact:	Bert Rogers, Director
	Ocean Classroom Foundation, Inc.
	PO Box 446
	Cornwall, NY 12518
	Tel: 800-724-7245 or 845-615-1412; Fax: 845-615-1414
	E-mail: mail@sailgamage.org
	Web site: http://www.sailgamage.org

Ocean Star

Launched in 1991 as the school ship for *Ocean Navigator* magazine, *Ocean Star* now sails under the banner of Sea-mester Programs as a college-level semester voyage. Sea-mester Programs offer 35 and 80-day semesters aboard and are based on principles of experiential and adventure education. Learning through interaction and practical activities, the primary academic foci of oceanography, marine science, communication, and leadership skills development are brought from the textbook into real-life application. Under the guidance of professional staff, including Ph.D. and Masters graduates, our students earn college credits for both academic and vocational activities, while piloting *Ocean Star* throughout the islands of the Lesser Antilles. Along the way, the crew visits up to 20 individual Caribbean islands, undertaking research and service projects with local government and private organizations while simultaneously working toward certifications in sailing and scuba

diving. No experience is necessary. Programs are available to high school seniors (Argo Academy), high school graduates and college-aged students. Sea-mester Programs are coeducational and non-competitive. The activities are not physically demanding, yet are challenging enough to teach the crew to work together. In the stimulating environment of the Caribbean islands, the expedition becomes the vehicle for gaining knowledge and understanding, confidence and skills.

OCEAN STAR

Flag:	UK
Rig:	Schooner, two-masted
Waters:	Eastern Caribbean
Who sails?	High school students (school year), high school graduates and college-aged students (summer).
Season:	Year-round
Program type:	Nine-month academic high school afloat. In summer, marine and nautical science mini-semesters.

Specifications:	LOA: 88'	Draft: 9'	Sail area: 4,600 sq. ft.
	LOD: 73'	Beam: 20'	Tons: 70 GRT
	LWL: 65'	Rig height: 92'	Power: 210 HP diesel
	Freeboard: 5'	Hull: steel	

Designer:	Bill Peterson
Built:	1991; Norfolk, Virginia, Marine Metals
Crew:	4. Trainees: 14
Contact:	Argo Academy/Sea-mester Programs
	PO Box 5477
	Sarasota, FL 34277
	Tel: 941-924-6789; Fax: 941-924-6075
	E-mail: seamester@msn.com
	Web site: http://www.argoacademy.com

Odyssey

research on Humpback Whale songs and his unparalleled long-term research on the Right Whale. Under Dr. Payne's leadership, WCI/OA has continually expanded benign Right Whale research techniques. The Institute combines rigorous science with a commitment to the welfare of whales and the ocean environment, and has helped people, regardless of their ideology, to better understand and appreciate the natural world. WCI/OA's Voyage of the *Odyssey*

The *Odyssey* is owned and operated by the Whale Conservation Institute/Ocean Alliance (WCI/OA), a nonprofit organization dedicated to the conservation of whales and their environment through research and education. Dr. Payne, President of WCI/OA and internationally acclaimed marine scientist, is best known for his pioneering Program, an assessment of the baseline levels of bio-persistent toxins in the oceans, is being conducted from the *Odyssey*. In 1995 the *Odyssey* was featured in PBS's "New Explorers Series", Discovery Channel's "Finite Oceans", BBC's "Paradise in Peril", and in 1996, the IMAX production "Whales."

Flag:	USA
Rig:	Ketch
Homeport/waters:	Key West, Florida and San Diego, California: Global
Who sails?	Scientists, college students and adults.
Program type:	WCI/OA is developing sea education programs on the Web in cooperation with accredited schools and colleges in marine science, including marine mammal research, education, and conservation programs. Dockside interpretation during port visits.

Specifications:			
	Sparred length: 94'	Draft: 11'	Sail area: 4,500 sq. ft.
	LOD: 85'	Beam: 18' 6"	Tons: 100 GRT
	LOA: 85'	Rig height: 89'	Power: Detroit diesel
	LWL: 69'	Freeboard: 6'	Hull: steel

Designer:	WECO/Whangarei, New Zealand
Built:	1976; New Zealand, WECO/Whangarei
Crew:	4. **Trainees:** 6 (2 science, 2 media, 2 interns)
Contact:	Iain Kerr, Vice President
	Whale Conservation Institute/Ocean Alliance
	191 Weston Road
	Lincoln, MA 01773
	Tel: 781-259-0423; Fax: 781-259-0288
	E-mail: interns@oceanalliance.org
	Web site: http://www.oceanalliance.org

OMF Ontario

On July 2, 1994, the hull of the schooner *OMF Ontario* was launched amidst the cheers of over 2,500 people from as for away as Florida and California. They came to applaud a six-year commitment by an all-volunteer crew to stimulate interest in and awareness of the Great Lakes. In 1998 all welding was completed, the final ballast in place, and spar construction begun. She will resemble many of the ships built at this location in the 19th century, except that she is built of welded steel to modern standards and will have backup diesel power. When complete, the schooner will serve as a floating classroom for the Education through Involvement program.

Participants of all ages will have a hands-on learning experience about the history, heritage, resources, ecology, and the future of the Great Lakes.

Flag:	USA
Rig:	Topsail schooner
Homeport/waters:	Oswego, New York: Great Lakes
Who sails?	School children, community groups, and senior citizens.
Program type:	Passenger day sails for organized groups such as schools, community organizations, and businesses. Dockside interpretation.

Specifications:			
	Sparred length: 85'	Draft: 8'	Sail area: 2,000 sq. ft.
	LOD: 60'	Beam: 16'	Power: 100 HP diesel
	LOA: 65'	Rig height: 70'	Tons: 42 GRT
	Freeboard: 6'	Hull: steel	

Designer:	Francis MacLachlan
Built:	1994; Oswego, New York
Coast Guard certification:	Passenger Vessel (Subchapter T)
Crew:	2, 4 instructors. **Trainees:** 25
Contact:	Dr. Henry Spang, Director
	Education Through Involvement Program Oswego Maritime Foundation
	41 Lake Street
	Oswego, NY 13126
	Tel: 315-342-5753

One and All

One and All was built to fulfill the dream of a dedicated group of South Australians to provide sail training in South Australia. This dream came to fruition on April 5, 1987 on her commissioning day. Since her commissioning, *One and All* has carried many thousands of trainees from South Australia and further afield from all states and territories of Australia and overseas.

One and All also caters to many other groups, including half and full-day educational trips for school groups, recreational day trips to the public, and adventure voyages of two to ten days for those who wish to experience the wonders of sailing on a square-rigged vessel.

One and All has participated in three Sydney to Hobart Races, a Darwin to Ambon Yacht Race, has been chartered to carry out scientific studies on the East Coast of Australia, and has participated in a number of tall ship events in Australia. *One and All* spends her time sailing the Australian coastline, but is equipped and certified to the highest Australian survey standard, which has allowed her to sail internationally in the past. No previous experience is needed to sail on board *One and All*, only a desire to experience sailing a square-rigger in Australian waters.

Flag:	Australia
Rig:	Brigantine
Homeport/waters:	Port Adelaide, Adelaide, South Australia, Australia: East Coast of Australia (summer), Gulfs of South Australia (winter)
Who sails?	High school students and individuals of all ages.
Season:	Year-round
Cost:	$3,000 AUS group rate per day, $120 AUS per person per day on extended voyages
Program type:	Sail training for paying trainees. Sea education based on informal, in-house programming. Dockside interpretation during port visits.

Specifications:

Sparred length: 140'	Draft: 9' 4"	Sail area: 6,251 sq. ft.
LOD: 98' 7"	Beam: 26' 11"	Tons: 121 GRT
LWL: 86' 11"	Rig height: 88' 7"	Power: 380 HP diesel
Hull: wood		

Designer:	Kell Steinman
Built:	1985, North Haven, South Australia, Australia, W.G. Porter and Sons Pty. Ltd.
Certification:	Australian Maritime Safety Authority Certificate for Australian and International Waters
Crew:	10. **Trainees:** 50 (day sails), 24 (overnight)
Contact:	Captain Ian Kuhl, CEO
	Sailing Ship Trust of South Australia, Inc.
	PO Box 222
	Port Adelaide, South Australia, 5015, Australia
	Tel: 61-8-8447-5144; Fax: 61-8-8341-0167
	E-mail: tallship@oneandall.org.au
	Web site: http://www.oneandall.org.au

Oosterschelde

Oosterschelde is a Dutch three-masted schooner, built in 1918. Owned by a family that also sailed her, the ship remained Dutch until the late 1930s. *Oosterschelde* was then Danish-owned and later Swedish-owned. Modernization took away the sailing power and the engine got bigger. In the 1980s she became a motor coaster, with no sails left.

In 1988, *Oosterschelde* was purchased by the current owners, who were interested in restoring her to her original condition. Many companies, private individuals, and governmental institutions supported the foundation "The Rotterdam Tall Ship" with a $1.7 million budget. Since the restoration (1988-1992), the ship has been run by a company established for that purpose. Voyages are sailed with a professional crew of eight, with berths for 24 passengers. Day sail trips are also available. *Oosterschelde* made a world voyage from 1996-1998.

OOSTERSCHELDE

Flag:	The Netherlands
Rig:	Schooner, three-masted
Homeport/waters:	Rotterdam, The Netherlands: Worldwide
Who sails?	High school students, adults, and families.
Cost:	$100-$200 per person per day
Program type:	Sail training for crew, volunteer, and paying trainees. Passenger day sails and overnight passages. Sea education based on informal, in-house programming.

Specifications:			
	Sparred length: 164'	Draft: 9' 8"	Sail area: 8,000 sq. ft.
	LOD: 121'	Beam: 24' 7"	Tons: 400 GRT
	LOA: 131'	Rig height: 115'	Power: 360 HP
	LWL: 115'	Freeboard: 4' 4"	Hull: steel

Built:	1918; The Netherlands, Apollo
Crew:	8. **Trainees:** 36 (day sails), 24 (overnight)
Contact:	Captain Dick van Andel
	BV Reederij Oosterschelde
	PO Box 23429
	3001 KK Rotterdam, The Netherlands
	Tel: 31-10-4364258; Fax: 31-10-4362100
	E-mail: info@oosterschelde.nl
	Web site: http://www.oosterschelde.nl

Pacific Grace

old ship, one of Canada's last original Grand Banks fishing schooners, have been carefully copied and a new replica vessel built using traditional methods. The boat building team consisting largely of skippers and crewmembers of other SALTS vessels, ably assisted by volunteers and past trainees.

The *Pacific Grace* is scheduled to begin sailing May 31, 2001, when she joins the *Pacific Swift* in providing coastal sail training programs in the cruising grounds of the Pacific Northwest. During the summer she will offer 10-day voyages open to anyone between the ages of 13 and 25, as well as shorter school programs during the spring and fall.

Since the retirement of SALTS' flagship, the *Robertson II*, at the end of the 1995 sail training season, *Pacific Grace* has been taking shape at the SALTS Heritage Shipyard and was launched in the harbor of Victoria, British Columbia on October 9, 1999. The lines of the

Flag:	Canada
Rig:	Gaff topsail schooner, two-masted
Homeport/waters:	Victoria, British Columbia, Canada: Pacific Northwest, Pacific Ocean
Who sails?	Students and young adults aged 13-25
Season:	March to October
Cost:	$85 CDN per 24 hours per trainee
Program type:	Sail training.

Specifications:			
	Sparred length: 130'	Draft: 11'	Sail area: 5,637 sq. ft.
	LOD: 105'	Beam: 22' 2"	Tons: 170 GRT
	LOA: 107' 10"	Rig height: 105'	Power: twin diesels
	LWL: 93'	Freeboard: 5'	Hull: wood

Built:	1999; Victoria, British Columbia, SALTS
Canadian Coast Guard certification:	Passenger Vessel, Sailing School Vessel
Crew:	5. Trainees: 30 (ages 13-25)
Contact:	Mr. Rob Howatson, Executive Director
	Sail and Life Training Society (SALTS)
	PO Box 5014, Station B
	Victoria, British Columbia V8R 6N3 Canada
	Tel: 250-383-6811; Fax: 250-383-7781
	E-mail: saltsociety@home.com
	Web site: http://www.saltsociety.com

Pacific Swift

Built as a working exhibit at Expo '86 in Vancouver, British Columbia, the *Pacific Swift* has sailed over 100,000 deep-sea miles on training voyages for young crewmembers. Her offshore travels have taken her to Australia and Europe, to remote communities on Easter and Pitcairn Islands, and to many other unusual and far-flung ports of call.

When not offshore, the *Swift* provides coastal sail training programs among the cruising grounds of the Pacific Northwest which include shorter school programs in the spring and fall and 10-day summer trips open to anyone aged 13 to 25.

Each year over one thousand young people participate in an experience which combines all aspects of shipboard life, from galley chores to helmsmanship, with formal instruction in navigation, pilotage, seamanship, and small boat handling. Rooted in Christian values, SALTS believes that training under sail provides the human spirit a real chance to develop and mature. SALTS received the 1998 Sail Training Program of the Year Award from the American Sail Training Association.

Flag:	Canada
Rig:	Square topsail schooner, two-masted
Homeport/waters:	Victoria, British Columbia, Canada: Pacific Northwest, North and South Pacific, Caribbean, and Atlantic
Who sails?	Individuals and groups.
Season:	Year-round
Cost:	$80 CDN per 24 hours per trainee
Program type:	Offshore and coastal sail training.

Specifications:

Sparred length: 111'	Draft: 10' 8"	Sail area: 4,111 sq. ft.
LOD: 78'	Beam: 20' 6"	Tons: 98 GRT
LOA: 83'	Rig height: 92'	Power: 220 HP diesel
LWL: 65'	Freeboard: 3' 6"	Hull: wood

Built: 1986; Vancouver, British Columbia, Canada, SALTS

Canadian Coast Guard certification: Passenger vessel, Sailing School Vessel

Crew: 5. **Trainees:** 30. **Age:** 13-25

Contact: Rob Howatson, Executive Director
Sail and Life Training Society (SALTS)
Box 5014, Station B
Victoria, British Columbia V8R 6N3, CANADA
Tel: 250-383-6811; Fax: 250-383-7781
Email: saltsociety@home.com
Web site: http://www.saltsociety.com

Palawan

Designed and built in 1965 as an ocean racer under the old Cruising Club of America rule, *Palawan* achieved a number of firsts. An early aluminum yacht, she was the first offshore boat to use the fin keel. Although she could not keep up with the newer hulls encouraged by the IOR rule, everyone spoke highly of the boat, and designer Olin Stephens declared her "perhaps the easiest steering boat I ever drew." Her racing career has been an active one, and she was used by the Maine Maritime Academy for over 10 years as a sail training vessel.

Palawan has operated as a passenger vessel since 1988 in Portland, Maine, serving both individuals and groups, and she is a popular vehicle for fundraising events for groups such as Friends of Casco Bay, Maine Island Trails, and others. A winter season may be spent as a yacht in warmer waters with up to six crew aboard.

Flag:	USA
Rig:	Cutter
Homeport/waters:	Portland, Maine: Casco Bay, Caribbean
Who sails?	Students, adults, and groups.
Cost:	$125 per person per day, $950 group rate
Program type:	Sail training with team-building activities for paying trainees. Passenger day sails and overnight passages.

Specifications:			
	Sparred length: 58'	Draft: 8' 1"	Sail area: 1,308 sq. ft.
	LOD: 58'	Beam: 12' 4"	Tons: 24 GRT
	LOA: 58'	Rig height: 68'	Power: 60 HP
	LWL: 40'	Freeboard: 4' 4"	Hull: aluminum

Designer:	Olin Stephens
Built:	1965; New York, New York, Derecktor
Coast Guard certification:	Passenger Vessel (Subchapter T)
Crew:	2 (day sails), 3 (overnight). **Trainees:** 24 (day sails), 6 (overnight)
Contact:	Captain Tom Woodruff
	Palawan Services, Inc.
	PO Box 9715-240
	Portland, ME 04104
	Tel: 207-773-2163; Fax: 207-781-5530
	E-mail: palawan@nlis.net
	Web site: http://www.sailpalawan.com

Pathfinder

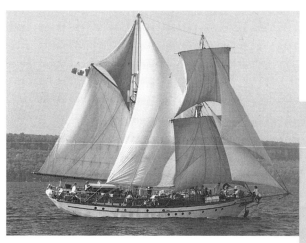

Tall Ship Adventures conducts sail training on board *Pathfinder*, a square-rigged ship designed specifically for youth sail training on the Great Lakes. Since 1964 over 15,000 young people have lived and worked aboard *Pathfinder* and her sister ship, *Playfair*.

Youth between the ages of 14 and 18 become the working crew on one or two-week adventures, making 24-hour passages from ports all over the Great Lakes. The program is delivered by youth officers between the ages of 15 and 18, trained and qualified during Tall Ship Adventures' Winter Training Programs. The captain and first mate are the only adults on board.

Every year each ship sails over 4,000 miles, spends over 40 nights at sea, and introduces 300 trainees to the tall ship experience. *Pathfinder* is owned and operated by Toronto Brigantine, Inc., a registered charity.

Flag:	Canada
Rig:	Brigantine
Homeport/waters:	Toronto, Ontario, Canada: Great Lakes
Who sails?	In July and August, youth programs for ages 14-18; in May, June, and September, school groups from middle school through college, and interested adult groups.
Cost:	$675 CDN for one week, $1,175 CDN for two weeks. Call for spring and fall group rates.
Program type:	Sail training for paying trainees, including seamanship and leadership training based on informal, in-house programming. Shoreside winter program. Dockside interpretation. Affiliated institutions include the Canadian Sail Training Association and the Ontario Camping Association.

Specifications:			
	Sparred length: 72'	Draft: 8'	Sail area: 2,600 sq. ft.
	LOD: 58'	Beam: 15' 3"	Tons: 31.63 GRT
	LOA: 60'	Rig height: 54'	Power: 150 HP diesel
	LWL: 45'	Freeboard: 4'	Hull: steel

Designer:	Francis A. Maclachlan
Built:	1963; Kingston, Ontario, Canada, Kingston Shipyards
Crew:	10. **Trainees:** 25 (day sails), 18 (overnight)
Contact:	Catharine McLean, Executive Director
	Toronto Brigantine, Inc.
	370 Queen's Quay West, Ste. 203
	Toronto, Ontario, M5V 3J3, Canada
	Tel: 416-596-7117; Fax: 416-596-9119
	E-mail: mail@tallshipadventures.on.ca
	Web site: http://www.tallshipadventures.on.ca

Peking

PHOTO BY NORMAN BROUWER

Peking was launched in 1911 at Hamburg, Germany by the Blohm & Voss shipyard. She was owned by the F. Laeisz Company of that port, who used her to carry fuel and manufactured goods to the West Coast of South America, around Cape Horn, and return to European ports with nitrate mined in northern Chile.

With her four-masted barque rig, steel hull and masts, and mid-ship bridge deck, *Peking* represents the final generation of sailing ships built for world trade. Though a product of the 20th century, she still sailed in the traditional way, with few labor-saving devices or safety features. Her crew followed the standard sailing vessel routine of four hours on duty and four hours off duty, around the clock, seven days a week.

Peking was retired in 1933, when steamers using the Panama Canal took over what was left of the nitrate trade. She served as a nautical school for boys, moored on a British River, until she was acquired by the South Street Seaport Museum in 1974. She now serves as a floating dockside exhibit. Educational programs for children and young adults take place on board, with a wet lab on the ship interpreting the biology of New York harbor.

Flag:	USA
Rig:	Barque, four-masted
Homeport/waters:	New York, New York
Cost:	$3 per person
Program type:	Sea education in marine science, maritime history, and ecology based on informal, in-house programming.

Specifications:	Sparred length: 377' 6"	Draft: 16'	Sail area: 44,132 sq. ft.
	LOD: 320'	Beam: 45' 8"	Tons: 3,100 GRT
	Rig height: 170' 5"	Hull: steel	

Built:	1911; Hamburg, Germany, Blohm & Voss
Contact:	Paula Mayo, Director of Programs
	South Street Seaport Museum
	207 Front Street
	New York, NY, 10038
	Tel: 212-748-8681; Fax: 212-748-8610
	Web site: http://www.southstseaport.org

Phoenix

The coastal schooner *Phoenix* was built on Long Island, New York and launched in 1984 as a replica of the type of vessels plying the waters of Long Island Sound at the turn of the century. *Phoenix* was first used as a cargo vessel between Port Jefferson, New York and Bridgeport, Connecticut, before carrying passengers over the same route for day trip excursions. In the mid-1980s the Nassau County Board of Cooperative Services used her as a platform for their marine biology public school education program. The vessel was later sold and moved to the Bahamas.

In 1993 *Phoenix* returned to Long Island and was acquired by the Coastal Ecology Learning Program, a nonprofit educational corporation. C.E.L.P. offers

shipboard environmental education programs for schoolchildren, families, and adults. *Phoenix* is the training ship for the Long Island US Naval Sea Cadets. The vessel is also available for private functions, children's birthday parties, corporate events, etc. *Phoenix* travels the length of Long Island Sound, offering programs throughout the region.

Flag:	USA
Rig:	Gaff schooner, two-masted
Homeport/waters:	Glen Cove, New York: Long Island Sound
Who sails?	Students of all ages, individuals and families.
Program type:	Sail training for volunteer and paying trainees. Sea education in marine science, ecology, and maritime history. Affiliated with the Long Island US Naval Sea Cadets.

Specifications:	Sparred length: 71'	Draft: 6'	Sail area: 1,600 sq. ft.
	LOD: 56'	Beam: 16'	Tons: 40 GRT
	LOA: 59'	Rig height: 60'	Power: 80 HP Ford/Lehman
	LWL: 54'	Freeboard: 4'	Hull: steel
	Hull color: white	Spar material: aluminum	

Designer:	Walter Merrit
Built:	1984; Patchogue, New York, Greg Brazier
Coast Guard certification:	Passenger Vessel (Subchapter T)
Crew:	3. **Trainees/passengers:** 2
Contact:	Captain Dennis F. Watson
	Coastal Ecology Learning Program, Inc.
	PO Box 473
	Huntington, NY 11743
	Tel: 631-385-CELP; Fax: 631-385-2357
	E-mail: celp@optonline.net
	Web site: http://www.coastalecology.org

PHOENIX

Phoenix

Built in Denmark in 1929 as a missionary schooner, *Phoenix* retired from missionary work after 20 years and carried cargo until her engine room was damaged by fire in 1972. In 1974 she was purchased and converted into a brigantine, before being purchased by Square Sail in 1988. In 1991 she was converted into a 15th-century Caravel, to replicate the *Santa Maria*, Christopher Columbus' flagship, for Ridley Scott's film "1492: Conquest of Paradise". In 1996 her name was changed back to *Phoenix* and she was converted into a two-masted brig.

All of Square Sail's ships are fully commissioned and work throughout the year. When not filming, they have a regular sailing program, giving people the chance to experience traditional square-rig sailing first-hand. These voyages typically run between four and seven days, and occasionally longer. They are either based from Square Sail's homeport of Charlestown, Cornwall, UK, or they work around the annual schedule offering voyages between the various ports.

Square Sail runs an annual course from February to October where trainees are given the opportunity to learn the skills associated with sailing these ships, and in addition to maintenance and shore-based instruction, they form part of the regular crew throughout the season.

Flag:	UK
Rig:	Brig, two-masted
Homeport/waters:	Charlestown Harbour, St. Austell, Cornwall, UK: UK and Europe
Who sails?	Individuals and families of all ages.
Season:	Year-round
Cost:	$160 per person per day, $5,600 group rate per day (charter)
Program type:	Sail training for professional crew, volunteer and paying trainees. Sea education in maritime history in cooperation with accredited institutions and as informal, in-house programming. Worldwide film work and corporate charters.

Specifications:			
	Sparred length: 112'	Draft: 8' 6"	Sail area: 4,000 sq. ft.
	LOD: 76'	Beam: 21'	Tons: 79 GRT
	LOA: 86'	Rig height: 81'	Power: 235 HP diesel
	LWL: 70'	Freeboard: 6'	Hull: oak on oak

Built:	1929; Frederickshavn, Denmark, Hjorne & Jakobsen
Certification:	MCA and MECAL (UK)
Crew:	10. **Trainees:** 12
Contact:	Chris Wilson, Marketing Manager, Square Sail
	Charlestown Harbour, St. Austell
	Cornwall PL25 3NJ, United Kingdom
	Tel: 44-1720-67526; Fax: 44-1726-61839
	E-mail: info@square-sail.com
	Web site: http://www.square-sail.com

Picara

The Nauset Sea Scouts have just celebrated more than 50 years of sail training. This program teaches seamanship and sailing to young people between the ages of 14 and 20 through education and annual cruises along the New England Coast. While on cruises, each scout takes part in every aspect of the voyage, including planning, cooking, navigation, sail repair, and sailing the vessel. The Nauset Sea Scouts have participated in such tall ships gatherings as the New York World's Fair 1964, Montreal's Expo '67, OpSail '76, Boston's 350th

anniversary in 1980, and the Grand Regatta 1992 Columbus Quincentenary in both New York and Boston.

Flag:	USA
Rig:	Sloop
Homeport/waters:	Eastham, Massachusetts: New England coast
Who sails?	Sea Explorers, middle school and high school students.
Program type:	Sail training for crew and apprentices. Sea education in maritime history and ecology in cooperation with Sea Scouts. Dockside interpretation during outport visits.

Specifications:	Sparred length: 36'	Draft: 5' 6"	Sail area: 750 sq. ft.
	LOA: 36'	Beam: 12'	Tons: 15 GRT
	LWL: 28'	Rig height: 49'	Power: 4,108 diesel
	Freeboard: 4'	Hull: fiberglass	

Designer:	S-2 Yachts
Built:	1982; Holland, Michigan, S-2 Yachts
Crew:	2. **Trainees:** 20 (day sails), 11 (overnight). **Age:** 14-20
Contact:	Captain Michael F. Allard
	Nauset Sea Explorers
	PO Box 1236
	Orleans, MA 02653
	Tel: 508-255-8150
	E-mail: mallard@capecod.net

Picton Castle

PICTON CASTLE

The 300-ton steel Barque *Picton Castle* is dedicated to making square-rig sailing ship voyages around the world. In her 2000-2002 voyage, the *Picton Castle* will visit 47 ports and islands in the South Pacific, the Far East, Africa, and the Caribbean. As a training ship, all on board work, stand watch, and learn the way of a ship. Workshops are conducted in rigging, sail making, boat handling, navigation and practical seamanship. While in the tropics, she carries much-needed supplies, schoolbooks, and trade goods to remote islands.

On her last world voyage, the *Picton Castle* served as flagship of UNESCO's "Year of the Ocean" program, delivering environmental education materials provided by NOAA throughout the South Pacific. On her current trip, two on-board educators for World Wise, Inc. create daily lessons for a Web-based distance learning program (found at http://www.beworldwise.org) that brings the sailing and cultural experiences of the crew and scientific information gathered at sea and ashore to school children around the world. The ship also carries a film crew who are creating a 13-part documentary of her voyage, the Tall Ship Chronicles, to be aired on Canadian television during 2001.

The *Picton Castle* is rigged following Germanischer Lloyds' rules for Cape Horners and outfitted to the highest standard with safety gear. She is a strong, seaworthy home for adventurers devoted to learning the art of square-rig seafaring. Captain Daniel Moreland welcomes trainee mariners to join the ongoing 2000-2002 World Voyage.

Flag:	Cook Islands
Rig:	Barque, 3-masted
Homeport/waters:	Lunenburg, Nova Scotia, Canada, Rarotonga, Cook Islands, South Pacific: worldwide.
Who sails?	Those over 18 years old on the world voyage, 16 years and up on shorter training cruises
Program type:	Deep-water sail training for expense-sharing trainees. Maritime education in cooperation with various institutes and organized groups. Comprehensive instruction in the arts of seafaring under sail. Dockside school visits and receptions. Charitable/educational outreach and supply to isolated islands.

Specifications:			
	Sparred length: 176'	Draft: 14'6"	Sail area: 12,450 sq. ft.
	LOD: 135'	Beam: 24'	Tons: 284 GRT
	LOA: 148'	Rig height: 100'	Power: 690 hp diesel
	LWL: 130'	Freeboard: 6'	Hull: steel

Designer:	Masting and rigging, decks and layout: Daniel Moreland, MM Stability calculations and ballasting: Daniel Blachley, NA/ME Webb Institute
Certificate:	Registered and certified as a Sail Training Vessel for worldwide service by the Cook Islands Ministry of Transportation and Tourism
Crew:	Permanent crew 10. Trainees: 38. Sex: Co-ed
Contact:	David Robinson, Coordinator
	Barque PICTON CASTLE Voyages
	1 Woodbine Lane
	Amherst, NH 03031-2102
	Tel: 603- 424-0219; Fax: 603-424-1849
	E-mail: wissco@juno.com
	Web site: http://www.picton-castle.com

Pilgrim

The *Pilgrim* is a full-scale replica of the ship immortalized by Richard Henry Dana in his classic book *Two Years Before the Mast*. Owned and operated by the Ocean Institute, *Pilgrim* is dedicated to multidisciplinary education. During the school year, the Ocean Institute offers an 18-hour, award-winning living history program that offers a hands-on exploration of literature, California history, and group problem solving in which crewmembers recreate the challenge of shipboard life. Students live like sailors of the 1830s as they hoist barrels, row in the harbor, stand night watches, swab the decks, and learn to cope with a stern captain.

On summer evenings, audiences are treated to the sights and sounds of the sea as the *Pilgrim*'s decks come alive with theatrical and musical performances. In late summer the *Pilgrim* sails on her annual cruise with an all-volunteer crew to ports along the California coast as a goodwill ambassador for the City of Dana Point. She returns in September to lead the annual tall ship parade and festival.

Flag:	USA
Rig:	Snow brig
Homeport/waters:	Dana Point, California: Point Conception to Ensenada, Mexico
Season:	Year-round
Who sails?	Student groups and individual volunteers.
Program type:	Maritime living history and volunteer sail training.

Specifications:			
	Sparred length: 130'	Draft: 9'	Sail area: 7,600 sq. ft.
	LOD: 98'	Beam: 24' 6"	Tons: 99 GRT
	Freeboard: 8'	Rig height: 104'	Power: diesel
	Hull: wood		

Designer:	Ray Wallace
Built:	1945; Holbaek, Denmark, A. Nielsen
Coast Guard certification:	Uninspected Vessel
Crew:	35. **Dockside visitors:** 50
Contact:	Daniel Stetson, Director of Maritime Affairs
	Ocean Institute
	24200 Dana Point
	Dana Point, CA 92629
	Tel: 949-496-2274; Fax: 949-496-4296
	E-mail: dstetson@ocean-institute.org
	Web site: http://www.ocean-institute.org

Pilgrim

Islands area of the St. Lawrence River. This schooner's main mission lies in creating an interest and appreciation of the Great Lakes maritime heritage and environment. The *Pilgrim* offers adult sail training, private charters, and participation in historical reenactments and festivals.

The captain and crew welcome the challenge of fulfilling your dreams through unique hands-on opportunities designed especially for you or your group.

The *Pilgrim* sails primarily the waters of Lake Ontario and the Thousand

Flag:	USA
Rig:	Gaff schooner, two-masted
Homeport/waters:	Oak Orchard River, New York: Lake Ontario, Thousand Islands area of St. Lawrence River
Who sails?	High school students, adults, and families.
Season:	May to October
Cost:	$100 per person per day, $600 group rate per day
Program type:	Sail training for paying trainees. Sea education in cooperation with organized groups and as part of informal, in-house programming.

Specifications:

Sparred length: 68'	Draft: 6'	Sail area: 1,850 sq. ft.
LOD: 52'	Beam: 15'	Tons: 33 GRT
LOA: 52'	Rig height: 58'	Power: 85 HP diesel
LWL: 44' 3"	Freeboard: 3' 6"	Hull: steel

Designer:	William Wood
Built:	1987; Norfolk, Virginia, Marine Metals
Coast Guard certification:	Uninspected Vessel
Crew:	3. **Trainees:** 6
Contact:	Captain Gary Kurtz
	Pilgrim Packet Company
	PO Box 491
	Kendall, NY 14476
	Tel: 716-682-4757

Pilgrim of Newport

Built by one man as a lifetime dream, *Pilgrim of Newport* was constructed over 13 years to plans purchased from the Smithsonian Institution. She is a traditionally built accurate replica of a 1770s privateer used during the American Revolution. Predecessor to the Baltimore Clipper, similar vessels were known for their speed and were used for smuggling and the slave trade. *Pilgrim of Newport*'s mission in the 20th century is marine education for children of all ages.

Sailing with the Catalina Island Marine Institute, *Pilgrim of Newport* does three and five-day marine science-based programs which include snorkeling and hiking on Catalina Island. The vessel is also used by the Ocean Institute in their living history programs. Whale watching, corporate team building, and cannon battles are just some of the activities available on *Pilgrim of Newport*. The goal is to provide a platform where dreams are realized and the ocean's strength, beauty, and history are directly experienced.

Flag:	USA
Rig:	Gaff topsail schooner
Homeport/waters:	Long Beach, California: Southern California
Who sails?	School groups from elementary school through college, adult education groups, and individuals and families of all ages.
Cost:	$45-$65 per person per day, $1,000-$2,000 group rate per day
Program type:	Sail training for volunteer crew or trainees. Sea education in marine science, maritime history, and ecology based on informal, in-house programming and in cooperation with other organizations. Day sails and overnight passages. Affiliated institutions include the Ocean Institute, other school education programs, and museums.

Specifications:	Sparred length: 118'	Draft: 10'	Sail area: 5,000 sq. ft.
	LOD: 83'	Beam: 25'	Power: diesel
	LOA: 83'	Rig height: 100'	Hull: wood
	LWL: 79'		

Designer:	Records from the Smithsonian Institution, working drawings by Howard Chapelle
Built:	1983; Costa Mesa, California, Dennis Holland
Coast Guard certification:	Passenger Vessel (Subchapter T)
Crew:	9. **Trainees:** 82 (day sails), 40 (overnight)
Contact:	Wade and Susan Hal
	Pilgrim of Newport
	611 9th St.
	Coronado, CA 92118
	Tel/Fax: 714-966-0686
	E-mail: sailpilgrim@earthlink.net
	Web site: http://www.sailpilgrim.com

PILGRIM OF NEWPORT

Pioneer

The first iron sloop built in the United States, *Pioneer* is the only surviving American iron-hulled sailing vessel. Built in 1885 by the Pioneer Iron Foundary in Chester, Pennsylvania, she sailed the Delaware River, hauling sand for use in the iron molding process. Ten years later *Pioneer* was converted to a schooner rig for ease of sail handling. In 1966, the then abandoned vessel was acquired and rebuilt by Russell Grinnell, Jr. of Gloucester, Massachusetts. In 1970 the fully restored schooner was donated to the South Street Seaport Museum.

Today historic *Pioneer* serves as a vital education platform. Students of all ages can come on board and experience New York history and other curricular subjects during the hands-on program. *Pioneer* also offers corporate and private charters, Elderhostel day programs, and public sails.

Flag:	USA
Rig:	Gaff topsail schooner, two-masted
Homeport/waters:	New York, New York: New York Harbor, Hudson River, and Atlantic Coast
Who sails?	School groups from elementary school through college, charter groups, museum members, and general public.
Season:	April through October
Program type:	Sail training for crew and volunteers, hand-on education sails designed to augment school curriculums in history, ecology, marine science, physics, and math. Corporate and private charters, Elderhostel programs, and public sails.

Specifications:	Sparred length: 102'	Draft: 4' 8" (min.), 12' (max.)	Sail area: 2,700 sq. ft.
	LOD: 65'	Beam: 21' 6"	Tons: 43 GRT
	LOA: 65'	Rig height: 79'	Power: diesel
	LWL: 58' 11"	Hull: steel	

Built:	1885; Marcus Hook, Pennsylvania, Pioneer Iron Works (rebuilt 1968; Somerset, Massachusetts)
Coast Guard certification:	Passenger Vessel (Subchapter T)
Crew:	3
Contact:	Captain Malcom Martin South Street Seaport Museum 207 Front Street New York, NY 10038 Tel: 212-748-8684; Fax: 212-748-8610 Web site: http://www.southstseaport.org

Playfair

Tall Ship Adventures conducts sail training on board *Playfair*, a square-rigged ship designed specifically for youth sail training on the Great Lakes. Since 1964 over 15,000 young people have lived and worked aboard *Playfair* and her sister ship, *Pathfinder*.

Youth between the ages of 14 and 18 become the working crew on one or two-week adventures, making 24-hour passages from ports all over the Great Lakes. The program is delivered by youth officers between the ages of 15 and 18. Our youth officers are trained and qualified during Tall Ship Adventures' Winter Training Programs. The captain and first mate are the only adults on board. Every year each ship sails over 4,000 miles, spends over 40 nights at sea, and introduces 300 trainees to the tall ship experience. *Playfair* is owned and operated by Toronto Brigantine, Inc., a registered charity.

PLAYFAIR

Flag:	Canada
Rig:	Brigantine
Homeport/waters:	Toronto, Ontario, Canada: Great Lakes
Who sails?	In July and August, youth programs for ages 14-18; in May, June, and September, school groups from middle school through college, and interested adult groups.
Cost:	$675 CDN for one week; $1,175 CDN for two weeks (summer youth rate). Call for spring and fall group rates. Also day sails and group rates.
Program type:	Sail training for paying trainees, including seamanship and leadership training based on in-house programming. Shoreside winter program. Dockside interpretation. Affiliated institutions include the Canadian Sail Training Association and the Ontario Camping Association.

Specifications:	Sparred length: 72'	Draft: 7' 6"	Sail area: 2,600 sq. ft.
	LOD: 58'	Beam: 16'	Tons: 32.98 GRT
	LOA: 60'	Rig height: 54'	Power: 110 HP diesel
	LWL: 45'	Freeboard: 4'	Hull: steel

Designer:	Francis A. Maclachlan
Built:	1973; Kingston, Ontario, Canada, Canada Dredge and Dock Co.
Crew:	10. **Trainees:** 25 (day sails), 18 (overnight)
Contact:	Catharine McLean, Executive Director
	Toronto Brigantine, Inc.
	370 Queen's Quay West, Ste. 203
	Toronto, Ontario, M5V 3J3, Canada
	Tel: 416-596-7117; Fax: 416-596-9119
	E-mail: mail@tallshipadventures.on.ca
	Web site: http://www.tallshipadventures.on.ca

Pride of Baltimore II

State of Maryland and operated by Pride of Baltimore, Inc., her primary mission is to promote tourism and economic development for Maryland and the Port of Baltimore internationally. She also serves as a unique electronic platform for Maryland's students through specially designed curricula used via the Internet. *Pride II* is available for charter and for dockside and sailing receptions in each of her destinations. She can accommodate up to six paying passengers for hire as "working guest crew" between ports of call.

The *Pride of Baltimore II* sails year-round with two full-time rotating captains and a crew of 11. Crew positions are open to qualified individuals. The *Pride of Baltimore II* maintains an international sailing schedule, most recently completing a tour of Asia. The 2001 tour schedule includes participation in ASTA's Tall Ships Challenge® race series in the Great Lakes.

The *Pride of Baltimore II* is a topsail schooner built to the lines of an 1812-era Baltimore Clipper. Owned by the

Flag:	USA
Rig:	Square topsail schooner, two-masted
Homeport/waters:	Baltimore, Maryland: Global
Who sails?	Corporate clients and residents of the State of Maryland and the City of Baltimore.
Season:	Year-round
Cost:	$150 per person per day (working guest crew); $750 per hour (dockside reception); $1,000 group rate per hour (sailing reception)
Program type:	Sea education and marketing development in cooperation with the State of Maryland. Passenger day sails and overnight passages, dockside school tours.

Specifications:			
	Sparred length: 170'	Draft: 12' 4"	Sail area: 10,442 sq. ft.
	LOD: 96' 6"	Beam: 26'	Tons: 97 GRT
	LOA: 108'	Rig height: 107'	Power: twin 165 HP diesels
	Freeboard: 6'	Hull: wood	

Designer:	Thomas C. Gillmer
Built:	1988; Baltimore, Maryland, G. Peter Boudreau
Coast Guard certification:	Passenger Vessel (Subchapter T)
Crew:	12. **Trainees:** 35 (day sails), 6 (overnight). **Age:** 18+
Contact:	Dale Hilliard, Executive Director
	Pride of Baltimore, Inc.
	401 East Pratt Street, Suite 222
	Baltimore, MD 21202
	Tel: 410-539-1151; Fax: 410-539-1190
	E-mail: pride2@pride2.org
	Web site: http://www.pride2.org

Pride of MANY

The *Pride of MANY* is a 65-foot Spanish Galleon modeled after the *Pinta* of Columbus fame. Owned and operated by the Youth Services Agency of Pennsylvania, Inc., and named for the Mid-Atlantic Network of Youth and Family Services (MANY), of which YSA is a member, she also serves as part of a comprehensive program for Community Development through Youth. *Pride of MANY's* mission is to enhance the character of youth through Adventure Challenge Therapy, perform community service projects in the region, and promote awareness of the marine environment, vocations, and heritage.

Clients of YSA can attend single-day events of exploration, fun, and an introduction to the sea and sailing, or multi-day adventures that typically provide a life-changing experience. The *Pride* and her crew provide an environment that nurtures and encourages the development of skills and attitudes necessary for the education of today's youth. Participants experience the value of communication, understanding, teamwork, and growth of awareness as well as a maturing of the

traits of patience, endurance, persistence, courage, and caution.

Marine communities can receive our assistance with creative community service projects that promote the awareness of the marine environment. These projects demonstrate the energy, talent, and desire that is our future—our youth.

PRIDE OF MANY

Flag:	USA
Rig:	Barque, three-masted
Homeport/waters:	Georgetown, Maryland: Delaware and Chesapeake Bays, Atlantic Coast
Who sails?	School groups from middle school through college. Individuals under age 25. Trainees are from existing Youth Services Agency of Pennsylvania programs.
Program type:	Sail training for trainees and agency related volunteers with an emphasis on self-esteem and team building. Sea education in maritime vocational opportunities based on informal, in-house programming. Affiliated institutions include Youth Services of Pennsylvania and MANY (Mid-Atlantic Network of Youth and Family Services).

Specifications:		
Sparred length: 75'	Draft: 7' 6"	Sail area: 3,700 sq. ft.
LOD: 60'	Beam: 17'	Tons: 50 GRT
LOA: 65'	Rig height: 70'	Power: 130 HP diesel
LWL: 55'	Freeboard: 5'	Hull: steel

Designer:	Steve Martin
Built:	1986; Port Stanley, Canada, Steve Martin
Coast Guard certification:	Uninspected Vessel
Crew:	3. **Trainees:** 6
Contact:	Roger Dawson, Youth Services of Pennsylvania
	PO Box 508, Jamison, PA 18929
	Tel: 215-343-7800
	E-mail: roger@ysaofpa.org
	Web site: http://www.ysaofpa.org

Providence

career in which she sank or captured 40 British ships, she earned the nickname "Lucky Sloop." John Paul Jones said of her, "She was the first and she was the best."

The Continental Sloop *Providence* is a statewide resource administered by the Providence Maritime Heritage Foundation and the City of Providence, Rhode Island. The primary mission of the *Providence* is to inspire and educate the thousands of Rhode Islanders served each year and to keep Rhode Island's rich maritime heritage alive. As Rhode Island's Flagship, the Sloop *Providence* serves youth and adults through the "Classroom Under Sail" programs, which illuminate Rhode Island's maritime history and the importance of the city of Providence in our nation's early development.

The Sloop *Providence* also serves as the Ocean State's sailing ambassador, representing Rhode Island at waterfront festivals along the East Coast. The *Providence* is available for charter for education, special events, corporate outings, documentary and film use, and historic reenactments.

The *Providence* is a replica of one of the first ships of the American Navy. Built as a merchant ship in the 1760s, the *Providence* (ex-*Katy*) went on to become the first command of John Paul Jones and one of the most successful American ships to fight in the Revolutionary War. After a successful

Flag:	USA
Rig:	Square topsail sloop
Homeport/waters:	Providence, Rhode Island: East Coast US
Who sails?	School groups from elementary school through college, individuals, and families.
Program type:	Sail training for crew and volunteers. Passenger day sails. Dockside interpretation at homeport and during port visits. Sea education in marine science, maritime history, Cadet program, and more for school groups of all ages.

Specifications:			
	Sparred length: 110'	Draft: 10'	Sail area: 3,470 sq. ft.
	LOD: 61' 1'	Beam: 20'	Tons: 59 GRT
	LOA: 65'	Rig height: 94'	Power: 170 HP diesel
	LWL: 59'	Freeboard: 8'	Hull: fiberglass and wood

Designer:	Charles W. Wittholz
Built:	1976; Melville, Rhode Island
Coast Guard certification:	Passenger vessel (Subchapter T)
Crew:	5-8. Trainees: 24-40 (day sails), 4-6 (overnight)
Contact:	Robert Hofmann, Executive Director
	Providence Maritime Heritage Foundation
	PO Box 1261
	Providence, RI 02901
	Tel: 401-274-7447; Fax: 401-751-0121
	E-mail: info@sloopprovidence.org, Web site: http://www.sloopprovidence.org

Quinnipiack

Built in 1984 for passenger service, *Quinnipiack* now serves as the primary vessel for Schooner Sound Learning, an organization dedicated to teaching about the ecology of Long Island Sound. Since 1975, Schooner Sound Learning has taught in classrooms, on the shores, and aboard a variety of vessels. Participants of all ages study under sail and explore the ecology of the estuary while getting an introduction to maritime heritage and seamanship. Students work alongside regular crew, learning the lessons in teamwork, self-reliance, flexibility, and interdependence that only sailing vessels can teach.

Quinnipiack programs complement traditional classroom studies in the sciences, mathematics, geography, history, literature, folklore, and social studies. Hands-on learning activities include collection, identification, and interpretation of estuarine organisms, land use, plankton study, piloting, sail handling, seamanship, sediment analysis, water chemistry, and weather.

Seafaring Scientists is a weeklong summer program in basic seamanship and

marine ecology for students entering grades 5-8. In the Cadet Program, high school students learn the operation and care of a traditional sailing vessel while sailing as a crew. The permanent crew consists of a licensed captain, mate, deckhands, and scientists, all of whom serve as educators in shipboard programs. The *Quinnipiack* is available for corporate charters and special events.

Flag:	USA
Rig:	Gaff schooner, two-masted
Homeport/waters:	New Haven, Connecticut: Long Island Sound
Who sails?	School groups from middle school through college, individuals, and families.
Season:	April to November
Program type:	Sail training for crew, apprentices, and trainees. Sea education in marine science, maritime history, and ecology in cooperation with accredited schools and colleges and as informal, in-house programming. Dockside interpretation during port visits. Passenger day sails.

Specifications:			
	Sparred length: 91'	Draft: 4' 6" - 11'	Sail area: 2,400 sq. ft.
	LOD: 65'	Beam: 20'	Tons: 41 GRT
	LOA: 65'	Rig height: 77'	Power: 119 HP diesel
	LWL: 58'	Freeboard: 5' 2"	Hull: wood

Designer:	Phil Sheldon
Built:	1984; Milbridge, Maine, Phil Sheldon
Coast Guard certification:	Passenger vessel (Subchapter T)
Crew:	4-8. **Trainees:** 40 (day sails), 4-6 (overnight)
Contact:	Beth McCabe, Executive Director, Schooner Sound Learning
	60 South Water Street, New Haven, CT 06519
	Tel: 203-865-1737; Fax: 203-624-8816
	E-mail: schooner@snet.net
	Web site: http://pages.cthome.net/schooner

Rachel B. Jackson

The *Rachel B. Jackson* is a one off design of an 1890s coastal schooner by Burt Frost. The keel was laid in Jonesport, Maine in 1974. She was planked and floated in Southwest Harbor where she sat unfinished at a mooring until 1979. The hull was pur- chased by George Emery and towed to Freeport, Maine. George, his brother Jim, and their father took the next three years to complete the *Rachel B. Jackson*, and launched her in 1982. George and Jim operated the boat out of Mystic Seaport as a sail training vessel. In 1984 she was sold and embarked on a three-year circumnavigation. She was sold again in 1990 and was put into the charter trade in Maine and the Virgin Islands. The *Rachel B.* was chartered by the National Geographic Society to do whale research off the coast of the Dominican Republic. The current owners, Steve and Andrew Keblinsky, just completed a two-year refit in May 1999. The *Rachel B. Jackson* now operates in Boston and Maine.

Flag:	USA
Rig:	Schooner, two-masted
Homeport/waters:	Southwest Harbor, Maine: Maine
Who sails?	School groups from elementary school through high school, individuals, and families.
Cost:	$2,000 group rate per day (charter)
Program type:	Sail training for volunteer and paying trainees. Sea education in marine science, maritime history, and ecology in cooperation with organized groups. Passenger day sails, dockside interpretation during port visits.

Specifications:			
	Sparred length: 75'	Draft: 8'	Sail area: 2,500 sq. ft.
	LOD: 52'	Beam: 17'	Tons: 52 GRT
	LOA: 52'	Rig height: 75'	Power: 108 HP diesel
	LWL: 43'	Freeboard: 4'	Hull: wood

Designer:	Burt Frost
Built:	1982; Freeport, Maine, George Emery
Coast Guard certification:	Passenger Vessel (Subchapter T)
Crew:	3. **Trainees/passengers:** 30
Contact:	Captain Steven Keblinsky
	Downeast Sailing Adventures, LLC
	PO Box 1252
	Southwest Harbor, ME 04679
	Tel: 207-244-7813
	E-mail: downeastsail@acadia.net
	Web site: http://www.downeastsail.com

Rainbow Chaser

Rainbow Chaser is a cutter rigged ketch, owned and operated by Rainbow Chaser Ltd. as a training and charter vessel. She was built by Gulfstar in 1976 as part of the Independence series. After several years of neglect, she was bought by the present owners and has been lovingly restored.

During the summer months, she takes part in the Boy Scouts of America High Adventure Program in the Abacos. Here, young people learn basic sailing and navigation skills as well as the traits of responsibility and cooperation.

In the fall, *Rainbow Chaser* is available for charter in her homeport of Melbourne, Florida, just south of Cape Canaveral Space Center. In the winter and spring she is available for charters in the Bahamas.

Flag:	USA
Rig:	Ketch
Homeport/waters:	Melbourne, Florida; Bahamas
Who sails?	Families, groups and individuals of all ages.
Program type:	Sail training for paying trainees. Sea education in cooperation with other organized groups.
Season:	Year-round

Specifications:	Sparred length: 56'	LOD: 50'	LOA: 52'
	LWL: 46'	Draft: 5'	Beam: 14'
	Tons: 29 GRT	Rig height: 59'	Power: Perkins 130 HP diesel
	Freeboard: 5'	Hull: Fiberglass	Hull color: white
	Spar material: aluminum		

Built:	1976; Tampa, Florida, Gulfstar
Crew:	2. Trainees/passengers: 12 (day sails), 12 (overnight)
Contact:	Captain Jack Leahy
	Rainbow Chaser Ltd.
	4 East Hill Drive
	Doylestown, PA 18901
	Tel: 267-880-0418
	E-mail: charter@rchaser.com
	Web site: http://www.rchaser.com

Raindancer II

Raindancer II was refurbished in 1997/98 and currently sails the Caribbean (including Cuba) and the East Coast of Canada. She is comfortably appointed with private cabins to serve six guests on weekly eco-sailing adventures combining hands-on shipboard activities with shore excursions and exploration.

Raindancer II is a unique modern classic. Fashioned from rare Angelique teak, she was finely crafted in Lunenburg, Nova Scotia, in 1981.

Flag:	Canada
Rig:	Staysail schooner
Homeport/waters:	Lunenburg, Nova Scotia, Canada
Who sails?	Individuals, families, and corporate groups.
Season:	Year-round
Program type:	Sail training for paying trainees. Passenger day sails and overnight voyages.

Specifications:	LOA: 75'	Draft: 8'	Sail area: 2,700 sq. ft.
	Rig height: 76'	Tons: 45 GRT	Power: 225 HP diesel
	Hull: teak		

Designer:	Stevens
Built:	1981; Nova Scotia, Canada, Stevens
Contact:	Captain Ron Lipscombe
	Raindancer Sailing
	10 Daleview Court
	Peterborough, Ontario K9J 8E5, Canada
	Tel: 613-542-6349
	E-mail: info@raindancerii.com
	Web site: http://www.raindancerii.com

The Ranger Foundation, Inc. was established in March 1999 to undertake one of the most exciting ventures in American maritime history—the rebuilding of John Paul Jones' famous warship, the *Ranger*. In 1777, no one expected that John Paul Jones and the Continental Sloop of War *Ranger* would help turn the tide of the American Revolution—no one but Jones himself. It was unthinkable for a lone ship to take on the world's mightiest navy in its own home waters, but that's exactly what Jones did.

It was the *Ranger* that first carried the new American flag into harm's way. When the French acknowledged that flag at Quiberon Bay off the coast of France, *Ranger* became the first ship under American colors to be recognized by a foreign power. Not long after,

Jones and the *Ranger* crew initiated a guerilla naval campaign against Britain that is the subject of books and ballads to this day. The Ranger Foundation is dedicated to bringing that story alive by creating a sailing and maritime education programs around a full-size replica of the famous ship.

RANGER

Flag:	USA
Rig:	Full-rigged ship, three-masted
Homeport/waters:	Portsmouth, New Hampshire: worldwide
Program type (planned):	Sail training and an extensive maritime education program integrated with other historical and maritime organizations throughout the region.
Coast Guard certification:	Undetermined
Crew (projected):	14
Contact:	Tom Cocchiaro, Chair
	The Ranger Foundation
	PO Box 6578
	Portsmouth, NH 03802-6578
	Tel: 603-436-2808; Fax: 603-436-2808
	Email: info@rangerfoundation.org
	Web site: http://www.rangerfoundation.org

...snake

waterfront in Jacksonville, Florida, and owned by the Maritime Heritage Foundation, Inc. A select group of the more than 200 members and volunteers of the Foundation is involved in the restoration of the vessel. These volunteers are learning boat-building skills and are preparing *Rattlesnake* to accommodate schoolchildren.

Much of Florida was originally explored and settled by people arriving in ships very similar to *Rattlesnake*. Once restoration is completed, the Foundation plans to use the vessel for excursions, nautical and environmental programs, and as a teaching aid for other programs along the Georgia and Florida coasts.

The *Rattlesnake* was built in Nova Scotia during the early 1980s by Captain David May and sailed to Florida. She was built as a two-thirds wooden replica of over 81 feet. *Rattlesnake* is moored on the downtown

Flag:	USA
Rig:	Barque, three-masted
Homeport/waters:	Jacksonville, Florida: St. Johns River, Atlantic Ocean
Who sails?	School groups from elementary school through college, individuals, and families. Affiliated groups include Boy Scouts, Police Athletic League, Duval County Schools.
Program type:	Sail training for volunteer trainees. Sea education in marine science, maritime history, ecology, art, and music in cooperation with other organized groups.

Specifications:	Sparred length: 81' 6"	Draft: 6'	Power: diesel
	LOD: 60'	Beam: 16'	Hull: wood
	LOA: 70'	Rig height: 66'	

Designer:	May/Millar via Royal Navy Archives
Built:	1983; Toronto, Canada, David May
Coast Guard certification:	Uninspected Vessel.
Crew:	n/a. **Trainees:** 16
Contact:	Captain David Damon, President
	Maritime Heritage Foundation, Inc.
	PO Box 806
	Jacksonville, FL 32201
	Tel: 904-741-3030 ext. 109; Fax: 904-741-4209
	E-mail: DavDamOne@aol.com
	Web site: http://rattlesnake.daci.net

Red Witch

A living tribute to US maritime history and her designer, John G. Alden, the *Red Witch* was built in the tradition of the vessels that were the workhorses of America's 19th-century transportation system. True to her ancestors, her block and tackle, wooden hull, and gaff rig capture the romance and adventure of sail.

Built expressly for chartering, she worked in San Diego and Hawaii from 1987 through 1997. In 1997 the *Red Witch* started plying the waters of western Lake Erie. From her new home in Port Clinton, she now sails from ports in Ohio from Toledo to Cleveland, and plans to visit Detroit soon. Available for walk-on day sails or private group charters, the *Red* *Witch* is also designing sail training programs for 2001. The *Red Witch* offers dockside interpretations, two-hour hands-on sails, and all-day island excursions.

Flag:	USA
Rig:	Gaff schooner
Homeport/waters:	Port Clinton, OH: Lake Erie
Who sails?	School groups from elementary school through college, individuals, and families.
Season:	May through October
Program type:	Sail training for volunteer or paying trainees. Sea education in marine science and maritime history in cooperation with accredited institutions and organized groups. Passenger day sails.

Specifications:			
	Sparred length: 77'	Draft: 6'6"	Sail area: 2,100 sq. ft.
	LOD: 54'	Beam: 17'6"	Tons: 41 GRT
	LOA: 57'	Rig height: 73'	Power: 125 HP diesel
	LWL: 49'	Hull: wood	Hull color: red
	Spar material: wood	Freeboard: 4'6"	

Designer:	John Alden
Built:	1986; Bayou La Batre, Alabama, Nathaniel Zirlott
Coast Guard certification:	Passenger Vessel (Subchapter T)
Crew:	4. **Trainees/passengers:** 49
Contact:	Captain Karl A. Busam
	Red Witch Charters
	PO Box 386
	Port Clinton, OH 43452
	Tel: 419-734-0734; Fax: 419-734-9339
	E-mail: schooner@redwitch.com
	Web site: http://www.redwitch.com

Resolute

Resolute was built in 1939 for the US Naval Academy at Annapolis, Maryland. She was the third of twelve Luders yawls built for the Navy, and over the course of twenty years it is estimated that some seventy thousand midshipmen trained aboard these yawls. During this time

Resolute was an active participant in intercollegiate and club racing circuits on the East Coast.

Resolute now finds her home on the West Coast. Purchased for one dollar by the Evergreen State College in 1972, she currently provides sail training opportunities and access to Pacific Northwest waters for students and volunteers. *Resolute* and her companion vessel *Sea Wulff* are used to teach a wide range of interdisciplinary programs, which vary from year to year. All of these classes are built around the fundamentals of sailing, seamanship, and navigation. Previous programs include Wooden Boat Building and Repair, Marine Biology and Field Work Methods, Native American Culture Studies, Pacific Northwest History and Development, and Maritime Literature.

Academic programs are available to students enrolled at Evergreen only, though outside charters are considered on a case by case basis. Student and community volunteers assist in maintaining *Resolute* and *Sea Wulff* in exchange for sailing opportunities.

Flag:	USA
Rig:	Yawl
Homeport/waters:	Olympia, Washington: Puget Sound and inland waters of British Columbia
Who sails?	Enrolled students at Evergreen State College. Outside charters on a case by case basis.
Cost:	$225 group rate per day
Program type:	Sail training for volunteer trainees. Fully accredited sea education in marine science, maritime history, ecology, and maritime studies.

Specifications:			
	Sparred length: 44'	Draft: 6'	Sail area: 1,050 sq. ft.
	LOD: 44'	Beam: 11'	Tons: 12 GRT
	LOA: 44'	Rig height: 60'	Power: diesel
	LWL: 30'	Freeboard: 3'	Hull: wood

Designer:	Luders
Built:	1939; Stamford, Connecticut, Luders Marine Construction Company
Coast Guard certification:	Passenger Vessel (Subchapter T)
Crew:	2. **Trainees:** 10 (day sails), 5 (overnight)
Contact:	Greg Buikema, Marine Operations Manager
	The Evergreen State College
	2700 Evergreen Parkway NW
	Olympia, WA 98505
	Tel: 360-866-6000; Fax: 360-867-5430
	E-mail: buikemag@evergreen.edu
	Web site: http://www.evergreen.edu

Roald Amundsen

The brig *Roald Amundsen* was originally built in 1952 as a motor-tanker for the East German Navy. After the German reunification she was bought and transformed into her present shape.

Since 1993, *Roald Amundsen* has sailed between Iceland, St. Petersburg, and the Canary Islands on voyages mainly dedicated to the education and understanding of young people. She has participated in several Cutty Sark Tall Ships Races.

Roald Amundsen is designed so that she will only sail with all hands onboard helping to sail the ship. Her permanent crew (well trained volunteers) undertakes the challenge of forming the new trainees into a group of enthusiastic young sailors.

While the rig of *Roald Amundsen* is designed like it was in the 19th century, the interior is built to high standards, with wood paneling and private heads. The vessel was built under the surveillance of Germanischer Lloyd and fully complies with the German

"Traditionsschiffsverordnung" (safety standards for traditional sail training vessels). Her safety standards are the highest available and she is licensed for worldwide voyaging.

Flag:	Germany
Rig:	Brig
Homeport/waters:	Wolgast, Germany: Baltic Sea, Canary Islands, Caribbean Sea
Who sails?	Youth trainees, school groups, families, and individuals over 16.
Cost:	Youth trainees, $70 per person per day; trainees over 26, $110 per person per day
Program type:	Sail training for apprentices and paying trainees. Accredited sea education. Day sails and overnight passages.

Specifications:			
	Sparred length: 165'	Draft: 15'	Sail area: 9,265 sq. ft.
	LOD: 139'	Beam: 25'	Tons: 252 GRT
	LOA: 140'	Rig height: 112'	Power: 300 HP
	LWL: 130'	Freeboard: 8' 6"	Hull: steel

Designer:	Detlev Löll
Built:	1952; Rorlau, Germany, Learn to Live on Sailing Ships
Certification:	German Lloyd Traditionsschiffsverordung
Crew:	14. **Trainees:** 65 (day sails), 32 (overnight)
Contact:	Contact: North Americans:

Contact: North Americans:	Others:
HANSA Foundation	LLaS
PO Box 69	Jungfernstieg 104
North Reading, MA 01864	24340 Eckernförde
Tel: 781-944-0304; Fax: 781-944-2469	Germany
E-mail: info@sailtraining.com	Tel: +49 4351 726074
Web-site: http://www.hansafoundation.org	Fax: +49 4351 726075
	E-mail: office@sailtraining.de
	Web site: http://www.sailtraining.de

Robertson II

1974, she was brought through the Panama Canal to Victoria, British Columbia, where for the last 20 years she has provided sail training programs for young people.

Officially retired in 1995 from active service, the *Robertson II* is open to the general public from May until September. The City of Victoria has provided a permanent dock in the inner harbor where the historic schooner is prominently exhibited.

One of the last original Canadian Grand Banks fisherman built, the *Robertson II* was launched at Shelburne, Nova Scotia in 1940. Fishing up to

Flag:	Canada
Rig:	Gaff schooner, two-masted
Homeport:	Victoria, British Columbia, Canada
Program type:	Interpretive programs.

Specifications:

Sparred length: 130'	Draft: 11' 1"	Sail area: 5,500 sq. ft.
LOD: 105'	Beam: 22' 1"	Tons: 170 GRT
Rig height: 105'	Hull: wood	Power: GM diesel

Built: 1940; Sherburne, Nova Scotia, Canada, McKay and Sons
Contact: Mr. Rob Howatson, Executive Director
Sail and Life Training Society (SALTS)
PO Box 5014, Station B
Victoria, British Columbia V8R 6N3 Canada
Tel: 250-383-6811; Fax: 250-383-7781
E-mail: saltsociety@home.com
Web site: http://www.saltsociety.com

"HMS

St.

PHOTO BY PHILIP PLISSON

The Tall Ship *Rose* is a three-masted full-rigged ship designed after an 18th-century colonial-era British frigate of the same name. She is currently the only Class A size ship certified by the US Coast Guard as a Sailing School Vessel, and may carry groups as large as 100 for day sailing or as many as 49 for overnight passages and live-aboard programs.

Carrying 19 professional crew and educators, *Rose* specializes in adventure-under-sail, experience-based education for youth groups, but also includes a number of sessions in her itinerary each year that are open to the public for general admission. Most general educational sessions are approximately one week long, but special arrangements are often made for longer or shorter programs. Corporate training, civic events, and other private functions may also be scheduled by groups or individuals. You might also catch an occasional glimpse of *Rose* in one of her many appearances in television documentaries and feature films both here and abroad.

Rose has sailed the waters of the US East Coast and Canada for many years, and sometimes ventures to the Caribbean and Western Europe, offering special extended sail training programs during her ocean passages. A comprehensive sailing schedule is published several times each year.

From time to time *Rose* offers two-week long summer term courses in maritime history accredited by Boston University.

Flag	USA		
Rig:	Full-rigged ship, 3-masted.		
Home port/waters:	Bridgeport, Connecticut: East Coast of North America (summer); overseas.		
Who sails?	Individuals and groups of all ages.		
Season:	Year-round.		
Cost:	Inquire		
Program type:	Fundamental sail training with additional education modules tailored for specific programs for middle and high school, college and university, adults and families, corporate team building, and more.		
Specifications:	Sparred length: 179'	Draft: 13'	Sail area: 13,000 sq. ft.
	LOD: 125'	Beam: 32'	Tons: 500 GRT
	LOA: 135'	Rig height: 130'	Power: twin diesels
	LWL: 105'	Freeboard: 13'	Hull: wood
Designer:	Original design by Hugh Blades, British Admiralty, in 1757; revised by Phil Bolger, 1970.		
Built:	1969-1970; Lunenberg, Nova Scotia, Smith & Rhuland (rebuilt: 1985-87; Bridgeport, Connecticut and Fairhaven, Massachusetts).		
Coast Guard certification:	Sailing School Vessel (Subchapter R).		
Crew:	18. Trainees: 85 (day sail), 31 (overnight). Age: junior high school to adult. Sex: coed.		
Contact:	"HMS" Rose Foundation, Inc. One Bostwick Avenue, Bridgeport, CT 06605 Tel: 203-335-0932; Fax: 203-335-1433; Fax: 203-335-6793. E-mail: sailrose@aol.com or onboard@tallshiprose.org Web site: http://www.tallshiprose.org		

Christopher

The *St. Christopher* is a classic three-masted schooner built (1932) just as the age of sail came to a close. Built in Delfzijl, Netherlands under the Germanischer Lloyd Certification, she is designed to operate in the roughest sea conditions in the world, the North Sea.

She has unfortunately been allowed to slide into very poor condition. Blown 4 1/2 miles from her mooring by Hurricane Georges into an estuary (salt-marsh), St. Christopher Services, LLC has acquired her and recovery is under-way. Through volunteers and donations, we will rebuild and upgrade her to full U.S. Coast Guard passenger carrying certification. We have a strong shipbuilding community here on the Gulf Coast, the best in the world. Individuals and companies are stepping forward with their contributions toward the restoration. Our purpose is a service of Christian love and evangelism, to provide for medical missions, storm recovery, etc. We are not sponsored by any particular church organization, but relying on God's provisions and our volunteers.

What could be more fun than to be able to experience this piece of sailing history and to participate in a gift of Christian love with your own hands. Indications are that our schedule will be full, and *St. Christopher* will be well maintained and active far into this century.

Flag:	USA		
Rig:	Schooner		
Homeport/waters:	Mobile, Alabama; US and Caribbean		
Season:	Summer		
Who sails?	Groups and individuals of all ages.		
Program type:	Christian missionary work/mercy ship		
Specifications:	Sparred length: 149'	LOD: 118'	LOA: 121'
	LWL: 103'	Draft: 6'6"	Power: Two GM 671 diesel
	Tons: 149 GRT	Rig height: 118'	Freeboard: 4'
	Beam: 19'	Hull: riveted steel	Hull color: white and blue
	Spar material: wood		
Built:	1932; Delfzijl, Netherlands, Niestern Delfzijl		
Coast Guard certification:	Mercy Ship		
Crew:	5		
Contact:	Mr. Bryan Leveritt, Chief Steward		
	St. Christopher Services, LLC		
	9275 Old Highway 43 South		
	Creola, AL 36525		
	Tel: 334-442-3247; Fax: 334-824-7768		
	E-mail: erumpf@iopener.net		
	Web site: http://www.in-city.com/stchristopher/inworks.htm		

St. Lawrence II

The *St. Lawrence II* is a purpose-built sail training vessel in operation since 1957, primarily on the Great Lakes. She was designed to be manageable by a young crew, yet complex enough with her brigantine rig to introduce teenagers to the challenge of square-rig sailing.

The ship is owned and operated by Brigantine, Inc., a nonprofit charity staffed by local volunteers who share the conviction that the lessons of responsibility, self-reliance, and teamwork provided by sail training are especially applicable to teenagers. With 42 years of operation, Brigantine, Inc. is one of the pioneering sail training programs in North America.

Cruises in this hands-on program range from six to ten days or more in length. *St. Lawrence II*'s crew complement of 28 comprises 18 new trainees, plus a crew of watch officers, petty officers, cook, and bosun, all aged 13 to 18.

The captain is usually the only adult onboard.

The ship's teenage officers are graduates of Brigantine, Inc.'s winter training program, involving lessons in seamanship, navigation, and ship's systems, as well as the ongoing maintenance of the ship. Every year the *St. Lawrence II* sails over 4,000 miles, spends more than 40 nights at sea, and introduces over 300 trainees to the rigors of life aboard ship on the Great Lakes.

Flag:	Canada
Rig:	Brigantine
Homeport/waters:	Kingston, Ontario, Canada: Lake Ontario and adjacent waters
Who sails?	School groups and individuals of all ages
Season:	April to November (sailing); October to March (winter program)
Cost:	$75 (US) per person per day. Scholarships available.
Program type:	Sail training with paying trainees.

Specifications:			
	Sparred length: 72'	Draft: 8' 6"	Sail area: 2,560 sq. ft.
	LOD: 57'	Beam: 15'	Tons: 34 GRT
	LOA: 60'	Rig height: 54'	Power: 165 HP diesel
	LWL: 46'	Freeboard: 4' 6"	Hull: steel

Designer:	Francis McLachlan/Michael Eames
Built:	1953; Kingston, Ontario, Canada, Kingston Shipyards
Crew:	10. **Trainees:** 36 (day sails), 18 (overnight)
Contact:	Carol Jeffrey, General Manager
	Brigantine, Inc.
	53 Yonge Street
	Kingston, Ontario K7M 6G4, CANADA
	Tel: 613-544-5175; Fax: 613-544-5175
	E-mail: briginc@kos.net
	Web site: http://www.brigantine.ca

Samana

in 1975 in The Netherlands, she has circumnavigated the globe and completed several noteworthy offshore passages.

Captain Larry Wheeler and Letty Wheeler are professional teachers with more than 25 years of classroom teaching experience and over 10 years of sail training experience. Based in Portland, Maine, courses span the Maine coast and reach the coastline of Nova Scotia. The curriculum is a rich blend of technical skills, confidence building, and common sense coupled with a spirit of adventure and romance.

The School of Ocean Sailing operates in the North Atlantic Ocean off the coast of Maine, offering courses in offshore ocean sailing and ocean navigation in a live-aboard setting. *Samana* is a modern, well-found, romantic, beautiful, fast, and very seakindly vessel. Built

The school offers courses in Advanced Ocean Sailing and Navigation, Celestial Navigation, and Offshore Passage Making. In each course, the trainees handle all offshore sailing operations. All instruction is delivered by mature, professional, Coast Guard-licensed teachers.

Flag:	USA
Rig:	Ketch
Homeport/waters:	Portland, Maine: Gulf of Maine to Nova Scotia (summer), Caribbean (winter)
Who sails?	Individuals of all ages
Cost:	$200 per person per day, $995 per person per five days
Program type:	Sail training for paying trainees. Ocean sailing, celestial navigation, offshore passage making.

Specifications:			
Sparred length: 63'	Draft: 7'	Sail area: 1,500 sq. ft.
LOD: 53'	Beam: 16'	Tons: 34 GRT
LOA: 63'	Rig height: 85'	Power: Ford Lehman 135
LWL: 45'	Freeboard: 4'	Hull: steel

Designer:	Van de Wiele
Built:	1975; The Netherlands
Crew:	3. **Trainees:** 6
Contact:	Captain Larry Wheeler
	School of Ocean Sailing
	PO Box 7359
	Portland, ME 04112
	Tel: 207-871-1315, 888-626-3557; Fax: 207-871-1315
	E-mail: svsamana@nlis.net
	Web site: http://www.sailingschool.com

Sarah Abbot

Built as an example of classic Nova Scotian schooner construction by master shipwright David Stevens in 1966, *Sarah Abbot* was a major player on the Nova Scotian schooner racing circuit until she moved to Massachusetts and began her career working for Phillips Academy in Andover, Massachusetts. For the last fifteen years *Sarah Abbot* has sailed the coast of Massachusetts, carrying Andover Summer Session students on summer research cruises. Highlights of the "Oceans" program include on-going studies of the Buzzards Bay ecosystem, a scallop restoration project in the Westport River, nonfiction writing instruction, and observation and tracking of whales on Stellwagen Bank. Experienced field biologists sail as faculty on *Sarah Abbot* and aim to give their students an experience akin to Charles Darwin's cruise on the *HMS Beagle*. Each

cruise carries six high school students, a scientist, mate, and licensed captain.

Flag:	USA
Rig:	Gaff schooner, two-masted
Homeport/waters:	Marion, Massachusetts: Coastal Massachusetts/Cape Cod
Who sails?	High school marine science students who attend Phillips Academy/Andover's Summer Session.
Season:	Summer
Cost:	$4,200 for six-week "Oceans" marine biology course which includes four weeks at Andover's campus and 11-day research cruise aboard Sarah Abbot.
Program type:	Academically challenging marine biology course which includes a major cruise project, labs, extensive field collection, and paper writing.

Specifications:		
Sparred length: 55'	Draft: 6' 6"	Tons: 15 GRT
LOD: 47' 6"	Beam: 11' 6"	Power: 36 HP diesel
Rig height: 61'	Hull: wood	

Designer:	David Stevens
Built:	1966, Lunenburg, Nova Scotia, Canada
Coast Guard certification:	Research Vessel (Subchapter U)
Crew:	3. **Trainees:** 6 (overnight). **Age:** 15-19
Contact:	Captain Randall Peffer, Program Coordinator
	Phillips Academy
	180 Main St.
	Andover, MA 01810
	Tel: 978-475-5967
	E-mail: rpeffer@andover.edu
	Web site: http://www.andover.edu

SEA's Sailing Research Vessel Project

Designed by Laurent Giles of Hampshire, England, the 134-foot steel brigantine will be the most sophisticated sailing research vessel ever built in the United States. Improvements in design and equipment, including a wet/dry laboratory and a larger library, classroom, and computer laboratory, will enhance the SEA academic program. The new vessel is slated for SEA Semesters in the Pacific for the two years following her delivery in the summer of 2001. Planned cruise tracks include Hawaii, Costa Rica, Alaska and Tahiti.

SEA's newest vessel, scheduled to be launched in the spring of 2001, is under construction at JM Martinac Shipbuilding in Tacoma, Washington.

Flag:	USA
Rig:	Brigantine
Homeport/waters:	Woods Hole, Massachusetts; worldwide
Season:	Year-round
Who sails?	Educators and students who are admitted by competitive selection. Over 150 colleges and universities award credit for SEA programs.
Program type:	Marine and maritime studies including oceanography, nautical science, history, literature, and contemporary maritime affairs. SEA programs include SEA Semester (college level, 12 weeks long, 17 credits), SEA Summer Session (college level, 8 weeks long, 12 credits), and SEA Seminars for high school students and K-12 teachers. All programs include a seagoing component on board one of the sailing school vessels.
Specifications:	Sparred length: 134'6" LOA: 119' Draft: 13'
	Sail area: 8,200 sq. ft. LWL: 87'6" Beam: 26'6"
	Power: Caterpillar 3408, 455 HP Hull: steel
	Displacement: 300 tons median load
Designer:	Laurent Giles, Hampshire, England
Built:	Under construction; Tacoma, Washington, JM Martinac Shipbuilding
Coast Guard certification:	Sailing School Vessel (Subchapter R)
Crew:	6 professional mariners and 4 scientists. Trainees: Up to 25 in all programs
Contact:	Sea Education Association, Inc.
	PO Box 6
	Woods Hole, MA 02543
	Tel: 508-540-3954; Fax: 508-457-4673
	E-mail: admission@sea.edu
	Web site: http://www.sea.edu

Seawulff

The *Sea Wulff* was originally conceived in 1974 by the faculty of The Evergreen State College as a sailing fishing vessel. Three years into its construction the vessel burned to the ground. Tremendous community support resulted in the project beginning anew. The design of the second vessel, launched in 1980, was revised to more fully meet the mission of the college. The fish hold was turned into laboratory space and sampling equipment was added. This gear enables the *Sea Wulff* to provide all the teaching opportunities afforded by a sailing vessel and to be used as a platform for marine research and education.

The *Sea Wulff* and her companion vessel *Resolute* are fundamental to a full range of academic programs at Evergreen. Previous classes have included Wooden Boat Design, Building, and Repair, Marine Biology and Fieldwork Methods, Native American Culture Studies, Pacific Northwest History, and Maritime Literature. Regardless of the focus of the class, students are always involved in all aspects of outfitting, operating, maintaining, and living

aboard the college's sailing vessels.

Academic programs using the *Sea Wulff* and *Resolute* change from year to year and are available to Evergreen State College students only. Student and community volunteers help maintain the vessels in exchange for sailing opportunities.

Flag:	USA
Rig:	Sloop
Homeport/waters:	Olympia, Washington: Puget Sound and inland waters of British Columbia
Who sails?	Evergreen State College students. Outside charters considered on a case by case basis.
Cost:	$225 group rate per day
Program type:	Sail training for volunteer trainees. Fully accredited sea education in marine science, maritime history, ecology, and maritime studies.

Specifications:	Sparred length: 39'	Draft: 6'	Sail area: 800 sq. ft.
	LOD: 36'	Beam: 12'	Tons: 12.5 GRT
	LOA: 36'	Rig height: 56'	Power: diesel
	LWL: 31'	Freeboard: 4'	Hull: wood

Designer:	Robert Perry and The Evergreen State College
Built:	1980; Olympia Washington, The Evergreen State College
Coast Guard **certification:**	Passenger Vessel (Subchapter T)
Crew:	2. **Trainees:** 10 (day sails), 4 (overnight)
Contact:	Greg Buikema, Marine Operations Manager
	The Evergreen State College
	2700 Evergreen Parkway NW
	Olympia, WA 98505
	Tel: 360-866-6000; Fax: 360-867-5430
	E-mail: buikemag@evergreen.edu
	Web site: http://www.evergreen.edu

Serenity

Virginia's Eastern Shore. Serenity is USCG certified to carry 34 passengers.

The Low Sea Company offers day sails and group charters designed to foster an understanding and appreciation of the maritime history and ecology of the Chesapeake Bay. She also offers birding trips every October, in conjunction with the Eastern Shore Birding Festival. Aboard the Serenity, a customized educational program, catering to groups of all ages interested in sail training, maritime history, the history of the Chesapeake seafood industry, and the ecology of

The Serenity is a two-masted, gaff rigged schooner designed by Tom Colvin and built by Custom Steel Boats in 1986. The Low Sea Company purchased her in the spring of 2000 and brought her to Cape Charles, on the Chesapeake Bay, is available.

Serenity sails out of historic Cape Charles harbor, located on the Eastern Shore of Virginia, 10 miles from the mouth of the Chesapeake Bay.

Flag:	USA		
Rig:	Gaff Schooner, 2-masted		
Homeport/waters:	Cape Charles, Virginia; Chesapeake Bay		
Who sails:	Individuals and groups of all ages		
Season:	April to November		
Cost:	$1500 - $2000 per day for group charters, $30 per person for day sails		
Program type:	Sail training for crew and apprentices. Sunset sails and eco-tour charters for groups and individuals of all ages.		
Specifications:	Sparred length: 63'	Draft: 5'6"	Sail area: 1,544 sq. ft.
	LOD: 50'	Beam: 14'	Tons: 26 GRT
	LOA: 63'	Rig Height: 55'	Power: 66 hp Yanmar Diesel
	LWL: 40'	Freeboard: 4'	Hull: steel
Designer:	Tom Colvin		
Built:	1986; Arapaho, North Carolina, Custom Steel Boats		
Coast Guard certification:	Passenger Vessel (Subchapter T)		
Crew:	3. **Trainees/passengers:** 34		
Contact:	Laura and Greg Lohse, Owners		
	Low Sea Company		
	505 Monroe Avenue		
	Cape Charles, VA 23310		
	Tel: 757-331-4361 or 757-710-1233		
	E-mail: lowsea@msn.com		
	Web site: www.schoonerserenity.com		

Shenandoah

While the *Shenandoah* is not a replica, the vessel's design bears a strong resemblance to that of the US Revenue Cutter *Joe Lane* of 1851. For her first 25 years, the rakish square topsail schooner was painted white, but she now wears the black and white checkerboard paint scheme of the 19th-century Revenue Service. Every summer *Shenandoah* plies the waters of southern New England and Long Island Sound, visiting the haunts of pirates and the homeports of whaling ships. *Shenandoah*'s economic bottom line is paying passengers. That reality includes sharing one's world with weekly passengers, which can be a satisfying and sometimes challenging endeavor.

Shenandoah runs 6-day sailing trips for kids ages 9-14 from late June through late August.

Flag:	USA
Rig:	Square topsail schooner, two-masted
Homeport/waters:	Vineyard Haven, Massachusetts: Southern New England
Who sails?	School groups from elementary through college and individuals ages 25 and under.
Season:	June to September
Cost:	$700 per person per week (Sunday night through Saturday noon)
Program type:	Sail training for paying trainees.

Specifications:	Sparred length: 152'	Draft: 11'	Sail area: 7,000 sq. ft.
	LOA: 108'	Beam: 23'	Tons: 85 GRT
	LWL: 101'	Rig height: 94'	
	Freeboard: 3' (amidships)		

Coast Guard certification:	Passenger Vessel (Subchapter T)
Crew:	6. **Trainees:** 49 (day sails), 27 (overnight)
Contact:	Captain Robert S. Douglas
	Coastwise Packet Co., Inc.
	PO Box 429
	Vineyard Haven, MA 02568
	Tel: 508-693-1699; Fax: 508-693-1881
	Web site: http://www.coastwisepacket.com

Sigsbee

as an oyster dredge boat until the early 1990s. She was named after Charles D. Sigsbee, who was the Commanding Officer of the battleship *Maine*. The vessel was rebuilt by the Living Classrooms Foundation in 1994, and now sails Chesapeake Bay with students on board. While sailing on board the *Sigsbee*, students learn the history of skipjacks and the oyster industry, marine and nautical science, and gain an appreciation of Chesapeake Bay and the hard work of the watermen of a bygone era.

The skipjack *Sigsbee* was built in 1901 in Deale Island, Maryland and worked

Flag:	USA
Rig:	Sloop
Homeport/waters:	Baltimore, Maryland: Chesapeake Bay and the Delaware River
Who sails?	Students and other organized groups, individuals, and families.
Season:	March through September
Program type:	Sail training with paying trainees. Sea education in marine and nautical science, maritime history, and ecology for school groups from elementary through college.

Specifications:	Sparred length: 76'	Draft: 3' 5"	Sail area: 1,767 sq. ft.
	LOD: 50'	Beam: 16'	Tons: 14 GRT
	Rig height: 68'	Freeboard: 2' 5"	Power: 150 HP diesel

Built:	1901; Deale Island, Maryland
Coast Guard certification:	Passenger Vessel (Subchapter T)
Crew:	4. **Trainees:** 30 (day sails), 15 (overnight). **Age:** 13+. **Dockside visitors:** 30
Contact:	Steve Bountress
	Living Classrooms Foundation
	802 South Caroline Street
	Baltimore, MD 21231-3311
	Tel: 410-685-0295; Fax: 410-752-8433
	Web site: http://www.livingclassrooms.org

Soren Larsen

Soren Larsen is one of the last wooden sailing ships built in Denmark. Restored by Captain Tony Davies and his family in the late 1970s, she initially starred in a number of films which helped to raise funds to fit her out to the high standards required by the British Maritime Coastguard Agency (MCA).

In 1982 the Davies realized their dream of taking people of all ages to sea under a three-year charter with the British Jubilee Sailing Trust, pioneering sailing for the disabled. In 1986 *Soren Larsen* embarked on a circumnavigation, rounding Cape Horn in 1991 and visiting New York and Boston for the Columbus Regatta.

In 1993 *Soren Larsen* sailed on a second world voyage to New Zealand via the Panama Canal. In 1999 she cruised the Pacific islands and was in New Zealand for millennial celebrations and the America's Cup races. In April 2000, *Soren Larsen* departed for Europe via the Pacific, Panama Canal, Caribbean, US, and Canada, participating in Tall

SOREN LARSEN

Ships 2000® and OpSail 2000 events.

Flag:	United Kingdom
Rig:	Brigantine
Homeport/waters:	Auckland, New Zealand: New Zealand coastal waters (summer), southwest Pacific islands (winter)
Who sails?	Families and individuals of all ages.
Cost:	$100 per person per day for overnight voyages.
Program type:	Sail training for paying trainees. Sea education in marine science, maritime history, and ecology as informal, in-house programming.

Specifications:			
	Sparred length: 140'	Draft: 11'	Sail area: 6,500 sq. ft.
	LOD: 98'	Beam: 25' 6"	Tons: 125 GRT
	LOA: 105' 6"	Rig height: 100'	Power: 240 HP diesel
	LWL: 90'	Freeboard: 3' 7"	Hull: wood

Designer:	Soren Larsen
Built:	1949; Denmark, Soren Larsen and Sons
Certification:	UK Maritime and CG Agency Loadline; Bureau Veritas Class Certificate.
Crew:	12. **Trainees:** 80 (day sails), 22 (overnight)
Contact:	Fleur Davies, Director
	Square Sail Pacific, Ltd.
	PO Box 310~Kumeu
	Auckland 1250, New Zealand
	Tel: 64-0-9-411-8755; Fax: 64-0-9-411-8484
	E-mail: sorenlarsen@voyager.co.nz
	Web site: http://squaresail.q.co.nz

SoundWaters

SOUNDWATERS

SoundWaters, Inc. is a non-profit organization dedicated to protecting Long Island Sound and its watershed through education. Annually, SoundWaters, Inc. offers shipboard and land-based programs to 15,000 children and adults from Connecticut and New York. The Floating Classroom, the schooner *SoundWaters*, features three-hour marine science and sail training experiences for school groups, scouts, and camps. The schooner also offers week-long summer camps, and week-long overnight pro-

grams, for middle and high school students. Instruction includes basic seamanship, navigation, helmsmanship, and field explorations of marine ecosystems.

The public may attend any of our Ecology, Sunset Lecture, or special Public Sails, which are offered several times each month, April through October. Call or visit our Web site for a schedule. The schooner is also available for evening or weekend charters for private groups and corporations.

SoundWaters, Inc. staff includes environmental educators, crew, and a licensed captain. College graduates with expertise in marine science, ecology, or sailing may apply for seasonal positions.

In addition, SoundWaters, Inc. operates the SoundWaters Community Center for Environmental Education, featuring educational exhibits and displays, classroom and community meeting space, as well as cutting-edge "green" construction. The organization also conducts many free outreach programs which are offered through public schools as well as community and senior centers.

Flag:	USA
Rig:	Gaff schooner, three-masted
Homeport/waters:	Stamford, Connecticut: Long Island Sound
Who sails?	School groups from elementary through college, individuals and families.
Season:	April to November
Cost:	$25 per person per two-hour sail, $700-$2,000 group rate for three-hour sail
Program type:	Sea education in marine science and ecology in cooperation with accredited institutions and other groups, and as informal, in-house programming.

Specifications:	Sparred length: 80'	Draft: 3'-8'	Sail area: 1,510 sq. ft.
	LOD: 65'	Beam: 14'	Tons: 32 GRT
	Rig height: 60'	Hull: steel	Power: diesel
	Freeboard: 3' 6"		

Designer:	William Ward
Built:	1986; Norfolk, Virginia, Marine Metals, Inc.
Coast Guard certification:	Passenger Vessel (Subchapter T)
Crew:	3, 5 instructors. **Trainees:** 42 (day sails). **Age:** 8+
Contact:	Captain Jonathan Boulware
	SoundWaters, Inc., Cove Island Park
	1281 Cove Road
	Stamford, CT 06902
	Tel: 203-323-1978; Fax: 203-967-8306
	E-mail: boat@soundwaters.org Web site: http://www.soundwaters.org

SAIL TALL SHIPS!

Spirit of Gloucester

The *Spirit of Gloucester* was originally built as a log carrier and still retains the log door in the bow. She later carried lumber to Iceland and salt fish on the return voyage. During World War II she was purposely sunk in a river so the Germans could not use her. Raised after the war, this Baltic trader continued to haul logs, lumber, salt, salt fish, and grain in bulk.

The *Spirit of Gloucester* was brought to the US in the late sixties, along with other Baltic Traders, to be converted into yachts. She was made over in the seventies in Maine, and brought to Gloucester in the late eighties to be used as a home.

Purchased by the Spirit of Gloucester

Foundation in the summer of 1999, the *Spirit of Gloucester* is currently being restored, with a new interior designed for sail training and maritime education.

Flag:	USA
Rig:	Ketch
Homeport/waters:	Gloucester, Massachusetts: New England
Who sails?	School groups from elementary school through high school, individuals, and families.
Cost:	$30 per person per day, $300 per person per week, $1,000 group rate per day
Program type:	Sail training for volunteer and paying trainees. Informal, in-house sea education in marine science.

Specifications:	Sparred length: 74'	Draft: 7' 8"	Sail area: 3,750 sq. ft.
	LOD: 74'	Beam: 21' 2"	Tons: 65 GRT
	LOA: 76' 9"	Rig height: 90'	Power: 6-71 Detroit diesel
	LWL: 68'	Freeboard: 4' 6"	Hull: wood

Built:	1914; Vejlc, Denmark
Coast Guard certification:	Sailing School Vessel (Subchapter R)
Crew:	4. **Trainees:** 40 (day sails), 20 (overnight)
Contact:	Graham Bell, Executive Director
	Spirit of Gloucester Foundation
	PO Box 281
	Gloucester, MA 01931-0281
	Tel: 978-283-3351

Spirit of Massachusetts

The schooner *Spirit of Massachusetts* is owned by the Ocean Classroom Foundation (formerly the Schooner Harvey Gamage Foundation). She sails on sea education programs ranging from 4 month semesters-at-sea to weeklong programs with schools and youth groups. All programs use the power of the sea and the challenge of traditional seafaring as the basis for the academic curriculum taught on board.

Ocean Classroom, a fully accredited high school semester-at-sea, is a true voyage of discovery for qualified sophomores, juniors and seniors. Young people come from all over the US to join this outstanding learning adventure. The voyage covers more than 4,000 nautical miles, connecting South American shores to the Canadian Maritimes. Students live and work as sailors while they study maritime history, maritime literature, marine science, applied mathematics, and navigation. Ocean Classroom is offered fall, spring, and summer terms.

Some other programs include SEAmester (a complete semester-at-sea for college credit), Marine Awareness Research Expeditions (also for college credit), and Summer Seafaring Camp (for teens age 13-17). The Ocean Classroom Foundation also owns and operates the schooner *Harvey Gamage*.

Flag:	USA
Rig:	Gaff topsail schooner, two-masted
Homeport/waters:	Boston, Massachusetts; Eastern US and Canada (summer), Caribbean and South America (winter)
Who sails?	School groups from middle school through college. Affiliated institutions include Proctor Academy, Long Island University, Franklin Pierce College and other schools.
Season:	Year-round
Program type:	Sail training with paying trainees/students. Fully accredited sea education in marine science, maritime history, maritime literature, marine applied mathematics, and navigation.

Specifications:			
	Sparred length: 125'	Draft: 10' 6"	Sail area: 7,000 sq. ft.
	LOD: 100'	Beam: 24'	Tons: 90 GRT
	LOA: 103'	Rig height: 103'	Power: 235 HP diesel
	LWL: 80'	Freeboard: 7'	Hull: wood

Designer:	Melbourne Smith and Andrew Davis
Built:	1984; Boston, Massachusetts, New England Historic Seaport
Coast Guard certification:	Sailing School Vessel (Subchapter R), Passenger Vessel (Subchapter T)
Crew:	7-11 including instructors. **Trainees/students:** 50 (day sails), 22 (overnight)
Contact:	Bert Rogers, Director
	Ocean Classroom Foundation, Inc.
	PO Box 446
	Cornwall, NY 12518
	Tel: 800-724-7245, 845-615-1412; Fax: 845-615-1414
	E-mail: mail@sailgamage.org
	Web site: http://www.sailgamage.org

Squaw

The *Squaw* was originally built in 1978 by shipwright Phil Shelton as a passenger and cruising schooner for Captain Steve Pagels. Her extremely shallow draft (2'6" with centerboard up) on a schooner with a 64-foot sparred length allowed exploring in coastal estuaries and bays that are not often visited by larger sailing craft. Recently re-acquired by Captain Pagels, the *Squaw* will again be offering coastal charters and day sails for groups of up to six. Waters sailed include Florida and the Carolinas in the winter and New England in the summer.

Based on the lines of a late 19th century sharpie schooner, the *Squaw* was built as a working vessel. With a large and easily handled sail plan for her size, the *Squaw* has a good turn of speed. With her centerboard and 30-inch draft, *Squaw* can explore coves and bays that are not often traveled.

Flag:	USA
Rig:	Schooner
Homeport/waters:	Cherryfield, Maine; Northeast (winter), Florida (summer)
Season:	Year-round
Who sails?	Groups and individuals of all ages.
Program type:	Sail training for volunteer crew or trainees. Passenger day sails.
Specifications:	Sparred length: 64' LOA: 52' Draft: 2'6"
	Beam: 12'6" Tons: 14 GRT Rig height: 42'
	Sail area: 1,030 sq. ft. Hull: wood Hull color: green
	Spar material: aluminum Power: 18 HP diesel
Designer:	Shelton/Pagels
Built:	1978; Brookhaven, New York, Phil Shelton
Crew:	2. **Trainees/passengers:** 6 (day sails), 6 (overnight)
Contact:	Captain Stephen F. Pagels
	Downeast Windjammer Cruises
	PO Box 28
	Cherryfield, ME 04622
	Tel: 207-546-2927 (winter), 207-288-4585 (summer); Fax: 207-546-2023
	Email: decruise@midmaine.com
	Web site: http://downeastwindjammer.com

Stad Amsterdam

The clipper *Stad Amsterdam* is an authentic reconstruction of the clipper frigate *Amsterdam*, which was built in 1854, towards the end of the heydays of the clipper era. The original clipper, a near sister ship of the *California*, sailed with precious cargoes until meeting her untimely end in a hurricane north of St. Helena in 1866.

Construction of the clipper *Stad Amsterdam* started in December of 1997, in Amsterdam, The Netherlands. During that time she served as a training opportunity for unemployed youngsters to gain valuable working experience. The clipper is designed to fulfill the requirements of luxurious cruising, training cruises, day trips, harbor receptions, and conferences and seminars.

Owned by the Municipality of Amsterdam and Randstad, an important employment agency, the clipper provides opportunities for young people to gain work experience in the areas of nautical engineering and hospitality management, while working alongside a professional sailing crew.

Stad Amsterdam plans to visit the US East Coast from January 7 until May 6, 2001.

Flag:	The Netherlands
Rig:	Full rigged ship, 3-masted
Homeport/waters:	Amsterdam, The Netherlands
Who sails?	Groups and individuals of all ages.
Program type:	Luxury cruises (coastal and passage), public relations activities, STA races, sail training, harbour parties, museum/historic activities

Specifications:	Sparred length: 250'	LOD: 199'	Beam: 34'6"
	Tons: 723 GRT	Sail area: 23,700 sq. ft.	Rig height: 152'
	Hull: welded steel	Power: Caterpillar 1000 HP, diesel	

Designer:	Gerard Dijkstra & Partners, NBJA, Amsterdam
Built:	Amsterdam, Damon Oranjewerf
Certification:	Sailing Passenger Vessel
Crew:	25. **Trainees/passengers:** 125 (day sails), 72 (overnight)
Contact:	Ton van der Helm, Fleet Manager RCSA
	Rederij Clipper Stad Amsterdam
	Postbus 12600
	1100 AP Amsterdam
	The Netherlands
	Tel: 31 20569 58 39; Fax: 31 20569 17 20
	E-mail: mail@stadamsterdam.nl
	Web site: http://www.stadamsterdam.nl

Star of India

The oldest active square-rigger in the world, *Star of India* has been around the globe 21 times and has never had an engine. Built as the full-rigged ship *Euterpe*, this former merchant ship has survived countless perils of the sea to survive as a fully restored square-rigger and National Historic Landmark. She embodies the term "tall ship" both in looks and spirit.

Star of India is the flagship of the San Diego Maritime Museum fleet. She sails on an annual basis. *Star* is host to thousands of schoolchildren each year, many of whom participate in overnight living history programs on board. *Star*'s decks are also used for highly acclaimed cultural events from theatrical performances of *Two Years Before the Mast* and sea chantey festivals, to Gilbert & Sullivan comic operas and "Movies Before the Mast." Volunteer sail handling is held every other Sunday, with the best sailors being selected to sail the tall ship when she goes to sea.

STAR OF INDIA

Flag:	USA
Rig:	Barque, three-masted
Homeport/waters:	San Diego, California: Coastal waters between San Diego, California, and northern Baja California, Mexico
Who sails?	Selected volunteers, permanent crew, and invited passengers.
Program type:	Sail training for crew and apprentices. Sea education in maritime history based on informal, in-house programming. Dockside interpretation.

Specifications:	Sparred length: 278'	Draft: 21' 6"	Sail area: 18,000 sq. ft.
	LOD: 210'	Beam: 35'	Tons: 1,197 GRT
	LWL: 200'	Freeboard: 15'	Hull: iron
	Rig height: 140'		

Designer:	Edward Arnold
Built:	1863; Ramsey, Isle of Man, United Kingdom, Gibson, McDonald & Arnold
Coast Guard certification:	Museum Attraction Vessel
Trainees:	50. **Dockside visitors:** 300
Contact:	Erninia Taranto, Office Manager
	San Diego Maritime Museum
	1306 North Harbor Drive
	San Diego, CA 92101
	Tel: 619-234-9153; Fax: 619-234-8345
	E-mail: info@sdmaritime.com
	Web site: http://www.sdmaritime.com/ourfleet/star.html

Sultana

tion of the 1767 schooner *Sultana* scheduled to be launched and operational by the summer of 2001.

Built as a cargo schooner in Boston, the original *Sultana* was purchased by the Royal Navy and used to enforce the notorious "Tea Taxes" on the Chesapeake, Delaware, and Narragansett Bays. *Sultana* is notable as one of the most thoroughly documented vessels from the time of the American Revolution. The schooner's original logbooks, crew lists, correspondence, and design drawings have all survived intact to the present day. Together these documents tell a vivid story of life along the coast of Revolutionary America - a story that has been incorporated into the schooner's educational programs.

The Schooner Sultana Project is a non-profit, 501(c)(3) organization based in the historic port of Chestertown, Maryland. The Sultana Project provides unique, hands-on educational opportunities for children and adults that focus on the history and natural environment of the Chesapeake Bay and its watershed. The principal classroom for the Sultana Project is a full-sized reproduc-

Sultana's educational programs are designed to compliment and support national, state and local curriculum goals - but just as importantly, they are meant to excite students about the process of learning. Again and again teachers have found that a day on *Sultana* can help to bring subjects like history, science, math and reading alive.

Rig:	Square topsail schooner, two-masted
Homeport/waters:	Chestertown, Maryland: Chesapeake Bay & Mid-Atlantic.
Who Sails?	School & adult groups as well as individuals of all ages.
Season:	April to November
Program Type:	Under-sail educational experiences in environmental science and history, including both day trips and live-aboard programming.

Specifications:		
Sparred length: 97'	LOD: 53'	LWL: 53'
Draft: 8'	Beam: 17'	Rig height: 72'
Freeboard: 5'	Tons: 50 GRT	Power: single screw diesel
Hull: wood		

Designer:	Benford Design Group, St. Michael's, Maryland
Built:	2001; Millington, Maryland, Swain Boatbuilders, LLC
Coast Guard certification:	Passenger Vessel (Subchapter T)
Crew:	5. Students: 32 (day sails), 11 (overnight)
Contact:	Drew McMullen, Director
	Schooner Sultana Project
	PO Box 524
	Chestertown, MD 21620
	Tel: 410-778-5954; Fax: 410-778-4531
	E-mail: dmcmullen@schoonersultana.com
	Website: http://www.schoonersultana.com

SULTANA

Susan Constant

Susan Constant is a full-scale re-creation of the flagship of a small fleet that brought America's first permanent English colonists to Virginia in 1607. Together with the smaller *Godspeed* and *Discovery*, *Susan Constant* is on exhibit at Jamestown Settlement, a living history museum of 17th-century Virginia, and hosts nearly a half-million visitors every year. Jamestown Settlement is administered by the Jamestown-Yorktown Foundation, an agency of the Commonwealth of Virginia.

Built on the museum grounds and commissioned in 1991, *Susan Constant* replaced a vessel built for the 1957 Jamestown Festival commemorating the 350th anniversary of the colony's founding. While no plans or renderings of the original *Susan Constant*, *Godspeed*, and *Discovery* have ever been located, the replicas are based on the documented tonnages of the 17th-century ships, and *Susan Constant*'s design incorporates research information that emerged after the first replicas were built.

With a crew of staff and volunteers, *Susan Constant* and *Godspeed* periodically sail to other ports in the Chesapeake Bay region to participate in commemorative and community events and host educational programs. A volunteer sail training program is offered to individuals of all ages. Participants are trained in sailing a 17th-century merchant vessel, including handling square sails, marlinespike seamanship, navigation, safety procedures, watch standing, and maritime history.

Flag:	USA
Rig:	Barque, three-masted (lateen mizzen)
Homeport/waters:	Jamestown Settlement, Virginia: Chesapeake Bay
Who sails?	Crew consisting of Jamestown Settlement staff and volunteers.
Program type:	Sail training for crew and apprentices. Dockside interpretation.

Specifications:			
	Sparred length: 116'	Draft: 11' 6"	Sail area: 3,902 sq. ft.
	LOD: 83'	Beam: 24' 10'	Tons: 180 GRT
	LOA: 96'	Rig height: 95'	Power: twin diesels
	LWL: 77'	Freeboard: 11'	Hull: wood

Designer:	Stanley Potter
Built:	1991; Jamestown Settlement, Virginia, Allen C. Rawl
Crew:	25
Contact:	Eric Speth, Maritime Program Manager
	Jamestown Settlement
	PO Box 1607
	Williamsburg, VA 23187
	Tel: 757-229-1607; Fax: 757-253-7350
	Web site: http://www.historyisfun.org

Svanen

both coastal and inshore waters. She maintains a yearly program to suit corporate sail training, general charter, and harbor commitments.

Sail training aboard *Svanen* provides team spirit, problem solving, coordination, and initiative opportunities, increasing self-confidence, self-worth, personal goals, and creating new horizons. Equally popular are offshore day sails, weekend packages and adventure holidays, and harbor cruises. *Svanen* will tailor programs to the client's voyage requirements.

Svanen is fully surveyed by the Maritime Service Board in conjunction with the Uniform Shipping Laws of Australia, which enables *Svanen* to operate as a charter and sail training vessel in

Flag:	Australia
Rig:	Barquentine, three-masted
Homeport/waters:	Port Jackson, Sydney, New South Wales, Australia: New South Wales and Queensland, Australia coast
Who sails?	Middle school students and individuals of all ages. Affiliated with organizations serving disadvantaged children.
Season:	Year-round
Cost:	$120 per person per day
Program type:	Sail training for professional crew and paying trainees. Sea education in cooperation with accredited institutions and organized groups. Passenger day sails and overnight passages.

Specifications:

Sparred length: 130'	Draft: 10' 1"	Sail area: 3,385 sq. ft.
LOD: 130'	Beam: 22' 4"	Tons: 119 GRT
LOA: 98' 4"	Rig height: 87' 3"	Power: diesel
LWL: 120'	Freeboard: 3'	Hull: Danish oak

Built:	1922; Frederikssund, Denmark
Certification:	Waterways Authority, New South Wales, Australia – 1E & 2C Survey
Crew:	5. Trainees: 25 (day sails), 30 (overnight)
Contact:	Laurence Nash Kalnin, Managing Director
	Svanen Charters Pty. Ltd.
	148-152 Regent St.
	Redfern, NSW 2016, AUSTRALIA
	Tel: 61-2-9698-4456; Fax: 61-2-9699-3399
	E-mail: medind@fl.net.au
	Web site: http://www.charterguide.com.au/main/search/boat/default.asp

Swan fan Makkum

The *Swan fan Makkum*, the largest brigantine in the world, was constructed in 1993, inspired by her 19th century predecessors. Present-day standards of safety and comfort are incorporated in a classical design that carries on the tradition of a ship type which made history in the previous century.

With her stylish and representative interior, the *Swan* offers countless possibilities. A day trip (as an incentive, for a presentation, a party or a reception, etc.) can be made for groups of up to 120 persons. For multiple day trips or cruises (individual or group travel), the *Swan* has 17 two-berth cabins, each with its own private bathroom.

As proud as her 19th century predecessors, the *Swan fan Makkum* sails the seven seas. During the summer in Europe, her sailing area extends from the Mediterranean Sea to Scandinavian waters. She calls in at events such as the Kieler Woche, Sail Amsterdam, Cannes Film Festival, the Rally of Monte Carlo and the starts of the Fastnet and Whitbread races. The *Swan* herself takes part in the Cutty Sark Tall Ships Races,

where she has built up a formidable reputation. She sets out for sunnier waters in the wintertime and visits such Caribbean destinations as the Grenadines and Virgin Islands as well as the Seychelles in the Indian Ocean.

Everyone who climbs aboard the *Swan* desires to simply push off at once. The towering masts and endless rope only need a pair of enthusiastic human hands and…wind, lots of wind. And the *Swan fan Makkum* is only in her element once the wind finds her sails and she cleaves the waves heeling over to starboard or port side.

SWAN FAN MAKKUM

Flag:	The Netherlands		
Rig:	Brigantine		
Homeport/waters:	Makkum, The Netherlands; world wide		
Who sails?	Groups and individuals of all ages.		
Program type:	Luxury cruises (coastal and passage), sail training for paying trainees, corporate team building, private charters.		
Season:	Year round		
Specifications:	Sparred length: 196'	LOD: 150'	LOA: 164'
LWL:	128'	Draft: 12'	Beam: 30'
	Rig height: 145'	Freeboard: 5'	Tons: 404 GRT
	Sail area: 14,500 sq. ft.	Hull: steel	Hull color: black
	Power:	Caterpillar 470 HP	Spar material: steel/wood
Designer:	Oliver van Mear		
Built:	1993; Gdansk, Poland		
Certification:	Passenger Vessel, Ocean		
Crew:	10. Trainees/passengers: 120 (day sails), 36 (ovenight)		
Contact:	Willem Sligting, Captain/Owner		
	Swan fan Makkum		
	Achterdijkje 8		
	NL 8754 EP Makkum		
	The Netherlands		
	Tel: +31 (0) 515 231712; Fax: +31 (0) 515 232998		
	E-mail: swanfan@wxs.nl Web site: http://www.swanfanmakkum.nl		

Swift of Ipswich

The Los Angeles Maritime Institute (LAMI), the educational affiliate of the Los Angeles Maritime Museum, operates the square topsail schooner *Swift of Ipswich* and the gaff topsail schooner *Bill of Rights.* LAMI staff use the ship to teach trainees how to sail and how to develop personal and "human skills" such as communication, cooperation, teamwork, persistence, self-reliance, and leadership in three different programs.

Topsail is the basic outreach program, with participants recommended by people who work with youth, including educators, youth leaders, and clergy. Cost is on an ability-to-pay basis. The program begins with a five-day series of day sails followed by a five-day voyage planned and organized by the participants. Participants are encouraged to continue as active members of the "*Swift* Family."

Swift Expeditions are more advanced and challenging voyages with specific purposes, goals, and durations. Cooperative programs afford organizations such as youth, church, school, and community groups to voyage on *Swift of Ipswich.* The Los Angeles Maritime Museum and its affiliates take pleasure in offering assistance to visiting tall ships and other "educationally significant" vessels.

Flag:	USA		
Rig:	Square topsail schooner, two-masted		
Homeport/waters:	Los Angeles, California: Coastal California and offshore islands		
Who sails?	Referred youth-at-risk and groups catering to students and adults.		
Season:	Year-round		
Program type:	Educational sailing adventures for "at-risk" youth and other youth or adult groups.		
Specifications:	Sparred length: 90'	Draft: 10'	Sail area: 5,166 sq. ft.
	LOD: 66'	Beam: 18'	Tons: 46 GRT
	LOA: 70'	Rig height: 74'	Power: diesel
	LWL: 62'	Freeboard: 5'	Hull: wood
Designer:	Howard I. Chappelle		
Built:	1938; Ipswich, Massachusetts, William A. Robinson		
Coast Guard certification:	Passenger Vessel (Subchapter T)		
Crew:	6. **Trainees:** 49 (day sails), 31 (overnight). **Age:** 12+		
Contact:	Captain Jim Gladson		
	Los Angeles Maritime Institute		
	Berth 84, Foot of Sixth Street		
	San Pedro, CA 90731		
	Tel: 310-833-6055; Fax: 310-548-2055		
	Web site: http://www.tollway.com/swift/		

Sylvina W. Beal

One of the last surviving examples of her type, the *Sylvina W. Beal* sails the Maine coast only a few miles from where she was launched at East Boothbay in 1911. Built as a sailing sardine carrier and mackerel seiner, the *Sylvina W. Beal* is a graceful and swift example of a Maine knockabout fishing schooner. Captain Ed Zimmerman takes great pride in this historic vessel's appearance and is also a part owner of the schooner.

Based in Boothbay Harbor, she sails most of her season on day sails but also has accommodations for overnight groups of up to 18. The *Sylvina W. Beal* can be chartered for educational and sail training programs that can be customized to suit the needs of the group. With her wood hull,

tarred rigging and wood/coal stove in the forecastle the *Sylvina W. Beal* is a living link to the working sail era of the past.

Flag:	USA
Rig:	Gaff schooner, two-masted
Homeport/waters:	Cherryfield, Maine; Boothbay Harbor, Maine
Who sails?	Individuals and groups.
Program type:	Sail training for volunteer and paying trainees. Passenger day sails and overnight passages.

Specifications:	Sparred length: 84'	Draft: 8'	Sail area: 2,200 sq. ft.
	LOA: 80'	Beam: 17'	Tons: 46 GRT
	LWL: 70'	Rig height: 56'	Hull: wood
	Freeboard: 4'		

Built:	1911; East Boothbay, Maine, Frank J. Adams Yard
Coast Guard certification:	Passenger Vessel (Subchapter T)
Contact:	Captain Stephen F. Pagels
	Downeast Windjammer Cruises
	PO Box 28
	Cherryfield, ME 04622
	Tel: 207-546-2927 (winter), 207-633-1109 (summer); Fax: 207-546-2023
	E-mail: decruise@midmaine.com
	Web site: http://downeastwindjammer.com

Tabor Boy

Tabor Boy has been engaged in sail training as a seagoing classroom for Tabor Academy students since 1954. Offshore voyaging and oceanographic studies go together in the curriculum, with cruises to destinations as distant as Mexico and Panama adding adventure to the experience. Many Tabor Academy graduates go on to the US Merchant Marine, Naval, or Coast Guard academies.

The schooner also offers seven summer orientation voyages for newly enrolled freshmen and sophomore students. During this time, trainees are fully involved in sail handling while studying Gulf of Maine marine wildlife and ecology. Winter programs feature sailing and snorkeling in the US and British Virgin Islands to observe and study coral reef ecosystems.

Flag:	USA
Rig:	Gaff schooner, two-masted
Homeport/waters:	Marion, Massachusetts: Coastal New England (summer), offshore Atlantic Ocean (school year)
Who sails?	Enrolled students at Tabor Academy.
Program type:	Seamanship and oceanography for high school students.

Specifications:	Sparred length: 115'	Draft: 10' 4"	Sail area: 3,540 sq. ft.
	LOD: 84' 6"	Beam: 21' 8"	Tons: 99.9 GRT
	LOA: 92' 10"	Rig height: 95'	Power: 295 HP diesel
	LWL: 78' 8"	Hull: iron	

Built:	1914; Amsterdam, The Netherlands, Scheepswerven & Machinefabrik
Coast Guard certification:	Sailing School Vessel (Subchapter R)
Crew:	6. **Trainees:** 23. **Age:** 14-18
Contact:	Captain James F. Geil, Master
	Tabor Boy, Tabor Academy
	66 Spring Street
	Marion, MA 02738-1599
	Tel: 508-748-2000; Fax: 508-748-0353
	E-mail: jgeil@taboracademy.org
	Web site: http://www.taboracademy.org

HMS *Tecumseth*

The original warship HMS *Tecumseth* was built at Chippewa on Lake Erie to be a part of Britain's defense fleet during the War of 1812. HMS *Tecumseth* spent two years as a supply ship on Lake Erie before her eventual transfer to the Naval Establishment at Penetanguishene, Ontario.

The *Tecumseth* replica is patterned from the original British Admiralty plans; built to appear as close to the original as possible, she is equipped to meet today's safety standards.

Owned by the Province of Ontario, and operated by the staff and volunteers of the Marine Heritage Association, the *Tecumseth* takes visitors back to the days of Nelson's Navy and England's "wooden walls." During port visits the officers and crew dress in historic uniform and interpret and present the life of a 19th century vessel to the public. Sail training in the art of 1812 seamanship for the crew and trainees of HMS *Tecumseth* is an intrinsic part of the vessel's operation.

The schooner *Tecumseth* is proud of her role as an ambassador for the Province of Ontario as she visits Canadian and American ports throughout the Great Lakes.

Flag:	Canada
Rig:	Square topsail schooner, two-masted
Homeport/waters:	Discovery Harbour, Penetanguishene, Ontario, Canada: Georgian Bay, Lake Huron
Who sails?	Individuals and groups.
Season:	June through September
Cost:	$26 CDN per person per two-hour sail
Program type:	Sail training and attraction vessel. New programs currently being developed.

Specifications:

Sparred length: 125'	Draft: 8'	Sail area: 4,700 sq. ft.
LOD: 70'	Beam: 29'	Tons: 146 GRT
LOA: 80'	Rig height: 90'	Power: 360 HP diesel
LWL: 63'	Hull: steel	
Hull color: black	Spar material: wood	

Designer:	Bob Johnston
Built:	1992; St. Thomas, Ontario, Canada, Kanter Yachts
Crew:	20. **Trainees/passengers:** 43 (day sails), 10 (overnight)
Contact:	The Marine Heritage Association
	PO Box 353
	Midland, Ontario L4R 4L1 Canada
	Tel: 705-549-5575 or 866-MHA-5577; Fax: 705-549-5576
	E-mail: marineheritage@on.aibn.com
	Web site: http://www.discoveryharbour.on.ca

Tenacious

JST promotes the integration of able-bodied and disabled people though the mediums of tall ship sailing and building. Such has been the success of the JST's first ship, *Lord Nelson*, that that JST decided to build *Tenacious*.

Bringing the ethos of integration ashore, the JST has developed the concept of Shorewatch, weeklong shipbuilding holidays. Professional shipwrights and mixed-ability volunteers have worked side-by-side as part of this amazing project.

Like the *Lord Nelson*, *Tenacious* enables all members of her crew to sail together on equal terms. Features include signs in Braille, power-assisted hydraulic steering, and points throughout the ship that enable wheelchairs to be secured during rough weather.

Voyages are open to anyone between 16 – 70+ and no previous experience is required. The crew of 40 is split 50/50 between able-bodied and physically disabled people, with eight wheelchair users. There is a permanent crew of 10, including a medical purser and cook.

The 213-foot, three-masted barque *Tenacious* is the Jubilee Sailing Trust's (JST) new, second ship. She is the largest wooden tall ship of her kind to be built in Great Britain this century.

Flag:	United Kingdom
Rig:	Barque, three-masted
Homeport/waters:	Southampton, United Kingdom: Northern Europe (summer), Canary Islands and Southern Europe (winter)
Who sails?	Physically disabled and able-bodied people, aged 16 to 70+.
Season:	Year-round
Cost:	$135 per person per day
Program type:	Sail training for paying trainees. Integration of physically disabled and able-bodied people through the medium of tall ship sailing.

Specifications:			
	Sparred length: 213' 3"	Draft: 14' 9"	Sail area: 12,956 sq. ft.
	LOD: 163' 6"	Beam: 34' 9"	Rig height: 129' 9"
	LOA: 177' 3"	Hull: wood/epoxy	Power: twin 400 HP
	LWL: 151' 3"	Freeboard: 7' 3"	

Designer:	Tony Castro, Ltd.
Built:	1996-2000; Woolston, Southampton, United Kingdom
Crew:	8. **Trainees:** 40
Contact:	Mrs. Lindsey Neve, Jubilee Sailing Trust
	Jubilee Yard, Hazel Road, Woolston,
	Southampton, Hampshire, SO19 7GB, United Kingdom
	Tel: 44-23-8044-9108; Fax: 44-23-8044-9145
	E-mail: jst@jst.org.uk
	Web site: http://www.jst.org.uk

Thomas E. Lannon

Over 4,000 schooners were built in the town of Essex, Massachusetts from the mid-1600s to 1948. Tom Ellis' dream of continuing that tradition came true when the sawn-framed trunnel-fastened schooner *Thomas E. Lannon* was launched at the Essex Shipbuilding Museum Shipyard in June 1997, just six months after her keel was laid. The *Lannon*, a fine new addition to the long line of Essex-built Gloucester fishing schooners, is similar to the schooner *Nokomis*, built in Essex by Mel McClain in 1903. The *Lannon* is named for Tom Ellis' grandfather, who came from Newfoundland and fished out of Gloucester from 1901-1943.

The schooner *Thomas E. Lannon* is berthed at Seven Seas Wharf at the Gloucester House Restaurant in Gloucester, Massachusetts, the oldest fishing port in America. The *Lannon* carries passengers on a variety of two-hour harbor sails from May to October. She is also available for charter to corpo-

rations, individuals, school groups, etc. for corporate outings, family gatherings, weddings, parties, field trips, and other special events.

Flag:	USA
Rig:	Gaff topsail schooner, two-masted
Homeport/waters:	Gloucester, Massachusetts: Cape Ann, Massachusetts
Who sails?	Individuals, groups, and families of all ages.
Season:	May to October
Cost:	$29 per person per two-hour sail, $400-$550 group rate per day (charter)
Program type:	Sail training for paying trainees. Sea education in marine science and maritime history based on informal, in-house programming. Passenger day sails.

Specifications:			
	Sparred length: 93'	Draft: 9'	Sail area: 2,000 sq. ft.
	LOD: 65'	Beam: 17' 6"	Tons: 51 GRT
	LOA: 83'	Rig height: 70'	Power: diesel
	LWL: 55'	Freeboard: 4'	Hull: wood

Designer:	Harold A. Burnham
Built:	1997; Essex, Massachusetts, Harold A. Burnham
Coast Guard certification:	Passenger Vessel (Subchapter T)
Contact:	Kay M. Ellis, President
	Thomas E. Lannon, Inc.
	5 Old Bray Street
	Gloucester, MA 01930
	Tel: 978-281-6634; Fax: 978-281-0369
	E-mail: k@schooner.org
	Web site: http://www.schooner.org

Three Hierarchs

(Work in Progress)

" ТРИ СВЯТИТИЛЯ "

On the island of Kodiak in the North Pacific the construction of a ship is underway. The *Three Hierarchs* is a replica of the ship that brought the first Russian settlers to America. In 1785 she landed on Kodiak Island to begin Russian life in the New World. These new pioneers relied on her to bring them supplies from Russia every year. After 10 years of sailing the treacherous waters of the North Pacific she was sent back to Russia on her most famous voyage. Before leaving port in Russia she picked up ten Russian Orthodox monks and brought them to Kodiak. These monks became the first Christian missionaries of the great land of Alaska.

Although the *Three Hierarchs* is little known, her importance is great. She is a legend in her own right, going down in history as the ship that brought two different worlds and peoples together, forming one unique heritage. This legendary ship, the *Three Hierarchs*, will always be remembered as the ship that connected Russia with America.

Now, 200 years later, the *Three Hierarchs* is rising again, being built by the at-risk youth of Alaska and, believe it or not, by monks.

Flag:	USA
Rig:	Galiot
Homeport/waters:	Kodiak, Alaska: North Pacific
Who sails?	School groups from elementary school through college, adults, and families. Affiliated with St. Innocent's Academy.
Program type:	Sail training for volunteer and paying trainees. Sea education in maritime history in cooperation with accredited schools. Dockside interpretation during port visits.
Specifications:	LOD: 78'
Designer:	Stuart Hoagland
Built:	Under construction; Kodiak, Alaska, St. Innocent's Academy
Coast Guard certification:	Sailing School Vessel (Subchapter R), Passenger Vessel (Subchapter T)
Contact:	Father John Marler, Manager
	Three Hierarchs
	St. Innocent's Academy
	PO Box 1517
	Kodiak, AK 99615
	Tel: 907-486-4376; Fax: 907-486-1758
	E-mail: innocent@ptialaska.net

Tole Mour

Built in 1988 to support primary health care and educational programs in Micronesia, *Tole Mour* ("gift of life and health") was named by the school children of the Marshall Islands. From 1988 through 1992, *Tole Mour* made regular teaching and medical "rounds" through the remote atolls of the Marshalls, serving 15,000 men, women, and children in 58 far-flung communities. She carried multinational teams of educators and health care professionals, most of whom served as volunteers. By the end of 1992, the volunteer professionals health teams had been replaced entirely by Marshallese counterparts using powered patrol craft, which allowed Marimed to phase out support and bring *Tole Mour* home.

Since 1992 *Tole Mour* has been used to support programs for special needs adolescents, including youth referred by juvenile courts and mental health agencies. The ship currently supports a 6 to 12-month residential treatment program

for Hawaiian youth who live, work, and attend school on board while receiving group, individual, and family therapy from a multidisciplinary treatment team.

Flag:	USA
Rig:	Square topsail schooner, three-masted
Homeport/waters:	Honolulu, Hawaii: South Pacific
Who sails?	Trainees include emotionally impaired youth referred by the Hawaiian Department of Health, Child, and Adolescent Mental Health Division.
Season:	Year-round
Program type:	Long-term residential treatment and education (including special education) for emotionally impaired male adolescents; vocational training leading to AB Sail MMD.
Specifications:	Sparred length: 156'
	LOD: 123'
	LWL: 101'
	Freeboard: 6'
Designer:	Ewbank, Brooke & Associates
Built:	1988; Seattle, Washington, Nichols Bros.
Coast Guard certification:	Sailing School Vessel (Subchapter R), Freight and Miscellaneous (Subchapter I)
Crew:	11, 10 instructors. **Trainees:** 80 (day sails), 28 (overnight). **Age:** 13-25
Contact:	David D. Higgins
	Marimed Foundation
	45-021 Likeke Place
	Kaneohe, HI 96744
	Tel: 808-236-2288; Fax: 808-235-1074
	E-mail: Kailana@pixi.com
	Web site: http://www.marimed.org

Specifications (continued): Draft: 13' 6" — Sail area: 8,500 sq. ft.; Beam: 31' — Tons: 229 GRT; Rig height: 110' — Power: 575 HP diesel; Hull: steel

Tree of Life

The schooner *Tree of Life*, launched in 1991, was built in Nova Scotia, Canada and Jacksonville, Florida. She sleeps 12 in three cabins and the foc'sle. Powered by 4,500 square feet of sail, she cruises at 8 to 10 knots. Her hull is a composite of strip planked clear fir and kevlar saturated in epoxy and sheathed in fiberglass. Her deck is fir, spars are spruce, and brightwork is Honduran mahogany. The interior is paneled in koa and teak.

In the past seven years, more than 200 trainees have crewed the *Tree* around the world, completing her first circumnavigation. The winter of 1998-1999 was spent in Spain, refitting for the 1999 Cutty Sark Tall Ships Race. The *Tree*'s crew roster has berths for the skipper and three permanent crew, plus six to eight trainees. Permanent crew includes skipper, first mate, provisioner, and engineer. All crewmembers share the cooking, cleaning, and navigation.

Tree of Life was chosen as one of the top ten yachts in North America by *Sail* magazine (1993), and in 1997 won the Bay of Islands Race.

Flag:	USA
Rig:	Gaff schooner
Homeport/waters:	Newport, Rhode Island
Who sails?	Adult individuals and families.
Program type:	Sail training for volunteer and paying trainees. Sea education in marine science and maritime history.

Specifications:	Sparred length: 93'	Draft: 8' 5"	Sail area: 4,200 sq. ft.
	LOD: 70'	Beam: 18' 6"	Tons: 70 GRT
	LOA: 70'	Rig height: 85'	Power: diesel
	LWL: 58'	Freeboard: 4' 5"	Hull: wood/epoxy

Designer:	Ted Brewer
Built:	1991; Covey Island, Canada
Crew:	4. **Trainees:** 6
Contact:	Sheri and John Laramee, Owners
	447 Bellevue Avenue
	Newport, RI 02840
	Tel: 401-847-0444 or 401-732-6464
	E-mail: JohnGL@aol.com
	Web site: http://www.schoonertreeoflife.com

True North of Toronto

True North of Toronto was built in 1947 as a North Sea Trawler. She was converted to sail in 1979 and has spent her years since then world voyaging for sail training and charter. *True North* is dedicated to promoting the preservation of traditional maritime life. This is accomplished by creating opportunities for people of all ages to participate in sail training voyages, fulfill professional crew positions, dockside visitations, and film work. *True North* was the proud recipient of the overall 1st place ranking for the 1998 ASTA Great Lakes Tall Ships® Race. Join *True North* and her crew for a voyage during the upcoming ASTA Tall Ship Challenge® Race/Rally Series in the Great Lakes.

Flag:	Canada
Rig:	Topsail schooner
Homeport/waters:	Toronto, Canada: Great Lakes, Atlantic, Caribbean
Who sails?	Individuals of all ages.
Program type:	Sail training for groups and individuals. Nautical curriculum, waterfront festivals, and film work.

Specifications:	Sparred length: 118'	Draft: 10'	Sail area: 9,688 sq. ft.
	LOD: 90'	Beam: 22'	Tons: 98 GRT
	LWL: 83'	Freeboard: 3' 6"	Power: 350 HP diesel
	Rig height: 90'	Hull: steel	

Built:	1947; Alphen, The Netherlands, Gouwsluis
Crew:	8. **Trainees:** 50 (day sails), 25 (overnight)
Contact:	Captain Doug Prothero
	Upper Canada Marine
	29 Euclid Avenue
	Toronto, Ontario M6J 2J7 Canada
	Tel: 416-603-0109 or 416-525-6321; Fax: 416-603-9270
	E-mail: doug.prothero@sympatico.ca
	Web site: http://www.tallship-truenorth.com

The Uncommon School

The Uncommon School presents a new model for teaching and learning. People in the 1800's created common schools to teach children by prescribing what they must know and by giving them formal instruction. This schooling is still given to young people today. Common schools work as if ideally everyone would learn the same things at the same time and in the same way. The Uncommon School works differently.

The Uncommon School is devoted to education, not schooling. We believe that it is best, as Mark Twain said, not to let your schooling interfere with your education. We provide you with a way to do this. Education—learning who you are and what you can do as an individual and as a member of the human race—doesn't necessarily result from schooling. The two aren't mutually exclusive, but they are different. And you can have one without the other.

The Uncommon School helps students educate themselves. Our students learn by asking questions and seeking answers. You learn from everything as you experience life, explore the world, and exercise your capabilities. Our teachers understand what you are trying to do and enjoy helping you realize your goals.

In our sailing program you learn to sail, earn an American Sailing Association certificate, explore some of the great literature of the sea (fiction and non-fiction), and explore Long Island Sound as you sail from Milford, Connecticut to Mystic, Connecticut and back. You spend the first five days of the two week program learning to sail the school's four J-22's. Then you sail the boats on the trip to Mystic. The fleet of students' sailboats is accompanied by a power boat and a thirty foot sailing auxiliary operated by the three teachers presenting the program.

Along the way, participants read and discuss works by Conrad, Melville, and others. It's interesting to read what these writer-sailors have to say while you're sailing yourself. In addition to these activities, you study nautical sciences like weather forecasting and navigation, and you have a close look at the marine ecology and environment of Long Island Sound. Participants live on board their sailboats, and plans each day include activities on shore. Accomodations are quite basic but adequate to meet your needs. You can anticipate living conditions like those you'd experience on a backpacking trip except with showers — sometimes! Admission to the program is open to students aged 15 and older.

Contact: Mr. Jamie Baldwin
            The Uncommon School
            173 Sunset Hill Road
            Redding, CT 06896
            Tel: 203-938-9297
            E-mail: uncommonschool@snet.net.
            Web site: http://www.uncommonschool.org

Victory Chimes

Built in Bethel, Delaware, in 1900, the schooner *Victory Chimes* is the largest commercial sailing vessel under the American flag and the only original three-master still working in America. Recently nominated for National Historic Landmark status, the *Victory Chimes* has been quietly supporting herself and a succession of private owners for the past 95 years. She has never been supported by foundations, grants, or endowments, and continues to be a well-maintained working vessel. Her current caretakers/owners, Captain Kip Files and Captain Paul

DeGaeta, offer Windjammer style vacations on Penobscot Bay. At over 200 gross tons, the *Victory Chimes* attracts career-minded professional crew and carries a crew of nine.

Flag:	USA
Rig:	Gaff schooner, three-masted
Homeport/waters:	Rockland, Maine: Coastal Maine
Who sails?	High school and college groups as well as individuals and adults of all ages. Affiliated institutions include Baylor Academy.
Season:	June through September
Cost:	$100 per person per day
Program type:	Sail training for crew, apprentices, and paying trainees. Sea education in marine science, maritime history, and ecology based on informal, in-house programming. Paying passengers on overnight passages.

Specifications:	Sparred length: 170'	Draft: 7' 5" (min.)	Sail area: 7,100 sq. ft.
	LOD: 132'	Beam: 25'	Tons: 208 GRT
	LOA: 140'	Rig height: 87'	Power: yawl boat with engine
	LWL: 127'	Freeboard: 11'	Hull: wood

Designer:	J.M.C. Moore
Built:	1900; Bethel, Delaware, Phillips & Co.
Coast Guard certification:	Passenger Vessel (Subchapter T)
Crew:	10. **Trainees:** 44. **Age:** 16-75
Contact:	Captain Kip Files
	Victory Chimes, Inc.
	PO Box 1401
	Rockland, ME 04841
	Tel: 207-265-5651
	E-mail: kipfiles@aol.com
	Web site: http://www.victorychimes.com

Viking

Puget Sound Naval Shipyard in 1939 for use in the Navy's fleet sailing program. As the US prepared for war, the Navy stripped its ships and whaleboats were sent ashore. The sailing program was never reinstated, and surplus Navy whaleboats found their way to Sea Scout units around the country, offering thousands of youth the opportunity to learn sailing, seamanship, and teamwork on the water. Of those boats, only a handful remain.

The Sea Scout Ship *Viking* has been serving the youth of the Bay Area for over 60 years, offering programs that teach sailing, seamanship, and leadership to young women aged 14-21. Her sister ship, *Corsair*, offers similar programs for young men. The two ships participate in many joint activities. In addition to the annual two-week summer cruise in the Sacramento Delta, the Sea Scouts organize day sails, races, weekend outings, dances, and regattas. New members are always welcomed, both young and adult.

Viking is a sailing whaleboat, an open boat designed to be launched from a larger ship while at sea, and was built at

Flag:	USA		
Rig:	Cutter		
Homeport/waters:	San Francisco, California: San Francisco Bay and tributaries		
Who sails?	High school students and individuals. Affiliated institutions include Sea Scouting, Boy Scouts of America, San Francisco Bay Area Council.		
Program type:	Sail training for female trainees, aged 14-21. Sea education in marine science and maritime history in cooperation with other groups.		
Specifications:	Sparred length: 30'	Draft: 4' 6"	Sail area: 600 sq. ft.
	LOD: 30'	Beam: 8'	Tons: 8 GRT
	LOA: 30'	Rig height: 35'	Hull: wood
	LWL: 28'	Freeboard: 2'	
Designer:	US Navy		
Built:	1939; US Navy, Puget Sound Naval Shipyard		
Coast Guard certification:	Uninspected Vessel		
Crew:	6-18		
Contact:	Nick Tarlson, Skipper		
	Sea Scout Ship Viking		
	220 Sansome Street, Ste. 900		
	San Francisco, CA 94104		
	Tel: 415-956-5700; Fax: 415-982-2528		
	E-mail: seascouts@dictyon.com		
	Web site: http://www.tbw.net/~chriss/scouts		

Virginia

The last of the great pilot schooners, the 118-foot *Virginia* served the Virginia Pilot Association from 1917 to 1926. Fast and seaworthy, *Virginia* remained in service long into an age where power vessels became the preferred platform for pilot station ships. *Virginia* was recognized in WWI for outstanding piloting services rendered to the convoy movements transiting in and out of Chesapeake Bay.

The Schooner Virginia Project, a 501(c) 3 not for profit corporation, seeks to build a replica of this historic ship along the Norfolk, Virginia waterfront. *Virginia*'s "living shipyard" will provide a unique educational experience, focusing on traditional wood ship construction, maritime history, and the vital role ship pilots and their vessels played throughout the history of the Commonwealth of Virginia.

A topsail schooner, *Virginia* will accommodate up to ten passengers in addition to eight full-time crew on overnight voyages. Day excursions will be limited to 35 passengers. In her mission as a goodwill ambassador for the Commonwealth, *Virginia* will maintain a international sailing schedule with crew positions open to qualified individuals.

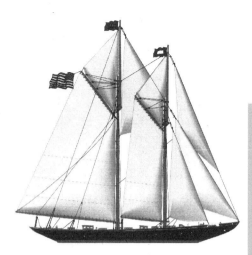

Flag:	USA
Rig:	Gaff topsail schooner, two-masted
Homeport/waters:	Hampton Roads, Virginia: worldwide
Who sails?	Students from elementary through college and individuals of all ages.
Season:	Year-round
Program type:	Sail training for volunteer crew and trainees. Sea education in marine science, maritime history, and ecology in cooperation with accredited institutions. Dockside interpretation during port visits.

Specifications:			
	Sparred length: 126'	Draft: 13'	Sail area: 7,000 sq. ft.
	LOD: 118'	Beam: 22'	Tons: 97 GRT
	LOA: 118'	Rig height: 105' 4"	Power: twin diesels
	LWL: 80'	Freeboard: 6'	Hull: wood

Built:	Construction to begin in 2001
Coast Guard certification:	Passenger Vessel (Subchapter T)
Crew:	8. **Trainees:** 35 (day sails), 10 (overnight)
Contact:	Rick Boesch, Executive Director
	Schooner Virginia Project
	PO Box 3126
	Norfolk, VA 23514
	Tel: 757-627-7400; Fax: 757-627-8300
	E-mail: schoonerva@aol.com
	Web site: http://www.schoonervirginia.com

Vita

Florida. Her cruising area includes Miami and the Florida Keys, the Dry Tortugas and the Bahamas. During the summer sailing season, she offers herself to the Boy Scouts of America as part of their High Adventure Program. Throughout the year, *Vita* is available for charter for school groups, for corporate and private functions, families, and individuals of all ages. Trainees learn sailing and basic coastal navigation. *Vita's* spacious interior provides comfortable accommodations for day sails and overnight trips. The 15-foot beam, uncluttered deck and tall rig make *Vita* an exceptional and fast training machine.

Designed by Charles Morgan at Heritage Yacht Corporation, this West Indies 46 Sloop was built in 1980, in

Flag:	USA
Rig:	Sloop
Homeport/waters:	Coconut Grove, Florida; Miami, Bahamas
Who sails?	Families, groups and individuals of all ages.
Program type:	Sail training for paying trainees. Passenger day sails.
Season:	Year-round
Cost:	$500 per group per day

Specifications:	Sparred length: 46'	Sail area: 900 sq. ft.	LOD: 42'
	LOA: 46'	LWL: 37'	Draft: 5'2"
	Beam: 15'3"	Rig height: 63'	Freeboard: 6'
	Tons: 29 GRT	Power: 85HP diesel	Hull: Fiberglass

Designer:	C. Morgan
Built:	1979; St. Petersburg, Florida, HYC
Coast Guard certification:	Uninspected Vessel
Crew:	1. **Trainees/passengers:** 6 (day sails), 6 (overnight)
Contact:	Captain Jim Sim
	2540 Inagua Avenue
	Coconut Grove, Fl 33133
	Tel: 305-801-3898 or 305-854-0031
	E-mail: sailvita@bellsouth.net

Wavertree

(Work in Progress)

Wavertree was built in Southampton, England in 1885. She was first employed to carry jute for use in making rope and burlap bags, voyaging between India and Scotland. Within two years, she entered the tramp trade, taking cargoes anywhere in the world. After 25 years, she limped into the Falkland Islands in 1911, having been almost dismasted in a gale off Cape Horn. Rather than re-rigging her, her owners sold her for use as a floating warehouse at Punta Arenas, Chile.

Wavertree was converted into a sand barge at Buenos Aires, Argentina in 1947, and was acquired there by the South Street Seaport Museum in 1968 for eventual restoration to her appearance as a sailing vessel. By the time *Wavertree* was built, she was nearly obsolete, being replaced by ocean-cross-ing steam ships. At the same time, iron—long the choice of shipbuilders in iron-producing countries such as England—was giving way to steel. *Wavertree* was one of the last large sailing ships built of wrought iron, and today is the largest afloat. Currently undergoing restoration, the *Wavertree* is expected to begin a limited sail training program in 2001.

Flag:	USA
Rig:	Full-rigged ship
Homeport/waters:	New York, New York
Program type:	Sea education in marine science, maritime history, and ecology in cooperation with accredited schools and other groups. Other education programs focused toward restoration.

Specifications:	Sparred length: 325'	Draft: 11' (min.), 22' (max.)	Sail area: 31,495 sq. ft.
	LOD: 263'	Beam: 40'	Tons: 2,170 GRT
	Rig height: 167'	Hull: iron	

Built:	1885; Southampton, England, Oswald Mordaunt & Co.
Contact:	Paula Mayo, Director of Programs
	South Street Seaport Museum
	207 Front Street
	New York, NY 10038
	Tel: 212-748-8681; Fax: 212-748-8610
	Web site: http://www.southstseaport.org

Weatherly

Australian challenger, *Gretel*, and won the Cup.

Weatherly is a classic; her mahogany hull has been restored by owner George Hill to her original lines and her varnished interior make her a beauty. She is part of America's Cup Charters' 12-meter fleet in Newport, Rhode Island, and is available for racing, corporate team building, and casual sails at the port of your choice from Maine down to the Chesapeake.

The fast and beautiful *Weatherly* is the only yacht in history to win the America's Cup without doing so when new. The legendary Emil "Bus" Mosbacher skippered her in 1962. In very close racing she defeated the first

Sail aboard an America's Cup winner— no sailing experience is necessary.

Flag:	USA
Rig:	Sloop
Homeport/waters:	Newport, Rhode Island: New England and Chesapeake Bay
Who sails?	Individuals of all ages.
Cost:	$1,800 group rate per day, $60 per person for evening sail
Program type:	Sail training for volunteer or paying trainees. Sea education based on informal, in-house programming. Passenger day sails.

Specifications:			
	Sparred length: 69'	Draft: 9'	Sail area: 1,850 sq. ft.
	LOD: 69'	Beam: 12'	Tons: 28 GRT
	LOA: 69'	Rig height: 90'	Power: diesel
	LWL: 46'	Freeboard: 4'	Hull: wood

Designer:	P. Rhodes
Built:	1958; Stamford, Connecticut, Luders
Coast Guard certification:	Passenger Vessel (Subchapter T)
Crew:	3. **Passengers/trainees:** 12
Contact:	George Hill/Herb Marshall
	America's Cup Charters
	PO Box 51
	Newport, RI 02840
	Tel: 401-849-5868; Fax: 401-849-3098
	Web site: http://www.americascupcharters.com

Welcome

The *Welcome* is a 55-foot sloop, a replica of the original *Welcome* built in 1775 at Fort Michimackinac during the Revolutionary War, which later became a British military vessel. The current *Welcome* is under reconstruction on a pier at the Great Lakes Maritime Academy in Traverse City, Michigan.

The Mackinac Island State Park Commission built the *Welcome* for the 200th anniversary of Independence Day. The vessel sailed the Great Lakes for a number of years before serving as a dockside museum in Mackinac City. In December of 1992, the Maritime Heritage Alliance (MHA), a nonprofit organization located in Traverse City, Michigan, was awarded the vessel for reconstruction.

Volunteers of the MHA, having built the schooner *Madeline*, are using their traditional boat building skills to restore this magnificent vessel. When completed, the *Welcome* will again serve as a living museum of Michigan's maritime tradition, from the era of the American Revolution.

Flag:	USA
Rig:	Square topsail sloop
Homeport/waters:	Traverse City, Michigan: Upper Great Lakes
Who sails?	Students from elementary school through high school and adult individuals.
Program type:	Sail training for volunteer trainees. Dockside sea education in maritime history during port visits.

Specifications:			
	Sparred length: 90'	Draft: 8'	Tons: 45 GRT
	LOA: 56'	Beam: 16'	Power: diesel
	LWL: 49'	Rig height: 96'	Hull: wood
	Freeboard: 6'		

Designer:	Ted McCutcheon
Built:	1976; Mackinaw City, Michigan, State of Michigan
Coast Guard certification:	Attraction Vessel
Crew:	5. **Trainees: 11. Age:** 13+
Contact:	Carole Hale, Office Manager
	Maritime Heritage Alliance
	322 Sixth
	Traverse City, MI 49684
	Tel: 231-946-2647; Fax: 231-946-6750
	E-mail: mha.tc@juno.com
	Web site: http://www.traverse.com/maritime/

Western Union

The *Western Union* is patterned after the schooners of the turn of the century that once roamed the high seas in the age of sail. Constructed of long leaf yellow pine with a Spanish Madeira mahogany-framed hull, the ship was built in Key West by the order of the Thompson Fish Company for operations they conducted on behalf of the Western Union Telegraph Company.

When launched in 1939, *Western Union* was among the last "working schooners" to be built in the United States. She was homeported in Key West during her 35 years of active service for Western Union as a cable repair vessel. In 1974 she was about to be converted into a barge when she was purchased by Captain John Krause and put into passenger service. *Western Union* was acquired by Vision Quest in 1984 and renamed *New Way* for the important role she would play in redirecting troubled youth.

In February 1997 the *Western Union* returned to Key West and was designated the flagship of the city. Already a national landmark, plans are underway to create a museum recalling the vessel's origins. She is now available for dockside tours, day sails, and special charters.

Flag:	USA
Rig:	Gaff topsail schooner, two-masted
Homeport/waters:	Key West, Florida
Who sails?	School groups from elementary school through high school and individuals of all ages.
Season:	Year-round
Program type:	Passenger day sails. Dockside interpretation while in port.

Specifications:			
Sparred length: 130'	Draft: 7' 9"	Sail area: 5,000 sq. ft.
LOD: 92'	Beam: 23'	Tons: 91 GRT
LWL: 85'	Rig height: 103'	Power: twin diesels
Hull: wood		

Built:	1939; Key West, Florida, Herbert Elroy Arch
Coast Guard certification:	Passenger Vessel (Subchapter T)
Contact:	Harry Bowman, General Manager
	202 (R) William Street
	Key West, FL 33040
	Tel: 305-292-9830; Fax: 305-292-1727
	E-mail: keywu@attglobal.net
	Web site: http://www.historictours.com/keywest/wunion.htm

Westward

Westward was built in 1961 as a private yacht for around-the-world service. She is modeled after the North Sea pilot schooners, which sailed offshore in rough seas to await incoming cargo vessels. She is owned and operated by the Sea Education Association (SEA) of Woods Hole, Massachusetts. SEA's founders located *Westward* through the late Captain Irving Johnson and purchased her to found SEA in 1971. During the last 28 years, SEA has refitted *Westward* several times to make her suitable as a seagoing classroom and research platform. Bunks were added below and the on-deck scientific laboratory was significantly upgraded in 1988. *Westward* also houses a small computer room/library

and an impressive array of oceanographic sampling gear, plus navigational and safety equipment. From 1971 to 1988, *Westward* sailed as a Research Vessel; she now meets the USCG specifications for Sailing School Vessels. See also: *Corwith Cramer.*

Flag:	USA
Rig:	Staysail schooner, two-masted
Homeport/waters:	Woods Hole, Massachusetts: Worldwide
Who sails?	SEA educational programs attract outstanding educators and a variety of motivated and adventuresome students who are admitted by competitive selection. More than 150 colleges and universities award full credit for SEA Semester.
Season:	Year-round
Program type:	Marine and maritime studies including oceanography, nautical science, history, literature, and contemporary maritime affairs. SEA programs include SEA Semester (college level, 12 weeks long), SEA Summer Session (college level, 8 weeks long), and SEA Seminars for high school students and K-12 teachers. All programs include a seagoing component on board the Sailing School Vessels *Westward* and/or *Corwith Cramer.*

Specifications:	LOA: 125'	Draft: 12'	Sail area: 7,000 sq. ft.
	LWL: 82'	Beam: 22'	Tons: 138 GRT
	Hull: steel	Power: 350 HP diesel	

Designer:	Eldridge McInnis
Built:	1961; Lemwerder, Germany, Abeking & Rasmussen
Coast Guard certification:	Sailing School Vessel (Subchapter R)
Crew:	10 instructors (6 professional mariners; 4 scientists). **Students/trainees:** up to 24.
Age:	primarily college-age students, with some high school and postgraduate students.
Contact:	Sea Education Association (SEA) Inc.
	PO Box 6
	Woods Hole, MA 02543
	Tel: 508-540-3954; 800-552-3633; Fax: 508-457-4673
	E-mail: admission@sea.edu
	Web site: http://www.sea.edu

Westwind

Owned and operated by Traverse Tall Ship Company, the schooner *Westwind* sails the spectacular waters of the Great Lakes. Able to accommodate 29 passengers for day sails, *Westwind* is fully certified by the US Coast Guard.

In conjunction with Inland Seas Education Association, *Westwind* offers the Schoolship Program, which provides an environmental, historical, and sail training education for students during the spring. The schooner offers partial as well as private charter service to family, company, motor coach, and corporate team building groups.

Flag:	USA
Rig:	Gaff topsail schooner, 2-masted
Homeport/waters:	Traverse City, Michigan; Great Lakes
Who sails?	Science and marine biology student groups from elementary school through junior high for educational programs; individual, family, and corporate groups on two-hour sails.
Program type:	Sail training for crew. Sea education in marine science, maritime history, ecology and corporate team-building workshops. Passenger day sails.
Season:	May to October

Specifications:			
	Sparred length: 65'	LOD: 58'	LWL: 49'
	Beam: 14'	Draft: 8'6"	Rig height: 63'6"
	Tons: 34 GRT	Freeboard: 4"	Power: 90 HP diesel
	Hull: steel	Hull color: white	Spar material: wood

Designer:	Bud McIntosh
Built:	1992; Palm Coast, Florida, Treworgy Yachts
Coast Guard certification:	Passenger Vessel (Subchapter T)
Crew:	3. **Trainees/passengers:** 29 (day sails)
Contact:	Captain David P. McGinnis, President
	Traverse Tall Ship Company
	13390 SW Bay Shore Drive
	Traverse City, MI 49684
	Tel: 231-941-2000; Fax: 231-941-0520
	E-mail: tallship@traverse.com
	Web site: http://www.traverse.com/tallship/

When and If

"*When* the next war is over, *and if* I live through it, Bea and I are going to sail her around the world." So said George S. Patton about the 63-foot Alden schooner he had commissioned in 1939. Built in Wicasset, Maine, *When and If*, as she was named, was perhaps the strongest Alden built. General Patton's dream was not to be, however—he was killed in an automobile accident shortly after the end of the war.

When and If remained in the Patton family until the 1970s, when Patton's nephew made a gift of her to the Landmark School in Pride's Crossing, Massachusetts, where she was the centerpiece of a sail training program for dyslexic children. In a storm in 1990, her mooring pennant broke and she was driven onto the rocks. Although the damage was extensive, the structural integrity of the boat was unaffected. She passed into private ownership, was rebuilt over the next three years, and relaunched in 1994.

When and If can now be seen cruising up and down the East Coast. With her majestic black hull and powerful rig, she turns heads wherever she goes.

Flag:	USA
Rig:	Schooner
Homeport/waters:	Vineyard Haven, Massachusetts: New England
Who sails?	School groups from elementary school through college, individuals, and families.
Program type:	Sail training for paying trainees. Sea education in cooperation with accredited schools and other groups. Special education arrangements are available. Dockside interpretation during port visits.

Specifications:			
	Sparred length: 85'	Draft: 9'	Power: GM 4-71
	LOD: 63' 5"	Beam: 15'	Hull: wood
	LOA: 63' 5"	LWL: 43' 3"	

Designer:	John G. Alden
Built:	1939; Wicasset, Maine, F.F. Pendleton. Rebuilt by Gannon and Benjamin, Vineyard Haven, Massachusetts.
Coast Guard certification:	Passenger Vessel (Subchapter T)
Crew:	3. **Passengers/trainees:** 15 (day sails), 6 (overnight)
Contact:	Virgina C. Jones
	Gannon and Benjamin Marine Railway
	Beach Road Box 1095
	Vineyard Haven, MA 02568
	Tel: 508-693-4658; Fax: 508-693-1818
	E-mail: gandb@gannonandbenjamin.com
	Web site: http://www.gannonandbenjamin.com

William H. Albury

them to a desk, counter, or workbench, Sea Exploring offers a learning-by-doing environment. Lessons of character building and teamwork apply to all facets of one's life. The Sea Explorer program requires that each trainee exert and extend him or herself physically, morally, and mentally to perform duties which contribute to the ship. The reward, over and above the experience of a world of beauty and challenge, is the satisfaction and self-assurance that contributes to self-discipline. The *William H. Albury*'s Sea Explorer Program offers lessons in ecology and international cooperation, as well as history, science, literature, and art. Subject to the dictates of nature, the Sea Explorer program is adventuresome while also a developer of character and a molder of lives. The *William H. Albury* is now in its 26th year of sail training.

In an era when the Atlantic crossing is measured in hours rather than weeks and most people's occupations anchor

Flag:	USA
Rig:	Gaff topsail schooner, two-masted
Homeport/waters:	Miami, Florida: Biscayne Bay, Florida Keys, and Bahamas
Who sails?	School and other groups and individuals. Affiliated institutions include Boy Scouts and schools in Dade County, Broward County and Abaco, Bahamas.
Cost:	$75 per person per day; $600 group rate
Program type:	Sail training with crew, apprentices, and paying trainees. Sea education in maritime history and ecology in cooperation with accredited schools and colleges and other groups. Passenger day sails and overnight passages.

Specifications:	Sparred length: 70'	Draft: 6'	Sail area: 2,100 sq. ft.
	LOD: 56'	Beam: 14'	Tons: 24 GRT
	LOA: 60'	Rig height: 64'	Power: 150 diesel
	LWL: 49'	Freeboard: 6'	Hull: wood

Built:	1964; Man o' War Cay, Abaco, Bahamas, William H. Albury
Coast Guard certification:	Uninspected Vessel
Crew:	3. **Trainees:** 30 (day sails), 14 (overnight)
Contact:	Captain Joseph A. Maggio, Marine Superintendent
	Inter-Island Schooner
	3145 Virginia St.
	Coconut Grove, FL 33133
	Tel: 305-442-9697; Fax: 305-442-0119
	E-mail: heritage2@mindspring.com
	Web site: http://www.heritageschooner.com

William H. Thorndike

The *William H. Thorndike* sails the coast of Maine in the summer. She has received several awards, including the "Most Photogenic" at the 1994 Antigua Wooden Boat Regatta. Formerly the schooner *Tyrone*, the *William H. Thorndike* is the fourth ship to be named for Dr. William H. Thorndike of Boston. Voyages feature traditional sailing with a spirit of light-hearted competition and camaraderie.

The Crocker Schooner is in Rockland Harbor for 2001, and is in reorganization, just completing a structural hull refit at Journey's End in Rockland, Maine.

Flag:	USA		
Rig:	Gaff schooner, two-masted		
Homeport/waters:	Maine		
Who sails?	Individuals and families		
Season:	Year-round		
Program type:	Sail training and seamanship for trainees of all ages.		
Specifications:	Sparred length: 75'	Draft: 8' 6"	Sail area: 2,200 sq. ft.
	LOD: 65'	Beam: 15'	Tons: 43 GRT
	LOA: 65'	Rig height: 80'	Power: diesel
	LWL: 50'	Hull: wood	
Designer:	Sam Crocker		
Built:	1939; Sims Brothers		
Coast Guard certification:	Uninspected Vessel		
Crew:	2. **Trainees:** 4		
Contact:	Townsend D. Thorndike		
	222 Whiteface Intervale Road		
	North Sandwich, NH 03259		
	Tel: 603-284-7174; Fax: 603-284-9258		
	E-mail: tdtfarm@worldpath.net		

Windy

Built as modern interpretations of the last days of commercial sail, the *Windy* and the *Windy II* are true to function while using modern materials and safety features. In 1996, *Windy* was the first four-masted commercial sailing vessel built since 1921, and *Windy II* was completed in 2001. They have many features not found on older tall ships like hot water showers, private bunks, great cabin, furling topsails, as well as bowthruster, shoal draft, and wing keel. Although sister ships, *Windy* is rigged as a schooner and *Windy II* as a barquen-

tine with three square sails. With their divided and easily managed multi-sail designs, there are ample opportunities for persons of all walks of life to participate in the sailing experience. During the summer at Navy Pier, Chicago, both vessels offer hands on sailing experiences to the public as well as private charters for corporations, weddings, team building, and private parties. In the fall and spring one of the vessels makes a voyage south through the Great Lakes, Erie Canal, Eastern Seaboard and south visiting any interesting port along the way.

Windy sail training programs include short introductory programs for schools and scouts which focus on maritime heritage and nautical science. The planned longer course will focus on the whole student in the four areas of nautical science, American heritage, social dynamics, and spiritual growth during a 6 to 8 week voyage including port visits to see Capitol Hill, the Liberty Bell, the Statue of Liberty, and more. Home-schoolers will have a particular interest in this program. Visit the Web site for details on all the programs and cruises.

Flag:	USA		
Rig:	Gaff topsail schooner, 4-masted		
Homeport/waters:	Chicago, IL; Great Lakes, Eastern Seaboard, and Caribbean.		
Who sails?	5th grade and up, Adults and Seniors of all ages		
Cost:	From $10/student program, $25 for Adults for short cruises.		
Season:	/ Great Lakes and Eastern Seaboard-spring and fall		
Specifications:	Sparred Length:148'	Draft: 8' 6"	Sail area: 4800' sq. ft.
	LOD: 109'	Beam 25'	Displacement: 142 tons
	LOA: 109'	Rig height: 85'	Power: 300 HP diesel
	LWL: 95'	Freeboard: 8'	Hull: steel
Designer:	R. Marthai		
Built:	1996/2001; Detyens Shipyard/Southern Windjammer, Ltd.		
Coast Guard certification:	Passenger Vessels (Subchapter T)		
Trainees:	150 (day sails), 26 (overnight). Coed.		
Contact:	In season:	Off Season:	
	Captain Bob Marthai	2044 Wappoo Hall Road	
	Windy of Chicago, Ltd.,	Charleston, SC 29412	
	600 E. Grand Avenue, Navy Pier	Tel: 843-762-1342	
	Chicago, IL 60611		
	Tel: 312-595-5472		
	Web site: http://www.tallshipwindy.com		

Wolf

The *Wolf* is a classic 74-foot topsail schooner built in 1982-1983 in Panama City, Florida by Master Builder Willis Ray and Finbar Gittleman. Designed by Merrit Walter, the *Wolf* is a Norfolk Rover class steel-hulled schooner.

Homeported in Key West, Florida, the vessel is owned and operated by Captain Finbar Gittleman of Key West Packet Lines, Inc. She is patterned after the blockade runners that plied the waters of the Florida Straits, Caribbean Sea, and Atlantic Ocean in the 19th century. The *Wolf* provides an ideal setting for dockside receptions, day sails, and sunset cruises.

The *Wolf* has been operating in Key West for more than 16 years and has come to symbolize the essence of that "island spirit" which draws visitors from all parts of the world. She often serves as the lead vessel in local harbor parades

and traditional events.

With Captain Gittleman at the helm, the *Wolf* has sailed extensively the waters of the Caribbean, Bahamas, and Gulf of Mexico, and is known for her humanitarian missions. She is showcased in many films and documentaries and is available for private charters, long-term voyages, and special events, including overnight Boy Scout excursions, weddings, and fundraising events..

WOLF

Flag:	USA
Rig:	Square topsail schooner
Homeport/waters:	Key West, Florida: Caribbean, Atlantic, Gulf of Mexico
Who sails?	Elementary and middle school groups, individuals, and families.
Cost:	$25 per person for two-hour sail, $800-$1,900 group rate per day
Program type:	Sail training for crew and volunteer trainees. Sea education in cooperation with organized groups and as informal, in-house programming. Passenger day sails and overnight passages. Dockside interpretation at home and during port visits.

Specifications:			
	Sparred length: 74'	Draft: 7'	Sail area: 2,500 sq. ft.
	LOD: 63'	Beam: 15'	Tons: 37 GRT
	LOA: 63'	Rig height: 56'	Power: 216 HP diesel
	LWL: 49'	Freeboard: 5'	Hull: steel

Designer:	Merrit Walter
Built:	1983; Panama City, Florida, Willis Ray/Captain Finbar Gittleman
Coast Guard certification:	Passenger Vessel (Subchapter T)
Crew:	4-5. **Trainees:** 44 (day sails), 6 (overnight)
Contact:	Captain Finbar Gittleman
	Wolf/Key West Packet Lines, Inc.
	PO Box 1153
	Key West, FL 33041
	Tel: 305-296-9653; Fax: 305-294-8388
	Web site: http://www.schoonerwolf.com

Zebu

prehensively rebuilt (to present as a vessel of the 1850s) for a four-year circumnavigation of the world as Adventure Flagship of Operation Raleigh, the International Youth Expedition. During this she was crewed by young adventurers from 23 nations, visited 41 countries, and sailed 69,000 miles.

In 1988 *Zebu* returned to a new homeport, the historic seaport of Liverpool, England. In 1996 a new Master, Susan Hanley-Place, was appointed to rebuild *Zebu* as a traditional adventure sailing ship for the 21st century, and return her to a role of international prominence as Heritage Flagship of the City of Liverpool.

This beautiful ship is also available for private charter and film work.

By the late 1980s, *Zebu*, a lovely brigantine originally built in the Baltic, had become one of the most internationally distinguished of windjammers. Following a trading career as a High Canvas Merchantman carrying timber around Northern Europe, she was com-

Flag:	UK
Rig:	Brigantine, rigged to circa 1850
Homeport/waters:	Liverpool, England: UK and international
Who sails?	Young people in training for youth leadership selected through youth organizations and individuals of all ages (group bookings preferred).
Season:	Sailing, April to October; education, year-round
Program type:	Personal development/adventure sailing. Dockside education while in port.

Specifications:

Sparred length: 110'	Draft: 8' 7"	Sail area: 4,800 sq. ft.
LOD: 72'	Beam: 22'	Tons: 123 GRT
LOA: 75'	Rig height: 87'	Power: 150 HP diesel
LWL: 64'	Freeboard: 6'	Hull: Kalmar pine on oak

Built:	1938; Holms Shipyard, Raa, Sweden
Certification:	UK Loadline
Crew:	8. Trainees: 16
Contact:	Captain Susan Hanley-Place
	SeaChallenge Shorebase
	11 Greenbank Drive
	Liverpool L17 1AN, United Kingdom
	Tel/Fax: +44 (0) 151-733-0699
	Email: seachallenge@btinternet.com

Zodiac

Designed to reflect the highest achievement of naval architecture under working sail, *Zodiac* was fundamentally a yacht. Built in 1924 for the Johnson & Johnson Pharmaceutical Company, she raced the Atlantic from Sandy Hook, New Jersey to Spain in 1928. The crash of 1929 forced her sale to the San Francisco Pilots Association in 1931.

Renamed *California*, she served forty years off the Golden Gate as the largest schooner ever operated by the Bar Pilots. She was bought in 1975 by a group of young craftsmen experienced in wooden boat restoration and was renamed *Zodiac*.

In 1982 she was placed on the National Register of Historic Places. Certified by the Coast Guard as a Passenger Vessel, she sails Puget Sound, the San Juan Islands, and the Canadian Gulf Coast. *Zodiac*'s spaciousness and amenities make her the ideal boat for sail training and education programs enjoyed by a wide range of people.

In early spring and late fall *Zodiac* hosts Elderhostel sessions, offering courses on

ZODIAC

sailing, navigation, Northwest Native American culture, legends of the Pig War Island, and geology and natural resources of the San Juan Islands. Summer sessions are open to sailing enthusiasts sixteen years and older.

Flag:	USA
Rig:	Gaff schooner, two-masted
Homeport/waters:	Seattle, Washington: Puget Sound, San Juan Islands, Canadian Gulf Islands
Who sails?	High school through college age students, adults, and families.
Season:	March to November
Cost:	$3200 per group per day
Program type:	Sail training for trainees sixteen and older, learning by standing watches on the helm, on sailing stations, and in the chart house.

Specifications:			
	Sparred length: 160'	Draft: 16'	Sail area: 7,000 sq. ft.
	LOD: 127'	Beam: 26'	Tons: 147 GRT
	LOA: 127'	Rig height: 101'	Power: diesel
	LWL: 101'	Freeboard: 5'	Hull: wood

Designer:	William Hand, Jr.
Built:	1924; East Boothbay, Maine, Hodgdon Brothers
Coast Guard certification:	Passenger Vessel (Subchapter T)
Crew:	8. **Trainees/passengers:** 49 (day sails), 24 (overnight)
Contact:	June Mehrer, Vice President
	Vessel Zodiac Corporation
	PO Box 322
	Snohomish, WA 98291-0322
	Tel: 425-483-4088; Fax: 360-563-2469
	Web site: http://www.nwschooner.org

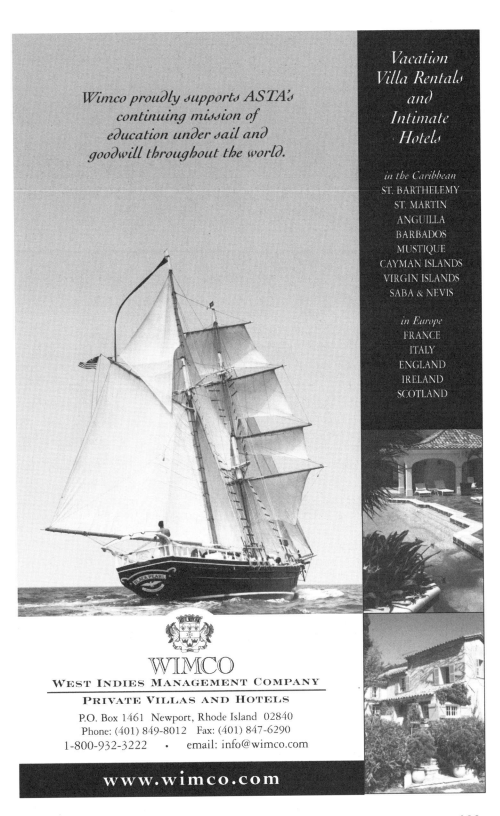

Wimco proudly supports ASTA's continuing mission of education under sail and goodwill throughout the world.

Vacation Villa Rentals and Intimate Hotels

in the Caribbean
ST. BARTHELEMY
ST. MARTIN
ANGUILLA
BARBADOS
MUSTIQUE
CAYMAN ISLANDS
VIRGIN ISLANDS
SABA & NEVIS

in Europe
FRANCE
ITALY
ENGLAND
IRELAND
SCOTLAND

WIMCO
WEST INDIES MANAGEMENT COMPANY
PRIVATE VILLAS AND HOTELS

P.O. Box 1461 Newport, Rhode Island 02840
Phone: (401) 849-8012 Fax: (401) 847-6290
1-800-932-3222 • email: info@wimco.com

www.wimco.com

SAIL TALL SHIPS!

299

On board the *Lord Nelson*

Affiliate Members

ORGANIZATIONS WHICH DO NOT OPERATE
VESSELS BUT DO OFFER SAIL TRAINING
OR SEA EDUCATION PROGRAMS

ActionQuest/Action Sail Programs

ActionQuest summer adventure programs offer teenagers the excitement of yachting while living aboard, developing new friendships through teamwork, and acquiring valuable, lifelong leadership skills. Shipmates gain certifications in sailing, scuba diving, marine science, water skiing, and windsurfing during their three weeks on board. Most shipmates arrive with no previous experience, yet the first time they set sail from the dock, it will be a shipmate who takes the helm under the guidance of licensed sailing masters. Programs operate in the Caribbean, Mediterranean, Galapagos, Australia, and South Pacific. Attracting over 450 teens from 37 states and 18 countries, ActionQuest creates an environment in which teens can discover the extraordinary in their lives and expand both geographical and personal horizons. ActionQuest also offers a high school semester afloat (Argo Academy) and 80-and 35-day college-level programs (Sea-mester Programs).

Contact: ActionQuest Programs
PO Box 5517
Sarasota, FL 34277
Tel: 941-924-6789 or 800-317-6789; Fax: 941-924-6075
E-mail: info@actionquest.com
Web site: http://www.actionquest.com

American Schooner Association

The American Schooner Association (ASA) fosters, promotes, and encourages interest in the preservation, traditions, and enjoyment of schooners and other traditionally rigged vessels. The ASA accomplishes these goals by providing a record of these vessels past and present, publishing a newsletter, Wing & Wing, and coordinating a program of cruising and racing. The ASA supports schooner classes in races in conjunction with other organizations that are dedicated to the preservation of maritime traditions such as Mystic Seaport Museum, South Street Seaport, and the Museum of Yachting. The organization also coordinates group participation in tall ship activities such as ASTA, OpSail and Sail Boston. The ASA has relished a rivalry with our Canadian brothers that continued the traditional races between fishing schooners that started in the 1800s. The ASA's annual meeting is held at Mystic Seaport Museum in Connecticut on the first Saturday in February.

Contact: American Schooner Association
PO Box 484
West Mystic, CT 06355
E-mail: schooner@massed.net
(Space donated by Mr. and Mrs. David Evan Thomas.)

America True Tall Ship Semester for Girls

The Tall Ship Semester is the only extended academic sail training program for high school girls. Provided through schools in the San Francisco area, the semester offers young women a chance to learn, to accept new challenges, and to succeed at new accomplishments. The students have an opportunity to develop confidence, life skills, and a sense of teamwork within a tangible community.

The program begins ashore in San Francisco, with students tackling their introductions to Oceanography, Maritime Literature, Coastal History, the Mathematics of Navigation, and Seamanship. The class then embarks on an eight-week voyage aboard a tall ship, where each student stands watch and performs the duties of a deckhand as they explore such regions as the Channel Islands, the Sea of Cortez, and Mexico's western coastline. Following the voyage, the students return to their school communities, completing their portfolios and projects such as videography, volunteering in marine-related activities, and teaching younger students.

Active as both crewmembers and scholars, the students learn to take risks and accept responsibility, discover new cultures, new possibilities, and new personal horizons. These lessons will serve them throughout their lives.

Contact: Gary Schwarzman, Coordinator
America True Tall Ship Semester for Girls
Pier 17
San Francisco, CA 94111
Tel: 415-433-4287; Fax: 415-433-9910
E-mail: TrueTSSG@AmericaTrue.org
Web site: http://www.AmericaTrue.org

Bermuda Sloop Foundation

The Bermuda Sloop Foundation is a nonprofit organization that is building an 88-foot reproduction of a Bermuda-rigged schooner to be used for sail training for Bermuda's youth.

The primary missions of the Foundation are to enhance and expand local opportunities for character development, teamwork, and community citizenship for youth through outdoor leadership and experience, and to teach Bermuda's maritime history to her people and visitors.

The vessel will be built over two years as a public event. The three-masted schooner will reach 1,500 students per year in a one-day school program and 240 students in eight teams on an ongoing basis.

Contact: Malcolm Kirkland
Bermuda Sloop Foundation
PO Box HM 3200
Hamilton HM NX Bermuda
Tel: 441-299-5110; Fax: 441-299-6517
E-mail: bdasloopfoundation@ibl.bm

Boston University Maritime Education Program

Boston University, one of the largest independent universities in the United States, is a hub of intellectual, scientific, and cultural activity. Our programs offer broad possibilities for combining career goals and personal interests. The University is a recognized innovator in education, as illustrated in the summer of 2000 when Boston University launched the Maritime Education Program, offering college credit courses on an historic tall ship. Recognition by ASTA as the "Sail Training Program of the Year" reaffirmed that we deliver excellence in programming.

Our courses are intensive educational experiences and range from management studies to the liberal arts. During one to two weeks aboard a tall ship, students learn sail training and complete a four-credit Boston University course. Students work as a team to experience the intellectual and physical challenges of our dynamic classes as they sail along the celebrated New England seacoast.

As a participant in the Maritime Education Program, we invite you to experience the Boston University community by visiting our campus located in historic Back Bay, extending westward along the south bank of the Charles River. The Maritime Education Program is offered from June through August.

Contact: Robyn Friedman, Coordinator Academic Services
Boston University Summer Term
Maritime Education Program
755 Commonwealth Avenue
Boston, MA 02215
Tel: 617-353-5124
E-mail: maritime@bu.edu
Web site: http://www.bu.edu/summer

Boy Scout Sea Base and *Argus*

The Orange County Boy Scout Sea Base uses the topsail ketch *Argus* as a sail training vessel for its members. Laid down and launched as a merchant vessel for work in the Baltic and Scandinavian waters, *Argus* probably began life as a salt fish carrier, but later carried a variety of cargoes including grain. In 1968 she was sailed from the Baltic to Spain, Canary Islands, then across the Atlantic to the Caribbean, through the Panama Canal, and north to Newport Beach, California. She has been used and loved by Sea Scouts ever since. *Argus* has a large diesel engine and a full component of working sails, which include three jibs, main, mizzen, and main topsail and course. She is supported by the "Friends of Argus," who enlist and train crewmembers, and the Orange County Council of the BSA, who bear the burden of financial support and arranging Sea Scout high adventure sails. *Argus* takes five-day and two-day trips at sea to Catalina Island and coastal ports for a working sail training cruise with trainees climbing the rigging, learning helmsmanship and small boat handling, snorkeling, swimming, beach hiking, and having the experience of night watches.

Contact: William Mountford, Sea Base Manager
Boy Scout Sea Base
1931 West Pacific Coast Highway
Newport Beach, CA 92663
Tel: 949-642-5031; Fax: 949-650-5407
E-mail: seabase_2000@yahoo.com
Web site: http://www.seabase.org

Buffalo Maritime Heritage Foundation, Inc.

The Buffalo Maritime Heritage Foundation was founded to promote visits of sail training vessels to the Great Lakes and the City of Buffalo. The Foundation promotes and supports sail training in the area. Visiting ships are berthed in the beautiful park setting of the Erie Basin Marina. Tall ships from around the world have visited, including *Christian Radich, Pride of Baltimore II, America,* and *Bounty.* Potable water, electricity, telephone service, showers, and waste disposal facilities are available. Stores are located close by in the downtown area. Buffalo is the western terminus of the Erie Canal, which made the city prosperous and famous. The canal is used today for yachts transiting from Albany on the Hudson River, and for recreational boating and barge traffic.

Contact: RADM J. Edmund Castro, NYNM, President

120 Delaware Avenue, Suite 100
Buffalo, NY 14202-2704
Tel: 716-847-2900; Fax: 716-856-6100
E-mail: jdecastro@jdecastro.com
Web site: http://www.transportation law.jdecastro.com

CIMI Tall Ship Expeditions

CIMI Tall Ship Expeditions builds character and develops minds by taking students and their teachers to sea. A subsidiary of Guided Discoveries, a non-profit organization dedicated to making a difference in the lives of children, our programs focus on marine science embedded in sail training. During the school year, students sail three, five, and seven day live-aboard expeditions to Catalina Island. Participants sail, study, snorkel, hike, kayak, sing, and work together to keep the vessel ship-shape. All instruction, equipment, and meals are provided. Topics covered on each expedition range from marlinspiking, navigation, and seamanship to plankton study, electronic oceanography and ichthyology. Live specimens are temporarily brought on board for study. The focus of instruction on each trip is customized by the group leader to fit their needs. During summer and winter months, programs of longer duration to other West Coast destinations are available. With its hands-on marine science, sail training, and adventure, CIMI Tall Ship Expeditions provides the experience of a lifetime!

Contact: For information, brochures and bookings:
CIMI Tall Ship Expeditions Coordinator
PO Box 1360
Claremont, CA 91711

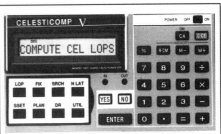

Tel: 800-645-1423; Fax: 909-625-7305
Web site: http://www.guideddiscoveries.org (follow prompts to tall ship)
For program specifics and employment:
Tim Hatler, Program Director
Tel: 310-508-0748
E-mail: thatler@guideddiscoveries.org

Coloma Outdoor Discovery School

The Coloma Outdoor Discovery School has added a California Gold Rush History and Science and Awareness program on board the 86-foot gaff-rigger schooner *Ka'iulani* to their well-established list of student educational adventures. With an experienced crew, talented naturalists, and a lot of enthusiasm, children will experience the voyage of a lifetime. Students engage in meaningful, dynamic, hands-on learning experiences while sailing on San Francisco Bay. The age-appropriate curriculum features social studies, science, math, history, and language arts. The experiential approach invites and maintains a high level of attention and enthusiasm throughout the program.

Contact: Coloma Outdoor Discovery School
PO Box 484
Coloma, CA 95613
Tel: 530-621-2298; Fax: 530-621-4960
E-mail: info@cods.org
Web site: http://www.cods.org

Dirigo Cruises, Ltd.

Since 1973, Dirigo Cruises has offered educational voyages with emphasis on celestial navigation, nature expeditions, sail training, and midshipman programs. Operating in New England, Canada, the Caribbean, and the South Pacific, Dirigo Cruises has programs for people of all ages.

Contact: Captain Eben M. Whitcomb, Jr.
39 Waterside Lane
Clinton, CT 06413
Tel: 860-669-7068; Fax: 860-669-2297

Drayton Harbor Maritime

Drayton Harbor Maritime (DHM) is a private, nonprofit, 501(c)(3) organization whose mission is "to preserve, restore, and interpret the past and present maritime, marine, and estuarine heritage of Drayton Harbor,Washington, and its associated waters." Headquartered in Blaine, Washington, DHM owns and operates the historic *Plover* pedestrian ferry. Built in 1944 to transport workers between the Alaska Packers Association (APA) cannery on Tongue Point (end of Semiahmoo Spit) and the City of Blaine, *Plover* travels her original route, providing visitors a voyage back in time and an interpretation of Drayton Harbor.

In co-operation with Whatcom County Parks, DHM also provides docents and staff for the Semiahmoo Park Museum, located on Semiahmoo Spit. The Museum houses a modest collection of displays and artifacts depicting the area's maritime history.

With grant funding and the assistance of Trillium Corporation, which owns Tongue Point, DHM is spear-heading the restoration of a portion of the old cannery wharf complex, against which, in its heyday, ships of the famous APA "star fleet" (*Star of India*, etc.) moored. Upon completion, the dock will be available for use by visiting tall ships, include interpretive signage, and will be the western terminus for *Plover's* route.

Contact: Richard Sturgill, Executive Director
Drayton Harbor Maritime
1218 4th Street
Blaine, WA 98230
Tel: 360-332-5742
or
Kenneth Ely, Chairman
E-mail: drkenely@juno.com

East End Seaport Museum and Marine Foundation

The mission of the East End Seaport Museum and Marine Foundation is to preserve the maritime history of Eastern Long Island. The Foundation operates the Seaport Museum, maintains the Long Beach "Bug" lighthouse at the entrance to Peconic Bay, runs educational sail training programs for Long Island school children, and produces the Maritime Festival the last weekend in September. The Museum features exhibits on aids to navigation, yacht racing (including the America's Cup), whaling, Revolutionary War, the Hooligan Navy (sailing yachts used to detect U Boats off the East Coast in World War II), and the history of local ship building. The museum has on display a clock works fourth-order lens from Plum Island and a second-order lens from Little Gull Island. The museum is located on the waterfront at the foot of Third Street.

Contact: East End Seaport Museum and Marine Foundation
PO Box 2095
Greenport, NY 11944
Tel: 516-477-0004; Fax: 516-477-3422
Web site: http://www.greenport.com/seaport

El Viento (The Wind)

El Viento will provide children and young adults with opportunities for success in life as responsible citizens through a long-term relationship based on leadership, mutual trust and respect, teamwork, learning, and skills building. Sea-related activities will be focused through partnerships with schools, colleges, development organizations, and other community constituencies. By using the sea and sailing as a metaphor for life, El Viento will introduce young people to their greater role in the environment while providing the tools and skills needed to create opportunities in life.

Contact: Ellen K. Shockro, Ph.D., Executive Director
El Viento Foundation
PO Box 3369
Newport Beach, CA 92659
Tel: 949-673-1654; Fax: 949-675-1794
Web site: http://www.elviento.org

Erie Maritime Museum

Erie Maritime Museum, homeport of U.S. Brig *Niagara* in Erie Pennsylvania, offers the story of *Niagara* from the warship that won the battle of Lake Erie in the War of 1812 to the reconstructed flagship of Pennsylvania. A range of multi-media and interactive exhibits coupled with lively interpretive programs vividly illustrate and teach *Niagara's* history and the region's rich maritime heritage.

When in homeport, the ship herself is the major "exhibit" berthed within yards of the Museum. Inside, the centerpiece exhibit of the Museum's large hall will engage not only the hearts and minds of visitors, but also their muscle: a reconstruction of the mid-ship section of the *Lawrence*, O.H. Perry's first flagship during the Battle of Lake Erie—complete with mast, spars and rigging—will foster hands-on learning in the ways of sail.

Other exhibits will tell the stories of the USS *Wolverine* (the nation's first iron-hulled warship), the environmental transformation of the Great Lakes ecosystem, former General Electric steam turbine (one of two left of this model, the other in the Smithsonian in Washington D.C.) and more. Future development includes our West Wing Gallery that will house the story of the industries and people who live along Lake Erie Shores, including the freshwater fishing industries, once the largest in the world.

There currently are spaces for two ships at the Maritime Museum. We invite all of our ASTA friends to use this docking space when needed.

> Contact: Rick Liebel, Public Relations Director
> Erie Maritime Museum
> 150 East Front Street, Suite 100
> Erie, PA 16507
> Tel: 814-452-2744; Fax: 814-455-6760
> E-mail: rliebel@brigniagara.org
> Web site: http://www.brigniagara.org

(Space donated by Captain Walter Rybka, Master of U.S. Brig Niagara.)

Foundation of the Los Angeles Maritime Museum

The Foundation of the Los Angeles Maritime Museum was founded in 1980 as an independent, non-profit corporation for the purpose of promoting and understanding the maritime historical development of the San Pedro Bay and adjacent areas. Its focus is based on educating through displays of the maritime industry, its history and the vision of the future.

The Los Angeles Maritime Museum is the largest maritime museum on the West Coast featuring seven galleries of exhibits. *Angels Gate*, the Museum's resident tugboat, is maintained and operated by volunteers. Other volunteer opportunities include: tour guides; building/repairing models; research; greeting visitors; and working in the Sea Chest Museum Store.

> Contact: Foundation of the Los Angeles Maritime Museum
> Berth 84-Foot of Sixth Street
> San Pedro, CA 90731
> Tel: 310-548-7618; Fax: 310-832-6537
> E-mail: museum@lamaritimemuseum.org
> Web site: http://www.lamaritimemuseum.org

Girl Scouts of the USA

More and more Girl Scouts are sailing in GirlSports, in boats small to tall. Whether learning from sailing around a pond or around the world, girls say the 'best part's the fun!' A sailing ship is a superb 'camp-of-the-sea,' where girls can focus on goals like teamwork and leadership through environmental action, international friendship, maritime heritage, arts, technology, science, careers, etc. Indeed, sail training is a great way to 'just add water' to Girl Scout handbooks, badges, interest projects and the progression of activities for every age level. Starting with basic safety for the youngest Daisy Girl Scouts through sailing adventures for teenage Senior Girl Scouts, Girl Scouts and volunteer leaders in over 300 local GS councils are always eager for more local, national and international opportunities for fun and learning under sail!

Notable Girl Scout sailors include Olympic medalists and tall ship captains, who, with thousands of others carry on a long tradition going back to 1935 with Girl Scout Mariners sailing the Johnson's *Yankee*. 2001 will continue the adventures: expanding the Connecticut Girl Scouts Friend Ship Amistad Ambassadors program; involving more Girl Scouts in Great Lakes ports and underway in Tall Ships Challenge® 2001; planning a GS Mariner reunion with the launch of the *Irving Johnson* and *Exy Johnson* in Los Angeles; and other exciting 'wider opportunities' under sail!

      Contact: Your local Girl Scout council listed under 'Girl Scouts,' the
      national Web site at or
      Nancy H. Richardson
      Sailing in GirlSports, GSUSA
      69 Burnet Street
      Maplewood, NJ 07040-2654
      Tel: 973-762-1430; Fax: 973-762-6720
      E-mail: marinergs@home.com

Glacier Society, Inc.

The purpose of the Glacier Society is to restore and operate the USS/USCG *Glacier* as a functioning museum ship honoring all who served in the exploration of the North and South Poles. The USS/USCG *Glacier* made 29 voyages to the Antarctic and 10 voyages to the Arctic under both the U.S. Navy and U.S. Coast Guard command—one of the few vessels to serve under the colors of both the USN and the USCG. Both in port and while underway, the Glacier Society will provide hands-on training to children and adults while teaching the history of exploration of the Poles. She will serve as a learning platform for K-12 students and as a scientific platform for university students including real-time Internet links to active polar research stations.

Picture yourself aboard the *Glacier* as her educational odyssey begins from San Francisco to the East Coast after restoration. We are looking for volunteers to participate in this exciting adventure! Volunteer opportunities include restoration, archival research and fundraising.

      Contact: Ben Koether, Chairman
      Glacier Society, Inc.
      905 Honeyspot Rd.
      Stratford, CT 06615
      Phone: 203-377-4414; Fax: 203-386-0416
      E-mail: bkoether@fastinc.com
      Web site: http://www.glaciersociety.org

Golden Gate Tall Ships Society

The Golden Gate Tall Ships Society (GGTSS) is a California nonprofit organization dedicated to educating people in nautical skills and supporting the preservation and operation of traditional sailing vessels, particularly tall ships.

Goals and Strategies:

• Provide opportunities for sail training experiences for young people.
• Provide sailing and shipboard education for members.
• Support shore-side education.
• Replenish the Cadet Scholarship Fund.
• Promote tall ships visits in San Francisco Bay.
• Increase the size and visibility of the organization.

Golden Gate Tall Ships Society (formerly Sausalito Tall Ships Society) supported Mercy High School's Tall Ship Semester for Girls aboard the *Californian* in 1999—a first for high school girls in San Francisco.

> Contact: Alice Cochran, President
> Golden Gate Tall Ships Society
> PO Box 926
> Sausalito, CA 94966
> Tel: 415-331-1009
> E-mail: info@stss.org
> Web site: http://www.stss.org

HANSA Foundation

The HANSA Foundation's goals are: to provide a sail training-based opportunity for North American and European young people, aged 15-25, principally from the Gulf of Maine community and the Hanseatic cities of the North Sea and the Baltic; to join an intercultural exchange with internationally mixed crews of trainees; to place North American trainees aboard Hanseatic sail training ships, and reciprocally European youth aboard North American ASTA ships; to provide programs on and in association with their partners, all of which are ASTA members; to make sail training opportunities available to all youth through need-blind scholarships, bridging the gap between the ASTA Sail Training Scholarship and STAG (Sail Training Association of Germany), whose trainee scholarships are restricted to German citizens or residents; and to build cultural and economic bridges with our largest European trading partner, Germany.

HANSA is the North American trainee coordinator for ASTA members *Esprit* and *Roald Amundsen*. They work actively with ASTA members *Amara Zee* and the Hurricane Island Outward Bound School, and work broadly in the German sailing community and with the German bluewater cruising club TRANS-OCEAN on Gulf of Maine awareness-raising issues.

> Contact: David Schurman, Executive Director
> HANSA Foundation
> PO Box 69
> North Reading, MA 01864
> Tel: 781-944-0304; Fax: 781-944-2469
> E-mail: info@sailtraining.com
> Web site: http://www.sailtraining.com

Headwaters to Ocean (H2O)

The only boat program of its kind in the Columbia River Basin, H2O is dedicated to fostering community-based stewardship of these awe-inspiring rivers through boat-based learning and hands-on experiences. Founded in 1995 by veterans of sail training programs world-wide, H2O uses the vintage 65' tugboat *Captain Conner*, stoutly built of timbers by prisoners at McNeil Island Penitentiary during World War II, to carry out its education-to-action mission.

To date, H2O has inspired 11,700 people to make small changes in their behavior to create healthier watersheds and stronger communities. H2O uses its floating platform to provide a great variety of on-water educational experiences for all ages, including: decision-maker briefings; teen overnight navigation voyages; youth field trips; tug and kayak 2-day adventures; summer day camps, and the popular "Shanghai" free boat rides for the general public. The *Captain Conner* travels on the Willamette River from Oregon City to the confluence with the Columbia River, and on the Columbia River, from Hood River, Oregon to the Pacific Ocean. With all eyes on the Pacific Northwest as it grapples with some of the most challenging environmental issues of our time, H2O is redefining boat-based education and environmentalism to meet the needs of a new era. H2O enjoys a diverse base of support from private grants, businesses, public agencies, individuals and volunteers.

> Contact: Kiirsten Flynn, Program Manager
> Headwaters to Ocean (H2O), Inc.
> 3945 SE Hawthorne Boulevard
> Portland, OR 97214
> Tel: 503-228-9600
> E-mail: HQ@h2ocean.org
> Web site: http://www.h2ocean.org

Historic Promotions

Historic Promotions is a full service company representing tall ships worldwide. We provide a variety services to our client ships, ports, communities and festivals. Historic Promotions places tall ships in events, as well as assists in event planning, funding, promotion and marketing. We specialize in sail racing events, historic reenactments, and motion pictures, and secure long-term ship sponsorships, corporate sponsors, advertising, and Web links.

> Contact: Ronald Prichep, CEO
> 11501 Gunston Road Way
> Mason Neck, VA 22079
> Tel: 703-541-0730; Fax: 703-541-0733
> E-mail: ronprichep@aol.com

Hull Lifesaving Museum

The Hull Lifesaving Museum translates the skills and ethics of the famous surfmen of Boston Harbor into experiential programs in traditional rowing craft for youth and adults alike. The Museum operates four sites: the restored, 19th century Point Allerton U.S. Life Saving Service Station and Windmill Point Boathouse in Hull, and the Navy Yard Rowing Center and Carriage House Maritime Resource Center in Boston's Charlestown Navy Yard.

Working out of 38-foot, 3-masted Bantry Bay gigs, 32-foot, six-oared Boston pilot gigs, and 24-foot, four-oared Whitehall gigs, the Museum's year-round, open-water rowing programs offer character and academic education, island and urban waterways exploration, and fun! Additionally, the Museum is the leadership organization for the development youth and education-focused open-water rowing programs in the U.S., with a special emphasis on those serving high-risk youth. Crews from throughout metropolitan Boston and the City's South Shore come from public schools, public housing projects, community organizations, and juvenile courts. Children and adults explore, race, build and maintain the Museum's fleet of 14 traditional rowing boats, and make daily discoveries about Boston Harbor.

> Contact: Lory Newmyer, Executive Director
> or Ed McCabe, Maritime Program Director
> 1117 Nantasket Avenue
> Hull, MA 02045
> Phone: 781-925-5433
> E-mail: hullmuse@channell.com
> Web site: http://www.bostonharborheritage.org

Independence Seaport Museum

The Independence Seaport Museum is located on the Delaware River at Penn's Landing in downtown Philadelphia. The Museum is a private, nonprofit institution dedicated to the collection, preservation, and interpretation of materials relating to maritime history, with a particular emphasis on the Delaware Bay and River.

Located in a newly renovated, multi-million dollar facility, the Museum houses permanent and changing exhibit galleries, classrooms, an active boat building shop, and a specialized maritime library. Museum visitors can tour the 1944 US Navy submarine BECUNA and the cruiser OLYMPIA, launched in 1895. The 1934 Trumpy motor yacht *Enticer* is maintained and operated in the charter trade.

The Museum regularly provides berths for visiting vessels and has jointly offered educational programs with sail training vessels such as *Niagara, A.J. Meerwald* and *Pioneer*.

> Contact: Paul DeOrsay, Assistant Director
> Independence Seaport Museum
> 211 South Columbus Boulevard
> Philadelphia, PA 19106
> Tel: 215-925-5439; Fax: 215-925-6713
> E-mail: pdeorsay@indsm.org
> Web site: http://www.seaport.philly.com

Maryland School of Sailing and Seamanship

The Maryland School of Sailing and Seamanship has conducted sail training courses from the basic through the advanced levels since 1991 and offshore sail training cruises since 1993 using Island Packet cruising yachts. Graduates of their courses earn certification from the American Sailing Association. This year's courses include Basic and Intermediate Sailing courses taught in the US Virgin Islands and the Chesapeake Bay; Intermediate Sailing/Cruising courses taught in coastal waters along the Atlantic Coast from Norfolk to Nantucket; Ocean Training Courses between Norfolk, Bermuda, and the US Virgin Islands; and classroom instruction including Coastal and Celestial Navigation and Offshore Passage Preparation.

> Contact: The Maryland School of Sailing and Seamanship, Inc.

PO Box 609
Rock Hall, MD 21661
Tel: 410-639-7030; Fax: 410-639-7038
E-mail: office@mdschool.com

Master Mariners Benevolent Association

The Master Mariners Benevolent Association (MMBA), formed in 1865, exists to encourage the restoration, maintenance, and active use of classic sailing vessels, and consists of nearly 200 such vessels, mostly in the San Francisco Bay area. Eight scheduled events from January to October provide opportunities for skippers and crew to race, cruise, parade, and swap equipment and ideas. The most popular events are the Master Mariners Regatta on Memorial Day weekend and the Wooden Boat Show late in June.

MMBA also manages an established charitable foundation to provide deserving local residents with sail training and maritime apprentice scholarships, and it has been instrumental in building a permanent host organization in conjunction with cadet sailing vessel visits to San Francisco Bay. Nearly a dozen of our largest member vessels are active as commercial charter sailing vessels, and several, most notably the *Californian*—the official tall ship ambassador for the state of California—double as cadet training ships.

Membership opportunities range from Regular (skippers of classic sailing vessels) to Friends, both at nominal cost. Membership inquiries should be directed to Jeff Stokes, 319 Strand Avenue, Pleasant Hill, CA 94523.

> Contact: Commodore Robert Rogers
> 60 Pamela Court
> Tiburon, CA 94920
> Tel: 925-287-4206; Fax: 925-934-0789
> E-mail: mastermariners@hotmail.com or robert.rogers@fmglobal.com
> Web site: http://www.mastermariners.org

National Outdoor Leadership School (NOLS)

The National Outdoor Leadership School (NOLS) has a 30-year history of excellence in outdoor education and leadership. Today, NOLS runs eight branch schools around the world and courses on five continents. Sail training is available on open boats in Baja California, Mexico, on keel boats in Desolation Sound, British Columbia, and as a cultural experience aboard dhows in Kenya, East Africa. These courses are run as self-reliant sailing expeditions. Training in a multitude of other skill areas is available from sea kayaking to mountaineering, hiking, horse packing, and more. Leadership, safety and judgment, and minimum-impact camping are central themes throughout every NOLS experience. College credit is available on most courses through the University of Utah. NOLS is a private, nonprofit educational corporation.

> Contact: Nathan Steele
> 288 Main Street
> Lander, WY 82520-3128
> Tel: 307-332-8800; Fax: 307-332-8811
> E-mail: nate_steele@nols.edu
> Web site: http://www.nols.edu

Northern S.T.A.R. (Sail Training and Renewal)

Northern S.T.A.R. offers academic programs focused on maritime history and ecological marine biology, with particular emphasis on crew experience, expeditionary learning, and early intervention.

> Contact: David Smith, Executive Director
> 1010 Stroud Court
> Charlevoix, MI 49720
> Tel: 616-547-1817

Northwest Schooner Society

Seattle's Northwest Schooner Society (NWSS) provides a unique opportunity for teens and adults to experience a piece of American history aboard fully restored "floating classrooms." The Society is a nonprofit, tax-exempt organization, founded in 1994 to allow more people to experience the excitement and challenge of old-fashioned seamanship, twenty-four hours a day.

The Northwest Schooner Society sponsors voyages of different lengths on historic ships through their own multidisciplinary educational program. Under billowing canvas, schools and youth groups experience real-life application of science, math, history, and geography. Programs are designed to bring out the best in teenagers, introducing youngsters to an inner strength they never knew they had while they haul sail to harness the elements. From their homeports in Bellingham and Seattle, they sail the stunning and protected waters of Washington State and British Columbia. The Society organizes environmental cruises on the 1924 schooner *Zodiac*, the largest sailing ship on the West Coast. The Society also owns and operates the 87-foot steel power yacht *Rebecca*, built in 1947.

> Contact: Bill Vonk
> Northwest Schooner Society
> PO Box 9504
> Seattle, WA 98109
> Tel: 800-551-6977; Fax: 206-633-2784
> E-mail: bvonk@nwschooner.org
> Web site: http://www.nwschooner.org

Ocean Navigator School of Seamanship

The Ocean Navigator School of Seamanship offers the following seminars for offshore sailors in approximately ten locations around the country:
- Introduction to Celestial Navigation
- Predicting Marine Weather I & II
- The Basics of Offshore Seamanship
- Introduction to Offshore Emergency Medicine
- Integrated Navigation Techniques
- Using Weather & Ocean Currents to Win
- Marine Diesel Engine Operation and Maintenance
- Ancillary Marine Systems Operation and Maintenance
- Marine Electrical Systems Operation and Maintenance
- The On Board Computer
- Marine Communication Systems and Operations
- Introduction to Yacht Design

The seminars are fast-paced and fairly intense, designed for experienced sailors. A knowledge of basic skills is assumed although most seminars begin with a review of those skills. In many cases the subject is too broad to produce experts overnight, but in every case you will go away with a full appreciation for the subject and the ability to go on learning from that day forward. The school's mission is to teach present and future offshore sailors important knowledge and techniques that will make them better voyagers and navigators.

Contact: Ocean Navigator School of Seamanship
PO Box 418
Rockport, ME 04856
Tel/Fax: 207-230-0385
E-mail: education@oceannavigator.com
Web site: http://www.oceannavigator.com

Ocean Voyages

Ocean Voyages was founded 22 years ago to provide participatory educational sailing programs throughout the world. Programs are open to sailing enthusiasts of all ages. Most programs run from one to four weeks in length. Ocean Voyages works with educators and institutions to design customized programs for youth participation for "youth of all ages." Ocean Voyages also has extensive experience in scientific research projects and documentary and feature films.

Ocean Voyages works toward preserving our maritime heritage and sailing arts, and providing opportunities for people to gain sailing education and seafaring experience. Coastal and inter-island programs are available in addition to offshore passage-making and around-the-world voyaging opportunities. Program areas include: Hawaii, California, the Pacific Northwest, Galapagos Islands, Aegean Sea, Caribbean, French Polynesia, and New Zealand, as well as Pacific and Atlantic Ocean crossings. Many of the international vessels that Ocean Voyages works with participated in Tall Ships 2000® and OpSail 2000, and are preparing to participate in ASTA's Tall Ships Challenge® race series.

Contact: Mary Crowley, Director
Ocean Voyages
1709 Bridgeway
Sausalito, CA 94965
Tel: 415-332-4681, 800-299-4444; Fax: 415-332-7460
E-mail: sail@voyages.com or voyages@ix.netcom.com

Philadelphia City Sail

Philadelphia City Sail is a nonprofit, maritime educational program working primarily with inner city youth of Philadelphia. The schoolship *Jolly II Rover*, a 73-foot topsail schooner, serves as an educational platform to introduce students to sailing, maritime history, and the marine sciences. While on board *Rover*, students set sail and have an opportunity to explore the world of plankton, study the water quality of the Delaware River, and learn about the past, present, and future of the Philadelphia waterfront.

Philadelphia City Sail's school-year program is a partnership with The Academy of Natural Sciences and is closely aligned with the Philadelphia School District. In combination with a summer program, the schoolship servces over 3,000 students each year.

>Contact: Mark Fallon, Education Director
>Philadelphia City Sail
>PO Box 43235
>Philadelphia, PA 19129
>Tel: 215-271-3400; Fax: 215-271-0234
>E-mail: Phcitysail@aol.com
>Web site: http://www.phillyfriend.com/citysail.htm

Project Link, Ltd.

Project Link was founded in 1984 to facilitate the incorporation of special-needs students into regular classroom settings. Project Link recently expanded the scope of its mission to include all students both before and after graduation. The new focus of the organization relates directly to the maritime world, taking special advantage of the coastal opportunities of Boston Harbor and vicinity.

Project Link is working with a number of Boston area schools to develop a program that will allow students to interact with personnel aboard several sailing vessels, providing real-life, real-time elements to issues and problems being discussed in class. Two such Internet links have been established with the *Picton Castle* and the USCG Barque *Eagle*. The study course will culminate with a sail aboard *Firebird*, a 47-foot Alden yawl. In addition to this program, Project Link helps students discover meaningful careers in the maritime field following high school graduation.

>Contact: John V. Henderson, Executive Director
>Project Link, Ltd.
>PO Box 167
>Manchester, MA 01944
>Tel: 978-768-7469; Fax: 617-357-5834
>E-mail: projlink@ma.ultranet.com

Rose Island Lighthouse Foundation

The Rose Island Lighthouse is located in lower Narragansett Bay, Rhode Island – a mile offshore and a century in the past. Beyond the reach of Newport's utility lines and services, the recently restored lighthouse is managed by the non-profit Rose Island Lighthouse Foundation as an independent, energy efficient, environmental education center that is directly dependent on forces of nature like rainwater and wind-powered electricity. The light in the tower was joyously relit on August 7, 1993 and is listed again on the charts. The Lighthouse is also listed on the National Register of Historic Places.

Home to historic keepers and their families for over a hundred years, the Lighthouse today abuts a 17 acre protected wildlife refuge that is owned by the Foundation. Both properties are maintained by modern keepers who sign on for a week at a time as part of our environmental education program, which also includes overnights in the museum, as well as school field trips and special group tours.

We welcome you to become part of our effort to keep the light shining in the hearts and minds of the next generation of the Earth's keepers. See how the past can provide answers for the future at Rose Island – a historic, living museum and environmental education center.

>Contact: Charlotte Johnson, Executive Director

Rose Island Lighthouse Foundation
PO Box 1419
Newport, RI 02840
Phone: 401-847-4242; Fax. 401-847-7462
E-mail: Charlotte@RoseIsland.org
Web site: http://www.RoseIslandLighthouse.org

Sail America

Sail America was founded in 1990 by members of the US sailing industry who wanted to play a very active role in growing sailing as a sport, an industry, and a way of life. Its nearly 500 members represent every segment of the industry, from manufacturers to sailing schools, charter companies to publications. It is the only nonprofit industry association exclusively working to promote the growth of sailing businesses.

Sail America's mission statement is: "To promote the growth of the sailing industry." To achieve this, they have developed programs and events which will significantly increase participation in sailing. Sail Expo® St. Petersburg, Sail Expo® Atlantic City, Pacific Sail Expo®, Strictly Sail® Chicago, and Strictly Sail® Miami not only boost sales for the businesses involved, but serve to educate sailors and non-sailors. Special events and over 300 seminars—a compilation of the best technical, safety, and entertainment presentations offered to the sailing public—take place during the Sail Expo® and Strictly Sail® events.

Contact: Scot West, Executive Director
850 Aquidneck Ave., Unit B-4
Middletown, RI 02842-7201

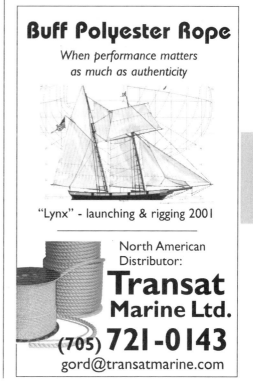

Tel: 401-841-0900; Fax: 401-847-2044
Web site: http://www.sailamerica.com

Sail Martha's Vineyard

Sail Martha's Vineyard is a 501(c)(3) nonprofit organization dedicated to celebrating and perpetuating Martha's Vineyard's maritime heritage and culture. Its activities encourage island children to be comfortable on the water by offering boat handling and sailing instruction free of charge, adult sailing classes, and support for the high school sailing team for competitive sailors.

Sail Martha's Vineyard supports educational programs in the public elementary schools that familiarize island children with the maritime traditions of Martha's Vineyard, such as their wooden boat project. It attracts interesting and historic vessels to the island, supports such local vessels, and serves as a clearinghouse for other maritime-related organizations and initiatives on the island.

Sail Martha's Vineyard depends entirely on its volunteers and is funded through individual and community contributions and grant support.

> Contact: John Christensen, President
> or Hope Callen, Administrator
> Sail Martha's Vineyard
> PO Box 1998
> Vineyard Haven, MA 02568
> Tel: 508-696-7644; Fax: 508-696-8819
> E-mail: sailmv@vineyard.net

Sail Newport

Sail Newport is a non-profit organization dedicated to offering public access to the sport of sailing. To accomplish its mission, we offer educational programs and foster one-design racing in Narragansett Bay. As Rhode Island's Public Sailing Center, the organization endeavors to make it easy and affordable to learn and enjoy the sport of sailing at any age, with its youngest students starting at age seven. Sail Newport also offers a rental fleet of J/22s and Rhodes 19s for use seven days a week during the sailing season.

The broad array of educational programs for youth and adults include novice, intermediate, and advanced levels of instruction. In addition, Sail Newport custom designs sailing programs for schools, colleges, community groups, municipal organizations, youth groups, and disabled organizations. The organization is especially proud of its Scholarship Program which provides financial aid to eligible community families.

Sail Newport has also earned a reputation for excellence in regatta management and is recognized as the leader in hosting world-class sailing competitions and premiere racing events in New England. Each year, we host a number of renowned national and international events with ample shoreside facilities serving regularly as race headquarters. Some of these events have included Sail Newport's own annual Newport Regatta™ , now in its eighteenth year, the Rolex International Women's Keelboat Championship, the Laser World Championship, Etchells North Americans, Junior Olympic Festivals, the 1998 Hartford World Disabled Championship, the 1998 J/24 North Americans, and the 2000 J/24 World Championship.

> Contact: Kim Hapgood, Program Director
> Sail Newport, Inc.

60 Fort Adams Drive
Newport, RI 02840
Tel: 401-846-1983
E-mail: kimh@sailnewport.org
Web site: http://www.sailnewport.org

Salish Sea Expeditions

Salish Sea Expeditions is a non-profit organization offering diverse science education and sail training programs on Puget Sound onboard the 61' yawl *Carlyn*. Salish provides students, educators, and citizens of all ages with the unique opportunity to directly experience and scientifically explore the Puget Sound marine ecosystem. With guidance from marine educators, Salish students develop a scientific hypothesis and detailed oceanographic sampling and navigation plans for a 2-5 day sailing/research expedition.

During their voyage, students work together to collect and analyze oceanographic samples, sail and navigate the ship, and help with cooking and shipboard chores. Conducting such a group project fosters cooperation, team building, and positive community problem-solving. It teaches students how to think critically and apply the scientific method. Furthermore, the unique and challenging shipboard environment allows students to master new skills, gain confidence, and see the world from a new vantage point.

Carlyn is designed and rigged to support maximum student participation. It is U.S. Coast Guard certified to carry 38 people and has the capacity to sleep 16. Please see our Web site or call for more information on our diverse array of program offerings. We can even custom-design programs to meet your group's special needs.

Contact: Sophy Johnston and Ellie Linen Low, Co-Directors
Salish Sea Expeditions
271 Wyatt Way, NE #102
Bainbridge Island, WA 98110
Tel/Fax: 206-780-7848
E-mail: info@salish.org
Web site: http://www.salish.org

Sea Scouts/Boy Scouts of America

Sea Scouting is adventure on sea and land – for you. Sea Scouting is a co-educational program offered to young adults between the ages of 14 and 21. It's a chance to learn and have fun at the same time.

Sea Scouting is organized to promote better citizenship and to improve members' boating skills and knowledge through instruction and practice in water safety, boating skills, outdoor, social, and service experiences, and knowledge of our maritime heritage.

You can learn to sail, SCUBA dive, row, and to keep a boat in shape; you can cruise local waters or go sailing on long cruises far from home. You'll also have a chance to develop maritime skills that can lead to careers later on.

Your local council service center can tell you where Sea Scout ships are and how to get in touch with them (look up "Boy Scouts of America" in your phone book). If there is more than one ship in your area, check them all out and decide which one looks best for you. Most ships' programs specialize in certain types of boating, and some will be closer to your interests than others.

A wealth of information on programs, training, activities and contact information is available from the Sea Scout Web site. It also includes an extensive library of training and program materials and artwork for downloading. Visit us at http://www.seascout.org

(Space donated by Mr. David A. Steen.)

SeaQuest Studio

SeaQuest Studio represents three generations of sailors passing on the seafaring arts as an integral discipline of maritime education. Through junior sailing outreach, scouts, teacher workshops, flotillas, and festival demonstrations, they are actively promoting the past and future of seafaring artistry.

For two years, the "Seafaring Artisan" crew has sailed the coast of North Carolina, involving sailors and educators in meaningful, practical, and decorative art forms of seamanship; i.e. wayfinding arts, logs/illustration, cartography, carving/scrimshaw, graphics, marlinespike, textiles, etc.

Training artists for the marine industry involves understanding dynamic innovation as a tradition, and it is this creative force that our sailors come to find within themselves. By exploring our artistic heritage under sail, they hope to nurture a genuine concern for our water planet.

      Contact: Susan R. Wallace Carr, Director
      SeaQuest Studio
      PO Box 5375
      Emerald Isle, NC 28594
      Tel: 252-354-8833
      E-mail: maritech@webtv.net

Seattle Area Sea Scouts and *Yankee Clipper*

Yankee Clipper, Sea Scout Ship 97, has trained youth between the ages of fourteen and twenty-one in nautical skills such as sailing, seamanship, navigation, aquatics, communications, leadership, as well as citizenship and character building. *Yankee Clipper* also uses a 14' C-Lark and Lido, and 10' Sea Scouter sailing dinghies.

Affiliated with the Boy Scouts of America and the West Seattle Lions Club, *Yankee Clipper* was built in 1943 by the US Navy, and lengthened and coverted to a sail training vessel in 1950. She sails the waters of Puget Sound and British Columbia. *Yankee Clipper* has participated in numerous events featuring classic vessels and is the recipient of awards and accolades including being named "historic tall ship" of the Southwest Seattle Historical Society.

Meetings are held weeky, overnight cruises monthly and longer cruises in the summer. In the fall, the crew conducts Ecology Tours on the Duwamish River.

      Contact: Captain John Kelly
      5271 45th Avenue SW
      Seattle, WA 98136
      Tel: 206-932-0971

Tall Ship Millenium Challenge

Tall Ship Millennium Challenge is a not-for-profit organization dedicated to promoting sail-training and tall ship adventure opportunities for people of all abilities. Through our booking service - www.bookaberth.com - TSMC serves as an agent for vessels and organisations booking supernumeraries. It acts as a referral service for clients seeking sail training adventure. We invite inquiries from vessels wishing to organise visits to Lunenburg or other maritime ports as well as inquiries from organisations and individuals interested in our sail-training promotion initiatives; booking opportunities; or service to mariners. TSMC also operates Redfish media that is providing information and support services in the development of Internet access and Web page for those in the marine service industries. Tall Ship Millenium Challenge is located in Lunenburg, Nova Scotia Canada, which was "ASTA's 1999 Port of the Year."

> Contact: Karen Acton-Bond
> 194 Montague Street, Box 1269
> Lunenburg, NS B0J 2C0 Canada
> Tel: 902-634-8171; Fax 902-634-8391
> E-mail: karen@tallshipmc.com

United States Merchant Marine Academy

The United States Merchant Marine Academy is located on Long Island Sound at Kings Point, New York. The USMMA, founded in 1943, is the fourth of the five federal service academies. Its mission is to train young men and women for civilian and military careers in the nation's maritime and intermodal transportation system. During a four-year course of study, midshipmen spend one year at sea as cadets aboard commercial merchant ships, where they gain valuable practical experience. The remaining three years are spent at the Academy. Upon graduation, individuals receive a Bachelor of Science degree, a US Coast Guard license as deck or engineer officer, and a commission as an Ensign in the US Naval Reserve. Tuition, room, and board are provided by the federal government, in exchange for a 5-8 year service obligation in the civilian transportation industry, active duty military, or Naval Reserve.

The Academy has long recognized the leadership and seamanship skills gained through sail training, and supports an extensive waterfront program. This includes a five-boat offshore sailing team, an inter-collegiate sailing team, and an extensive instructional and recreational fleet. All midshipmen are required to learn to sail, and nearly 20% participate in the extracurricular programs. Midshipmen operate and maintain all small craft and serve in all billets, from skippers to watch captains and navigators.

> Contact: CDR Eric Wallischeck, USMS, Sailing Master
> Yocum Sailing Center
> US Merchant Marine Academy
> Kings Point, NY 11024-1699
> Tel: 516-773-5396
> E-mail: wallischecke@usmma.edu
> Web site: http://www.usmma.edu

Urban Harbors Institute

The Urban Harbors Institute conducts multidisciplinary research on urban harbor issues ranging from water quality to waterfront development. The Institute sponsors workshops, symposia, and educational programs. It publishes reports and proceedings, provides technical assistance to community and business leaders and the general public, and maintains a resource library. It also co-sponsors an annual expedition aboard the schooner *Ernestina* (for six geography credits), and day programs are offered aboard various schooners from the New England region.

The Institute is associated with the University of Massachusetts' programs in environmental sciences, geography, and management. Its core staff, senior associates, and researchers have expertise in public policy, coastal resource management, marine law, economics, waterfront planning, international coastal zone management, and education.

> Contact: Madeleine Walsh
> Urban Harbors Institute
> University of Massachusetts-Boston
> 100 Morrissey Blvd.
> Boston, MA 02125
> Tel: 617-287-5570; Fax: 617-287-5575

Ventura County Maritime Museum

Located on Fisherman's Wharf at the corner of Channel Islands Boulevard and Victoria Avenue in Oxnard, California, the Ventura County Maritime Museum is the focal point of Channel Islands Harbor's entertainment center, and where maritime history comes alive.

The Museum is dedicated to the interpretation of world maritime history, and is acknowledged as housing the finest collection of marine art and ship models on the Pacific Coast. The art collection spans four centuries of marine painters, beginning with the 17th century Dutch and Flemish masters and ending with the work of contemporary artists such as John Stobart and David Thimgan. An international parade of models of historic ships make up a "Genealogy Of Sail" presentation representing nearly 5,000 years of sailing history. Temporary exhibits featuring both local and internationally recognized artists, as well as timely subjects of maritime interest, assure that there is always something new to appeal to and attract repeat as well as first-time visitors.

The Museum also has an active elementary education program targeted to grades 4 through 7, featuring California, American, and ancient maritime history. The Museum combines its programs with the Channel Islands Marine Floating Lab, which offers an oceanography program, to provide students with a rich, rewarding field trip to Channel Islands Harbor. These programs touch about 4500 students each year.

The Museum is open seven days a week; hours are 11 to 5. Suggested donation is $3.00 for adults, $1.00 for children under 12. Group tours, special activities for school groups, and social events can be arranged.

> Contact: David Leach, Operations Manager
> Ventura County Maritime Museum
> 2731 S. Victoria Avenue
> Oxnard, CA 93035
> Tel: 805-984-6260; Fax: 805-984-5970
> E-mail: VCMM@aol.com

Williams-Mystic Maritime Studies Program

The Maritime Studies program of Williams College and Mystic Seaport offers undergraduates the opportunity to focus a semester on the study of the sea. Students take four Williams College courses at Mystic Seaport: maritime history, literature of the sea, marine science (either oceanography or marine ecology), and marine policy. Academics are enhanced by hands-on maritime skills classes in sailing, shipsmithing, celestial navigation, or sea music. There are opportunities to climb aloft on square-riggers.

Four field seminars are incorporated into the curriculum each semester. Aboard a 130-foot staysail schooner, students voyage offshore for nearly two weeks in the North Atlantic each fall and in the Caribbean each spring semester. These expeditions involve intensive student participation. Students also travel to Nantucket and the Port of New York for the Atlantic Coast Field Seminar, and out west to California and Oregon to compare and contrast the flora, fauna, history, and environmental issues of the Pacific Coast.

Students return to Mystic and apply knowledge gained in their field experiences toward research projects in history, marine science, and marine policy. A full semester of credit is granted through Williams College (equivalent to 18 transfer credits). Financial aid is available.

Contact: Rush Hambleton, Assistant Director of Admissions
Williams-Mystic Maritime Studies Program
Mystic Seaport
75 Greenmanville Avenue-PO Box 6000
Mystic, CT 06355-0990
Tel: 860-572-5359; Fax: 860-572-5329
E-mail: admissions@williamsmystic.org
Web site: http://www.williamsmystic.org

The Wooden Boat Foundation

The Wooden Boat Foundation is a nonprofit organization located in Port Townsend, Washington, committed to fostering respect for self, community, and environment by providing a center for unique educational experiences through the exploration of traditional maritime skills.

The Foundation offers its members and the community access to a maritime bookstore and library, and educational courses and events. Current maritime programs include regattas, community rowing, small boat sailing and sail training for youth and adults, and specialized charters aboard the longboat Townsend.

The Wooden Boat Foundation's annual fundraiser, the Wooden Boat Festival, takes place Friday, Saturday, and Sunday following Labor Day. With up to 30,000 visitors, the Festival features hundreds of finely crafted wooden boats displayed in the water and on land, demonstrations, lectures, regattas, young mariners' boat building, regional music, food, and fun for the entire family. Proceeds from the Festival support the Wooden Boat Foundation's educational mission.

Contact: Aletia Alvarez
Cupola House
380 Jefferson Street
Port Townsend, WA 98368
Tel: 360-385-3628; Fax: 360-385-4742
E-mail: info@woodenboat.org
Web site: http://www.woodenboat.org

WoodenBoat School

The WoodenBoat School is located on a 64-acre waterfront campus in Brooklin,

Maine. Founded in 1981, the school's twin focus is on wooden boat building and seamanship taught by experienced professionals in the marine industry. Sailing courses are taught by experienced, licensed instructors on cutters, Friendship sloops, ketches, and more than 20 assorted small craft ranging from sailing prams to Herreshoff 12 1/2 s. Instruction in related crafts such as lofting, marine mechanics, marine survey, painting and varnishing, marine photography, navigation, and marine art is also offered. Accommodations are available at the school. Courses are also offered at various off-site locations around the country.

> Contact: Rich Hilsinger, Director
> WoodenBoat School
> PO Box 78
> Brooklin, ME 04616
> Tel: 207-359-4651; Fax: 207-359-8920
> Web site: http://www.woodenboat.com

Youth Adventure, Inc.

Youth Adventure, Inc. is the oldest nonprofit sail training organization in the Pacific Northwest. Founded in 1959, Youth Adventure purchased the 1913 schooner *Adventuress* and began to offer a sail training program for "youth of all ages." This limited program became more active in the late 60s when stewardship of the historic schooner was assumed by Ernestine "Erni" Bennett. For the next 25 years, Erni and a dedicated group of volunteers operated sail training programs aboard the venerable ship for thousands of youth, adults, and seniors in Girl and Boy Scout, school, environmental education, Elderhostel, and other groups.

In 1991, Youth Adventure passed ownership and stewardship of the *Adventuress* to Sound Experience, a nonprofit environmental education and sail training organization. Since then, Youth Adventure has continued to help fund regional sail training and sea education programs, youth scholarships, and related activities. Today, the 40-year-old organization envisions an expanded support role for Pacific Northwest groups that provide sea-related educational experiences aboard a variety of traditional sailcraft—from large tall ships to small longboats.

In recognition of her commitment to sail training, Erni Bennett was presented the ASTA Lifetime Achievement Award in 1998. Youth Adventure is dedicated to continuing this proud legacy, supporting and promoting sailing-based, lifelong learning opportunities for "youth of all ages."

> Contact: Ernestine "Erni" Bennett
> Youth Adventure, Inc.
> PO Box 23
> Mercer Island, WA 98040
> Tel: 206-232-4024
> or
> Chuck Fowler
> 2518 Walnut Road NW
> Olympia, WA 98502-4110
> Tel: 360-943-2858; Fax: 360-943-5411
> E-mail: nwnx@olywa.net

Supporting Members

Newport, Rhode Island

PORTS, BUSINESSES, AND ASSOCIATES OF TALL SHIPS

Acheson Ventures, LLC

Acheson Ventures, LLC is committed to showcasing the marine lore of the Port Huron, Michigan area, in addition to providing educational experiences to the public. One of Michigan's oldest settlements, Port Huron is located where Lake Huron becomes the St. Clair River and is affectionately referred to as the Blue Water Area. Port Huron is home to the historic Fort Gratiot Lighthouse, oldest lighthouse in Michigan, the Huron Lightship Museum, historic Downtown District as well as host to a number of cultural events annually. The Museum of Arts and History hosts a number of annual events including the Feast of the St. Clair, a fascinating reenactment of the fur trading rendezvous, and the Thomas Edison Festival celebrating the great inventor and his youthful years in Port Huron, and Native American celebrations. Every fall the Classic Boat Show features some of the great pleasure boats from area boat builders.

We are very interested in attracting tall ships and tall ship enthusiasts to help celebrate the maritime history of the Blue Water Area.

> Contact: Robert Lafean
> Acheson Ventures LLC
> 600 Fort Street, Suite 101
> Port Huron, MI 48060
> Tel: 810-966-0900 Fax: 810-966-0990
> E-mail: RCLaf@juno.com

Alliance Marine Risk Managers, Inc.

Alliance Marine Risk Managers, Inc. specializes in the consultation and placement of marine insurance for yacht owners and seaman worldwide. Founded and operated by lifelong sailors, Alliance Marine provides the product knowledge and insurance market experience one expects from highly regarded marine insurance professionals. Equally important to the owner of traditional and historic vessels, Alliance honors and shares the values these vessels represent to the past, present, and future of America's maritime heritage.

> Contact: Fredric A. Silberman, President
> Alliance Marine Risk Managers, Inc.
> 1400 Old Country Road, Suite 307
> Westbury, NY 11590
> Tel: 516-333-7000, 800-976-2676; Fax: 516-333-9529
> Email: AMRM-NY@worldnet.att.net

Atlantic City & The Casino Reinvestment Development Authority

Atlantic City was a "shore" bet for tall ships participating in Tall Ships 2000®. Several dozen tall ships made Atlantic City a port of call during the cruise-in-company period and were greeted by enthusiastic crowds! Crewmembers and trainees experienced the world's most famous boardwalk, fabulous casinos and gourmet restaurants in addition to partnering in activities involving the City's community youth organizations.

America's favorite playground is extending another warm welcome to those vessels wishing to visit our port en route to the Great Lakes this summer. Based on an overwhelming response from and to the tall ships that visited last summer, the City of Atlantic City and the Casino Reinvestment Development Authority anticipate offering some unique opportunities to those vessels interested in visiting our port in late May/early June, 2001. If you are interested in visiting Atlantic City this summer, please contact:

Contact: Bunny Loper, Senior Project Officer
Casino Reinvestment Development Authority
1014 Atlantic Avenue
Atlantic City, NJ 08401
Tel: 609-347-0500 extension 3118; Fax: 609-347-7009

Battle of Georgian Bay 2001

On August 23-26, 2001, the Battle of Georgian Bay, a fictional War of 1812/Revolutionary War naval and military reenactment, will be hosted by the historic towns of Midland, Penetanguishene, Tiny Township and Discovery Harbour—Canada's leading marine heritage site on the beautiful shores of Georgian Bay. The Battle will feature authentic tactics, street fighting, marine assault landings, artillery duels, tall ship battles, pillaging, cavalry charges and much more! A living history encampment at Discovery Harbour will feature 19th century merchants, artisans, demonstrations and other family activities. Period entertainment at Jack's Nasty Face Tavern will fill the air for three nights; Tanglefoot will perform in concert, and the American Originals Fife and Drum Corps from Washington, DC will entertain on the battlefield.

The scenario of this fictional event involves an invasion by American forces that capture the township of Tiny, the towns of Midland and Penetanguishene and the secret naval base nearby. British and Canadian troops, along with native allies and militia, spend the weekend attempting to recover the towns and the base. Participate with over a thousand other reenactors as they celebrate victories and mourn defeats or join the public as they observe the pageantry in this critically acclaimed reenactment. For all who dare to come!

Contact: David J. Brunelle, Chairman
Battle of Georgian Bay 2001
22 Fox Street
Penetanguishene, ONT L9M 1R9 Canada
Fax: 705-549-6625
E-mail: brunelle@csolve.net
Web site: http://www.battleofgeorgianbay.huronia.com

Bowen's Wharf, Newport, Rhode Island

Brick walks, granite quays, and 18th-century commercial wharf buildings bring you back to Newport's beginnings as a thriving seaport in one of the finest natural harbors in New England. Trading with all corners of the world then and now, Bowen's Wharf is central to Newport's commerce and culture. Explore unique shops and galleries carrying scrimshaw, pottery, hand-blown glass, canvas, furniture, toys, art, jewelry, clothing, and more. From the romantic ambiance of sunsets over the harbor to the colorful dynamics of a historic working waterfront, a day at Bowen's Wharf is a day well spent. The central location offers plentiful parking. Open all year, seven days a week.

Contact: Bart Dunbar

Bowen's Wharf
PO Box 814
Newport, RI 02840
Tel: 401-849-2243; Fax: 401-849-4322
Web site: http://www.bowenswharf.com

Buffalo, New York Inner Harbor Waterfront Project

Buffalo, New York—"Queen City of the Great Lakes"—celebrates its rich waterfront heritage with the Inner Harbor Development Project. The site was once the western terminus of the Erie Canal. The heritage of the Erie Canal is acknowledged in the site design by creating a setting where authentic maritime uses are organized along with a newly created inland slip for visitors. The new Inner Harbor will open with a grand celebration July 4, 2001. Buffalo's capacity to harbor maritime activity will dramatically increase with the addition of three boat basins. Commercial maritime activities are grouped together in the South Basin's three finger piers located adjacent to Buffalo's Marine Midland Arena. A Canal Slip, bordered by the new naval museum and canal park for Erie Canal touring vessels and visitors, is the centerpiece of harbor activity. Buffalo extends a warm invitation to visit the "Queen of the Great Lakes."

Contact: Peggy Beardsley
Buffalo Place, Inc.
671 Main Street
Buffalo, NY 14203
Tel: 716-856-3150; Fax: 716-852-8490
Web site: http://www.buffaloplace.com

Clayton, New York Chamber of Commerce

Nestled among the Thousand Islands, Clayton, New York is a community that caters to the needs of visiting boaters. Sitting on a peninsula surrounded by the St. Lawrence River, the area provides and endless variety of recreational opportunities.

In the past, the village was home to small boat builders and large shipyards, turning out three-masted schooners that plied the Great Lakes. Clayton offers a full range of services, including marinas, ship's stores, and repair facilities. Ample dockage is available along the picturesque waterfront.

Contact: Karen Goetz
Clayton Chamber of Commerce
510 Riverside Drive
Clayton, NY 13624
Tel: 315-686-3771, 800-252-9806; Fax: 315-686-5564
E-mail: ccoc@gisco.net
Web site: http://www.1000islands-clayton.com

Coos Bay/North Bend PCB

Oregon's Bay Area—Coos Bay, North Bend, and Charleston—invites you to visit our beautiful bay area on the southern Oregon Coast. The Port of Coos Bay is a deepwater port and well equipped to handle tall ships. The Coos Bay Pilots Association and the U.S. Coast Guard have the expertise needed to bring vessels into Coos Bay and guide them safely to dockside. Should you offer tours to the public, we also have funds to advertise on major television networks, newspapers and magazines to help promote your visit. We will consider financial assistance to visiting tall ships to help offset costs. Coos Bay City Dock is located across the street from city center, and we welcome the opportunity to host tall ships and sail training vessels. Should you consider our port, we would be happy to make special arrangements to welcome your tall ship!

Contact: Beverly Saukko, Executive Director
Coos Bay/North Bend Promotion & Convention Bureau
500 Central – Room 10
Coos Bay, OR 97420
Tel: 541-269-8921; Fax: 541-267-5615
E-mail: tourism@harborside.com
Web site: http://www.oregonbayarea.com

Euro Products, Inc./ Randers Ropeworks

Euro Products, Inc. is a fully owned subsidiary of Randers Reb a/s, and Brd. Markussen a/s, both out of Denmark. Randers Reb a/s is an ISO 9001 certified company, which celebrated its 150- year anniversary in 1994, and is one of the oldest rope manufacturers in Europe. Brd. Markussen is a well-recognized manufacturer of hardware sold to the fishing and lifting industry worldwide.

Euro Products exclusively imports and distributes products in North America, manufactured by the principals in Denmark. Among other products, this includes Randers Navy Flex rope, a synthetic fiber rope with the look of natural fiber rope, but with all the advantages of a modern rope. The product is extensively used for running rigging on many tall ships worldwide.

Euro Products also distributes different kinds of hardware used for rigging such as stay wire, wooden blocks, thimbles, chain, etc. Although headquartered in Seattle, Washington, distribution takes place from five different warehouses across the US.

Contact: Lars O. Pedersen
Euro Products, Inc./Randers Ropeworks
1557 NW Ballard Way
Seattle, WA 98107
Tel: 206-789-6468; Fax: 206-784-9848
E-mail: randersrope@msn.com
Web site: http://www.europroductsinc.com

Fall River Celebrates America

The 15th annual Fall River Celebrates America Waterfront Festival, August 9-12, 2001, will be a family-oriented, alcohol-free series of events and exhibits at Battleship Cove and Heritage State Park on the historic Fall River, Massachusetts waterfront. Tall ships, Portuguese Night, multi-cultural exhibits, Country Night, three entertainment stages, fireworks, children's entertainment, sailing regattas, International Food and Desserts Fairs, arts and crafts, six-division parade, and water ski shows are a few of the many events available. In addition, there are year-round attractions such as Battleship MASSACHUSETTS, the Marine Museum at Fall River, the Old Colony and Fall River Railroad Museum, and the Fall River Carousel.

The festival is produced by the Chamber of Commerce in cooperation with the

City of Fall River, the Fall River Cultural Council, The FIRSTFED Charitable Foundation, and other businesses. Tall ships interested in participating and for further information, please contact Donna Futoransky.

> Contact: Donna Futoransky, Executive Director
> Fall River Celebrates America
> 200 Pocasset Street
> Fall River, MA 02721
> Tel: 508-676-8226; Fax: 508-675-5932
> E-mail: donnaf@fallriverchamber.com
> Web site: http://www.frchamber.com

Village of Greenport, New York

Located in the beautiful, deep and superbly protected waters of the Gardiners/Peconic Bay system of eastern Long Island, Greenport Harbor has been a uniquely appealing destination for mariners since the dawn of American history. Modern-day Greenport remains true to this heritage. A sea-born visitor arriving today steps off the boat, and back in time, to enjoy an authentic working seaport where a car is unnecessary.

Deep water dockage for large and small vessels is available at a municipally owned marina in the heart of a downtown waterfront listed on the National Register of Historic Places. Stores, galleries, and services including those catering to mariners such as welding, hauling, carpentry, and marine hardware, even a hospital, are but steps away. A waterfront park is currently being developed upland of the marina which will boast a vintage carousel, outdoor amphitheater, and a boardwalk con-

necting the marina to a transportation center where bus, rail, and ferry connections are available to Shelter Island, New York City, and destinations throughout Long Island.

Greenport is keenly interested in visits by tall ships and sail training vessels and will make special arrangements to host traditional sailing vessels, their crews and trainees.

Contact: Mayor David E. Kapell
Village of Greenport
236 Third Street
Greenport, NY 11944
Tel: 631-477-3000; Fax: 631-477-1877
Greenport Harbormaster monitors VHF Channel 9

Port of Oswego, New York

The Port of Oswego is the first U.S. port-of-call on the Great Lakes from the magnificent St. Lawrence Seaway and is the gateway to the picturesque New York State Barge Canal System. There is no end to our waterways, and no end to the ways they can be enjoyed. Visitors and residents launch their craft from one of three marinas, walk the waterfront on scenic linear parks, sail before the wind, or relax at a lakeside restaurant or right on the beach, watching magnificent commercial ships and pleasure boats arrive at port.

In the Historic Maritime District, the Port of Oswego Authority accommodates the Oswego Maritime Foundation and its 1850-style Great Lakes Schooner, the *OMF Ontario*, and the H. Lee White Marine Museum. The Museum, which pre-

serves Oswego's rich history, owns and operates the Tug LT-5, a National Historic Landmark, and the Derrick Barge, the last steam-powered vessel on the Barge Canal. The Port of Oswego Authority also supports numerous local programs, including Harborfest — four days of fun under the sun and stars. Fest goers enjoy over 200 free performances including top-name entertainment, arts and crafts, children's activities and parade, showstopping fireworks, tall ships, antiques, nautical events and international cuisine.

Contact: Thomas H. McAuslan, Executive Director
Port of Oswego Authority
PO Box 387
Foot of East First Street
Oswego, NY 13126
Tel: 315-343-4503; Fax: 315-343-5498
E-mail: shipping@dreamscape.comWeb site: http://www.portoswego.com

Piscataqua Maritime Commission

The Piscataqua Maritime Commission (PMC) was formed in January 1998 to meet several needs within the community—to promote the region's rich maritime history through special programs and projects and to provide a means of organizing support for visiting ships. The organization's first project was providing support for the HM Bark *Endeavour*, a replica of Captain James Cook's 18th-century ship of discovery. The ship, which visited Portsmouth in September 1998, drew more than 60,000 visitors, including 1,500 school children, who were thrilled to get the chance to experience the age of sail first-hand. PMC continues to be committed to providing programs like the *Endeavour* to the Greater Portsmouth community and welcomes sail training organizations that would like to show off their vessels and programs in the Portsmouth, New Hampshire area (prime display season is May 30 - October 15).

PMC is made up of more than 300 volunteers and representatives from the Port of New Hampshire, Portsmouth City Council, Portsmouth Naval Shipyard, the Navy League, and other local maritime groups.

Contact: Sue Cobler
Piscataqua Maritime Commission
PO Box 545
Portsmouth, NH 03802-0545
Tel: 603-431-7447

City of Port Colborne, Ontario

The Tall Ships are Coming® to Port Colborne, July 5-9, 2001! Experience the majesty of the tall ships as they sail across the Great Lakes and into Port Colborne. This once in a lifetime event summons more than fifteen of these great vessels as they embark on the 2001 Tall Ships Challenge® race series. Reach out and touch a piece of history and witness a spectacle of unmatched beauty and elegance. The City of Port Colborne will welcome thousands of visitors to this international event and promises excitement and hospitality that will leave lifelong memories. Tall ship tours and cruises, "Tall Ships® Town", live concerts, fireworks, food festival and more!

Canal Days Marine Heritage Festival is scheduled for August 3-6, 2001. The City of Port Colborne is preparing for its 23rd Annual Canal Days Marine Heritage

Festival. Every year, thousands of people fill the streets overlooking the beautiful Welland Canal. Come out and experience tall ship tours and cruises, live concerts, children's entertainment, food festival and fabulous fireworks display. Enjoy the car show, kite flying display, boat parade of lights and more!

> Contact: City of Port Colborne
> 66 Charlotte Street
> Port Colborne, ONT L3K 3C8 Canada
> Tel: 1-888-PORT FUN or 1-905-835-2901 ext. 310
> E-mail: edo@portcolborne.com
> Web site: http://www.portcolborne.com

Sail Baltimore

Sail Baltimore is a nonprofit, community organization dedicated to offering maritime educational experiences to the general public, visitors, local citizens, children, and disadvantaged youth. Other goals are to stimulate the economy of the City of Baltimore and surrounding communities, to increase regional tourism, provide a forum and network for encouraging business development opportunities, and to foster international cultural exchange.

This mission is accomplished through recruiting, planning, and hosting visits of various types of ships whose presence in the harbor offers an educational but noncommercial experience. Sail Baltimore also produces special events designed to attract people to the city's waterfront, including several successful tall ship events and water parades over the past 25 years.

> Contact: Sail Baltimore
> 1809 Thames Street
> Baltimore, MD 21231
> Tel: 410-752-7300; Fax: 410-522-3405
> E-mail: info@sailbaltimore.org
> Web site: http://www.sailbaltimore.org

Sail San Francisco

Sail San Francisco is a nonprofit organization founded to foster international friendships and good will in the San Francisco Bay Area. The organization hosts events such as international tall ship gatherings and supports local youth focused tall ship sailing programs which are designed to enhance leadership skills, self-esteem and experience with intercultural exchanges. Special emphasis is placed on community outreach during international tall ships visits. Sail San Francisco strives to offer a variety of free events and ensure that these events are accessible to disabled individuals. Exchanges between local and foreign tall ship crews and under-served residents and students of the Bay Area who share the same language are also a priority.

Sail San Francisco successfully brought the 'Gold Rush Sail' visit of international tall ships, their crew and many educational and cultural events to more than two million Bay Area visitors and residents in July, 1999. Work is underway to host the next international tall ship visit to San Francisco in 2002.

> Contact: Alison Healy, Director
> Sail San Francisco
> 2905 Hyde Street
> San Francisco, CA 94109

Tel: 415-447-9822; Fax: 415-556-0149
E-mail: sailingangel@hotmail.com
Web site: http://www.sailsanfrancisco.org

Savannah Waterfront Association

In the 1970s, the city of Savannah, Georgia implemented a major urban renewal program to revitalize the waterfront. Old cotton warehouses have been transformed, and the Savannah Waterfront Association hosts many exciting festivals to bring people to the river. Today, Savannah's historic waterfront is lined with more than 100 unique shops and galleries, fabulous restaurants, seductive nightspots, and elegant inns and hotels. The docking facilities were updated in the last six years, and Savannah has hosted several tall ships and has plans for an annual tall ship festival. The Savannah Waterfront Association is a nonprofit organization whose purpose is the promotion and preservation of the historic waterfront.

> Contact: Gordon Varnedoe, Executive Director
> Savannah Waterfront Association
> PO Box 572
> Savannah, GA 31402
> Tel: 912-234-0295; Fax: 912-234-4904
> E-mail: waterfests@aol.com
> Web site: http://www.savriverstreet.com

Société du Vieux-Port de Montréal (Old Port of Montreal Corporation, Inc.)

Since May 1992, the Old Port of Montréal has been offering Montréalers, yachting tourists, and tall ships a quality marina—The Port d'Escale. Located in the Jacques Cartier Basin, the Port d'Escale is equipped with a full range of up-to-date facilities to accommodate sailboats over 200 feet, docking on floating docks. Tucked into the heart of the Old Port, a few steps away from downtown Montréal, this secure facility provides a quiet haven for tall ships mooring there. Because of its varied activities and its unique atmosphere, the Old Port is an important site for recreation and tourism in Montréal. Set a heading for the Port d'Escale, and discover Montréal in style.

> Contact: Sylvain A. Deschamps, Harbourmaster
> 333 de la Commune Street West
> Montréal, QUE H2Y 2E2 Canada
> Tel: 514-283-5414; Fax: 514-283-8423

Greater South Haven Area Chamber of Commerce

Located on the Eastern Shore of Lake Michigan in Southwest Michigan, the South Haven area combines an idyllic setting with a strong community spirit to make it one of the region's most promising locals.

Prior to its founding, South Haven was a trading area for members of the Potowatami tribe who stored birchbark in the sands along the beaches and referred to the area as Ni-Ko-Nong, beautiful sunsets. At various points in its 140 year-old history, South Haven has been an agricultural center, industrial hot spot, and tourist mecca.

The community has a strong commercial and recreational maritime history. From the early days of Great Lakes sailing schooners through passenger steamship runs from Chicago to South Haven, Lake Michigan and the maritime tradition are part of the community. Since 1976 the community hosted three gatherings of tall ships and receives individual visits periodically. With the strength of the Michigan Maritime Museum in South Haven, those maritime traditions will continue to prosper. In 2001 the community is proud to host WoodenBoat Magazine's 2001 WoodenBoat Show June 22-24. Come see why South Haven was selected ASTA's 1998 Port City of the Year!

> Contact: Larry King, Executive Director
> Greater South Haven Area Chamber of Commerce
> 300 Broadway
> South Haven, MI 49090
> Tel: 616-637-5171; Fax: 616-639-1570
> E-mail: cofc@southhavenmi.com
> Web site: http://www.Southhavenmi.com

Tall Ships® Newport

Come to legendary Newport, Rhode Island where entertaining tall ships and their crews is a well-practiced tradition. Often referred to as the birthplace of the American Navy, Newport's nautical history is evident everywhere. Founded in 1639 as a haven for those seeking religious freedom, today the City by the Sea is a favored spot of competitive sailors and a resort destination for those seeking an extraordinary travel experience.

A cruise-in-company port for last year's tall ship festivities, Newport hosted 50 tall ships and their crews delighting enthusiasts with parades, concerts, family activities, sports competitions, and tours. While we plan no formal tall ship festival in 2001, we do plan educational activities in conjunction with Sail Newport.

Newport has active ship repair facilities, sail lofts and chandleries. Visiting tall ships are welcome any time. If your traditional sailing vessel is planning to visit historic Newport on beautiful Narragansett Bay, please contact our office for assistance.

> Contact: CAPT Eric J. Williams, USCG (Ret.)
> Tall Ships® Newport
> 47 Bowen's Wharf
> Newport, RI 02840
> Tel: 401-847-8206; Fax: 401-847-8508
> E-mail: talshipsnpt@aol.com

Tall Ships®Travel Club

The Tall Ships® Travel Club (TSTC) is a division of the Landings Travel Agency of Sarasota, Florida. Dedicated to bringing luxury level cruises to the tall ships experience, the TSTC delivers on three levels of travel experience.

Since 1997 the TSTC has planned a cruise rendezvous with a major port maritime festival and the start of a leg of the annual tall ships races. In 1997, *Crystal Harmony* was in Stavanger, Norway; in 1998, *Crystal Symphony* visited Lerwick, Scotland; and in 1999 it was Stockholm, Sweden. For 2001 a rendezvous in Bergen, Norway is planned. For 2002, the TSTC has arranged with the *Silver Pride* of the Silver Seas Line to meet the fleet of tall ships in La Coruna, Spain. In 2003, aboard the brand-new Crystal ship, the TSTC will return to St. Petersburg, Russia for the 300th anniversary of that magnificent port city.

The TSTC is also committed to arranging and scheduling group cruises on board the tall cruise ships, *Star Clipper* and *Royal Clipper.*

Finally, the Tall Ships® Travel Club is designing maritime heritage land-tours to the grand maritime museums and nautical venues of the UK, Ireland, France, and Europe.

Contact: Dewey Kennell
Tall Ships® Travel Club
Landings Travel Agency
4986 S. Tamiami Trail
Sarasota, FL 34231
Tel: 800-299-1123
E-mail: deweykennell@earthlink.net

Technology Law Offices

Technology Law Offices specializes in developing companies around new innovative ideas, patenting the ideas, and assisting the new business owner in commercializing the ideas. We are especially interested in working with sailing individuals to protect and commercialize new ideas pertaining to sailboats such as new pulleys, line, boat construction, sail materials, and other inventions that make the art of sailing a more exciting and exacting sport. We are located in Northern Virginia in Middleburg and in the Corporate Research Center of Virginia Tech in Blacksburg, Virginia.

While we are a law firm we are also business people who can assist you in taking your idea and commercializing it in a business structure to maximize your return. We have started many new hi-tech and bio-tech companies over the years and represent such companies worldwide.

Contact: Jim Hiney, Senior Partner
Technology Law Offices
PO Box 818
Middleburg, VA 20118
Tel: 703-754-1860 or 540-552-4400; Fax: 703-753-9481
E-mail: TEKLAW2000@aol.com
Web site: http://www.TEKLAW2000.com

About Sail Training

It takes teamwork to raise the mainsail on the *Bill of Rights*.

INFORMATION TO HELP YOU
PLAN YOUR SAIL TRAINING
EXPERIENCE

Take Responsibility for Your Adventure!

BY MICHAEL J. RAUWORTH

One of the most important products of sail training is the development of a sense of judgment about what and whom you can rely on, and to what degree. This applies to: the compass, the weather forecast, your shipmates, the depths on the chart, the strength of the anchor cable, the vigilance of the lookout on the other ship, and many other things. Sail training also builds a reasoned sense of self-reliance. All of this starts from the moment you begin to think about a voyage. Use the information in this Directory to begin to evaluate and decide what might be the best sail training experience for you.

Recognize who you are dealing with and what is included. When you book a sail training trip, you are dealing with the vessel owner or its representatives—ASTA is not involved. You must evaluate whether the financial and business arrangements make sense for you. If there is connecting travel involved, for example, find out if you must make the arrangements, or if it is somehow tied into those you make with the vessel. What happens if you miss your ship because your plane is delayed, or vice versa? Do you need trip insurance? Have you confirmed with the vessel owner any possible customs or immigration issues? Will you need a passport or a pre-purchased air ticket? You must seek out the answers to these questions.

Make informed, responsible decisions about risk and safety, level of challenge, physical suitability and other important issues. One of the important reasons to embark on a sail training trip is to engage the world in a different, stimulating, and challenging way—if you want to stay warm and dry, you should stay at home by the fireplace. Much of the point is to come face-to-face with the elements. At the very least, this probably means that you will find yourself wet, chilled, or tired at some point in a challenging voyage. But everyone's threshold for this is different, and you need to find out what you are likely to be experiencing in order to find out if it is well matched for you.

Since the beginning of time, going to sea has been recognized as carrying an element of risk. These days, we more commonly think about risk in connection with highway travel or aviation, but the idea is the same: you get a pre-flight safety brief on an airliner, you get a lifeboat drill on a cruise ship. Part of the value of sail training is addressing these issues head on. You need to decide whether you are comfortable with the combination of risks and safety measures connected with your proposed sail training trip.

For example, will you be able to go aloft? Will trips in smaller craft be involved? Will you be expected to stand watch at night? Do the demands of the ship match your physical and health capabilities? Are you on medication that will (or may) become necessary during the voyage, or do you have a condition (for example, hemophilia or epilepsy) that may require special access to medical attention; if so, is the vessel operator aware of this? Will you be able to get up and down the ladders, in and out of your berth, and along a heeled-over deck? If there is an emergency, will you be needed to handle safety equipment or to help operate the vessel?

Remember that sail training is often not intended to be like a vacation. Some vessels, on the other hand, may offer leisurely voyages, where very little will be asked of you. You should arrive at a clear understanding of these issues prior to setting sail.

In short, you must satisfy yourself that the trip you are looking into is the right thing for you to do, considering safety, risk, suitability, challenge, comfort, convenience, educational value, cost, and any other factors you consider important.

Does the American Sail Training Association have a hand in any of this? In a word—no! ASTA is your "bulletin board" to introduce you to opportunities. However, the American Sail Training Association does not operate any vessels, and has no ability or authority to inspect, approve, or even recommend vessels or programs because programs are constantly evolving and changing.

The American Sail Training Association is a nonprofit organization with a limited staff. It serves as a forum for the sail training community, but it has no authority over what programs are offered, or how vessels are operated. The information in this Directory is supplied by the vessel operators, and ASTA can not possibly verify all the information, nor visit all the ships in order to evaluate programs. For these reasons, you must take the information in this Directory as a starting point only, subject to change and correction, and proceed directly with the vessel operator. The American Sail Training Association is not an agent or business partner for the vessel operators, and is not a travel agent.

ASTA believes in the value of sail training as a concept, but remember, from the moment you step beyond looking at this book, the decision and the resulting experiences rest with you.

Raising the sails on the *Swift of Ipswich*

Choosing a Sail Training Program

The four essential components of any sail training program are a seaworthy vessel, a competent captain and crew, qualified instructors, and a sound educational program appropriate and suited to the needs of the trainees on board.

There are as many sail training programs as there are ships, and choosing the right one depends a great deal on your personal needs and desires. Sail training differs from going on a cruise ship, in that you are expected to take part in the running of the ship by handling sail and line and standing watch, as well as working in the galley (the ship's kitchen) or performing routine cleaning or maintenance duties. To what degree depends on the sail training program you select.

Do you want a program that specializes in marine biology or adventure travel? Would you like to ship out for a day, a week, a school semester—or, for as long as it takes to circumnavigate the world? Are you interested in maritime history? In celestial navigation? Whales? Do you want the unique challenge of climbing aloft in a square-rigger? A race across the Atlantic? Maine lobster dinners aboard classic windjammers? Exotic ports of call? Will you be bringing your wheelchair? Would you like to receive academic credit?

The answers to the above questions provide a profile for just some of the options available to you. As to what sail training programs require of you— beyond an eager willingness to get the most out of your voyage—the requirements are few:

Safety First!

Take a close look at the vessel's credentials. In the US, check to see if the vessel operates under United States Coast Guard regulations. Does the vessel currently hold a USCG-issued Certificate of Inspection (see page 312, "Regulations for US Sailing Vessels") or comparable certification from the authorities of the country in which it is registered? If it is a non-US vessel you should ensure that the vessel operates in accordance with the maritime safety rules of that country. In most cases this is supervised by a government agency similar to the US Coast Guard. The resources section of the ASTA Web site lists the latest known Web sites of some of these agencies.

Talk to the program provider! Ask questions! Read the organization or company's literature; check out their Web site. Most important: visit the ship if you can. Get a sense of the professionalism of the operation and the quality of its program. Find out about the experience level of the captain and officers. How long have they served the ship you are looking into? If you will be joining the vessel in a distant port, or if it does not hold a current USCG Certificate of Inspection, be especially diligent in your research. Ask the program operator for the names of past trainees or clients and give them a call and ask about their experience. The amazingly diverse range of opportunities featured in this book provides each of us with a variety of options.

Many ships venture no more than 20 miles from a harbor and are rarely underway overnight; others offer offshore voyaging and the challenge of distant passages where severe weather and water conditions may be unavoidable. Being underway around the clock requires watch duties night and day, demanding both physical and mental stamina and perseverance.

Experience

With very few exceptions, no prior sailing experience is required of trainees. Some programs do accept non-paying volunteers as crewmembers, but typically require experience in similar vessels or a long-term commitment—or both. Paying positions typically require a license—"Able-bodied Seaman" papers document a minimum of 180 days spent underway and successfully passing an exam administered by the US Coast Guard. Licenses are awarded to crew based on additional time underway, the tonnage of vessels served in, waters sailed, technical training, and additional testing.

Swimming ability

Trainees are encouraged to have the ability to feel comfortable in and around the water; however, many programs have no formal swimming requirements.

Age

Most voyages are planned with a specific age group in mind. This varies from program to program, but many sail training programs start accepting unaccompanied trainees from the age of 14 (ninth grade). Ask what the composition of the ship's complement will be and, if you plan to send a young person on an extended voyage, what the in-port supervisory arrangements will be. Day sails and dockside education programs are readily available for elementary school students and overnight trips can be arranged for older school groups as well. There are a tremendous variety of adventure programs for adults of all ages, including "Elderhostel" voyages for seniors.

Academic credit

Some vessels are tied directly to academic institutions that grant academic credit to trainees who successfully complete sail training programs as part of a course of study or project in a wide range of subjects. Some educational institutions will also grant credit for on-board independent study.

Co-education

Just about every sail training vessel in the US sails with both male and female professional crew and programs are typically co-ed. Others are designed specifically for groups such as the Girl Scouts or in conjunction with a single-gender school or affiliated program.

Cost

Prices vary considerably, ranging from $25 to $150 per person per day, depending on the nature and the duration of the program and the type of vessel.

Financial aid

A few vessels have limited financial assistance available, and some trainees, Scouting, and school groups have successfully sought private, business, and/or community support to help defray the cost of sail training. In addition, there are a small number of independent organizations that provide financial aid to trainees, usually through matching grants. Check with the sail training program you are interested in to see what opportunities may be available.

Regulation of US Sailing Vessels

Virtually all vessels are subject to some form of regulation by the national maritime authority of their "flag state"-the country in which they are registered. In the United States, these regulations are written and enforced by the US Coast Guard, pursuant to laws enacted by Congress. Under the Safety of Life at Sea (SOLAS) Convention, administered by the International Maritime Organization (IMO), vessels of any nation signatory to the convention and over a certain size or carrying more than 12 passengers and operating internationally must comply with the requirements of the Convention with regard to construction, safety equipment, manning, crew training, etc. Compliance is documented in a "SOLAS Certificate" issued by the ship's national maritime authority.

US-registered vessels listed in this directory will generally fall into one of the following categories: Small Passenger Vessel, Sailing School Vessel, Oceanographic Research Vessel, and Uninspected Vessel. For each category there is a comprehensive set of regulatory requirements governing construction and arrangement, watertight integrity and stability, lifesaving and firefighting equipment, machinery and electrical systems, vessel control and equipment, and operations.

With the exception of Uninspected Vessels, all categories of US-registered vessel are subject to Coast Guard inspection on an annual basis. Upon satisfactory completion of the inspection, a Certificate of Inspection (COI) is issued, and must be permanently displayed on board the vessel. The COI spells out what waters the vessel may operate in (its authorized route), how many passengers or sailing school students may be carried, how many crew must be carried and what qualifications the master and crew must have, the requirement for and location of lifesaving and firefighting equipment, and so forth. Although not inspected annually, Uninspected Vessels (which are generally vessels less than 65 feet in length and carrying 6 or fewer passengers for hire) must still comply with requirements for safety equipment and a licensed skipper. The type of COI to be issued to inspected vessels is determined by both the size and construction of the vessel and the operating intentions of the owner. Some vessels carry dual certification.

The Coast Guard also prescribes the qualifications for the officers and crew of inspected vessels, and requires both that they have certain minimum levels of experience and training and that they be examined and issued licenses or documents before they can lawfully serve on board.

Following is a brief description of the various types of certifications governing the operation of US-flagged vessels:

Sailing School Vessels (SSV) are inspected under Title 46, Subchapter R of the Code of Federal Regulations (CFR). An SSV is a vessel of less than 500 gross tons carrying six or more sailing school students or instructors, principally propelled by sail, and operated by a nonprofit educational organization exclusively for the purpose of sailing education. Sailing School Vessels are required to pass regular inspection by the USCG in order to maintain their certification.

Passenger Vessels are certified according to size and number of passengers (not engaged in educational activities or in the operation of the vessel) carried under Title 46 of the CFR:

> **Subchapter C** - Uninspected vessels which operate with no more than six passengers.

> **Subchapter T** - Small passenger vessels of under 100 gross tons that carry more than six passengers and are required to pass regular USCG inspection of the ship and all onboard equipment.

> **Subchapter K** - Small passenger vessels of under 100 gross tons that carry more than 150 passengers and are required to pass regular USCG inspection of the ship and all onboard equipment.

> **Subchapter H** - Passenger vessels more than 100 gross tons that carry passengers for hire and are required to pass regular USCG inspection of the ship and all onboard equipment.

Attraction Vessel certification is required whenever a vessel is open to public boarding or conducts dockside programs. The vessel may be permanently moored to a pier, or it may also be certified under one or more of the above subchapters, but the Attraction Vessel COI (ATCOI) certifies its safety for dockside programs and visitation only.

Oceanographic Research Vessels (ORV) are certified under Subchapter U of Title 46 of the CFR. An ORV is a vessel employed exclusively in either oceanographic (saltwater) or limnologic (freshwater) instruction and/or research, and is not necessarily equipped for passengers or other non-professionals.

For more information, access the United States Coast Guard through the link on ASTA's Web site or contact the Government Printing Office for the above listed sections of the Code of Federal Regulations.

Shipping Out

Each year, ASTA asks one of its Member Organizations for the equipment list they provide to potential trainees, for use in this Directory. This list is a general guide only. Requirements may vary from vessel to vessel. Check for specific requirements of the program you are considering. The following "Guest Crew Information and Guidelines" was provided by Pride of Baltimore, Inc., owner and operator of *Pride of Baltimore II*.

ABOUT YOUR PASSAGE

You have expressed an interest in sailing aboard *Pride of Baltimore II* on the adventure of a lifetime as a Working Guest Crew member. The following information regarding the selection process, guidelines, a travel check list, and a passage price list have been provided to better inform and prepare you for the possibility of a passage aboard *Pride II*.

Please understand that as a Working Guest Crew member, you will be working alongside the crew during your passage. Remember, THIS IS NOT A CRUISE VESSEL! You should be prepared to handle sails, work as a deckhand, stand watch, and adhere to the vessel's chain of command. The accommodations are 3 co-ed guest crew cabins with 2 berths per cabin. You will be provided three meals a day as prepared by the ship's cook, and eat alongside the crew.

GUIDELINES

Listed below are guidelines that help define the passenger experience. They should assist you in determining whether you are ready to accept the challenge of working as a Guest Crew member aboard *Pride II*. Please review them prior to your conversation with one of the Captains.

1. Unless otherwise arranged, passengers are invited to board after 7:00 pm on the evening before departure. You are responsible for your meals on arrival day.

2. Sheets, towels and blankets are provided. If the weather will be cold, we rec-ommend that you bring a sleeping bag.

3. Your gear should be packed in a duffle bag or other soft luggage. Cabin space is ample but not generous.

4. Always remember that it is colder on the water. Dress wisely and bring plenty of layers of clothing. The vessel's heat is provided by the galley stove, and there is no air conditioning!

5. To fully participate in the watch system, you should bring full foul-weather gear. At minimum, a waterproof jacket or slicker is required. Remember that you will be exposed to the elements while on watch.

6. Do not bring hair dryers, electric razors, or other small appliances that require electricity.

7. Each passenger cabin has two bunks (one above another). They are assigned on a first-come, first-served basis. Like our crew accommodations, passenger space is co-ed.

8. After boarding, you will be taken on a brief tour of the vessel by one of the crew members who will describe life onboard. He/she will fully explain the watch system...we expect you will participate!

9. All recreational items (camera, books, games, cards, etc.) should be brought with you. Please keep in mind that the

gear you bring must stow in your cabin.

10. *Pride II*'s supply of fresh water is limited. Hot showers are restricted while underway and are generally available every other day.

11. Three meals are provided daily and served according to the watch routine. You will be advised of the times when you come aboard.

12. You are encouraged to take part in the day-to-day operation of the vessel by handling sail, standing watch, maintaining the vessel and fulfilling the other duties of a deckhand. Participating in the watch system is the most rewarding part of the passenger experience.

13. *Pride II*'s mission is to serve as Maryland's Goodwill Ambassador. As such, she often hosts sailing or dockside receptions for individual, corporate, or government groups. If part of your passage involves a port visit where receptions are scheduled, you may choose to stay aboard while these activities take place, or take this opportunity to pursue interests you may have on shore.

14. Sailing aboard a traditional vessel such as *Pride II* is a unique experience. In the finest tradition of the sailor's craft, we ask that you be courteous and respect the rights and privacy of your shipmates.

15. While the ship is underway, there is to be quiet after 2200 hours (10:00 PM)

16. There will be no alcohol consumed while the ship is underway, unless otherwise specified by the Captain.

17. Smoking is only allowed on deck.

18. "Check out" time is 1600 hours (4:00 PM) on the day that *Pride II* arrives in port (unless her itinerary requires different arrangements), but you may leave earlier if you wish. If you decide to leave earlier, please be sure to tell the Captain and ship's cook of your plans.

19. Please bring with you a valid Passport if the ship will be leaving the country or entering international waters. If you are not sure whether this will be necessary, please contact the office.

FOR YOUR SAFETY, PLEASE FOLLOW ALL INSTRUCTIONS GIVEN BY THE CAPTAIN AND CREW!

TRAVEL CHECK LIST

There are a number of items which you will need to bring with you during your passage aboard *Pride of Baltimore II*. In order to better prepare you, we have provided the following list:

• Foul weather gear and sea boots
• Heavyweight sweater or sweatshirt
• Knit turtleneck/pullover
• Waterproof shoes with non-skid soles
• Sturdy jeans or khakis
• Shorts, tee shirts and underwear
• Several pairs of socks
• Hat/gloves/scarf
• Books, cards or other recreational items
• A sturdy coffee mug
• Toiletries, including sunscreen
• Valid U.S. Passport (International including Canada)

Above, *Pride of Baltimore II* sailing in Chesapeake Bay, Summer 2000. Below, *Pride of Baltimore II* making a grand entrance in to Milwaukee Harbor, Summer 1999.

ASTA Programs and
Services

ASTA's Annual Conference on Sail Training and Tall Ships

ASTA's Annual Conference on Sail Training and Tall Ships gathers ships' masters, port representatives, public officials, marine suppliers, naval architects, program administrators, festival managers, preservationists, environmentalists, crewmembers, and educators. Topics concerning vessel operations, regulatory issues, management, educational programming, and safety at sea are addressed each year, as are sessions on media relations, marketing, funding, communications, and port event organization.

The American Sail Training Association invites you to the

28th Annual Conference on Sail Training and Tall Ships

"Sail Training in the New Millennium"
November 1-3, 2000

and the

The 1st Biennial Education Under Sail Forum
November 4, 2000

Holiday Inn Chicago City Centre, Chicago, Illinois

Briefings: 2001 and 2002
Tall Ships Challenge™ Series
Interactive Web Site Development
Marketing
Safety Under Sail
Sponsorship
Curriculum Development
Grant Writing
Port Event Planning and Management
Business Plan Development
Crisis Management
Technology Workshop
Regulatory Issues
Benefits for Crew
ASTA Regional Meetings
ASTA Committee Meetings
2000 Sail Training Awards

Held annually during the first week in November, the ASTA Conference on Sail Training and Tall Ships is both fun and informative and offers oceans of networking opportunities.

Plan to join us in November of 2001 for the 29th Annual Conference to be held in Victoria, BC, Canada.

The International Sail Training Safety Forum

The International Sail Training Safety Forum, initiated in 1992 in cooperation with the ISTA, expands the international dialogue among professional mariners by presenting case studies of actual incidents at sea, discussing emerging technologies, and sharing "best practices" so as to constantly insure a high level of safety and professionalism in the sail training industry. Professionals engaged in sail training, sea education, vessel operations, and tall ship events from throughout the world partici-

pate in this annual symposium, which take place in conjunction with ASTA's Annual Conference during odd-numbered years and in Europe during even-numbered years.

The 8th Annual ASTA/ISTA International Sail Training Safety Forum held in Boston, MA in November, 1999. The 1999 Safety Forum Proceedings on CD ROM are available for purchase through the Ships Store on page 360.

ASTA Biennial Education Under Sail Forum

ASTA's new Education Under Sail Forum made it's grand premiere in Chicago in 2000! This was the first of what is planned to be a program-focused complement to the International Safety Forums biennial series.   Inspired by a night watch suggestion from Captain Jesse Briggs and led by Captain Jim Gladson from LA Maritime Institute, the theme for 2000 was "How Do You Know if You're Making a Difference? Outcomes Measurement and Sail Training."

Designed to inform and inspire excellence in the development and delivery of educational experiences under sail, the forum overflows with creative exchanges among captains, crew, administrators, teachers, program developers, curriculum designers, and others.

Ideas and questions are welcomed by the ASTA Sail Training and Education Committee, Contact: Nancy H. Richardson, 973-762-1430 or email marinergs@home.com

Above, Nancy Richardson and Captain Jim Gladson, Co-organizers of the first Biennial Education Under Sail Forum held in Chicago in November of 2000. Left, Dr. Sidney Thompson, keynote speaker.

ASTA Regional Meetings

Top, during the 1999 Atlantic Regional Meeting on board the *Eagle,* Coast Guard Cadets and guests of ASTA "man-the-yards." Above, ASTA Board Members Nancy Richardson and Michael Ream on board the *Eagle.*

Regional-Atlantic, Pacific and Great Lakes-meetings are held late winter/early spring. These meetings are less formal than our annual Conference, but like the Conference, we encourage our professional members to submit ideas for locations and topics.

The regional meetings offer an opportunity for the host to showcase their facility and programs while providing an intimate setting for attendees to network. A typical regional meeting may include a tour, special presentation, safety demonstration, day sail and luncheon.

In 1999, the Atlantic Regional Meeting was held in Mystic and New London, CT. On the first day of the meeting, attendees enjoyed free admission to Mystic Seaport where ASTA members were treated to a celestial navigation presentation at the planetarium, a tour of the boat shed where *Amistad* was taking shape, and an update as preparations were underway for *Brilliant's* transatlantic voyage. Afterwards, attendees toured the seaport village and visited the gift shop.

On the second day of the meeting, all hands mustered at the USCG Academy for a safety briefing prior to training alongside the cadets aboard *Eagle* where ASTA members climbed aloft and set and stowed sail. After a full morning of line handling, attendees were treated to a hearty meal and camaraderie on the mess deck.

The Great Lakes Regional Meeting is usually held in conjunction with the Canadian Sail Training Association's annual meeting and safety forum. We hope to include a Gulf Coast Regional Meeting in the near future.

Recent regional meetings have been hosted by Living Classrooms Foundation, San Diego Maritime Museum, Great Lakes Schooner Company, and the Center for Wooden Boats. Planning usually starts in November with meetings held February, March or April. If your organization would like to host a regional meeting, please send a letter of interest along with a proposed agenda to ASTA.

The USCG Barque *Eagle* at home in New London, CT plays host to the 1999 ASTA Atlantic Regional Meeting.

The ASTA Sail Training Rally

Bucket Brigade

Rowing

Knot-Tying

In the 1980s, ASTA developed the concept of the Sail Training Rally; a competition among crews, both at sea and ashore. These rallies provide trainees with an opportunity to demonstrate their seamanship skills in a friendly but competitive format. Shoreside events such as knot tying, tug-of war, bucket brigade, rowing, walk the plank, and heaving line toss/hawser pull, allow the general public to observe the sort of teamwork and maritime skills that are learned on board sail training vessels at sea.

Tug-of-War

Heaving Line Toss
and Hawser Pull

SAIL TALL SHIPS!

Henry H. Anderson, Jr. Sail Training Scholarship

ASTA Sailing Vessel Assistance Grant

ASTA Crew Development Grant

The Henry H. Anderson, Jr. Sail Training Scholarship, ASTA Sailing Vessel Assistance Grant, and ASTA Crew Development Grant programs were established in 1999. The first is designed to assist young people between 14 and 19 to achieve a sail training experience aboard USCG-inspected ASTA member vessels. Scholarships are available to both individuals and groups. The second is designed to assist ASTA member vessels which may not be USCG-inspected in maintenance and improvement projects that will better enable them to further ASTA's missions. The Crew Development Grant program is designed to help keep motivated crewmembers in the ASTA fleet by assisting them in upgrading their professional qualifications through training.

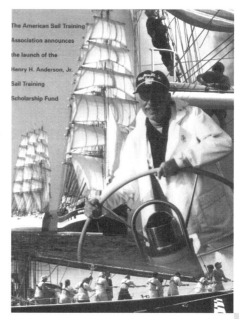

The ASTA Marine Insurance Program

The American Sail Training Association Marine Insurance Program provides ASTA Member Vessels the ability to secure comprehensive commercial insurance for all vessels, whether they are navigating, permanently berthed, or under construction, and includes benefits such as personal effects coverage for crew and trainees, separate deductibles for theft of electronics, and extension of liability coverage for piers, docks, and ticket areas. (See ad on page 14)

AN INSURANCE PROGRAM FOR MEMBER VESSELS OF THE **AMERICAN SAIL TRAINING ASSOCIATION** FROM **ALLIANCE MARINE** RISK MANAGERS, INC.

The ASTA Web Site

http://tallships.sailtraining.org links you to the world of sail training. Links to ASTA member vessels and affiliates make it easy to learn more about opportunities under sail, the ships that can take you to sea, and shore-based programs. The ASTA Web site also provides links to tall ship events such as Tall Ships Challenge® and to international sail training associations and resources around the world.

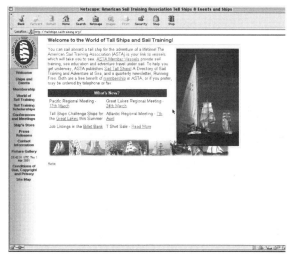

An on-line Billet Bank provides notice of positions available aboard ASTA member vessels. ASTA Professional Members are invited to post available positions using the standardized form found on the ASTA Web site. New information is added on a daily basis and billets remain posted for 90 days unless ASTA is otherwise advised. ASTA does not endorse any specific program or individual, but simply shares information as it becomes available.

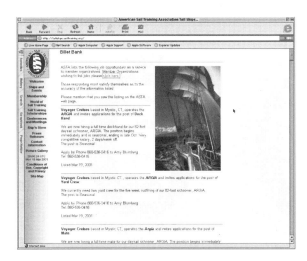

ASTA Publications

Sail Tall Ships! A Directory of Sail Training and Adventure at Sea first appeared in 1980, and is now in its thirteenth edition. The directory provides program and contact information for member vessels and sail training associations throughout the world. To help fulfill ASTA's mission, the directory is also distributed through maritime museums and their affiliated shops, marinas, maritime events, and sail training programs, as well as bookstores, libraries, high school guidance counselors, university career resource centers, and education conferences throughout the United States and Canada.

Guidelines for Educational Programs Under Sail defines ASTA standards for sail training and sea education within the framework of the Sailing School Vessels Act. This manual defines criteria and indicators of effectiveness for the design, delivery, and evaluation of curricula, instruction, and program administration. In addition to the core of safe seamanship education, the guidelines apply to all aspects of sail training: adventure, education, environmental science, maritime heritage, and leadership development.

The ASTA Training Logbook enables trainees to keep a personal log of their sea time and to document their progress in sail training, and records a progression of skill-building activities in nautical science, safety, seamanship, and navigation. Completion of course work and sea time must be certified by either the instructor or the ship's master.

The International Safety Forum Proceedings, an annual publication of the International Safety Forum, is a record of the papers submitted and discussions held on various aspects of sail training safety and operations, emergency procedures, professional training and qualifications, vessel design and construction, etc. The Forum has been held each year since 1992, and copies of each year's proceedings are available through ASTA's Ship's Store.

A Quick Guide to the Regulations Pertaining to Sail Training Vessels Visiting US Waters gives non-US vessels a sense of the regulations governing all ships visiting ports in the United States and provides contact information for each of the federal authorities enforcing those regulations.

Tall Ships by Thad Koza, published by TideMark Press with a foreword by ASTA's former Executive Director, Pamela Dewell Smith, is available through the ASTA office. This beautiful book features four-color photographs of 150 sail training vessels in the international fleet.

ASTA Membership Opportunities

Membership benefits are subject to change, but an item or service of comparable value will be substituted. ASTA's logo merchandise changes seasonally. Membership dues are increased periodically. All prices are US dollars. This listing is as of February, 2001.

Individual $45/year (tax-deductible value is $15)
• Complimentary copy of Sail Tall Ships! A Directory of Sail Training and Adventure at Sea.
• Subcription to Running Free, ASTA's quarterly newsletter covering tall ship news, events and job opportunities. ASTA anticipates publishing this newsletter on-line in the near future. Members who have provided their e-mail address will receive notification that the newsletter has been posted.
• Discounts to attend ASTA's Annual Conference on Sail Training and Tall Ships.
• Invitations to attend ASTA's Regional Meetings, education and safety forums, and other special events.

Junior $30/year (tax-deductible value is $0)
• Open to sailors 22 years of age and younger.
• All of the benefits of Individual Membership above.

Family $75/year (tax-deductible value is $35)
• Open to two members at the same address.
• All of the benefits of Individual Membership above plus two lapel pins.
• Member discounts applicable to two.

Supporting $250/year (tax-deductible value is $215)
• For ports, businesses and associates of sail training and tall ships.
• All of the benefits of Individual Membership above plus two lapel pins and two coffee mugs.
• Listing in Sail Tall Ships! A Directory of Sail Training and Adventure at Sea.
• Listing in Running Free, ASTA's quarterly newsletter, and editorial opportunities.

Corporate $1,000/year (tax-deductible value is $990)
• For businesses and individuals wishing to express a greater commitment to ASTA's mission.
• All of the benefits of Supporting Membership above plus an ASTA ballcap.
• Two complimentary tickets to ASTA's annual awards dinner or ASTA's summer fundraiser.

Sail Training Organizations

• Organizations operating sail training vessels or tall ships are enrolled for the calendar year (January through December) renewable between January and May. Membership dues are based on the organization's annual budget. For budgets less than $250,000, membership dues are $225. For budgets between $250,000 and $500,000, dues are $300. For budgets greater than $500,000, dues are $375.

• Full-page listing (including a photo of your vessel) in Sail Tall Ships! A Directory of Sail Training and Adventure at Sea.
• 10 complimentary copies of the Directory for your staff and key volunteers.
• Subscription to Running Free, ASTA's quarterly newsletter, and editorial opportunities.
• A listing on ASTA's Web site with a link to your Web site (reciprocation appreciated).
• Listing of your job opportunities in ASTA's Billet Bank.
• Access to ASTA's Marine Insurance Program.
• Discounts for staff to attend ASTA's Annual Conference on Sail Training and Tall Ships.
• Invitations to participate in sail training races, cruises-in-company, and nautical rallies.
• Invitations to attend ASTA's Regional Meetings, educational and safety forums, and other special events.
• Opportunity to apply for ASTA's Sailing Vessel Assistance Grants and Professional Development Grants for Crew.

Affiliate $150/year (tax-deductible value is $0)

Open to non-profit organizations which do not operate their own sail training vessel, but do offer sail training, sea education or maritime history programs (Scouts, schools, colleges, etc.)
• Listing in Sail Tall Ships! A Directory of Sail Training and Adventure at Sea.
• 10 complimentary copies of the Directory for your staff and key volunteers.
• Subscription to Running Free, ASTA's quarterly newsletter, and editorial opportunities.
• A listing on ASTA's Web site with a link to your Web site (reciprocation appreciated).
• Listing of your job opportunities in ASTA's Billet Bank.
• Discounts for staff to attend ASTA's Annual Conference on Sail Training and Tall Ships.
• Invitations to participate in sail training races, cruises-in-company, and nautical rallies.
• Invitations to attend ASTA's Regional Meetings, educational and safety forums, and other special events.
• Opportunity to apply for ASTA's Professional Development Grants for Crew.

Membership Form

Yes, I/we want to join the American Sail Training Association!

Name_____

Organization_____

Mailing Address_____

City_____ State_____ Zip_____

Country_____

Phone_____ Fax_____

E-mail_____

Please enroll me/us in the following membership category:

Associate Memberships Associate memberships are renewable on date of anniversary.

- ❑ Individual $45
- ❑ Junior $30
- ❑ Family $75
- ❑ Supporting $250
- ❑ Corporate $1,000

Professional Memberships Professional Memberships are for calendar year (January through December).

- ❑ Affiliate (youth groups and schools) $150

Sail Training Organizations

- ❑ Budget less than $250,000 $225
- ❑ Budget between $250,000 and $500,000 $300
- ❑ Budget greater than $500,000 $375

*Associate memberships are renewable on date of anniversary.
**Professional memberships are for calendar year.

•Addresses in Canada/Mexico please add US $16 to cover additional postage and handling cost. Memberships outside North America please add US $24.

- ❑ Check enclosed (US dollars drawn on US bank only)
- ❑ Visa or MasterCard

Card number_____ Expiration date_____

Name on card_____

Mail or fax this form to: ASTA
PO Box 1459
Newport, RI 02840 USA
FAX: + 1 401-849-5400
or join via ASTA's Web site:
http://tallships.sailtraining.org

ASTA Ship's Store

Sail Tall Ships! A Directory of Sail Training and Adventure at Sea. $18.00
13th edition. 240 member vessels!

Guidelines for Educational Programs Under Sail $14.00
For vessel operators and curriculum developers seeking guidance as to safe practice and procedures within the sail training industry. If you are considering starting a sail training program or are considering using sail training to further your educational program this book contains valuable information.

1999 International Safety Forum Proceedings $20.00
(CD-ROM) Proceedings and papers or the 8th annual forum sponsored by the American Sail Training Association and the International Sail Training Association. (Includes bonus NOAA Hurricane Manual.)

1997 International Safety Forum Proceedings $8.00
Proceedings from 1997 still available. (soft cover book)

ASTA Logbook - New, revised edition!
A valuable aid for trainees and crew of all levels used to track their training
progress.   1-10 copies $5.00 ea.
                   11-25 copies $3.50 ea. + shipping
                   26 or more   @2.00 ea. + shipping

Tall Ships, by Thad Koza $28.00
New edition for the 21st Century - 150 color photographs of some of the world's great ships by the country's premiere tall ship photographer. (soft cover)

2002 Tall Ships Calendar $15.00
Featuring tall ships from around the world, photographed by Thad Koza and with an introduction by the ASTA Chairman.

American Photographers at the Turn of the Century $23.00
Beautifully reproduced photo essays on world travel by a number of renowned photographers, including Roger Archibald's photos of experiences aboard ASTA vessels.

By Force of Arms, signed by author James Nelson. $15.00
The first in the Revolution at Sea Saga. (soft cover)

The Maddest Idea, signed by author James Nelson. $15.00
The second in the Revolution at Sea Saga. (soft cover)

The Continental Risque, signed by author James Nelson. $15.00
The third in the Revolution at Sea Saga. (soft cover)

Lords of the Ocean, signed by author James Nelson. $15.00
    The fourth in the Revolution at Sea Saga. (soft cover)

All the Brave Fellows, signed by author James Nelson. $22.00
    The newest in the Revolution at Sea Saga. (hard cover)

ASTA Baseball Cap $18.00
    "Adams" pre-washed cotton. Available in Khaki w/ Navy Bill and Blue
Embroidered ASTA Logo, Blue w/ White Embroidered ASTA Logo, and
Nantucket Rose w/ White or Blue Embroidered ASTA Logo - one size fits all.

ASTA "Cruise Hat" $20.00
    Cotton Full Brimmed Sun Hat - Blue w/ White Embroidered ASTA Logo
or Khaki w/ Navy Embroidered ASTA Logo.

ASTA Canvas Web Belt $24.00
    Repeating ASTA ship Logo (Navy Blue w/ White Logo). Available with
buckle or "D" ring closure - standard sizes.

ASTA Flags - Navy with white ASTA logo. Fly from your ship, home, or office.

12" x 18" -	$20.00
2' x 3' -	$30.00
3' x 5' -	$40.00
4' x 6'	$60.00
5' x 8' -	$70.00

    For additional products, information, and pictures please visit the Ship's
Store on the ASTA Web site at http://tallships.sailtraining.org.

    *All prices include shipping and handling to US addresses, except where noted.
Please inquire for shipment outside the US. Payment may be made with US bank check,
Visa, or MasterCard. Please allow 4 weeks for delivery.*

Mail or fax order information to:

    ASTA
    PO Box 1459
    Newport, RI 02840 USA
    FAX: + 1 401.849.5400
    or call the ASTA office: +1 401.846.1775
    order via the Web: http://tallships.sailtraining.org/shipsstr.htm

Ships' Shapes

Sail training vessels are as varied as the programs operated on board them. Below are examples of the different rig configurations used by ASTA's Member Vessels. At right is a diagram of the different sails carried by a full-rigged ship.

Two-Masted Schooner   Brigantine   Topsail Schoone

Full-Rigged Ship   Barquentine

Three-Masted Schooner

Brig

SAIL NAMES

1. Fore mast
2. Main mast
3. Mizzen mast
4. Flying jib
5. Outer jib
6. Inner jib
7. Fore topmast staysail
8. Fore sail, fore course
9. Fore lower topsail
10. Fore upper topsail
11. Fore lower topgallant sail
12. Fore upper topgallant sail
13. Fore royal
14. Main royal staysail
15. Main topgallant staysail
16. Main topmast staysail
17. Main sail, main course
18. Main lower topsail
19. Main upper topsail
20. Main lower topgallant sail
21. Main upper topgallant sail
22. Main royal
23. Mizzen royal staysail
24. Mizzen topgallant staysail
25. Mizzen topmast staysail
26. Main spencer
27. Crossjack, mizzen course
28. Mizzen lower topsail
29. Mizzen upper topsail
30. Mizzen lower topgallant sail
31. Mizzen upper topgallant sail
32. Mizzen royal
33. Spanker

What is a Tall Ship?

"... how tall is a tall ship? The answer to this is rather similar to that of 'How long is a piece of string?' Perhaps John Masefield stated it best in his famous poem Sea Fever:

'And all I ask is a tall ship and a star to steer her by.' "

from *Sail Training, The Message of the Tall Ships* by John Hamilton

A "tall ship" is not a strictly defined type of sailing vessel. Most of us use the term to mean a large, traditionally rigged sailing vessel, whether or not it is technically a "ship." The United States Coast Guard's training ship *Eagle,* for example, is technically a barque. A tall ship can also be a schooner, brigantine, barquentine, brig, ketch, sloop, or a full-rigged ship depending on the number of masts and the cut of the sails.

For the purpose of classification and race rating, the International Sail Training Association divides tall ships into three classes and several sub-classes:

Class A: All vessels over 160 feet in overall length, regardless of rig, and all square-rigged vessels over 120 feet (Square-rigged vessels include ships, barques, barquentines, brigs, and brigantines, but not square-topsail schooners)

Class A Division II: All square-rigged vessels less than 120 feet in length

Class B: Fore-and-aft rigged vessels between 100 feet and 160 feet in length

Class C: All other fore-and-aft rigged vessels at least 30 feet long at the waterline

The American Sail Training Association owns the registered trademark Tall Ships® as it relates to the organization of sailing events and races and related commercial activity.

Indices

GEOGRAPHICAL, ADVERTISERS',
AND ALPHABETICAL INDICES

Geographical Listing of Vessels

Great Lakes, US

Bay City, MI: APPLEDORE IV, 77
Chicago, IL: WINDY, 294
Chicago, IL: WINDY II, 294
Duluth, MN: GRAND NELLIE, 144
Erie, PA: NIAGARA, 210
Grand Marais, MN: HJORDIS, 156
Milwaukee, WI: DENIS SULLIVAN, 111
Northport, MI: MANITOU, 199
Oswego, NY: OMF ONTARIO, 219
Port Clinton, OH: RED WITCH, 245
Suttons Bay, MI: INLAND SEAS, 162
Traverse City, MI: MADELINE, 195
Traverse City, MI: WELCOME, 287
Traverse City, MI: WESTWIND, 290

Great Lakes and St. Lawrence, Canada

Kingston, Ontario, Canada: ST LAWRENCE II, 251
Montreal, Quebec, Canada: CONCORDIA, 103
Ottawa, Ontario, Canada: BLACK JACK, 87
Ottawa, Ontario, Canada: FAIR JEANNE, 130
Penetanguishene, Ontario, Canada: HMS BEE, 85
Penetanguishene, Ontario, Canada: HMS TECUMSETH, 273
Toronto, Ontario, Canada: CHALLENGE, 99
Toronto, Ontario, Canada: EMPIRE SANDY, 122
Toronto, Ontario, Canada: KAJAMA, 173
Toronto, Ontario, Canada: PATHFINDER, 225
Toronto, Ontario, Canada: PLAYFAIR, 235
Toronto, Ontario, Canada: TRUE NORTH OF TORONTO, 279

Canadian Maritimes

Halifax, Nova Scotia, Canada: DOROTHEA, 114
Halifax, Nova Scotia, Canada: HIGHLANDER SEA, 154
Lunenburg, Nova Scotia, Canada: AVON SPIRIT, 81
Lunenburg, Nova Scotia, Canada: BLUENOSE II, 89
Lunenburg, Nova Scotia, Canada: PICTON CASTLE, 230
Lunenburg, Nova Scotia, Canada: RAINDANCER II, 242

New England

Bath, ME: MAINE, 196
Boothbay Harbor, ME: EASTWIND, 118
Boston, MA: LIBERTY, 187
Boston, MA: LIBERTY CLIPPER, 188
Boston, MA: SPIRIT OF MASSACHUSETTS, 262
Bridgeport, CT: BLACK PEARL, 88
Bridgeport, CT: JOHN E. PFRIEM, 169
Bridgeport, CT: ROSE, 249
Camden, ME: APPLEDORE II, 76
Camden, ME: MARY DAY, 201
Castine, ME: BOWDOIN, 92
Charlestown, MA: USS CONSTITUTION, 105
Cherryfield, ME: LITTLE JENNIE, 190
Cherryfield, ME: MALABAR, 197
Cherryfield, ME: MARGARET TODD, 200
Cherryfield, ME: SQUAW, 263
Cherryfield, ME: SYLVINA W. BEAL, 271
Duxbury, MA: ARIES, 79
Eastham, MA: PICARA, 229
Gloucester, MA: ADVENTURE, 62

Mid-Atlantic

Cobb Island, MD: MABEL STEVENS, 194

Croton-on-Hudson, NY: HALF MOON, 147

Georgetown, MD: PRIDE OF MANY, 237

Glen Cove, NY: PHOENIX (NY), 227

Hampton Roads, VA: VIRGINIA, 283

Hampton, VA: MISTY ISLES, 206

Jamestown, VA: DISCOVERY, 267

Jamestown, VA: GODSPEED, 267

Jamestown, VA: SUSAN CONSTANT, 267

Jersey City, NJ: GALLANT, 137

Long Island, NY: BOUNTY, 91

New York, NY: ADIRONDACK, 60

New York, NY: LETTIE G. HOWARD, 185

New York, NY: PEKING, 226

New York, NY: PIONEER, 234

New York, NY: WAVERTREE, 285

Norfolk, VA: AMERICAN ROVER, 73

Norfolk, VA: NORFOLK REBEL, 213

Oak Orchard River, NY: PILGRIM (NY), 232

Oakley, MD: FYRDRACA, 136

Philadelphia, PA: GAZELA PHILADELPHIA, 138

Philadelphia, PA: JOLLY II ROVER, 315

Potomac River, MD: H. M. KRENTZ, 157

Poughkeepsie, NY: CLEARWATER, 100

St. Michaels, MD: KATHRYN M. LEE, 178

Wilmington, DE: KALMAR NYCKEL, 175

Wilmington, DE: LISA, 189

Wilmington, DE: NINA, 212

Wilmington, DE: NORSEMAN, 214

Wilmington, DE: SANTA CLARA, 212

Southeast and Gulf Coast

Apalachicola, FL: GOVERNOR STONE, 143

Biloxi, MS: GLENN L. SWETMAN, 141

Biloxi, MS: MIKE SEKUL, 202

Bokeelia, FL: KALAHA, 174

Charleston, SC: 777, 58

Charleston, SC: TRIPLE SEVEN, 58

Coconut Grove, FL: VITA, 284

Eastern Caribbean: OCEAN STAR, 217

Fort Lauderdale, FL: MISS MAVIS, 205

Hilton Head, SC: CAMELOT, 96

Jacksonville, FL: RATTLESNAKE, 244

Key West, FL: AMERICA, 70

Key West, FL: DREAM CATCHER, 115

Key West, FL: LIBERTY, 187

Key West, FL: LIBERTY CLIPPER, 188

Key West, FL: ODYSSEY, 218

Key West, FL: WESTERN UNION, 288

Key West, FL: WOLF, 295

Melbourne, FL: RAINBOW CHASER, 241

Miami, FL: EYRIE, 129

Miami, FL: HERITAGE OF MIAMI II, 151

Miami, FL: HIBISCUS, 153

Miami, FL: WILLIAM H. ALBURY, 292

Mobile, AL: ST CHRISTOPHER, 250

St. Petersburg, FL: AMARA ZEE, 69

California and Pacific Northwest

Aberdeen, WA: HEWITT R. JACKSON, 152

Aberdeen, WA: LADY WASHINGTON, 182

Coupeville, WA: CUTTY SARK, 109

Dana Point, CA: PILGRIM (CA), 231

Galveston, TX: ELISSA, 120

Kodiak, AK: THREE HIERARCHS, 276

Long Beach, CA: AMERICAN PRIDE, 72

Long Beach, CA: CALIFORNIAN, 95

Long Beach, CA: PILGRIM OF NEWPORT, 233

Los Angeles, CA: BILL OF RIGHTS, 86

Los Angeles, CA: EXY JOHNSON, 128

Los Angeles, CA: IRVING JOHNSON, 165

Los Angeles, CA: SWIFT OF IPSWICH, 270

Manteo, NC: ELIZABETH II, 121
Newport Beach, CA: ALASKA EAGLE, 66
Newport Beach, CA: ARGUS, 304
Newport Beach, CA: LYNX, 193
Olympia, WA: RESOLUTE, 246
Olympia, WA: SEAWULFF, 255
Port Townsend, WA: ADVENTURESS (WA), 63
Richmond, CA: NEHEMIAH, 209
San Diego, CA: DISTANT STAR, 113
San Diego, CA: ODYSSEY, 218
San Diego, CA: STAR OF INDIA, 265
San Francisco, CA: ALMA, 67
San Francisco, CA: BAGHEERA, 82
San Francisco, CA: BALCLUTHA, 83
San Francisco, CA: C.A. THAYER, 98
San Francisco, CA: CORSAIR, 107
San Francisco, CA: VIKING, 282
Sausalito, CA: DARIABAR, 110
Sausalito, CA: HAWAIIAN CHIEF-TAIN, 149
Sausalito, CA: KA'IULANI, 172
Seattle, WA: MALLORY TODD, 198
Seattle, WA: YANKEE CLIPPER, 320
Seattle, WA: ZODIAC, 297
Victoria, British Columbia, Canada: PACIFIC GRACE, 222
Victoria, British Columbia, Canada: PACIFIC SWIFT, 223
Victoria, British Columbia, Canada: ROBERTSON II, 248

Europe and Russia

Amsterdam, The Netherlands: EUROPA, 126
Amsterdam, The Netherlands: STAD AMSTERDAM, 264
Blennerville, Tralee, County Kerry, Ireland: JEANIE JOHNSTON, 168
Bremen-Vegesack, Germany: ESPRIT, 125, 310
Charlestown, Cornwall, United Kingdom: KASKELOT, 176
Kalingrad, Russia: KRUZENSHTERN, 180
Kyiv, Ukraine: BAT'KIVSHCHYNA, 84
Liverpool, United Kingdom: ZEBU, 296
Makkum, The Netherlands: SWAN FAN MAKKUM, 269

Monfalcone, Italy: LYCIA, 192
Otrano, Italy: IDEA DUE, 160
Rotterdam, The Netherlands: OOST-ERSCHELDE, 221
Southampton, United Kingdom: JOLIE BRISE, 170
Southampton, United Kingdom: LORD NELSON, 191
Southampton, United Kingdom: TENACIOUS, 274
St. Austell, Cornwall, United Kingdom: EARL OF PEMBROKE, 117
St. Austell, Cornwall, United Kingdom: PHOENIX (UK), 228
St. Petersburg, Russia: MIR, 204
Stavoren, The Netherlands: APHRODITE, 75
Upnor, Kent, United Kingdom: ARETHUSA, 78
Wolgast, Germany: ROALD AMUND-SEN, 247, 310

Pacific and Indian Oceans

Auckland, New Zealand: SOREN LARSEN, 259
Honolulu, HI: TOLE MOUR, 277
Nassau, Bahamas: CONCORDIA, 103
Port Adelaide, South Australia, Australia: ONE AND ALL, 220
Port Jackson, Sydney, Australia: SVA-NEN, 268
Rarotonga, Cook Islands: PICTON CASTLE, 230
Surabaya, Indonesia: DEWARUCI, 112
Sydney, Australia: ENDEAVOUR, 123

South America and Caribbean

Abaco, Bahamas: KEEWATIN, 179
Buenos Aires, Argentina: LIBERTAD, 186
Cartegena, Colombia: GLORIA, 142
Castries, St. Lucia, Bahamas: FANTASY, 131
Eastern Caribbean: OCEAN STAR, 217
Guayquil, Ecuador: GUAYAS, 145
Port Vila, Republic of Vanuatu: ALVEI, 68
St. Thomas, USVI: GRAND NELLIE, 144

Advertisers' Index

Index

Photo Gallery

The 2000 ASTA Scholarship Fundraiser on board the US Brig *Niagara*, Fort Adams, Newport, RI.

Top, *Hawaiian Chieftain* crewmembers and ASTA's Christine attend a fundraiser on board *Dewa Ruci* in Oakland, CA

Below, Jon Dickinson and Lori Aguiar man the ASTA booth in Wilmington, DE during Tall Ships 2000® this past summer.

Above, Captain and crew of the Continental Sloop *Providence* during Tall Ships® Newport Salute 2000.

Above, Christine Highsmith, ASTA Race Secretary for the Boston to Halifax leg of Tall Ships 2000®, poses outside the North American equivalent of ISTA's "Yellow Caravan" during Tall Ships 2000® Halifax.

Right, ASTA Race Director, Steve Baker, on board the "HMS" *Rose*.

Captain Larry Mahan and wife Linda of the schooner *Larinda*, and Gordon Varnedoe of the Savannah Waterfront Association during ASTA's Conference in Chicago last November.

Left, Captain Jan Miles of the *Pride of Baltimore II* and Patti Lock, port organizer for Tall Ships Challenge® Cleveland, during a reception at the ASTA Conference in Chicago, hosted by the ports of Tall Ships Challenge® Great Lakes 2001.

Below, ASTA Board Members (left to right) Nancy Richardson, Chris Rowsom, and Mike Rauworth, at the ASTA Conference in Chicago.

SAIL TALL SHIPS!

ASTA's Christine and Lori with Captain Austin Becker of the *Providence*, at the ASTA Conference in Chicago last November.

Jon Dickinson stands in front of the *Kruzenshtern* during Tall Ships® Delaware.

Steve Baker and Lori Aguiar in front of the *USS Constitution* following the ASTA Tall Ships Challenge® press conference in Boston last May.

The mission of the American Sail Training Association is to encourage character building through sail training, promote sail training to the North American public, and support education under sail.